Singing the French Revolution

✦

Singing the French Revolution

◆

Popular Culture and Politics, 1787–1799

LAURA MASON

Cornell University Press

Ithaca and London

First published 1996 by Cornell University Press.

Library of Congress Cataloging-in-Publication Data
Mason, Laura.
   Singing the French Revolution : popular culture and politics
  1787–1799 / Laura Mason.
      p.   cm.
   Includes bibliographical references (p.   ) and index.
   ISBN 0–8014–3233–2 (cloth : alk. paper)
    1. Revolutionary ballads and songs—France—History and criticism.
  2. Popular culture—France—History—18th century. 3. France—History—
  Revolution, 1787–1799.   I. Title.
  ML3621.R48M37   1996
781.5'99'094409033—dc20   96–17694

Printed in the United States of America

This book is printed on Lyons Falls Turin Book,
a paper that is totally chlorine-free and acid-free.

for Michael

Contents

Contents

Part III *Ending the Revolution*

Subsequent research and writing were supported by a postdoctoral fellowship from the Princeton University Department of History and by two Sarah Moss Fellowships from the University of Georgia. Private generosity played its part too, and I am grateful to Pat and Christine Murray for their friendship and for the peaceful room with a view of the Eiffel Tower that they so kindly provided during a crucial summer.

Numerous others have contributed immensely in a broad range of ways and, in so doing, they have reminded me of the satisfactions of belonging to a lively intellectual and human community. Above all, I thank Suzanne Desan who, I feel reasonably certain, has read this manuscript more often than any other person. Her enthusiasm for the project, her thoughtful criticism, and her perceptive interpretations of the Revolution not only helped me to make this a better book but rejuvenated my own enthusiasm. Similarly, Dena Goodman's advice and assistance and her stimulating pep talk one day in Chicago played no small part in boosting me over some of the final hurdles of completing a first book.

I have had occasion to share this work with several reading groups which gave generous attention to it. At an early stage, I presented several chapters to the members of the Berkeley French History group. The discussion was enormously helpful to me. Thanks to all the readers there, especially to Susanna Barrows, who, as many can attest better than I, creates an atmosphere that encourages creative and critical exchange, and to Cathy Kudlick, who helped to make that visit possible. As I neared the end of the writing process, I had the opportunity to present my work to the members of the Early Modern Group at Emory University. There too I benefited from the suggestions of several readers, in particular from Judith Miller's generous and penetrating comments. Finally, thanks to Christian Jouhaud for organizing and animating a discussion of revolutionary song lyrics in Paris that suggested to me new ways of treating songs.

In Athens, Jean Friedman and David Schoenbrun generously offered advice, encouragement, and friendship—not always in that order—while successive department chairs—Lester Stephens, John Morrow, and David Roberts—did all that they could to facilitate my completion of this book. And, although she has long since flown Athens, it was there that I first met Amy Forbes, whose remarkable warmth and highly original approach to history have made her a fine colleague and the best of friends. Marybeth Hamilton began to foster my appreciation for the peculiarities of popular culture well before I began this project, and she has been, throughout, an irreplaceable friend and ally. Thanks as well to Betsy Colwill for advice and encouragement on several key points, especially as I

Acknowledgments

✦ IN THE DECADE since I began this project, I have incurred innumerable debts—intellectual, emotional, and material—for which these acknowledgments can serve only as meager recompense. I hope that this book as a whole will be taken as a kind of thanks too. I began working on revolutionary songs as a graduate student at Princeton University, where the advice of Robert Darnton and Natalie Davis shaped the questions I asked. Their comments, insights, and continued enthusiasm for this book have sustained and enlightened me throughout. I also thank Lynn Hunt and Philip Nord, who provided thoughtful commentary and perceptive suggestions. I hope that I have answered some of their questions here. In Paris, Roger Chartier kindly allowed me to participate in his ongoing seminar at the Ecole des Hautes Etudes. I cannot overstate the value of these seminars and of my conversations with him for shaping my historical conceptualization and broadening my imagination as a researcher. Finally, lest it be thought that I began to become a historian only in the past decade, I want to acknowledge the contributions of Jonathan Beecher and Peter Kenez, who first nourished and channeled my love of history during my years as an undergraduate at the University of California, Santa Cruz. There I found the kind of attentive and intensive teaching that I fear is becoming all too rare in publicly funded universities and without which I might not have continued.

This book itself would not have been possible without the public and private funding that subsidized much of my research and writing. Early research trips were supported by a Bourse Chateaubriand from the French government and a grant from the Fulbright-Hayes Foundation.

was rethinking the Terror; to Bill Weber, Peter Jones, Tom Kaiser, Jim Halpert, and Pasquale Pasquino, who raised questions or offered insights that found their way into my manuscript; to John Carson, for his renowned editorial skills, which improved an earlier version of this work; and to Regina Sweeney, who kindly shared with me some of her beautifully imaginative and perceptive work on World War I songs. Last but not least, Andrew Wallis offered helpful and often witty suggestions to improve and enliven my translations of song lyrics.

I thank the following publishers for permission to use material here from previously published articles. Part of Chapter 2 was published as "*Ça ira* and the Birth of the Revolutionary Song," in *History Workshop* 28 (Autumn 1989): 22–38, © 1989 by Routledge. Parts of Chapters 4 and 5 were published in "Songs: Mixing Media," in Robert Darnton and Daniel Roche, editors, *Revolution in Print: The Press in France, 1775–1800* (Berkeley: University of California Press, 1989), © The New York Public Library, Astor, Lenox, and Tilden Foundations.

Finally, this work emerged as well from tribal relations. Above all, the members of my large and still-growing family have been a source of encouragement and inspiration throughout and, although they may not see it, each has found her or his way into my work. The Kwass clan made an enormous contribution too, offering unexpected interest and enthusiasm for the project that enlivened and challenged me. And then there is Michael Kwass, who contributed his keen analytic skills, an incomparable level of support, and more. It is because I owe him more than I can readily say that I simply say thank you and dedicate this book to him.

L. M.

Athens, Georgia

Singing the French Revolution

✦

Introduction

✦

Revolutionary Scholarship and Popular Culture

✦ WERE IT POSSIBLE to endow books with soundtracks, this one might begin with a simple, unaccompanied performance of the *Marseillaise*.

> Allons enfants de la patrie
> Le jour de gloire est arrivé;
> Contre nous de la tyrannie
> L'étendard sanglant est levé

The tune, like the lyrics, is inviting; it declares itself simply and proudly. Upon hearing it, one can scarcely doubt that "the day of glory" has, in fact, arrived. Then, suddenly, the voice sinks, to ask in a tone of outrage that barely skirts fear:

> Entendez-vous dans les campagnes
> Mugir ces féroces soldats?
> Ils viennent jusque dans vos bras
> Egorger vos fils, vos compagnes.

Finally, it rises again, to swell into a celebratory and determined chorus: *Aux armes, citoyens!*

But this is too much a twentieth-century conception of revolutionary singing: a single voice performing, with almost classical poise, the almost classical song that we now remember as the hymn of the French Revolution. Few revolutionaries sang so formally or with such well-trained voices, and none could possibly be certain what their anthem would finally be. These are retrospective additions. So let us begin again, less anachronistically. Let us endow this book with a soundtrack that seems at first to be an unrecognizable jumble of voices and sounds. As we listen more closely, we recognize snatches of song amid street noises, shouts, and more practiced speeches. We may hear a bit of the gay and aggressively lively *Ça ira*, or a slow and sober lament of the king's execution, even a phrase or two of the *Marseillaise*, but sung now in a coarse, full-throated voice that confuses some of the difficult and learned lyrics.

This is how I imagine Paris in the last decade of the eighteenth century. It was a city that encompassed a cacophony of voices as revolutionaries and royalists filled streets, theaters, and cafés, organizing festivals, giving speeches, rioting and, throughout all, singing. Common citizens rhymed political opinions, which some sang privately even as others trumpeted them forth before legislative and sectional assemblies. Theatrical composers capitalized on revolutionary enthusiasm with songs which commemorated recent events or which, by their ambiguity, provoked heated debate that attracted new customers. Even revolutionary governments participated, producing songs for festivals and the army, only to turn later to disciplining the street singing that legislators rightly saw as a form of popular activism. In short, during the final decade of the eighteenth century, songs overleapt boundaries between politics, entertainment, and the market, to become one of the most commonly used means of communication of the French Revolution.

Singing was a fluid and highly improvisational means of expression that moved easily between oral and print cultures. Because most songs were "composed" by rhyming new verses to familiar tunes, anyone who had the most rudimentary sense of rhyme was qualified to become a "songwriter." Easy composition made songs a timely means of communication which, like newspapers and cheap engravings, was highly responsive to the movement of events. The advantages of easy composition were reinforced by the facility with which songs were reproduced and communicated. A songsheet was cheap, usually no more than a few *liards* (the equivalent of a few pennies), and often smaller than the palm of one's hand, so easy to transport and easy to hide. But, more important, the songs that such sheets carried were not confined to the page. Words are learned quickly when set to a familiar tune; thus singing offered special advantages to a society which was only partially literate and in which the free circulation of information was intermittent at best. Songs allowed anyone to commit news and controversial opinions to memory and relay them across city or countryside, outpacing printing presses and police alike. And just as such oral circulation immeasurably increased the number of "composers" and the size of audiences, it created a wealth of possibilities for the appropriation and transformation of songs. In short, throughout the Revolution, songs were a uniquely accessible means of communication.

These dimensions of revolutionary songs are already well known; even before the Revolution was over, memorialists were commenting on revolutionaries' rage for singing.[1] In the twentieth century, historians have turned to the thousands of revolutionary songsheets preserved in Paris to remind us of the songs' popularity and their ability to accurately reflect revolutionary opinion.[2] And yet, few have considered the moment when a song achieved its full expressive potential: the moment of performance.[3] A song came fully to life only in being sung, for then the latitude for reinforcing, appropriating, and manipulating lyrics was enormous. Singers made songs their own with vocal inflections, gestures, and the particular circumstances under which they chose to sing. And audiences helped to shape a song's meaning by reacting to the singer's interpretation and expressing their own opinions with shouts and applause, or even another song. Song lyrics made statements about revolutionary events and ideas, but it was through the performance of those lyrics that singers and audience "discussed" and reshaped such statements. Clearly, performance did more than simply extend the vitality of this genre. Even as ease of composition and dissemination broadened the accessibility of songs, performance lent singular weight to individual appropriations, shifting emphasis from the content of a particular song to the ways in which it was used. Individuals of all social backgrounds and every political stripe composed their own songs, but they also reshaped those of others, mocking or distorting lyrics whose meaning may have once seemed fixed. More than that of any other genre, the meaning of a song was as much dependent on appropriation and contexts of performance as it was upon content, format, or presumed authorial intent.[4]

Because of these qualities, songs were accessible to competing uses and interpretations, permitting singers, composers, and audiences to shape them to reflect their particular experiences of the Revolution. Since revolutionary song culture was available to all, it would prove to be heterogeneous, capable of expressing the fears and aspirations of revolutionaries and counterrevolutionaries alike while embodying the different competencies and modes of expression of amateurs and professionals. As such, it reflected an exceptionally broad range of interpretations of the Revolution. This fluidity gave rise to multiple temporal shifts as song culture expressed the emerging expectations and the realignments of social and political power that stretched across the decade.

Songs were not, however, an exclusively revolutionary means of expression.[5] In adopting them, revolutionaries and counterrevolutionaries turned to a genre that had been firmly rooted in the Old Regime, and so they found themselves compelled to struggle with traditional practices and old habits of mind. Throughout the nineties, singers in the most broadly accessible arena, the street, adapted and repeatedly transformed available practices, using songs in increasingly self-conscious ways to express allegiance and engage in political debate. Meanwhile, in the more restricted arenas of theatrical and print culture, revolutionaries and royalists wrestled with representations of songs as a form of "popular" culture. In response to evolving singing practices and the shifting political currents of the revolutionary movement, they would come to change such representations gradually but decisively. Thus, while song culture revealed singularly broad dimensions of the Revolution, the Revolution was in the process of changing that culture.

My aim is to investigate both these phenomena, treating song culture as a lens through which to consider the cultural activity of the Revolution, and as a form of popular culture that was dramatically changed by the Revolution. On the one hand, song-writing and singing practices reveal the extent to which all French citizens contributed to the very constitution of revolutionary culture, and the degree to which such a culture was shaped and reshaped by contest and antagonism. This, in turn, helps to explain the urgency with which successive governments set about constituting an official political culture. Their own claims to the contrary, legislators had not taken on the relatively simple task of educating and indoctrinating a backward populace. Rather, they sought to impose representational homogeneity on a multifaceted and activist population that included both counterrevolutionaries and popular radicals. The debate over representation that all these groups engaged in would become highly charged because all citizens recognized the importance of anthems and icons for promoting their interpretations of revolutionary events, publicizing their definitions of political representation, and championing their aspirations for the Revolution's outcome. In the end, the inability of song culture in particular, and of revolutionary political culture in general, to encompass the breadth of its constituency would help to bring about its demise.

At the same time, songs reveal the extent to which the Revolution changed cultural practices and representation. By creating new arenas of cultural production and by broadening access to those already in existence, revolutionaries threw open new worlds of creativity. This process of innovation was further intensified by the tendency of revolutionaries and counterrevolutionaries alike to make explicit the relationships that existed between culture and politics, thereby encouraging new conceptions of both. It was against this background that all citizens considered and reconsidered the political seriousness of singing, the relationship between a means of expression and its content, and the use of different genres to influence the course of the Revolution. The revolutionary experience would show how fully traditional cultural practices could be reshaped to accord with radically new circumstances, even as it bestowed new respectability on a popular cultural form. These transformations would be among the Revolution's legacies to the modern world.

MAKING SENSE OF THE FRENCH REVOLUTION

Few doubt any longer that one of the distinctive innovations of French revolutionaries was their elaboration of a wholly new political culture. In the past two decades, Maurice Agulhon, Mona Ozouf, François Furet, Lynn Hunt, and others, have shifted attention away from social interpretations of the French Revolution by arguing that the Revolution was distinctive not because it brought a loosely defined bourgeoisie to power but because it created new political language, practices, and symbolism.[6] Drawing upon the evidence of festivals, rhetoric, and iconography, these scholars have advanced powerful analyses that affirm the importance of linguistic and cultural practices to the development of revolutionary politics. As Lynn Hunt has explained, such work reveals, "the ways in which 'the Revolution' took shape as a coherent experience."[7]

As these scholars describe it, a relatively small group of men and women worked steadily from 1789 onward to promote new rhetoric, iconography, festivals, and political practices that could rejuvenate an adult population come of age under the Old Regime, ridding them of ancient habits and superstitions and reorienting them toward a modern republicanism. In sum, revolutionary political culture was an instrument forged by legislators and cultural elites to educate and contain an unruly citizenry. This is not to say that these men and women were members of a homogeneous elite: often divided by politics, legislators and others occasionally expressed their rivalries by reshaping shared ceremonies and icons.[8] Nor does this mean that the populace was wholly excluded from the process of creation: revolutionary elites sometimes appropriated popular practices and incorporated them into the same ceremonies and icons over which they themselves struggled. But when such qualifications have been made, we are left with a picture of a remarkably uniform political culture that was elaborated by a relatively small number of people.

It is this final image that is problematic, for it accords poorly with what we know of the political practices of the Revolution. Most fundamental was the opposition between revolutionaries and counterrevolutionaries. Throughout much of the Revolution, counterrevolutionaries constituted a vocal and highly creative opposition. They produced their own symbols and anthems, and many drew freely on satire and burlesque in their efforts to destabilize revolutionary political symbolism and turn it back on itself. In other words, even as they produced a blatantly oppositional culture, counterrevolutionaries also helped to create uncertainty about the political implications of means of expression upon which revolutionaries drew.[9] Meanwhile, revolutionaries were divided among themselves. Tension between the legislature and an increasingly radical popular movement drove the Revolution onward during the first half of the nineties. Deputies, journalists, and other elites developed a variety of attitudes toward a diverse and activist populace that included proponents of direct democracy, advocates for the recognition of women's political sovereignty, and critics of unrestricted private property. Concessions and compromises were reached with difficulty, and the vast majority of revolutionary alliances proved to be temporary.[10]

Given such political and social tensions, it is hardly surprising that legislators would seek to construct a culture that could unite and organize a mobilized and heterogeneous population. And yet, for exactly the same reasons, there is little reason to believe that the populace would unproblematically assimilate such a culture, or that legislators and cultural elites alone would try to establish particular representations of new political rights and relationships. Certainly, political opinions, education, material needs, and even personal experience must have affected the ways in which audiences interpreted and appropriated official culture. We cannot assume that the culture simply imprinted official forms of patriotism and republicanism. Might not words and images have been turned back on the Revolution and used in ways that the government never intended?

In recent years, a handful of scholars have begun to answer this question by suggesting that revolutionary legislators were no more capable of establishing stable meanings for "liberty," "sovereignty," or "fraternity" than they were of determining the parameters of political participation. Some of these historians have even argued that it was their very malleability that gave revolutionary words their force, for it enabled them to encompass a variety of definitions and serve a multiplicity of aspirations.[11] I propose to go still further and demonstrate that different fractions of the French citizenry did not merely appropriate political culture in different ways; they contributed to its very constitution.

The creative activities of revolutionary elites were more than matched by those of a mass of smaller producers, men and women who held a broad range of political opinions and whose creative expressions achieved varying degrees of publicity, popularity, and aesthetic legitimacy. Revolutionary song culture emerged from the dynamic tensions among many individuals and groups, as revolutionaries opposed counterrevolutionaries and as appropriation moved in both directions between government and populace. Shared compositional and singing practices were neither summoned into existence nor controlled by revolutionary governments; rather, they emerged from negotiations and conflicts within an engaged and activist populace. In this sense, revolutionary song culture was very much like revolutionary politics, born of contestation between opposing political factions and between the legislature and a popular political movement that it could neither assimilate nor will away.

By describing the precise means by which revolutionaries and counterrevolutionaries of all sorts contributed to the constitution of song culture, I shall demonstrate that political culture was not the sole possession of revolutionary legislators and cultural elites. It was instead a contested terrain over which countless individuals and political factions struggled, unable to agree and therefore unable to end the Revolution. By restoring a greater sense of conflict and heterogeneity to our conception of the Revolution, we reach a better understanding of why legislators and private citizens were unable to bring the Revolution to a successful close and, as well, sketch a better picture of the political culture that revolutionaries bequeathed to the nineteenth century. For, as Maurice Agulhon and others have made abundantly clear, the republican legacy to the nineteenth century was by no means coherent or uniform.[12]

Seeing political culture as a field of contestation on which all French citizens met also draws attention to the experience of the Directory. Accounts of revolutionary culture usually emphasize the early years of the Revolution, when new symbols were first elaborated and opposition was most dramatic. These studies suggest, either implicitly or explicitly, that the later period—the second half of the nineties—left political culture relatively unchanged or that it witnessed a "normalization" of political and cultural practices.[13] But long after the fall of Robespierre and the

Committee of Public Safety, legislators and private citizens of all sorts continued to experiment with new means to organize society, politics, and culture. The experiments of the later years were more restrained than those initiated during the first half of the Revolution, but they were to have lasting consequences. In particular, directorial singing practices suggest the conservative dimensions of revolutionary cultural experimentation. Directorial culture was conservative in both senses of the word: while legislators worked to institutionalize and thus preserve the new republican symbolism, citizens turned to culture as a means to restore social and political order, often reinstituting older, formalized standards of expression and behavior that helped to silence some and marginalize others. As we shall see, new cultural and political practices in the late nineties combined to prepare the way for the regime that Napoleon Bonaparte would begin to construct in 1799. Perhaps more important still, those cultural practices were important in the long term in bridging the radical Revolution of the early nineties and the nineteenth century.

SINGING AS A FORM OF POPULAR CULTURE

But this book is not only about revolutionary political culture; it is also about the how the Revolution transformed popular culture. Like historians of the Revolution, scholars of popular culture have abandoned strictly social interpretations of their subject to develop broader and more inclusive definitions. As the editors of one collection put it, we now understand "popular culture" to be constituted by "beliefs and practices, and the objects through which they are organized, that are widely shared among a population."[14] This definition acknowledges that a broad range of cultural forms—songs among them—are available to all members of a given population, so it sidesteps the once-common tendency to identify particular practices as the unique province of specific socioeconomic groups. But such a definition also risks doing away altogether with the notion of the "popular" by defining a democratic, common culture from which all might freely appropriate. At least one historian of eighteenth-century France has, in fact, already gone this far, arguing that "there is no such thing as popular culture . . . if by that term one means amusements for common people as opposed to those for the elite."[15]

But culture is one of the principal means by which any given part of a population distinguishes itself from others, by marking differences that express and reinforce social hierarchy.[16] To be sure, certain cultural objects and practices are shared universally. Their meanings do not, however, appear transparently, for they are mediated and reshaped by descriptions, observations, and judgments. And it is here, at the level of representation, that the idea of popular culture emerges. In the eighteenth century, the most potent representations were elaborated and deployed by men and women of letters, by royal authorities, and by members of the church: in other words, by those whose education or institutional affiliations lent publicity and credibility to their accounts.[17] Furthermore, as Jacques Revel has argued, these representations were not intended merely to label and classify particular practices but, as well, to reaffirm the status of the men and women who formulated them.[18] Referring to learned ideals of truth, rationality, and convention, cultural authorities classified as "popular" that which opposed or departed from those ideals. Thus, in considering cultural conventions "the propriety of legitimate practices was set against the marginality of non-regulated uses of language (which were, of course, the uses of the majority). The norm had become classificatory; while the term 'popular' remained socially pejorative, it lost all reference to a specific social identity."[19] Although the term lacked a specific social identity, it had powerful political implications, for to label a means of expression "popular" was to circumscribe the arenas in which it might legitimately be used, and to undermine the credibility of those who had access to few other means of expression.

Song culture was "popular," therefore, not because only common people sang—singing practices were shared throughout old-regime and revolutionary society—but because cultural authorities commonly represented it as the expression of working people. In France during the Old Regime, the very word *chanson* was embedded with notions of cultural hierarchy, as Furetière's *Dictionnaire universel* underscored in 1690 when it claimed that, above all else, the word referred to "a small bit of verse . . . that is sung by common people [*le peuple*]." More than a half century later, Diderot's *Encyclopédie* added, "The authors of our songs' lyrics are hardly ever known: such lyrics are mere fragments of meager thought, produced by several hands and, for the most part, born from the pleasure of the moment."[20] Frivolous, unreflective, the special expression of *le peuple*: these distinctions would persist into the Revolution to inform the representations that would be elaborated by politicians, journalists, and even theatrical composers.

The Old Regime conception of popular culture emerged from the distinction between practices and representations, but the Revolution would temporarily abolish this distinction and so transform popular culture. Revolutionaries made possible the emergence of new relationships between practices and representations by fundamentally altering the parameters of cultural production and judgment. By opening up new arenas of cultural activity and broadening access to arenas already in existence, they permitted a much larger and more diverse population to engage in cultural production and exchange. They abolished privilege, sweeping away the central pillar of the Old Regime's cultural hierarchy and thus allowing French citizens to reconsider aesthetic hierarchies and the determinants of good taste. Finally and perhaps most radically, they made political criteria an explicit dimension of cultural experience, thereby validating new kinds of creative activity and suggesting new implications of cultural production. As citizens in streets and cafés elaborated their revolutionary singing practices and working people acquired a new political status, the gap between practices and representations narrowed. For a brief moment during the early years of the Republic, the gap seemed to close altogether as both practices and representations suggested that all revolutionaries shared a common song culture.

The Revolution marked a turning point for popular culture, which shifted from an essentially conservative to a potentially radical means of expression.[21] In the early modern period, artisans and peasants used common cultural symbols to express complaint, but they did so without transgressing defining social and political boundaries. In other words, such men and women made very specific demands—relief from taxation, lower bread prices, restoration of traditional labor practices—but they did not call into question, in Y.-M. Bercé's words, "the totality of power."[22] Rather, early modern protest either sought the return of earlier, allegedly more "just" regimes or invoked a transcendent order; it did not seek to reconfigure state power (which was, in any case, still in the process of emerging) or to reorder social hierarchy. By the nineteenth and twentieth centuries, however, the magnitude and objectives of oppositional struggles had changed. The focus was now on contests over the structure of state power, the allocation of resources, and the social and cultural hierarchies that marginalized and disciplined working people. Popular culture came to serve more radical movements effectively as workers drew upon available songs, language, and iconography in their struggles for suffrage and political representation and against industrialization and the imposition of bourgeois mores. The French Revolution marks the turning point between these different uses of popular culture, for it was here that common people first elaborated the cultural means to critique the foundations of social and political organization and to suggest worldly alternatives. In short, a genuinely oppositional popular culture emerged from the French Revolution.

In bringing together practices and representations that expressed the politically transformative power of singing, the Revolution made songs and singing a legitimate and respectable means of political expression. The Revolution bequeathed to the nineteenth century an anthem, a tradition of political singing, and the memory of countless politically engaged singers. Henceforth, singing did not simply entertain or express anonymous complaint; it evoked a concrete political heritage and a set of claims for a more equitable and inclusive polity. This is a legacy to which worker-poets and elite songwriters alike would turn in the nineteenth century.

PROJECT OF THE BOOK

I have confined this enquiry to Paris, in part because only within the confines of a specific geographic area is it possible to describe how a common set of cultural artifacts were manipulated by different social and political groups. More important, the city's status as the political and cultural center of France makes it an ideal location in which to examine the broadest possible range of compositional and singing practices. Relations between unofficial activists and the government were most focused in Paris, where one could find an enormous range of cultural productions representing the entire spectrum of political opinion.

I have chosen a chronological structure for this book because my interest is in the unfolding of specific events; but I have not tried to impose a neat, unidirectional narrative. A uniform history cannot do justice to popular song-writing and singing practices, which developed in a diffuse and open-ended way giving rise to competing interpretations and appropriations. Each chapter describes and analyzes a different face of revolutionary song culture as it emerged at a particular point in the Revolution, highlighting the interaction of songs with other expressive forms and indicating moments when the culture coalesced around particular political ideas and practices.

I argue that revolutionary culture in general, and song culture in particular, was the product of a fragmented society whose members pursued different and often competing social and political objectives. All members of French society sang, but the act of singing carried particular resonances for members of different social groups as well as for revolutionaries and counterrevolutionaries. As the revolutionary movement increasingly incorporated members of diverse social groups and effectively silenced its opposition, the songs' satiric character was stripped away and their association with common people became a representational asset. For a brief moment in the early years of the Republic, songs ceased to be defined pejoratively as a form of popular culture; instead, they were represented as a legitimate means of expression for the whole revolutionary community. But the social and political tensions that divided revolutionary France could not be conjured away, nor could they be permanently silenced. As singing practices came to express different visions of the Revolution and as the gap between practices and representations widened, song culture fragmented once more.

Song-writing and singing practices were reshaped yet again in the second half of the Revolution: this time by the reemergence of social distinctions and by a marked privatization of politics. As fractions of the population increasingly isolated themselves, they developed distinct compositional and singing practices. While official song writing was centralized and professionalized, elites worked to re-create an explicitly apolitical culture of art and entertainment songs, and common people retreated from the shared spaces of parks and streets to local bars and cafés. But these fractions shared a common desire to use culture to bury the political turmoil of the Terror and to celebrate the ostensibly apolitical program of foreign war. The genres and cultural practices elaborated in the final years of the Directory would prove to be wholly suited to the repressive years of the Empire.

Part I

✦

*From Old Regime
to Revolution*

Chapter One

✦

Songs under the Old Regime

✦ THE EVENINGS IN Paris are comfortable during the summer, and the days are long. From mid-June until late August the twilight lingers for hours. Had one gone in search of entertainment on such an evening in 1783, it would have been possible to head to the Quai de la Ferraille, on the bank of the Seine near the pont Neuf, to watch Baptiste "called *le Divertissant*."[1] There, each night between seven and nine, Baptiste and his partner, Madame Baptiste, stationed themselves to sing and sell romances to passers-by, who had been drawn in by the sound of a familiar tune, and to regulars, who had seen the pair before or knew of their whereabouts from notices printed on their songsheets.[2] Baptiste and his partner were streetsingers, *chansonniers*, who earned their livelihoods by singing and hawking cheap songbooks which held their lyrics and named the popular tunes to which they were meant to be sung.

Streetsingers such as these had long been celebrated as the standard-bearers of Parisian song culture. But however colorful these men and women, they were only a few of the many who used songs to express themselves. There were, as well, amateurs of all sorts who penned songs to mock and scold the injustices of the powerful; members of singing societies who met together regularly to share new compositions and entertain one another; religious and political foes of the crown, who included songs in their arsenal of oppositional tactics; and average men and women who simply sang to amuse themselves when they met in neighborhood cafés or in wine shops at the city gates.

Together these men and women helped to create the song culture of the Old Regime. It was a culture of remarkable vitality and richness, one that possessed histories both real and legendary and was closely inter-twined with the broader entertainment and political cultures of eigh-teenth-century Paris. The songs, singing practices, and habits of mind that grew up here would serve both as a foundation upon which revolu-tionaries would build and, like so much else from the Old Regime, as a problematic legacy. A sketch of this milieu will serve as a useful back-ground to debates and innovations that would emerge during the Revo-lution. We must focus in particular on the contradictions and deep ambivalences in Old Regime culture, which would present a special set of problems to the men and women who set out to remake themselves and their society at the end of the century. Above all, revolutionaries would confront contradictions between the widespread practices of singing and song writing and censorious representations of them.

Old Regime songs were undeniably popular, but they were so in two very different ways. On the one hand, singing was popular because it was a broadly accessible and widely used means of expression. Songs were composed and performed by men and women of all ranks of society; even the crown, which censored and chased disrespectful songs, used popular tunes to celebrate noteworthy events and disseminate important news. Songs were popular in much the same way that Robert Isherwood has claimed all eighteenth-century entertainment culture was popular: audiences and genres were so much intermingled that one could not truthfully sort them out according to social hierarchy or distinct "taste publics."[3] And yet, we should not conclude, as Isherwood does, that the alternate meaning of popular—with its connotation of commonness, even vulgarity—is no longer relevant. For although singing practices were found in all social classes, political authorities and cultural elites repre-sented singing as the peculiar expression of common people.

It was, in fact, the very breadth of practice that gave rise to such nar-row representations. There was, first, enormous social diversity amongst the devotees of song. Singers and composers reached all the way up the social hierarchy, but they also extended all the way down, where they in-cluded the culture's most visible representatives: streetsingers. And as we shall see, streetsingers were highly problematic representatives, for they had no corporation of their own and no proper place in Old Regime so-ciety; they were recognizable as a coherent group only through the con-tradictory images found in idealized literary representations and largely hostile police reports. Second, songs and singing were put to many uses. Fully integrated into the world of street, fair, and theatrical entertain-ment, songs were also used to voice political complaint and insult ene-mies. These diverse, often intermingled uses, combined with the uncertain identity of singers, gave rise to considerable anxiety among political and cultural authorities alike. Rarely able to distinguish between entertainment and political songs, disturbed by a song's ability to attack honor and undermine reputation, and unsettled by the fleeting and ephemeral quality of singing itself, cultivated men and women marginalized song culture by asserting that they possessed more serious modes of expression.

THE PLACE OF SONGS IN THE OLD REGIME

Singing was an integral element of the overwhelmingly oral and gestural world in which Parisians lived under the Old Regime.[4] For in spite of the steady progress of literacy over the course of the century, this was a city that continued to sustain a culture that was largely oral and visual. Beyond those who simply could not read were the many whose access to print was limited by time, condition, or the uncertainties of royal censorship.[5] Without a reliable and unregulated press, even the well educated had to rely upon word of mouth for information and opinion. In the wake of every noteworthy event, rumors and gossip flew through the city, linking poor to well-born on a loose chain of genuine knowledge and conjecture.[6] And this news, both real and imaginary, inevitably made its way into songs.

Songs and singing did more, however, than simply entertain and inform. They were fully integrated into the richly aural and visual culture of the eighteenth century. Sound and vision did not exist in opposition to one another, as some scholars have suggested; rather, they formed a sensually complex whole.[7] The ears attended not only to spoken words but to tone, volume, rhythm, and inflection as well, while the eyes sought an almost infinite number of details. Dress revealed social status as surely as accent betrayed geographic origin. The city itself was rich in visible signs; locals and strangers alike oriented themselves by landmarks—buildings, statues, cafés—rather than by street names and numbers. Gesture was of enormous importance, and Parisians were skilled in untangling the wealth of meanings conveyed by posture and movement.[8] Even the king's power was demonstrated, made palpable by festivals, *Te Deums*, and public executions that made plain the extent of his reach.[9] Having spent their lives in this resonant culture, singers were well versed in its articulations, and they drew upon a rich repertoire of gesture and inflection to suggest what could not be said openly. Thus, men and women of every rank used rhythm and inflection, gesture and costume as they sang—their songs spreading news and gossip, criticizing arbitrary sovereign powers, and responding to or reinforcing the great and petty humiliations of a rigid social hierarchy.

Song culture was active and vibrant because it was sustained by such performative richness and because, in serving so many different ends, it became intimately entwined with the political events, social structures, and cultural enterprises that shaped daily life. Entertainment songs dominated the culture most visibly during the eighteenth century whereas political songs lived more elusively, shielded by Parisians against the gaze of the police. Such elusiveness as was found within eighteenth-century song culture was not, however, timeless. Rather, song-writing and singing practices had a history which shaped policing and popular practices alike, although this was not readily apparent to all Parisians. For in preceding centuries the political possibilities of singing had been fully and openly exploited each time the crown's authority weakened. At these moments the singers' capacity to mold songs into powerful weapons of indoctrination and opposition became most apparent.

During the Reformation and the Wars of Religion, for example, Protestants used songs to win adherents and extend instruction in the new faith. Relying on the traditional practice of rhyming new verses to popular tunes, they changed popular romances to pious chants by altering a phrase or even a single word: thus, converts who once sang, "Ma chère Dame, ayez de moi mercy" (My beloved Lady, have mercy upon me), might now intone, "Mon créateur, ayez de moi mercy / Et regardez mon coeur" (My creator, have mercy upon me / And look into my heart).[10] Such songs did not simply advertise the new doctrine. They permitted singers to replace "licentious" ideas with religious sentiment, repeating a song that was both familiar and new until it became an integral and almost unconscious part of daily life, shaping and improving the singer's spirituality.[11] These compositional practices permitted all believers to become composers, turning song writing into a powerful means of communication and persuasion.

Singing formed an integral part of the new faith. In France, Huguenots instructed and sang together on Sundays, associating certain songs so closely with their movement that they recognized one another from a distance by the sound of their tunes.[12] A hostile Catholic Church and a hostile monarchy acknowledged the effectiveness of Protestant singing practices by mimicking them even as they tried to repress them. Thus, Jesuits set about altering popular songs to reinforce and reiterate Catholic doctrine, while the French crown forbade Huguenot singing in the streets and threatened charges of heresy against those who refused to relinquish their Protestant songbooks.[13]

In the seventeenth century, the political crisis of the Fronde produced a similar dynamic as songs became part of a struggle for power that pitted princes and urban notables against regents.[14] Wielded for and against the Royal party, the songs of the Fronde resembled those of the Reformation in their ability to become emblematic: people were so familiar with certain songs that pamphleteers had only to cite their refrains to make a particular point.[15] And once again, the crown met this oppositional singing by parrying song with song even as it tried to impose silence.[16] These were important moments of rupture in the political culture of the Old Regime. As authority weakened and daily life was politicized, songs became powerful instruments of faction. Openly oppositional and highly emblematic, they announced political or religious affiliation, struck verbal blows against opponents, and sought support from the undecided. The crown, its authority contested and weakened, did not content itself with mere repression; it contributed to the cacophony by singing its case as well.

The accession of Louis XIV in 1661 put an end to such openly confrontational singing by initiating a period of domestic peace and relative political stability that would last for almost a century and a half. The singing practices of the Reformation and the Fronde became only memory, legend, or fear, creating a backdrop against which more surreptitious practices were elaborated and policed. Song culture would not regain its visibly combative power until the end of the eighteenth century, when revolutionaries and counterrevolutionaries began to incorporate songs into their political arsenals, drawing upon their educative possibilities and using them to stir the devotion of allies and the rancor of enemies.

But in the years between the rise of Louis XIV and the decline of Louis XVI, singing practices became more subtle as they were elaborated in the shadow of a stable and increasingly intrusive state. Henceforth the audible power of songs served primarily as a means of entertainment, while their use for protest became more discreet. But even as certain dimensions of the culture became less visible, singing did not decline. Songs were wildly popular throughout the eighteenth century. Produced by streetsingers and theatrical entrepreneurs, by working people and courtiers, songs encompassed the commercial and the amateur, the entertaining and the political. Subject to the fleeting concerns of Parisians, most songs were ephemeral, catching on and dying out in the space of a few weeks. They resonated through the system of honor that shaped French society, able to make and unmake reputations and seeming to fray ties of social and political obedience. Finally, singing was subject to conflicting representations. It was both celebrated for its wit and gaiety and scorned as frivolous and common. Old Regime song culture was at odds with itself, for even as it emerged from practices that were shared throughout society, it continued to be represented as an inherently "popular" means of expression.

STREETSINGERS AND THE COMMERCE IN SONGS

The exemplary figures who promoted urban, commercial songs were streetsingers: Baptiste, Madame Baptiste, and many others who tried to turn a meager profit by singing. No description of the city was complete without reference to these men and women who, day after day, returned to the same spot to sing and sell *pont-neufs*, songs that they had composed by rhyming new verses to traditional or popular tunes.[17] There was Phillipot, the blind Savoyard who, as Boileau and others claimed, took his songs on the road once they had been successful in Paris. There were retailers of religious hymns and of rowdy songs, who vied for customers within forty feet of one another: "One offers you a blessed scapulary that frightens the devil . . . the other celebrates the famous victory that has been won; all of it is raised to the level of miracles; and the auditors stand, with their ears divided between the sacred and the profane." Less picturesque were the streetsingers whom Restif de la Bretonne described as "wretches without morals, idlers, useless characters."[18]

Chansonniers sought areas where they were likely to find the large, slow-moving crowds upon which the livelihoods of all street performers depend. Until midcentury, the pont Neuf—the main thoroughfare between Right and Left Banks and the site of an active market—was especially popular and famous.[19] But even before the market declined, and certainly afterward, singers found other arenas of performance. Baptiste and his wife probably established themselves on the Quai de la Ferraille, which abutted the pont Neuf, to take advantage of the crowds drawn by the animal and flower markets. Fanchon, reputed to have bought a *hôtel* with her earnings as a streetsinger, performed along the boulevards where the "little theaters" sprang up in the 1760s and 1770s. Jean-Baptiste Cligny and his partner Roussel didn't bother with bridges or boulevards at all; they hawked their "dissolute songs" in cafés, where they were less likely to draw the attention of the police but still able to find an established clientele.[20] As the careers of these men and women suggest, finding an audience was probably the least difficult of the *chansonnier*'s tasks. For, while the well-to-do and the well educated congregated at court and in private salons, most Parisians spent the better part of their lives out of doors. Adults marketed and socialized, children played in the streets or ran errands, and all were easily drawn out of doors by disturbances or spectacles.[21] A singer who found no audience present could, with the proper song, draw listeners to their windows, just as vegetable dealers drew maids into the street with their cries.[22]

There was no single locale for singing, nor was there a uniform type of *chansonnier*. Truly successful ones like the Fanchons, who were able to raise children and buy *hôtels* on their earnings, were few and far between. The absence of a professional organization of streetsingers and their uneven policing meant that this was an occupation that people joined and left with some frequency, relying on perhaps meager skills of musicianship and forming temporary relationships with printers who produced their songsheets. Thus, of three young women arrested for singing "infamous songs" in the fossés St. Germain in 1717, one identified herself as the wife of a paper dealer, another as a crier of decrees, and the third as simply "a maiden."[23] Louis George Nichon was a day laborer, but the woman he was arrested with was a colporteur, while Marie-Anne Bie was the daughter of a seller of songs who lived in the home of a water merchant.[24] Roussel and Cligny claimed that they were musicians, but neither was ever heard singing the songs that they sold.[25] Because street singing and song selling were occupations that one might practice sporadically and without special training, these men and women needed only a few songsheets to go into business. And unlike colporteurs, whose numbers were restricted and who were subject to specific regulations, *chansonniers* were regulated only to the extent of having to present their compositions to the police for approbation before printing.[26]

The same qualities that favored a casual plying of the trade made it a difficult undertaking for those who practiced it full time. François Lebas, a *chansonnier* for twenty years, made this point in a letter to the lieutenant general of police. He argued that by limiting the number of *chansonniers* who might practice in Paris, the police would protect them from the competition of all sorts of lawbreakers, including those who smuggled brochures into Paris and "women and girls of ill repute who contort themselves in the street and, sometimes drunken, expose themselves to public view, often adding things that are not in the songs and . . . frequently acting out what does not merit description."[27]

Lebas was undoubtedly choosing the most egregious cases to secure his argument, but the truth was that, apart from a few legendary characters, streetsingers were elusive and marginal figures. Musicians who sold songs that they never sang, criers of decrees who sang only on Sundays, and colporteurs who stuffed a few songsheets into their baskets of decrees and broadsheets, all found their way into this irregular trade. Beyond the great legends, only a handful actually identified themselves as *chansonniers*. For most, selling songs was but one of many means of earning a livelihood. And the songs themselves contributed to the ephemeral nature of the trade and the difficulty of policing it. Because songs had a fixed and special place in oral culture, those that were obscene or overtly political could easily be memorized, which enhanced their circulation and enabled them to elude police confiscation in a way that the printed page could not.

Finally, streetsingers were marginal because they existed outside of the juridical framework that shaped Old Regime society; they had neither a guild nor the most basic legal guidelines to regulate their numbers and practices. Eighteenth-century chroniclers and nineteenth-century historians have written of the wealth of French songs and spread a handful of anecdotes about famous *chansonniers*, but they have had little or nothing to say about the mass of common singers on street corners who drew the attention only of passers-by. Contemporaries occasionally compared singers and song vendors to colporteurs and criers of decrees, or lumped them together with sellers of magic elixirs and shoeshine boys, but streetsingers only became distinctly visible before the law when they transgressed it.[28] So far were they from being considered recognizable tradesmen, that they even fell beneath the attention of the Encyclopedists. For, while the *Encyclopédie* praised songs and vaudevilles as true expressions of French *esprit*, the chevalier de Jaucourt passed over *chansonniers* altogether, naming only vaudevillists of some literary accomplishment.[29]

Streetsingers were often arrested for singing obscene or otherwise offensive songs but because of the *chansonnier*'s irregular status and informal habits, the Paris police applied the most consistent regulation of songs at the level of publication, the point at which the trade was most regular. The police required that all songs be read and approved by the lieutenant general before printing. When this regulation was circumvented, royal authorities not only turned against *chansonniers*; they sought as well the printers and booksellers who were implicated, for these men were members of corporations against whom heavy fines could be levied, and they were, in some cases, expelled from their guilds for such activity.[30]

Songs provided both information and entertainment, and song books rarely retailed a single type of song (nor, doubtless, did performances).

Just as legal pamphlets mingled drinking songs and romances with celebrations of military victories and royal births, so the illegal mixed pornography with insults to the powerful.[31] In both cases, variety made the songbook a better value for the customer.

Song booklets that were sold on the streets were not printed with music: that would have raised their prices from two or three sous to a livre or more—beyond the reach of the many who could not read music.[32] Instead, cheap songs were printed with the names or choruses of the tunes to which they were meant to be sung, and because these tunes were popular or traditional, most buyers already knew them. If not, singers like Baptiste and his contemporary LaJoye printed addresses on their songsheets, where "those who are ignorant of the tunes" might find them to learn new melodies.[33]

Songs were a useful source of news in a society with limited literacy and circumscribed access to information. All noteworthy events were cause for song, and many an account in Barbier's journal closes with "this busied the *chansonniers* of our good city of Paris." Although the police would not approve songs like the one that described a public debauch involving several dancers of the Opéra or the one that advertised a student rebellion at the Collège Louis le Grand, they usually passed on songs that celebrated royal weddings and births, and they actively encouraged songs about executions and the exploits of victorious generals.[34] Openly pornographic songs were never given approbation, while songs of political scandal could arouse the ire of victims, whose response was sometimes more dangerous than that of the police.

> Saint-Amant [a singer on the pont Neuf during the reign of Louis XIV] decided suddenly one day to circulate one of his songs against M. le Prince, the refrain of which, *Laire, lan, laire,* was in itself an insult. . . . A few days afterward, the poet was found bludgeoned one fine morning, beaten to death right in the middle of the pont Neuf. M. le Prince wanted to take his revenge right where he had been insulted.[35]

To make a successful appeal to customers, the streetsinger had to draw on those same qualities that nourished the songs generally: timeliness, scandal, and wit. Timeliness mattered because songs were expected to broadcast current events: "always ready to celebrate all that happens, [*chansonniers*] often precede gazetteers and publicize the most important events with a vaudeville."[36] Then, as an event faded from memory, the songs that celebrated it declined rapidly in popularity.[37] The scandals could be anyone's, even the songwriter's, perhaps because he had been arrested or pursued for compositional audacity. In fact, the knowledge that a song had been prohibited or its author arrested would boost its popularity, sending all of Paris scrambling to find the forbidden object.[38] Meanwhile, wit and gaiety were the songs' very essence. "The French prevail over all the peoples of Europe for the wit and grace of their songs: they have always enjoyed this entertainment and have always excelled at it; . . . Our songs are of several varieties but, in general, we favor love, or wine, or satire."[39] And the vaudeville in particular, "a child of joy and gaiety," was meant to have an "unrestricted, lively, and playful character."[40] Finally, as the editor of the 1765 *Anthologie française* reminds us, songs often won audiences simply because of their charming tunes or graceful singing.[41]

Chansonniers were the most visible producers of commercial songs, but there were others. Off the streets, songs played an integral part in all fairs and boulevard theaters, where they served as a means to circumvent the Comédie-Française's monopoly on spoken dialogue.[42] Introduced as weapons in the struggle against privilege, these songs—often called *vaudevilles* but compositionally the same as *pont-neufs*—quickly became an enormously popular draw. Those that were most successful on the stage were printed and sold on the street.

Theatrical songwriters included their share of legends: Piron, Collé, Desfontaines, Piis. But these men earned a greater degree of respect than did ordinary *chansonniers* in the streets, in large part because they possessed education, literary reputation, and social contacts that won them entry into salons and singing societies and, occasionally, noble patronage. Institutional affiliation with boulevard theaters, the increasingly respectable Opéra Comique, and even the privileged Comédie-Française also gave these men an established place in Old Regime society.[43] Theatrical songwriters may have been better established and more respected than streetsingers, but all shared an intimate association with song which, however witty and broadly consumed, was nonetheless considered frivolous and foreign to the privileged establishment of Old Regime culture and society.

POLITICAL SINGING AND SONG WRITING

Although they were the most visible, commercial entertainers were not alone in writing songs and singing them for others. For even as production and performance became more discreet after the mid-seventeenth century, songs remained a common and potent means of political expression for all the king's subjects. But political songs did not simply voice complaint; they resonated through Old Regime culture, drawing enormous power from their ability to impugn personal honor and undermine reputations at all levels of society. In so doing, they troubled authorities who were concerned that songs, extraordinarily difficult to police, could weaken social and political hierarchies that structured Old Regime society.

While political songs were written and sung by all of the king's subjects, the well born and the well educated were allowed the greatest freedom of expression. Salons and affiliation with the court conferred privacy and privilege. Parisian authorities reserved their gravest suspicions for popular street singing, which they considered most dangerous to public order. Ironically, few aspects of court politics escaped being set to music. Although some such songs were meant simply to entertain, most were weapons against the enemy, like the song that advertised Madame du Barry's common origins after she helped to engineer the fall of the duc de Choiseul.[44] Greater liberty did not, however, mean complete freedom, and the severity of punishments meted out indicates the seriousness with which both the crown and the police regarded compositions that were insulting. In 1738, for example, the abbé Jean Leonard Dalainval and a cohort spent a week in the Bastille for circulating *nouvelles à la main* and "slanderous songs about different well-placed persons"; in 1749, Pidanset de Mairobert spent almost a year in the Bastille for possessing verses and songs against the king and Mme. de Pompadour, "which he showed to his friends, allowing them to make copies."[45] But of course such songs remained enormously popular.

The ease with which songs could be memorized meant that they were disseminated more widely than just as manuscripts or printed songsheets, and it helps to explain the popular use of songs to criticize and complain. In the largely oral culture of the eighteenth century, memories were honed by regular practice. Some singers acquired the remarkable mnemonic powers to which Siméon Hardy alluded when he described a thirty-four verse song against the king and queen, "which dwells in an infinite number of heads . . . so hard did people work to learn it by heart and so avoid having to transcribe it."[46] This ease of dissemination and the song's ability to pass between written and oral forms set it apart from other media. The stock of tunes that most Parisians knew enabled them to learn new lyrics quickly, and melodic simplicity allowed them to acquire still more tunes when the need arose.[47]

Print and oral cultures formed a compatible and mutually reinforcing pair in which each compensated for weaknesses of the other. A song remembered orally was safe from police and censor, while printed and manuscript copies guarded against faults of memory and facilitated broad distribution. The compatibility of written and oral forms is most apparent in the songs printed on handbills. Posted at moments of political crisis—like the Jansenist controversy of midcentury and later the calling of the Assembly of Notables—handbills served as an anonymous means to criticize the crown and its agents.[48] The police worked quickly to remove them, but Parisians were able to memorize the songs first and circulate them orally long after the originals had been confiscated.

Songs about famous people and current events served a multitude of purposes. Above all, they helped to circulate information through a society where privilege and censorship, limited literacy, and a scarcity of official news restricted communication. Like other kinds of informative media, songs varied in their degree of reliability, since they carried official news, rumor, and gossip. And like other kinds of informative media, songs varied in their degree of legality. The crown permitted, and at times even encouraged, flattering songs like this one, printed with police approbation in 1744:

Roi des Français;	King of the French;
Tu étais né pour la Couronne,	You were born for the crown,
Roi des Français;	King of the French;
Ton Sang nous impose des lois:	Your blood imposes laws upon us:
Mais nous chérissons ta Personne,	But we cherish you,
Et c'est notre coeur qui te nomme	And our heart names you
ROI DES FRANÇAIS.[49]	KING OF THE FRENCH.

It censored and chased mocking, bitter, or angry songs, like that celebrating the fall of Maupeou in 1774:

Chanson sur l'air, du haut en bas

La poule au pot	The chicken in the pot
Depuis longtemps était promise	Had long been promised
La poule au pot	The chicken in the pot
Attendait dès longtemps *Turgot*	Has long awaited *Turgot*
Terray n'est plus, la nappe est mise	*Terray* is no more, the table is set
L'on va bientôt mettre à sa guise	We'll soon put him in his spot
La poule au pot.	The chicken in the pot.
Maupeou n'est plus,	*Maupeou* is no more,
Thémis reprendre la balance;	Thémis recaptures the scale;
Maupeou n'est plus,	*Maupeou* is no more,

Ce monstre a fait place aux vertus	This monster has given way to virtues
Reparaissez Dieu d'abondance	Reappear God of plenty
Riez français, faites bombance	Laugh, Frenchmen, and revel
Maupeou n'est plus.[50]	*Maupeou* is no more.

A song's legality was tied to the commentary that it advertised, but that itself was a complex matter. Commentary was not based simply on what one sang; it drew power from the way singing resonated with political practices and notions of honor as well as from the songs' associations. Old Regime politics was based on negotiations for power at all levels of society. Louis-Sebastien Mercier claimed that public life was rife with subtle expressions of approval or disapproval of court politics, expressions that the crown heeded because it was keenly aware of the wealth and numbers that lay behind them.

> The Court is very attentive to the talk among Parisians; it calls them *frogs*. What do the frogs say? the princes often ask one another. And when the frogs applaud their appearance at the theater, or on the road to Sainte Geneviève, they are very happy. Sometimes the frogs punish them with silence; in short, the princes can read opinions about themselves in the behavior of the people.[51]

Rather than openly combating the crown, as they had done during the Fronde, Parisians expressed dissatisfaction by singing satiric or bitter songs and epigrams or by refusing to offer shouts of *vive le roi*. Alternately, they signaled pleasure by applause and vocal acclamation. Mercier was critical of such behavior, which he argued was the product of Parisians' indifference to their political condition—an indifference they sustained as long as their ills did not become too oppressive.[52] But applause offered or withheld and studied indifference did more than shape political dialogue; they were motivated by the knowledge that words and seemingly petty acts played an important part in the system of honor that sustained all members of French society. Whether one was minister of state or a washerwoman in the faubourg St. Antoine, a sound reputation was a valuable asset. At the upper reaches of society, honor was essential to successfully navigating court politics and international credit systems alike, and the importance of a good name often outweighed possession of the right skills.[53] At the opposite end of the social scale, working people cultivated their reputations as ends in themselves and as instruments of negotiation with neighbors, merchants, or police.[54]

Song writing and singing could damage a good name in a variety of ways. Simply penning songs discredited the marquis de Pezai who, in a letter whose length belied its casual tone, sought to persuade the lieutenant general of police of how little consequence had been his youthful compositions of songs and comic operas. He beseeched Sartine to intervene with the dauphin, who had been led to believe that Pezai, as an occasional composer, was unfit to become a maréchal of France.[55] Others, however, were damned by songs whose express intent was to shame and embarrass.

> M. Dodun, controller general of finances and extremely rich, acquired the marquisat of Herbault. . . . Considering it too bourgeois to remain an *homme de robe*, above all now that he possessed the *cordon bleu*, he took the sword [and] had himself called Monsieur the marquis of Herbault. . . . Since the *sieur* Dodun is roundly hated, his origins were investigated and it was discovered that his grandfather had been a footman. In the end, songs were written about him and his wife that even the shoeshiners sang. Madame Dodun did not sleep for eight days.[56]

Songs were cruelly effective in undermining an enemy's honor because they literally took that person's name into the street, spreading insults far and wide with little hope of silence. Once a song had gained currency, the only possible responses were ignoring it or countering it with a song of one's own.[57] And, as the case of the marquis de Pezai suggests, a song need not openly attack to damage a reputation; often it was enough merely to associate a name with this particular means of expression. Songs were defined as witty, frivolous, sarcastic, and ridiculing: to pair a respected name with such an inherently irreverent means of expression clearly implied insult. Some songs, of course, were legal announcements of royal births and marriages, but these circulated because they served the crown's interests, functioning as one of the signs of approbation about which Mercier spoke. However, singers were forbidden to do more than that: songs that referred too explicitly to persons of rank were likely to attract the hostility of the crown and its authorities.[58]

The crown's agents chased disrespectful songs for the same reasons that they tracked rumor, tried to silence gossip about the well born, and punished those who had merely penned denunciations of the king on slips of paper.[59] The crown pursued all of these not because it feared that words lead to actions but because words *were* actions. Living within an oral culture based on honor and ceremony, the French king and his subjects used language as a means of power; words did not refer abstractly to other ideas or possible actions, they were things in themselves.[60] Even if words and the music behind them rarely galvanized crowds into action, they could sully reputations, undermine respect, and weaken social and political hierarchies.

One might expect, therefore, that the policing of songs was only a game of cat and mouse between police and songwriter. However, singing was one of many activities that formed a spectrum of resistance which ranged from the monarchy's unrealizable ideal of total obedience to open riot and rebellion. While crown and police chased hostile and irreverent songs, men and women of letters argued that—like writing anagrams, epigrams, and verse—composing and performing such songs served as a necessary pressure valve for the release of tensions that might otherwise overturn the social order.

> The Italians cool their anger with *pasquinades*, and the majority of Frenchmen let theirs shine in songs.[61]
>
> There have fallen into my hands two small satiric pieces, ordinary productions of the Parisian imagination which, happily, no longer knows of other means to revenge itself or satisfy its discontent than with the arms of wit alone.[62]

Such writers illuminated a facet of song culture that Mercier's criticism ignored. Parisians were not wholly indifferent to their condition, and they had means other than riot and rebellion to make their opinions felt. Songs could be used in daily struggles for power because they resonated within the existing system of honor and respect: all knew that hostile or mocking songs did not simply release individual frustrations, they were darts that could very well hit their mark.[63]

Thus, while the crown's agents attempted to censor songs, some writers argued that singing facilitated the smooth functioning of society and that silence was the more dangrous expression. Silence might mean that social tensions were no longer being released gradually or, worse, that public anger had risen to a level for which songs could no longer compensate. Thus, when the Paris Parlement was exiled in 1787 and crowds began to riot, Siméon Hardy worried: "We see with uneasiness that the light-heartedness of Parisians seems to have been extinguished by a general indignation which cannot restrain itself even in public; they no longer compose satiric songs nor circulate malicious little epigrams."[64] The court had quite clearly made a very serious mistake.

THE REPRESENTATION OF SONGS AND THE PROBLEM OF POPULAR CULTURE

Here we must stop and look back to our starting point: the pont Neuf and other such places where streetsingers and others sang simply for entertainment.

> It was 10:30. . . . Returning by way of the boulevard Saintmarcel, we heard a few young people of both sexes singing before a door. They laughed and sang. Sara was naturally a happy person. One of the young men having sung a verse of the romance, *Gabrielle De-Vergi*, Sara hid in a patch of rye and responded with the second. Her sparkling voice caused a profound silence and lively admiration. They listened to her.[65]

Singing for entertainment was common throughout Paris, crossing class and age lines. Songs about court scandals and royal family affairs were matched by noisy drinking songs, outrageous pornographic songs, romances, and complaints about drunken or violent husbands.[66] And political songs could be entertaining too. There was, after all, no reason why an attack upon the king's minister or his mistress or his policies should not also get a good laugh. So, for example, an anonymous songwriter might denounce and mock the collapse of Law's system all in one breath.

Lundi, je pris des actions,	Monday, I bought some stock,
Mardi, je gagnis des millions,	Tuesday, I earned milions,
Mercredi, je pris equipage,	Wednesday, I outfitted myself,
Jeudi, j'arrangis mon ménage,	Thursday, I furnished my house,
Vendredi, je m'en fus au bal,	Friday, I went to a ball,
Et Samedi, à l'hôpital![67]	And Saturday, hocked it all!

The line between political and entertainment singing was not always fixed or clear, and the anger that gave rise to a song did not necessarily keep it from being playful. Parisians were famous for their love of language and word games. Mercier described the rivers of words that flowed through the city daily, as conversations were struck up among waiting coachmen, between merchants and customers, or across adjoining tables in any café.[68] Hardy filled his seven-volume journal with innumerable examples of the songs, anagrams, epigrams, and poems that "passed through his hands" after any noteworthy event. Who but a devotee of language (and an implacable enemy of Maupeou) would expend the effort necessary to discover that the minister's full name was an anagram for "nous chancelier mauvais, né pour le dégât" (governs us badly, born for havoc)?[69] And those lovers of jokes and language who did not make up their own songs might still appreciate the talent in others, and so learn and repeat the songs they heard on street corners or in fair and boulevard theaters.

The characteristics described here—the active role of songs in unregulated and theatrical entertainment, the lowly and uncertain status of streetsingers, and the confusion between politicizing and entertaining—explain the silences and outright ambivalence that prevailed in literary representations of song culture. For while songs were celebrated in print, certain of their qualities were also the object of scorn. Thus Mercier, grousing about the rage for rhyming, implied that songs were incapable of voicing serious thought. "This repetition of consonants, this puerile tinkling, [which] costs the language its clarity, its precision, its very flexibility," was, he suggested, best left to songs and vaudevilles, "for which alone it seems appropriate."[70] Restif, as we have seen, voiced his disgust with the daily practitioners of an irregular occupation when he dismissed *chansonniers* as a pack of miserable idlers, speaking no better of them than did the police agents who pursued singers of illegal songs. Even Siméon Hardy, far less irritable than either Mercier or Restif, occasionally suggested that songs—dozens if not hundreds of which he had transcribed into his journals—constituted a frivolous response to serious matters: in 1771 he castigated "the French nation which takes frivolity to the point of amusing itself with ridiculous pleasantries under the most disastrous circumstances."[71]

Even literary rhetoric that celebrated popular songs tended to circumvent or exclude its less picturesque traits. It either represented "song" as an entity that somehow sang itself or relied on standard tales about legendary *chansonniers* with picturesque reputations and harmless qualities. The uniform worn by the coachman of Verthamont, the Savoyard's blindness, Fanchon's (real or imagined) *hôtel*, and the like were features that set these streetsingers apart as colorfully unusual while bestowing a recognizable identity that kept them from becoming too marginal. Public chroniclers who sought to praise *chansonniers* secured their colorful and amusing reputations by describing them as having sung legal songs—complaints, romances, hymns—or illegal ones that (unlike those found in police files) were free of obscenities and anger. And when these commentators spoke about the more popular political singing against obnoxious ministers or crown policies, their language rarely conjured up visions of angry voices or faces. Certainly Parisians relied on mockery and satire to express frustration and discontent, but the other, more frightening face of the carnivalesque, the very real anger expressed when the needs of the populace seemed to have been completely dismissed, was often disregarded in print.

The chroniclers and Encyclopedists, even poets and educated vaudevillists who described Parisian song culture actively negotiated between the ideal and the real.[72] Their negotiations probably reflected the conflicted attitudes of many cultured Parisians. Just as the unpleasant realities of song culture did not keep authors from celebrating songs, so it did not keep Parisians from singing. The chaotic reality of song culture did mean, however, that singing was hedged with unflattering associations. The well born and well educated penned songs, sang, and laughed at what they heard on street corners, but they continued to place songs at the bottom of their cultural hierarchies.[73] Others doubtless saw matters in the same terms as the Norman *parlementaire* LeCerf de la Vieville, who simply ignored the greatest number of people when speaking of a "popular" taste in music. For him, "popular" meant "people of quality . . . who frequent the theaters," and certainly not "shop boys, porters, waitresses, and cooks who listen to songs by the pont Neuf and never go to the Opéra."[74] In short, with other means of expression and information available to them, such men and women did not worry that singing cheapened them or undermined their reputations; a few probably believed that they were slumming, but most saw singing as one means of expression and amusement among many.

This was truly a common culture. Men and women throughout Old Regime society composed and sang political songs and entertainment songs alike, and apart from certain refinements of language, songs destined for the pont Neuf or for a private salon formulated insults in roughly the same terms. However, while Parisians shared a common set of cultural practices, they did not necessarily believe that they were all doing the same thing, or that their actions had the same implications. Although the cultivated praised the culture of song and actually sang quite regularly, they, like the crown and its agents, had grave suspicions about those who used only this means of expression or who used it too often. Literary celebrations of a few mythically picturesque *chansonniers* aside, most streetsingers were marginal figures who evoked the hostility of police and earned little respect from chroniclers of daily life. Memorialists and Encyclopedists represented singing as cheap entertainment and as an effective means of expressing anger. In their view it was not a serious cultural form, nor were songwriters capable of developed reasoned critiques of politics; singing was a fleeting means of expression that reflected popular passions or passing fancies. Of course, those who cast these judgments had access to other kinds of entertainment and other means of political expression.

Thus, song culture was characterized by a sharp distinction between, on the one hand, compositional and performative practices that were shared by French men and women from the court to the pont Neuf and, on the other hand, by cultivated representations which described singing as a vulgar means of expression that was not to be taken seriously as cultural or political expression. It is this distinction that permits us to treat songs and singing as forms of "popular culture." For although singing practices were shared, definitions of what it meant to sing most definitely were not. More importantly, this distinction between shared practices and critical representations did not simply vanish in 1789; it persisted to help shape revolutionary song culture as revolutionaries and counterrevolutionaries struggled both to understand and to redefine the political implications of singing.

Chapter Two

✦

Songs in the Street (1787–July 1792)

✦ IF, AS SIMÉON HARDY has told us, the exile of Parlement in August 1787 filled Parisians with such indignation that they ceased writing satiric songs, then Parlement's return in September must have rescued Parisian *esprit*. Celebrants gathered around the Palais de Justice, most notably in place Dauphine, to set off fireworks and throw rocks at soldiers. Many sang a new song that celebrated Parlement's return, and which was circulated in manuscript and in print:

Sur l'air: ah! le bel oiseau

Elle est enfin de retour	It has at last returned
Cette auguste compagnie.	This august company.
Français, en cet heureux jour,	Frenchmen, on this happy day,
Chantons tous malgré l'envie:	Let's sing despite jealousy:
Vive, vive le Parlement!	Long live the Parlement!
Adieu la mélancolie	Goodbye to melancholy
Vive, vive le Parlement	Long live the Parlement
Et son premier Président![1]	And its first President

As was usual, such a noteworthy event improved the business of the most quick-witted *chansonniers*. Two particularly enterprising singers erected an arbor of laurel branches and ribbons directly opposite the main gate of the Palais de Justice, where they proceeded to sing and sell their latest: a song with the refrain "Vive le Roi, le Parlement" (Long live the king and Parlement), whose tune was lifted from the Beaumarchais opera, *Tarare*.[2] Printed copies of this song were no more than "a small square of paper the size of an in-12° page . . . unadorned by police per-mission," and in Hardy's opinion not worth their price of two sous, but they sold well. When the singers returned to the Palais for a second day of business, they had scarcely enough songsheets to meet the demands of the crowd that surrounded them.[3]

Historians have become used to thinking of the period during which these events occurred as the "pre-Revolution," when old means of polit-ical negotiation and representation broke down, setting in motion the sequence of events that would lead to the Revolution in 1789. But how-ever radical the political events that singers in place Dauphine cele-brated, their songs and singing practices remained rooted in the Old Regime. Like most eighteenth-century songs, these were set to well-known tunes, and they drew their popularity from the news worthiness of the events that they celebrated. Fleetingly current, they would disap-pear within a week or two, when Parisians turned their attention else-where.

But this moment in place Dauphine marks an endpoint. In the course of the next few years, singers, auditors, and critics would re-shape traditional practices and representations before abandoning them altogether and creating a new and recognizably revolutionary song culture. Streetsingers would soon cease to be exemplary public singers, as amateurs moved to the representational foreground, to sing choruses that advertised political opinions or commemorated recent events. Songs themselves changed: lyrics offered new descriptions of politics and suggested novel representations of popular activism. Even singing practices would undergo transformation as a new song, *Ça ira*, acquired emblematic status in the eyes of revolutionaries and royalists alike.

As songs and singing practices were reshaped to meet the needs and experiences of a revolutionary society, a new song culture emerged which, flexible and pluralistic, was capable of expressing a broad range of opinions. But as the Revolution moved onward, this culture would os-sify as songs both expressed and helped to reinforce the polarized poli-tics that would become characteristic of revolutionary society in the mid-nineties. And throughout this period, revolutionaries would strug-gle with Old Regime characterizations of songs as a "popular" means of expression. For rather than simply abandoning old ideas, many journal-ists and politicians translated traditional ambivalence into revolutionary terms by expressing doubts about the political seriousness of singing. But as practices changed, new kinds of representations began to emerge. By 1792, many of the cultural elites who claimed to speak for the revolutionary movement would be expressing novel ideas about the political and pedagogic strengths of singing.

EMERGING FROM THE OLD REGIME

Parisian political culture developed rapidly but unevenly after 1787. Political practice and the emerging periodical press radicalized quickly as ministers, deputies, journalists, and pamphleteers abandoned traditional means of debate and resolution. The rich citywide web of informal expressions—songs, rumors, handbills, demonstrations, occasionally riots—evolved more slowly, however, as Parisians appropriated traditional media to respond to and participate in new political events. These media were vital in disseminating the new political crisis beyond the walls of government, but as they did so, they were in turn altered.

The popular action that led to the taking of the Bastille was among the most dramatic examples of traditional expression become revolutionary, but there were more discreet cases as well. In August and September 1789, for example, market women revolutionized traditional processions of thanks to the city's patron saint simply by organizing them. By initiating these processions they were assuming a role that had once belonged to the Paris Parlement itself.[4] Processions took on new significance. Hardy observed that "many people find them frightening in their arrangement, their composition, and their size. A few find these public actions ridiculous, as they are impossible to interrupt and, sadly, are not entirely motivated by piety."[5] Ceremonial could, of course, be appropriated in less threatening ways. For example, under the Old Regime, Parisians had commonly made offerings to the royal couple in celebration of special events like the queen's name day or a royal entry into Paris.[6] But as the events of 1788 and 1789 enlarged the group of public figures beloved by the people, Louis XVI and Marie-Antoinette found themselves part of an ever-expanding company that included Necker, Lafayette, Bailly, and other deputies to the National Assembly, as well as the Parisian electors for the third estate. All were now celebrated in song, and many received offerings from the hands of Parisian market women.[7]

Like demonstrations and ceremony, song culture quickly came to include both the old and the new; singers adapted traditional practices to revolutionary events, and songwriters produced lyrics that expressed new perspectives. As we saw in the preceeding chapter, Old Regime singers did not always state their opinions openly: often only the song's tone or even its tune, like Saint-Amant's *laire, lan, laire*, communicated a singer's sense of approbation or injustice. Similarly, Old Regime theater audiences used noisy and disruptive applause to indicate that a particular song applied to a recent event or a famous personality.[8] These practices were carried into the Revolution with lasting consequences.

Revolutionary singers began by using well-known tunes, already understood to have allusive meaning, to signal peaceful intent and hostility alike. For example, the women of Paris who marched on Versailles in October 1789 hid their cannon as they neared the palace and began to sing *Vive Henri IV*, proclaiming their loyalty to that king.[9] Conversely, in the spring of 1790, when a crowd tried to clear the Capuchins St. Honoré of clergy speaking against the suppression of church property, "scorn and ridicule were the only arms with which to disperse that gang. . . . The crowd was enormous. M. de Virieux climbed onto a chair to call for the floor and silence. Seeing that he was accorded neither the floor nor silence, he shouted: *People! people! You are being misled!* Hoots kept the speaker from going any further, and an oboe began to play the tune *Marlboroug s'en vat en guerre* [sic]."[10]

Journalists did not simply report such incidents as they happened to witness them; like theater audiences, they sought performances of music that they considered "analogous to the circumstances" and used them rhetorically to suggest the hopes of those present or to reveal what they believed to be the essential truth of circumstances at hand. It was for this reason that the journalist A.-J. Gorsas claimed that the song *Où peut-on être mieux qu'au sein de sa famille?* (Where is one happier than in the bosom of his family?) was "analogous to the circumstances" when it was played for the king's first visit to Paris after the taking of the Bastille. In so describing the song, Gorsas emphasized the day's festivities and the Parisians' hopefulness rather than the king's manifest uneasiness at finding himself surrounded by an armed citizenry.[11]

Songs too were undergoing subtle changes as new was grafted onto old. Cheap songsheets carried lyrics that described current events as they had always done, but which were also slowly elevating common people to the center stage, formerly occupied by kings and ministers.[12] Traditionally, song lyrics had represented events as the outcome of actions taken by political elites: kings and queens, ministers, nobles, and, perhaps, a tiny handful of influential outsiders. Thus, even songs that mocked the powerful—like the anonymous *Pot Pourri* against the Assembly of Notables of 1787—gave voice only to the elite and implied that average men and women could do no more than bear witness to events and react with joy or anguish.

Or Messieurs, cette assemblée,	Now good men, this assembly,
Qui tient en ces tristes jours;	Which meets in these sad days;
A la France désolée,	To troubled France,
Ne pouvant porter secours	Can bring no help
Bientôt sera expulsée,	Soon it will be evicted,
Et sans de bonnes raisons	And without good reasons
Finira par des chansons.[13]	All will finish with a song.

After July 1789, when common people entered political life by seizing the Bastille, they became more conspicuous in lyrics. So, for example, the *Récit historique de ce qui s'est passé dans la ville de Paris depuis le commencement de Juillet* (Historical account of what happened in Paris since the beginning of July) only briefly attended to the king before looking elsewhere:

Le Peuple enfin s'irrite de voir que l'on s'agite	The people, at last angered to see these goings-on,
Et qu'on n'avance à rien, il met en évidence	Which lead nowhere, give ample proof
Que tout sujet de France doit être Citoyen.	That every French subject must be a citizen.

Subsequent verses went still further, identifying specific individuals who executed concrete actions within the crowd:

A l'assaut, sans attendre, qui d'abord a monté,	To the assault, without delay, who first climbed up,
Comme l'on doit entendre, ce fut le sieur Harné,	As you must hear tell, it was Master Harné,
Brave Soldat des Gardes, que partout l'on regarde,	Courageous soldier of the Guard, watched from everywhere,
Suivi du sieur Humbert, qui sur les embrasures	Followed by Master Humbert, who at the breach,
Montrent en belle figure, drapeaux à découvert.	Shows a fine figure, flags waving in the air.
Bientôt le sieur Hélie, que l'on avait cru mort,	Soon Master Hélie, once believed dead,
Reparaît plein de vie, glorieux dans ce fort,	Reappears full of life, glorious in this fortress,
• • • • • • • • • • •	• • • • • • • • • • •
Le sieur Maillard ensuite, portant drapeau d'honneur,	Master Maillard next, carrying the flag of honor,
Tous deux vont au plus vite d'abord au Gouverneur;	Side by side they fly quickly to the Governer;

Le saisissent et l'emmenant et son	They seize him, taking him and
épée qu' il tiennent,	the sword he wields,
Dont il veut se percer, jusqu'à	With which he hopes to pierce
l'Hôtel de Ville.[14]	himself, off to the City Hall.

This song and others like it reflected the politics of the Revolution, which now included popular as well as royal or ministerial activity. But these songs did not simply describe; their lyrics encouraged singers to identify with the actors they celebrated: "Adieu Bastille . . ./ Nous voilà maîtres" (So long Bastille . . . / We are the masters now).[15] Such identification would broaden steadily over the years. By 1791, singers would go beyond identifying with Parisian crowds to identify with the larger polity, singing of *their* deputies, *their* laws, *their* Nation.

Camarades, buvons; chantons	Comrades, let's drink; let's sing
L'honneur de notre nation,	Our nation's honor,
Nos braves députées seront	Our courageous deputies will be
Au temple de gloire	In the temple of glory
Gravé dans l'histoire,	Engraved in history,
De tout notre coeur publions,	With all our hearts, let's proclaim
Vive la constitution.[16]	Long live the constitution.

Faced with a radically new political situation, Parisians were responding with the only means of expression at their disposal, those acquired during a lifetime under what was now an "old regime." Cultural practices and means of expression were flexible enough to encompass new events and changed political relations, and they would continue to be reshaped over the next several years. For this reason, change during the early years of the Revolution was often a rapid process of growth and accretion. A revolutionary culture was emerging from tensions between street activities, newspaper accounts, the force of events, and developing oppositions between revolutionaries and royalists.

The first years of the Revolution witnessed extraordinary cultural ferment, as revolutionaries and royalists alike experimented with different ways to represent their experiences and new states of mind. While private citizens improvised demonstrations and celebrations in the streets of Paris, journalists and correspondents conducted lively exchanges in print about how to reshape French culture in accord with revolutionary ideals. They did more than demand that aristocratic tropes be purged from language and literature; they developed explanations for the new symbols like the Phrygian cap; they recounted anecdotes that they hoped would serve as models of correct revolutionary behavior; and they sometimes simply puzzled over seemingly opaque gestures. Revolutionary culture was, during these years, both flexible and uncertain, because revolutionaries themselves were uncertain. Divided in their political aspirations and still vague in their self-definition, revolutionaries were unsure how to represent themselves and their project. But it was an exhilarating and liberal uncertainty, which permitted experimentation and a plurality of opinions.

While citizens in the streets used singing to participate in and celebrate the Revolution from its outset, revolutionary newspapers only intermittently reported such activity. For in spite of the emergence of revolutionary lyrics and the growing popularity of singing in the streets, journalists and their correspondents continued to treat singing with mistrust and even scorn, thus helping to sustain a distinction between broadly shared practices and the representation of singing as a vulgar and marginal means of expression. In the revolutionary press, Old Regime cultural hierarchies were recycled in the form of revolutionary critiques of songs' political capacity.

At a performance of the *The Marriage of Figaro* in December 1789, the lyric that would later be the opening epigram of many a song collection and the closing remark of many a discussion met with a decidedly unfavorable reaction. "When someone in the loges shouted encore after the couplet *everything finishes with a song*, a patriot in the parterre stood up, singing *everything finishes with cannons*; the occupant of the loges did not shout encore for him."[17] Although this reaction was reported in the context of a performance, it was more often explicated in print. A reader of the *Chronique de Paris* explained it best. Responding to an article claiming that the ancient Greeks used the same word for "songs" and "laws" because they knew that one might use songs to govern, the reader protested, "The Greeks never considered governing with songs; little children know that Mazarin said of the French: *Let them sing, they'll pay anyway*; and what frightens the aristocracy today is that we talk, we write, we arm ourselves, and we do not sing."[18]

As critics saw it, the French nation had made a political revolution and transformed the relationship between the people and the king. This relationship, although still qualified by adoration of royalty, was founded on a new maturity that arose from the third estate's participation in the government. And such maturity implied a seriousness of character that disdained songs as the frivolous distractions of a politically impotent people. As the Abbé Fauchet put it, "friends of the Constitution and of the mores appropriate to a newly liberated people produce writings that are solemn, strict, and just."[19] The frivolity of the song, rooted in its lightness and gaiety and its Old Regime value as entertainment, meant that it might easily be turned to ill effect and fall prey to the machinations of the aristocracy. Camille Desmoulins, who admitted that he sometimes listened to streetsingers whose couplets lacked "neither gaiety nor *esprit*," cautioned his readers that "song merchants have never been required to hold principles or a sense of honor; it is enough that they don't grate on the ears of passers-by as they scrape on their violins."[20]

No one actually suggested abolishing songs or clearing the streets of singers. Some singers even received the backhanded compliments of newspaper correspondents who expressed delighted surprise that, despite the essentially frivolous nature of the genre, they heard songs "composed in the spirit of revolution."[21] But given its tarnished reputation, the most favorable printed accounts typified singing as a harmless amusement which entertained and intermittently reminded passers-by of liberty. Songs were far from being accorded the morality, purpose, and pedagogic efficaciousness that had already been granted to both the press and the theater.[22]

The degree to which representations of song culture continued to be shaped by Old Regime ideas and stereotypes was underscored by discussions of festival hymns. Critics were suspicious of popular songs, but those who wrote about hymns had only praise for a form that they associated with the church and the military. This tiny group of writers saw themselves carrying hymns boldly into the revolutionary future, where they would instruct and inspire. Describing an ideal performance of his imagined *Hymn to Liberty*, one author rhapsodized, "It is with such simple means that men of state in all countries have accomplished great things. . . . A people becomes invincible, and there is nothing of which they are not capable, when one can inspire them to say, as Horace proclaimed to the Romans, *dulce et decorum est pro patria mori.*"[23] Another writer criticized the *Te Deum*, which he or she associated with war and the injustices of the Inquisition, but did so in order to demand "a French hymn, which can only improve on the *Te Deum*," for the festival of Federation.[24]

But hymns were generically associated with poetry, and their performance conjured up visions of trained and tightly organized orchestras and choirs, far different from street singing. Singing ceremonial hymns corresponded more closely to the activities of schools and churches than to the undisciplined popular invention of street songs. For a more tolerant and sophisticated discussion of street songs to take place, a significant change in the prevailing point of view was necessary. The initiative for this change came from the most likely and yet the least expected source: popular invention in the streets of Paris.

REVOLUTIONIZING PRACTICE

In the first week of July 1790, Parisians volunteered by the thousands to help level the Champ de Mars in preparation for the first festival of Federation, and it was during these days of common labor that the first truly revolutionary song, *Ça ira*, was born. The festival of Federation closed the first year of the Revolution, a year characterized by hopefulness and common efforts to reconstitute French society, as well as by sporadic episodes of urban and rural violence. People traveled from all parts of France to watch the king, the Assembly, and the armed forces swear to protect the state and the constitution. The festival, which marked the first anniversary of the taking of the Bastille, was believed to open a new era made possible by the success of the Revolution.[25]

It was about this time that *Ça ira*'s reputation as the anthem of the Revolution was born. Regardless of when *Ça ira* was written, it was christened and given symbolic value by the days that preceded the first festival of Federation, when seemingly all of Paris joined together to prepare the Champ de Mars.[26] Over the next two years, *Ça ira* would transcend the ephemeral popularity characteristic of most songs as it moved beyond entertaining, informing, or complaint to become an emblem of revolutionary aspirations. And as *Ça ira* and the singing practices associated with it became revolutionary, representations of song culture would begin to change as well.

When, in early July, rumors began to circulate that the Champ de Mars would not be cleared in time for the festival, Parisians began coming to the work site to help. As early as 4 July, a district battalion passed a motion organizing workers, and the number of volunteers from throughout the city grew steadily over subsequent days. Camille Desmoulins claimed that 150,000 people labored there, Prud'homme reported that there were 300,000.[27] If the upcoming festival of Federation was to mark the beginning of a new era, then the preparation of the Champ de Mars symbolized the hopes of what it might be. Stories were told repeatedly of the willingness of all to do whatever they could, of the mixing of classes working shoulder to shoulder, of the peace, order, and single-minded purpose that existed throughout.

> In this arena, the disheveled courtesan found herself next to the prudish citizenness; the Capuchin boozed with the Knight of Saint-Louis, as did the porter with the libertine of the Palais Royal; the robust market woman pushed the wheelbarrow filled by a lady of fashion. The well-to-do, the indigent, people in tailored clothes and those in tatters, the aged, women, religious communities, academicians, actors, etc. formed this mighty and animated workshop . . . and everywhere were to be found the feelings that

arise from the common labor of men who are animated by enthusiasm, exhilaration, and appreciative rivalry.[28]

A merchant contributed a barrel of wine to ease the thirst of those who had worked hardest; a young man left two watches lying on top of his jacket while he labored at some distance without fear of theft; deputies to the Federation and members of the National Assembly came to dig and drag away cartloads of dirt. Even the king came to witness this fraternal activity, and he too took up a shovel for a few moments.[29]

But if the preparations of the Champ de Mars suggested the brightest and most hopeful vision of the Revolution, it also carried reminders of tensions and hostilities. For example, after a day spent working at the Champ de Mars, the colliers of Paris "marched by the light of torches. They were preceded by a banner on which was written: *The last gasp of the aristocracy.* Immediately following the banner was one of their own who they had tied up and dressed in black with a short coat. This was the aristocracy, which they represented in the costume of the Abbé Maury."[30] Meanwhile, the butchers worked beneath a banner that bore a large knife and the warning: "tremble aristocrats, here are the butchers."[31] The journalist Prud'homme reminded his readers that "the nature of a free people is to tame the arrogant and PARDON THE VANQISHED. Aristocrats no longer deserve your wrath," at the same time that rumors circulated that the entire Champ de Mars had been mined by counterrevolutionary conspirators who were going to blow it up, along with the Ecole Militaire, on the day of the Federation.[32] Throughout the entire week those who worked at the Champ de Mars sang, and above all they favored "a new song called the *Carillon national.* Everyone sings at once: *ça ira, ça ira, ça ira.*"[33]

Ça ira is a simple song with a quick, bright tune. Its rapid chorus, interspersed with staccato repetitions of *ça ira* (things will work out) calls to mind nothing so much as dancers breathless from whirling about. The song is lyrically simple, too, which permitted a broad range of invention; for the song to continue to be recognizable as the *Ça ira* all it need do was retain tune and chorus.[34] Almost immediately it had several different versions. Printed lyrics celebrated the upcoming festival of Federation:

Ah! ça ira, ça ira, ça ira	Ah! ça ira, ça ira, ça ira
Réjouissons nous le bon temps viendra,	Let's rejoice, good times will come,
Les gens des Halles jadis *a quia*	The market people, once overwhelmed
Peuvent chanter *alléluia.*[35]	Can now sing hallelujah.

or commemorated its occurrence in the recent past:

Ah! ça ira, ça ira, ça ira	Ah! ça ira, ça ira, ça ira
Il nous faut chanter en réjouis- sance	We must sing in celebration
Ah! ça ira, ça ira, ça ira	Ah! ça ira, ça ira, ça ira
De la grande fête on se souvien- dra.[36]	All will remember the great festival.

Such lyrics sometimes included a brief reference to the Revolution's op-position: "Malgré les mutins tout réussira / Nos ennemis confus en restent là" (In spite of rebels everything will succeed / Our bewildered enemies will stay put),[37] but generally they were hopeful and concilia-tory. They celebrated a Revolution that faced only the task of legislative consolidation, and they proclaimed the possibility of peaceful coopera-tion between all members of the former estates. These were not, how-ever, the only versions of *Ça ira*. Others, more belligerent, seem not to have been printed at the time: "the chorus of most of the songs was, *ça ira, Hang the aristocrats!*"[38] The *Chronique de Paris* remarked, "We cannot describe all the songs that people sang . . .; suffice it to say that the aris-tocrats were not spared."[39]

Ça ira grew up around the first festival of Federation, and acquired its significance from the preparations that preceded it. The song's symbolic importance emerged from the combination of official sanction and pop-ular initiative that was apparent in the choice of the date of the anniver-sary and in the organization of the festival. In declaring the first official festival of the Revolution, the members of the National Assembly were not commemorating a royal or legislative action but a popular uprising, one that had been entirely independent of official guidance or sanc-tion.[40] With this celebration, the Assembly officially acknowledged a date that already held a central place in popular memory.[41] But no revolu-tionary anthem emerged from the festival itself, for several reasons.

Quite simply, no song was composed for the festival of Federation that could be carried back into the streets and sung on succeeding days. There were only tunes played by military musicians and a *Te Deum* writ-ten especially for the occasion by Gossec. Although the *Te Deum* was writ-ten in *plein chant*, meaning that the music was relatively easy to learn, it was still a *Te Deum*, and it was still in Latin. Hardly the sort of piece to have wide popular appeal. But there were also important differences be-tween the festival and the events that surrounded it, and these provide a clearer understanding of the importance bestowed upon *Ça ira*.

The preparation of the Champ de Mars had a special significance because it actively represented the highest ideals of the Revolution. Populace cooperated with government and the former estates cooperated among themselves to build an arena for the first national festival of the Revolution. The spontaneous, popular initiative that went into these activities made them that much dearer to popular memory: this was an event in which the populace was intimately involved and for which they were directly responsible. Rather than being consigned to the edge of a circle to watch the king and the National Guard swear to protect the Revolution on their behalf, they participated in acts of commemoration and celebration.[42] Finally, in spite of the great spectacle of the Federation, the ceremony of the 14th was a solemn event. Almost silent but for military and religious music, it contrasted sharply with the days that preceded and followed, when there was much singing, dancing, and celebration. On Sunday the 18th, for example, "The ruins of the Bastille offered a third arena of celebration. The eight towers of the fortress were represented by 83 trees covered with leaves . . . a chain of lanterns, festively suspended, ran from tree to tree. In the middle, a pole 60 feet high . . . carried a banner on which was written the word LIBERTY in huge letters. . . . A sign, made merry by the contrast that it evoked, adorned the door of this room: *Here, we dance.*"[43]

Closely associated with the popularly initiated and celebratory preparations of the Champ de Mars, *Ça ira* reflected two faces of the Revolution. Its lyrics were as fluid as the culture within which it was born. By July 1790, two dominant visions of the Revolution's future were emerging: one aspired to a peaceful resolution of political differences and a successful cooperation among former estates; the other saw French society and politics being pulled with ever-increasing force between the Right and the Left. In July 1789, Gorsas had tried, in the *Courrier*, to simply dismiss the tensions between the desired "analogousness" of *Où peut-on être mieux qu'au sein de sa famille?* and the painfully real circumstance of the king looking fearfully at the armed crowd that surrounded him. By July 1790, however, newspapers that recorded and endorsed the hopeful vision suggested by the work at the Champ de Mars were cognizant, as well, of the political and social tensions manifest there. *Ça ira,* gaining popularity in a revolutionary society that had not yet established a coherent definition of itself, fit well. Conciliatory and hostile versions reflected the two most common ideas of the Revolution, and this song expressed both.

The birth of *Ça ira* elicited a response that showed the other face of the Revolution. Once revolutionaries had adopted their anthem, royalists replied with an emblematic song of their own: *O Richard, ô mon Roi.* *O Richard,* like *Ça ira,* was associated with a very particular set of circumstances that gave it special significance. *O Richard, ô mon Roi* had first been sung in a revolutionary context almost a year before the appearance of *Ça ira,* at the beginning of October 1789. But although the events of October obviously bestowed special significance on *O Richard,* this did not become clear until after *Ça ira* had become popular.

O Richard, ô mon Roi is an aria from the opera *Richard the Lion-Hearted,* by Grétry. In marked contrast to *Ça ira,* this song's tune is slow, solemn, and musically more difficult. In the opera it is sung to the imprisoned king by his faithful servant, Blondel:

ô Richard, ô mon Roi,	O Richard, O my king,
L'univers t'abandonne,	The universe abandons you,
Sur la terre il n'est donc que moi,	In the whole world, there is none but I,
Qui s'interesse à ta personne.	Who takes care for you.
Moi seul dans l'univers,	I alone, in all the universe,
Voudrais briser tes fers,	Would like to break your chains,
Et tout le reste t'abandonne.	And all the rest abandon you.

This became and remained the anthem of royalism throughout the Revolution, maintaining more consistent popularity than even the *Marseillaise.* The special meaning of the song came from its performance at a dinner given to welcome the Flanders Regiment to Versailles on 1 October 1789. Rumors of outrageous behavior at the dinner reached Paris two days later where, together with the continuing scarcity of bread, they triggered the march of the Parisian market women to Versailles on 5 October.

The taking of the Bastille in July helped to resolve the most immediate impasse between the king and the Assembly, but other divisive issues remained. Bread prices had fallen in midsummer, but scarcity continued because drought made the regular milling of grain impossible. Meanwhile, a factional movement was afoot to settle the legislative battle over the royal veto by bringing the king to Paris. When public disorder and political dissent increased in September, the Flanders Regiment was invited to Versailles to provide reinforcements in case of trouble.[44] When the Flanders Regiment arrived at Versailles, they were housed with the king's guards. As was customary, the company in place organized a dinner to welcome the newcomers.[45] This was to be the scene of the infamous performance. Initially, the dinner was kept within the bounds of decency, and the royal family stopped in briefly to allow the dauphin to see the festivities. However, "Soon the party . . . changed into a complete orgy. The wine, poured with a truly royal munificence, went to every-one's heads; the musicians played several pieces appropriate to exalting people's spirits still further, such as *O Richard, ô mon Roi, l'univers t'aban-donne!* the perfidious allusion of which could not be lost upon any one at this moment."[46] A.-J. Gorsas used the telling phrase once more when he reported that *O Richard* had been sung following the performance of several tunes "all analogous to the circumstances."[47]

When news reached Paris of the dinner, it was not the singing of *O Richard* nor even the idea that the officers present might have considered the song to be "analogous to the circumstances" that angered Parisians. The real source of fury were stories of what was done to the tricolor cock-ade after *O Richard* had been sung: officers wearing the tricolor cockades were said to have torn them off and taken up black ones. No one in Paris seemed to know whose livery the black was meant to represent; it was clear only that this signified hostility against the Revolution.[48] The day after reports of the dinner reached Paris, Siméon Hardy noted that "this afternoon, at the Palais Royal as well as at the place de Grève and the Luxembourg Gardens, quarrels broke out between some soldiers and of-ficers of the Paris National Guard and some officers of different troops . . . who, quite unwisely, decided to announce their disdain for the na-tional cockade by putting on black cockades; it's even said that some were torn off rather violently, which only feeds the rumor that the black cockade is a rallying sign, especially after what we have heard from Ver-sailles."[49] By the following summer details of the dinner had become still more lurid. The tricolor cockade had not simply been replaced by the black; it had been trampled underfoot and torn to pieces.[50]

The point here is that the wearing (or purported wearing) of the black cockade and the stories about the trampling of the tricolor turned the dinner into an event of unmistakable meaning. It was remembered as a manifestation of arrogant royalism and hostility toward the Revolution, and *O Richard, ô mon Roi* had been sung at this gathering. Although dis-cussion of the song itself did not arise for almost a year, when it was again performed publicly it was rich with counterrevolutionary associations. But all of this lay dormant until the summer of 1790 when, as the newly popu-lar *Ça ira* began to fly through the streets of Paris in late July and August, testimony was given in the municipal courts about the events that had led to 6 October and the royal family's return to Paris. This testimony and newspaper discussions revived the increasingly lurid details of the guard's dinner and reminded the public of the infamous performance of *O Richard.* Then, only a few weeks after the hearings had ceased, the Comédie-Italienne decided to perform *Richard the Lion-Hearted,* the opera

from which *O Richard* had been taken. This would be the first Parisian production of the piece since the events of October 1789.

The royalist *Ami du Roi* applauded the *comédiens'* choice and claimed
that *le peuple* had done so, too: the audience was reputed to have expressed noisy admiration for the faithful Blondel, "who had the rare
courage to take the part of his king" and to have shed tears when the
king was freed from his imprisonment.[51] There was no more news of the
piece until the following month, when its performance was interrupted
for almost two hours as shouts were raised on the theater floor against
occupants of the loges, who began to applaud loudly as soon as they
heard the opening notes of *O Richard, ô mon Roi*. The republican
Chronique and the *Courrier de Paris* both reported the incident; the *Courrier* added that the *comédiens* would be well advised to cease performing
an opera that excited such dolorous memories and which could only appeal to the Revolution's enemies.[52] The matter, and the song, then disappeared from the newspapers for several months.

Just as revolutionaries heckled and condemned *O Richard*, royalists
mocked *Ça ira*. Hardly had the celebrants of the festival of Federation
left the Champs de Mars before royalists began to complain, "Everywhere people sing the worse than awful song ÇA IRA. I have even seen
the parterre audience in various theaters shout out the demand that the
orchestra play it."[53] In Chatillon-sur-Seine, that October, a "former
noble" went so far as to lodge a complaint against a shopkeeper he had
overheard singing *Ça ira*, claiming that the song was a personal insult.
When the acting mayor responded with the declaration that "it will be
forbidden to insult any citizen, by means of speech, song, or otherwise,"
the townspeople gathered outside the nobleman's and mayor's homes,
"singing the proscribed song louder than ever."[54]

With a few exceptions, like the report from Chatillon-sur-Seine, most
published references to *Ça ira* during the late summer and fall of 1790
were the jokes and jabs of royalists, who took note of popular singing for
the same reason that revolutionaries disdained it in print: songs did not
signify political seriousness. *Les Actes des Apôtres* set the tone by archly describing a performance of *Ça ira* at a fraternal dinner on 17 July and
printing what they claimed had been sung:

Le pauvre qu'on opprimera	The oppressed poor
Jamais en vain ne réclamera.	Will never beg in vain.
A jamais dans l'histoire,	Forever throughout history,
Notre siècle on citera,	Our century will be distinguished,
Comme ça ira	For everything working out

The *réponse* that followed inverted the song, turning all of its hopes back on themselves:

En vain le roi sanctionnera,	In vain will the king sanction,
Tous les décrets que l'on voudra,	All the decrees they want,
Espérance illusoire,	Illusory hope,
Rien n'ira mieux pour cela.	Nothing will be better for that.
Ah! ça ira[55]	Ah! ça ira

L'Ami du Roi acknowledged divisions among revolutionaries by recounting an anecdote in which a group of foolishly wild-eyed revolutionaries sought to pry open a pair of trunks rumored to contain gold for the counterrevolution, all the while singing, "Ah! ça ira . . . hang the aristocrats." Their project was thwarted by a commandant who also sang *Ça ira*, but who added a threat to kill the first man who broke the trunks' seals; they were in his safekeeping and contained only the old clothes and pious books of a departed curé.[56]

This state of affairs did not continue long, however. Although royalists used representations of *Ça ira* as shorthand with which to mock the Revolution, they could not take possession of the song's meaning and its potential application. In practice, revolutionaries turned the song to their ends, and their singing reflected the hardening and narrowing of political positions. Over the course of 1791, performances of *Ça ira* would reflect the widening fissures in French society caused by the oath to the Civil Constitution of the Clergy, the king's flight to Varennes, and the growing tensions between revolutionaries and royalists.

On 12 July 1790, the National Assembly formally adopted the Civil Constitution of the Clergy, making church officials salaried employees of the state and placing them under lay authority. The constitution did not, however, become a source of dissension until early 1791, when authorities moved to implement a decree requiring clergy to publicly swear allegiance to the constitution or face dismissal. The administration of the church then erupted into a religious debate that divided urban and rural parishes alike. In some regions, crowds gathered to prevent administration of the oath; in others, they publicly celebrated their priest's acceptance of the constitution. Opposition over the oath even created the potential for violence, a scenario that was especially common in Paris. Newspapers on both the Left and the Right printed accounts of acceptances and refusals, and what was already a deeply divisive issue became still more difficult when, in March, Pius VI issued a bull condemning both the constitution and the Revolution.[57]

Music found its way into the affair when revolutionaries began to signal their indignation at refusals with impromptu performances of *Ça ira.*
These performances humiliated refractory clerics at the same time that they defused tense and, under other circumstances, possibly violent situations. For example, when several refractory clerics tried to force an "uncivil" *Te Deum* on a company of National Guard in Pontarlier, the guard responded with a "general salvo of *Ça ira*" that drowned out the voices of their opponents; they continued until they had driven away the ecclesiastics and then performed a "civil" *Te Deum* themselves.[58] Mercier described a similar scene when the curé of Saint-Sulpice tried to deliver a sermon against the Civil Constitution and the National Assembly to a church filled with revolutionaries.

> A universal cry of indignation reverberated through the arches of the church. [The curé] paled, believing that he saw the crown of martyrdom descending on his head. . . . Suddenly, the majestic organ filled the church with its harmonious music and echoed through every heart the famous tune: *Ah! ça ira! ça ira!* Indignation became patriotic jubilation, and the counterrevolutionary instigator was invited to sing *Ça ira.* He climbed down from his chair, covered with laughter, shame, and sweat.[59]

Anticlerical performances of *Ça ira* did not immediately overshadow more hopeful and celebratory performances, but such conflictory singing practices were broadened and reinforced by the events of the summer. On 20 June 1791, the royal family slipped away from the Tuileries Palace and fled Paris, hoping to cross the French border at Montmédy to join counterrevolutionary forces being amassed there by the Princes of the Blood. Once the king and queen had been arrested and returned to Paris, the Assembly faced the task of deciding whether to try the king. Voices were raised inside and outside the legislature calling for Louis's removal and replacement by a regent or, more radically, for the establishment of a republic. But the Assembly finally voted, on 15 July, to claim that the king had been kidnapped, to guarantee his inviolability and restore him to his functions. That same day, the Cordelier Club, a vocal advocate of democratic principles, began to circulate a petition that reiterated demands for the king's trial and the establishment of a republic. Within two days, the Cordeliers gathered several thousand signatures for the petition, which they took to the Champ de Mars to place on an altar. As supporters gathered, two men were discovered hiding under a table and, mistakenly identified as spies, they were killed by the crowd.[60] When news of the violence at the Champ de Mars reached the

Assembly, it responded by declaring martial law, while Bailly, the mayor of Paris, ordered Lafayette and the National Guard to clear the crowd gathered at the site of the Federation. The troops charged and fired, killing perhaps fifty people and wounding many more.[61]

These events had a tremendous impact on the people of Paris. Under the conditions of martial law, fraternal societies were outlawed and a number of leading political figures, including both Danton and Marat, fled or went into hiding. Many common people reacted with both fear and anger; in the next several weeks quite a few were arrested and interrogated for having shouted insults against Lafayette, the National Guard, and Bailly. A certain Destrumel even went so far as to sing a "filthy song" against the guard, to which he added the observation that "M. de Lafayette is a villain and a rascal. He fired upon the citizens at the Champs de Mars."[62]

The events of June and July were critical in the development of the ideas and attitudes of royalists and revolutionaries alike. Royalists believed that the king's flight proved beyond the shadow of a doubt what they had long suspected: that Louis repudiated the Revolution and was being held in France against his will. Revolutionaries faced a twofold dilemma. In spite of the government-sponsored fiction that Louis had been kidnapped, many continued to believe that he had freely chosen to flee the country. Once it was clear that the king himself approved of counterrevolution, the revolutionary effort became still more precarious. Second, the imposition of martial law and, above all, the massacre at the Champ de Mars were the worst possible representations of the divisions among revolutionaries. Not only had a large fraction of the revolutionary party shown itself willing to shield the king in his attempts to desert his people but, under adverse conditions, they allowed guns to be turned on their fellows. By the end of the summer of 1791, the threat of the counterrevolution was unmistakable, and there was a growing sense of urgency and suspicion. These tensions, and a keener sense of opposition, were reflected in singing practices that were becoming increasingly confrontational.

Such was the political environment in Paris when the Comédie-Italienne again staged *Richard the Lion-Hearted*. The *comédiens* underscored their provocation by offering a free performance of the opera, in imitation of revolutionary theaters that had just given free performances to celebrate the king's acceptance of the Constitution. On the designated day, the *Courrier* warned its readers that royalists had prepared for the event in advance by making paper crowns, writing *impromptus*,[63] and circulating a new song that was set to the tune of *O Richard*:

O Louis, ô mon Roi!	O Louis, ô my king!
Notre amour t'environne:	Our love encircles you:
Pour notre coeur c'est une loi	Only one law rules our hearts
D'être fidèle à ta personne.	To be faithful to you.
Aux yeux de l'Univers	Before the eyes of the Universe
Nous briserons tes fers,	We will break your chains,
Et nous te rendrons ta couronne.[64]	And return to you your crown.

The *Courrier*'s warning and the royalists' advance preparations had their desired effects: audience members were so unruly that the police were required to restore order.[65] The opera was not produced again during the Revolution.

In spite of the closing of *Richard the Lion-Hearted*, revolutionary newspapers continued to report and discuss the events of its final performance for several days. Above all, they sought to deny that any association could be drawn between the activities of royalist audience members, the *comédiens*, and the situation of the king. The *Chronique* distinguished between "this constitutional royalism that every good Frenchman carries in his heart, like the love of the Law" and "that stupid royalism which slanders the monarchy," while the *Courrier* printed a brutally disparaging biography of Richard the Lion-Hearted which closed by asking if the directors of the Comédie-Italienne really thought that they were honoring Louis by comparing him to such a monster.[66]

The dispute here was not only a confrontation between revolutionaries and counterrevolutionaries over the singing of a song laden with unhappy associations; it was also a means of debating the king's relationship to the Revolution, and whether he had tried to flee France or had been kidnapped. Royalists who sang *O Richard* or, still more pointedly, *O Louis*, were expressing their conviction that the king was being held hostage by the Revolution. This implied, of course, that his acceptance of the constitution was a sham: an implication that was underscored by the Comédie-Italienne's aping of revolutionary theaters by presenting a free performance of *Richard the Lion-Hearted*. The shouts raised against royalists inside the theater, like the efforts of the *Courrier* and the *Chronique* to dissociate Louis from the activities of the *comédiens* and their patrons, were the revolutionaries' way of denying of these accusations.

Although revolutionary Parisians responded to royalist activity at the theater with shouts and foot stomping, they did not confine themselves to this reaction for long: the following February, they began to interrupt plays that contained counterrevolutionary allusions by singing *Ça ira*. In the space of a few days, a play by Cousin Jacques at the théâtre de Monsieur unintentionally provoked the song, as did an actress at the Comédie-Italienne who overplayed her role and, turning her eyes upon the queen (who was in the audience), "conveyed the most disgusting flattery."[67] At the théâtre du Vaudeville, the audience demanded that the orchestra play *Ça ira* while a copy of a particularly offensive play was burned onstage "and not to stop until the piece had been burned rhythmically."[68] In all of these cases, *Ça ira* was not only a means of expressing disdain of aristocratic jokes and allusions; it was also a way of "purging" or "purifying" the theaters in which those jokes were repeatedly told.[69]

While confrontation was explicit in the theaters, it was implicit in cafés and public celebrations where the threat of the aristocracy was hounded and chased away figuratively. In August revolutionaries took over the royalist Pavillon de Foi, where they held a mock religious ceremony of purification and then danced and sang *Ça ira* until late into the night.[70] Several months later, several "patriots" announced that they would sing the song at the site of a stabbing, and the regulars at the café de la Civette held a private civic ceremony where they sang a version of *Ça ira* that heaped scorn on Russians, Austrians, émigrés, and "fanatical priests," verse by verse.[71]

Conciliatory versions of *Ça ira* that celebrated the Revolution and expressed faith in its future had given way almost entirely to hostile versions that announced distrust of aristocrats and the threat that they represented. As political positions hardened, there was a corresponding narrowing of the varieties of *Ça ira* that could be sung. The hostile versions, too, had undergone transformation since the summer of 1790, because the purpose of singing them had changed. No longer a simple expression of growing political tensions, *Ça ira* had become a verbal weapon wielded against counterrevolution.

For royalists, too, the meaning of *Ça ira* changed. It ceased to be an emblem of revolutionary foolishness and became one of potential violence. In the summer and fall of 1790, royalists had used this song to represent the rabble of the streets and the thoughtless disordering of tradition, which they considered typical of the Revolution. But such characterizations had some flexibility: *L'Ami du Roi* distinguished between orderly and disorderly singers of the *Ça ira*, and the sophisticated parody in *Les Actes des Apôtres* was aimed at a cosmopolitan audience that was more interested in laughing at the revolution than in fighting it. By the fall of 1791, however, the song was being set in a very different context. *Ça ira* was still associated with the mob, but this was a mob that had moved from vandalizing property to committing acts of physical violence, and which had gained in strength from the organization and authority offered by the Jacobins.

> Since the Club has finished closing our churches, the Jaquets [Jacobins]
> are unbearably violent. They gather together at night with their wives and
> children, and run through the streets bellowing out the most infamous
> songs and shouting at the tops of the voices, *Hang the aristocrats.*[72]

Royalists and revolutionaries alike had been appropriating and reshaping this malleable song to represent their fluid politics and their changing perceptions of the Revolution. But over the course of 1791 *Ça ira*,
like the political culture of which it was a part, became increasingly rigid
and confrontational.

In late February 1792, during the same week that impromptu performances of *Ça ira* were censoring offensive theater pieces, a deputy of the
Assembly became embroiled in a dispute at the café Herculanium over
his request that the orchestra play this song. The orchestra's compliance
excited the anger of several royalists, who then demanded, and received,
a performance of *O Richard*. Newspapers reported the incident differ-
ently: which party was drunken and unruly and which song found
greater favor depended on the editor's political persuasion.[73] The following week saw a more one-sided dispute; revolutionary youths dressed
a café in tricolor ribbons and sang *Ça ira* while the café musicians
burned copies of *O Richard, ô mon Roi.*[74]

Rising political tensions and the increasingly confrontational use of
songs and singing encouraged partisans of opposing camps to hoot at
and assail the anthem of their opponents. Finally, they had only to sing
their songs in direct opposition to one another. From as far away as London came the report: "three or four . . . émigrés went to the shop of a famous piano maker, one of them tried a few tunes on a piano and
accompanied himself while singing *O Richard, ô mon Roi*. Two profoundly silent Englishmen were in the same room. The more serious
one sat down at the place that the Frenchman had just vacated and
played the famous tune *Ça ira* with the greatest perfection. Tonight
there is talk of nothing other than this little anecdote, which has done
no small service in revealing the thoughts of many people."[75] The account was printed without commentary: the songs spoke for themselves.
Ça ira had ceased to represent a plurality of opinions and instead stood
for a Revolution that, publicly at least, was increasingly homogeneous;
one either supported or opposed it.

Ca ira and *O Richard, ô mon Roi* had such multidimensional and visible
careers because they seemed able to represent political positions with
great transparency and, in so doing, they acquired increasingly evocative
associations. In the space of a year, the two songs became so much a part

of Parisian political culture that they could be used as emblems, sung against one another as representatives of whole ensembles of political beliefs. In becoming emblematic, however, *Ça ira* lost its ability to represent more than one kind of political opinion. Whereas rigidity was hardly a problem for royalists, whose ambitions were relatively consistent throughout the Revolution, it would create difficulties both great and small for revolutionaries. In the short term, it limited the representational life of *Ça ira* because it inhibited the song's ability to keep pace when revolutionary culture took a new turn, as it would with the declaration of war in 1792. More broadly and more significantly, in becoming an emblem of the Revolution that one could only accept or reject outright, *Ça ira* revealed what would become a profound difficulty in later years. Having forged their anthem as they engaged in increasingly polarized opposition, revolutionaries would later find themselves unable to promote a song that evoked the pluralism of the Revolution's early years, a song onto which citizens could project a variety of political aspirations and opinions. This problem would, however, lie dormant until revolutionaries stabilized the Republic and began to seek compromise among themselves.

Ça ira and *O Richard* were not, of course, the only songs performed in Paris between 1790 and 1792, they were simply the most dramatic and innovative. Throughout this period other popular songs sustained very different kinds of careers. Ephemeral songs, they appeared and disappeared with every turn of the Revolution. Traditional tunes persisted as well, and two of them sustained a lengthy popularity, similar to that of *Ça ira* and *O Richard* but with narrower representational possibilities. *Vive Henri IV* and *Où peut-on être mieux qu'au sein de sa famille?* were already well known by 1789, and their modest revolutionary careers suggest other dimensions of song culture between 1787 and 1792 even as they underscore the unique status of *Ça ira*.

As readers may recall, Parisian market women sang *Vive Henri IV* when they marched on Versailles in October 1789, in the hope that the tune would reassure Louis of their loyalty and peaceful intent. Dating to the sixteenth century, the song originally celebrated the king who ended the Wars of Religion:

Vive Henri IV, vive ce roy vaillant!	Long live Henri IV, long live this valiant king!
Ce diable à quatre a le triple talent	This fine rascal has a triple talent
De boire et de battre et d'être un vert galant.[76]	For drinking, and fighting, and acting the galant.

Henri IV was, in company with Saint Louis, the favorite king of Parisians. Now two kings of France could be said to have ended civil strife and restored happiness to the realm:

Au diable guerres, rancunes et partis,	To hell with wars, grudges, and parties,
Comme nos pères, chantons en vrais amis,	Like our fathers before us, let's sing as true friends,
Au choc des verres, les roses et les lys!	To the clinking of glasses, roses and lilies!

Because the song was so closely associated with the institution of the monarchy and with Louis XVI himself, its popularity could not long survive the flight to Varennes. In spite of the fiction of the king's kidnapping, *Vive Henri IV* quickly became representative of aristocratic machinations and of an attachment to the king that was increasingly difficult to reconcile with revolutionary sympathies. This is why the editor of the *Courrier* complained bitterly only a few days after the king's acceptance of the constitution, that *Ça ira* had been played just once on the afternoon that Bailly visited Louis, while *Vive Henri IV* was played repeatedly.[77] Similarly, the royalist *A deux liards* exulted a few months later, "The tune *Ça ira* no longer excites delight, especially not among *le peuple*. It was performed a few days ago at the Nicolet Theater; no one applauded it. Immediately afterward, *Vive Henri IV* was requested, and the clapping of hands was universal. Quite certainly, *Ça ira* no longer pertains to anyone but royalists."[78]

Où peut-on être mieux qu'au sein de sa famille? fared better in navigating the shifting currents of revolutionary sentiment between 1789 and 1792. This was the song considered "analogous to the circumstances" when the king visited Paris just after the taking of the Bastille, and it was the standard celebratory piece played when the royal family attended the theater. The song was an aria from *Lucile*, another opera by Grétry, which celebrated the intimacy of the bourgeois family and the triumph of virtue over caste.[79] Other than its title, taken from the song's first two lines, lyrics were of little importance: the sentimental tune alone evoked the appropriate associations. *Où peut-on être mieux?* had a more successful revolutionary career than *Vive Henri IV* because it was devoid of aristocratic allusions and emphasized the life of the nation rather than the person of the king. Its primary emphasis was on family, the head of which could be changed, so even when *Où peut-on être mieux?* no longer celebrated Louis XVI and Marie-Antoinette, it was still played in honor of the mayors of Paris: first Bailly and later Petion.[80]

Vive Henri IV and *Où peut-on être mieux?* reflected some of the political currents of the early Revolution, but they did so without achieving the extraordinary success of *Ça ira* and *O Richard* for two important reasons. In the first place, neither song was associated with a founding event that rooted it firmly within the chronology of the Revolution. Rather, *Vive Henri IV* and *Où peut-on être mieux?* belonged to the period before the summer of 1790: they were old, popular songs whose flexibility allowed them to be adapted to new circumstances without gaining an independent identity. Second, both songs had limited representational possibilities: because each was so closely linked to a specific idea (king, family), neither could be abstracted and used for the broad range of issues to which *Ça ira* was initially applied.

REVOLUTIONIZING REPRESENTATION

The sustained popularity of *Ça ira* and *O Richard* and their increasingly emblematic status distinguished them from their musical predecessors and their more traditional counterparts. As these songs and the singing practices associated with them became explicitly revolutionary, representations of singing began to change. Initially, the change took the form not of new opinions but of subtle shifts in attitude and a greater importance accorded to singing in print. Derogatory comments about the suspicious and aristocratic character of songs died away after the summer of 1790. Revolutionaries still accused royalists of using songs to woo common people away from the Revolution, but they now placed the blame on royalist machinations rather than on the essential nature of songs. Meanwhile the *Chronique de Paris* and Gorsas' *Courrier*, newspapers published by men who were evolving into moderate republicans, began to print more anecdotes about street singing and incidents involving song. *Ça ira* had helped to reshape singing practices; it had given name and revolutionary character to what until then had been considered cheap and disorganized entertainment. This development facilitated journalistic use of both *Ça ira* and *O Richard* as shorthand for political opinions; and as some newspapers reported and celebrated new practices of singing, they helped to reinforce and broaden them.

By the summer of 1791, singing had been linked closely enough to the revolutionary position that royalists were no longer the only political group claimed to use songs to win converts. Royalists now turned the accusation on their enemies. Thus, while the Assembly debated the king's fate, *L'Ami du Roi* bemoaned the variety of means used by the "execrable factions" of Republicanism to undermine the monarchy. Beyond subsidizing reprehensible engravings and encouraging rumors, these factions "scatter public singers through all the intersections, and practically under the windows of the Tuileries Palace, each more audacious than the last; they ceaselessly sing abomination upon abomination; there is not a single word in their songs that is not a blasphemy against religion, the king, the queen, and the monarchy."[81]

While royalists and some moderate republicans drew attention to the revolutionizing of singing practices, however, Jacobins remained suspicious. As those who sought to break most decisively with the past and create cultural forms that would exalt, instruct, and encourage revolutionary commitment, Jacobins believed that they had sound reasons for mistrusting songs. Songs had, after all, been firmly rooted in the frivolous entertainments and coercive political life of the Old Regime. As a form of entertainment, they seemed incapable of improving their audiences the way a regenerated revolutionary theater or a didactic festival could. As means of communication, songs served the illiteracy that Jacobins hoped to extirpate. Finally, and no doubt most damning, as a means of political expression, songs seemed to recall the old hierarchies and servitude that were meant to inhibit complaint and which certainly did not promote legitimate political action.

Jacobins relinquished their prejudices more slowly and, as we shall see, less completely than did many other revolutionaries, but in the face of new practices even they began to see that singing might become a powerful instrument. So, for example, in an address to the Jacobin Club in the fall of 1791, J. M. Coupé suggested that songs might be as useful as the press and the theater in disseminating revolutionary principles throughout rural France. In his *Vues proposées . . . pour éclairer le peuple de la campagne* (Proposals. . . . for the enlightenment of the people of the countryside), Coupé, a deputy from the Oise, argued that those who loved liberty must purify the means of communication that an oppressive government had corrupted, turning them instead toward enlightenment and the eradication of old habits of thought. The contested genres that he mentioned included journals, almanacs, dance, traveling players, and songs.

Opening his discussion on an old note, Coupé reminded his audience that the crown had employed songs to circulate obscenities and beguile the populace. But, he continued, songs turned to a salutary end became all-powerful and were readily adopted by young villagers, who never allowed a happy tune to escape them. "If we put the principal traits of our Revolution in varied stanzas, tastefully and simply give them the rhythm of dances, the lightness of little melodies, the emotion of romances, they will carry patriotism into all souls, enlightening them and delighting our youth."[82] He concluded by reassuring the Jacobins that they need feel no shame about encouraging their own pastoral poets to replace the miserable government songsters, who trafficked in burlesque vulgarities.

Thus, in the face of innovative and undeniably politicized practices, revolutionary political and cultural leaders began to describe singing and song writing as revolutionary activities that could legitimately be shared by all French citizens. As practice and representation moved into closer agreement, journalists began to describe *Ça ira* in terms that would inform the more developed transcendental language used to describe songs during the Terror. In June 1791, when describing the *Ça ira* that had been played by the National Guard, the *Chronique* did not refer to the song's more common associations but characterized it as "the tune which has the greatest effect on the patriotic spirit."[83]

The following spring, in April 1792, the *Chronique de Paris* went even further in heaping praise upon the song. Who could doubt the power of music among the ancients, it asked, after seeing the effect of the *Ça ira* on the French? "Has music ever made such an impression? If Tyrtée's verse . . . could restore the shattered courage of the Lacedemonians and make them victors, there is nothing we may not hope from Frenchmen animated by this tune when they go into battle against the enemies of liberty."[84] The article went on to suggest that military bands should promenade through Paris playing the piece on Sundays, and that theaters play it at the end of their programs, so that audiences could leave singing the "patriotic refrain." Here was the most abstract language possible being applied to a song: *Ça ira* was characterized as having superseded representational status and achieved an independent meaning. As it became an emblem, *Ça ira* revolutionized song culture by resolving the tension between practice and representation—a tension that had initially led many revolutionaries to regard singing as necessarily outside of politics. Increasingly political performances of *Ça ira* encouraged the cultural and political leaders of the Revolution to forge new definitions of revolutionary songs and revolutionary singing.

Even though revolutionaries and royalists could agree on little else by 1792, most knew a revolutionary (or counterrevolutionary) song when they heard one. Here *Ça ira* played a profoundly important role in helping to constitute revolutionary political culture, for not only did it serve as a means by which revolutionaries could express an increasingly certain notion of themselves but, as well, it helped to determine what constituted a revolutionary means of expression. Even during the early years of the Revolution, song culture did more than simply express a politics that had prior existence; singing helped to create the political life of the nation. *Ça ira* shaped what could be said about the Revolution and, along with *O Richard*, it offered a means of discussion in which all members of revolutionary society could share. Furthermore, this anthem strengthened revolutionary political culture in the same way as did other, seemingly more traditional songs. *Ça ira*, like all songs, could go anywhere. Restricted neither to theaters nor printed pages, singing moved from street to café to home: in every arena it was capable of stirring deep feelings of loyalty and affiliation, or of opposition and hostility. In all cases, songs and singing were fundamentally important in disseminating the idea that the Revolution was a far-reaching event that touched people's lives at all points and in all ways.

But singing practices were not the only site of innovation during the early years of the Revolution. Even as some revolutionary elites expressed concerns about the political seriousness of singing, others—revolutionary and royalist alike—played upon the traditional associations of songs: gaiety and frivolity. In newspapers and theaters, these men and women enlarged on the satiric dimension of songs, elaborating representations that their critics feared would give rise to counterrevolutionary practices. This dimension of song culture is important for two reasons. First, it reminds us of the continuing heterogeneity of revolutionary culture. Just as members of revolutionary society disagreed over political objectives and solutions, so many of them experimented with vastly different modes of expression. While a growing consensus emerged around one dimension of song culture, dissension continued about others. Second, and in consequence, a measure of force was ultimately required to achieve a recognizably revolutionary song culture. For although citizens achieved consensus around certain issues, they would impose the outcomes of others. This would have significant consequences for the development of song culture in the later years of the Revolution.

Chapter Three

✦

Songs off the Street:
Newspapers, Theaters, and Satire
(1789–September 1793)

✦ *ÇA IRA* WAS TRANSFORMED into an emblem of political belief in the streets, parks, and cafés of Paris, but song culture did not reside only in such open, public arenas. Malleability, ease of composition, and ready movement between oral and print culture allowed songs to play different roles in diverse cultural spheres and to be reshaped to suit distinct and often conflicting purposes. As well as in the streets, songs were to be found in the newspapers and theaters that flourished after 1789, freed from Old Regime commercial practices and censorship by revolutionary legislation. This freedom would initially make possible a varied and subtle manipulation of songs.

Serious revolutionary and royalist newspapers accorded attention to singing slowly and unevenly. The editors of these papers were less interested in providing ostensibly unbiased information than in promoting particular political philosophies. Conversely, satiric newspapers immediately seized upon songs, exploiting associations of commonness and frivolity that survived from the Old Regime when they incorporated singing into their polemical comedy. In both cases, newspaper editors would increasingly turn songs to explicitly political ends, in so doing, revealing their aspirations for the Revolution and their changing ideas about song culture. Meanwhile, in the small theaters that sprang up in Paris after January 1791, songs and singing would serve commercial purposes. Theatrical entrepreneurs would add political songs to their programs to render older plays more timely, and seek out lively or controversial songs to outdo their rivals in an increasingly crowded market. Both these arenas, political and commercial, were dominated by cultural elites intent on exploring a broad range of linguistic and gestural possibilities and the revolutionary implications of their Old Regime representations. These elites did not produce songs in isolation, however; between 1790 and 1793, they came into increasingly close contact with activists in the streets, with whom they debated revolutionary politics and the politics of entertainment.

Much of this debate would be provoked by the journalistic and theatrical use of a kind of song not common in the streets of Paris: the satire. As the Revolution progressed, the publication and performance of satiric songs became ever more explosive as such songs, with meanings that were neither fixed nor uniform, came to be associated with political opposition. Royalists and others would broaden the oppositional associations of satiric songs by integrating them into disputes about the nature and objectives of the Revolution. This explicitly political use of satiric songs would not, however, remain confined to that arena; it came to affect commercial songs as well in the form of the vaudeville, a genre closely associated with the stage. For even after revolutionaries had silenced many of their internal opponents, they sustained an intense argument about which means of expression and entertainment could justifiably be called revolutionary. Having first freed journalistic and theatrical expression, revolutionaries would gradually move toward imposing new limits as circumstances and priorities changed. In the end, several entrepreneurs would quite self-consciously revolutionize the vaudeville form for political and commercial reasons. By 1793, combined legislative and popular activity would eliminate much of the nuance and diversity that became possible only four years before.

SONGS IN THE PRESS AND SATIRE

Free expression of thought and opinions is one of the most precious rights of man. Accordingly every citizen may speak, write and publish freely, subject to the penalties for the abuse of this freedom provided by the law.[1]

On 24 August 1789, the National Assembly adopted the eleventh article of the Declaration of the Rights of Man, which formally declared the freedom of the press. The publication of political pamphlets had been rising steadily since 1787, but the eleventh article had a remarkable impact on the periodical press.[2] Newspaper publication rates skyrocketed in 1789 and continued to rise throughout the following year: from the four papers published in Paris in 1788, their numbers leapt to 184 in 1789 and 335 in 1790.[3] Most newspapers established during this first flush of freedom were in fact little more than political pamphlets that appeared perhaps once or twice before vanishing in a flood of printed matter. Whether ephemeral or enduring, these papers broadened the information available to readers at the same time that they advertised the editor's political principles and offered interpretations of current events. And just as ideology helped to determine what kinds of events were reported and how they were treated, it also affected what songs were printed and how incidents of singing were reshaped in print.[4]

As we have already seen, journalists were slow to include song lyrics or news of singing practices in the pages of their newspapers. Even as *Ça ira* became increasingly popular and singing practices more revolutionary, the decision to print news of songs and singing depended, in the early years of the revolution, on journalists' political opinions. Given the radicals' support of popular democracy, it is perhaps surprising that they were not among the first to celebrate revolutionary singing practices. Instead, more moderate revolutionary newspaper editors led the way in turning public attention to singing. Before the revolution of August 1792, the *Chronique de Paris* and Gorsas' *Courrier* were the foremost purveyors of songs within the informative press, giving singing far more complete coverage than did the radical journals to their left or the royalist one to their right.[5] Moderate editors printed descriptions of unofficial ceremonies and impromptu performances of song which, they believed, suggested that revolutionary culture was being elaborated, albeit somewhat uncertainly, in the streets. Meanwhile, radical newspapers, like Prudhomme's *Révolutions de Paris* and Camille Desmoulins's *Révolutions de France et de Brabant*, continued to shun singing because its disorganized character was at odds with the serious, pedagogically sound, and virtuous body of revolutionary arts to which they aspired.[6] Although capable of recognizing occasional instances of revolutionary singing, many radicals would not truly embrace song culture until after the republican revolution. Meanwhile, serious royalist newspapers, like *L'Ami du Roi* and the *Gazette de Paris*, often regarded singing as merely one more example of the anarchic, popular activism unleashed by the Revolution.

Ideology affected more than just the frequency with which songs or incidents of singing were printed. It also shaped how journalists reflected about the Revolution or about song culture. Thus, when the moderate *Courrier* and the radical *Révolutions de France et de Brabant* reported that the king had been overheard singing, "je suis démocrate, moi" (I am a democrat), they imputed different meanings to the ditty and suggested different perspectives on the Revolution. Gorsas, in the *Courrier*, began by asking rhetorically, "Why do we allow the king to remain surrounded by men who are so despicable as to affect feelings similar to his in front of him while they so badly compromise his patriotism behind his back!" By claiming that the king had sung "I am a democrat" as he escaped the company of such scoundrels, Gorsas simultaneously affirmed faith in the king's patriotism and in the capacity of songs to express that patriotism.[7] But Camille Desmoulins preceded his account, in the *Révolutions de France et de Brabant*, with reflections on the National Assembly's declaration that the executive, the sovereign, and the people "have the same goals and the same interests." "Considering Rabelais' saying *that a king doesn't live on a little*, it decreed him such a great sum for his civil list that, if it is in the people's interest to love the constitution, it is undeniably also in the prince's."[8] For Desmoulins, the king's singing "I am a democrat" could only have the most cynical implication, suggesting that neither the crown nor the practice of singing were politically sound.[9]

Just as newspapers encouraged popular activism by reporting it, they broadened the circulation of songs by printing them. The songs they printed, with the tune included, could be sung by literate and illiterate alike. In satirizing the women of the markets, *Les Actes des Apôtres* painted a revealing picture of songs moving from the printed page to the wider arena of the street:

> [The market women] have been caught quite often this summer using your *actes des apôtres* to wrap [all the fish] that they sold . . . When they catch sight of your songs, which happens every time your antinational tunes happen to be noted . . . they ask the militia or the victors of the Bastille to read or sing them.[10]

Similarly, streets and newspapers often shared in the elaboration of singing practices. Consider, for instance, the uproar over the performance of *Richard the Lion-Hearted* in September 1791. That dispute did not take place independently and spontaneously: royalist newspapers advertised the lyrics of *O Louis*, priming audience members before the performance began, and Gorsas responded with editorial comments in which he implicitly encouraged revolutionaries attending the opera to be prepared to counterattack.[11] Newspapers helped to disseminate and reinforce singing in streets, cafés, and theaters by advertising it. This openness to dialogue encouraged readers to send songs and notices of their activities to newspapers, making possible a still broader advertisement of popular commitment to or rejection of the Revolution.

> Here is a song that has been sent to us . . . We believe our readers will be pleased to look it over to judge how far the aristocracy will carry its guilty frenzy: it makes one shudder.[12]

Until late 1792, however, such activity involved a limited number of songs and informative newspapers alike. Songs played a far more important role in the other kind of press common before the revolution of August 1792: the satiric press. Unlike the informative press, which represented all political opinions but was dominated by revolutionaries, the satiric press was the special domain of royalists.[13] Although the songs published here were not meant to be sung by people in the streets, and perhaps not by anyone, they played a pivotal role in royalist political criticism. Here, royalists played upon the Old Regime prejudice that represented songs as a lowly means of expression, using songs to underscore their vision of the Revolution as a foolishly inconsistent and anarchically popular event.

The earliest and most famous example of the satiric press was *Les Actes des Apôtres*.[14] The paper first appeared in 1789 on the Day of the Dead (2 November) and was probably founded by Jean-Gabriel Peltier. Peltier, the son of a wealthy Breton merchant, had spent several years trying unsuccessfully to establish banks in Paris and Santo Domingo. Returning to France in time for the opening of the Estates General, he was initially sympathetic to the Revolution, to the point of marching to the Bastille alongside Camille Desmoulins. But his sympathy waned with startling alacrity. He produced his first counterrevolutionary pamphlet only three months after the fall of the Bastille and, a week later, began to publish *Les Actes*. While Peltier was assisted in his new task by several prominent journalists and politicians, two shining wits dominated the paper: Antoine Rivarol, a writer who spent his youth rubbing shoulders with some of the greatest figures of the Enlightenment and who claimed the Berlin Academy prize in 1784, and François Suleau, another son of provincial commerce, who had already been imprisoned for counterrevolutionary activism by the time he joined the company of *Les Actes* in 1790.

Les Actes des Apôtres was said to be the product of dinners in a café at the Palais Royal, where the authors exchanged news of the day's events and scribbled their best jokes, epigrams, and verse on tablecloths. Although these reactionary wits espoused different varieties of royalism, they shared a consistent reliance on satire which, as Jean-Paul Bertaud has pointed out, cleverly combined double entendre with subtle, moralizing messages. The paper's most obvious comic poses were rooted in double entendre: it made exaggerated claims and sweeping statements that were exact negatives of the editors' true opinions. But having laughed at the authors' preposterous lies, the attentive reader might also consider the more serious criticism that was embedded in these same statements. Even the title itself permitted such interpretation, for while the authors claimed that they were the "apostles of Revolution" whose sole aim was to sing its praises—a clear and outright lie—they were also "good apostles," true friends of the king devoted to denouncing the Revolution's crimes.[15]

Songs were integral to the satire of *Les Actes*, and its pages were filled with couplets, verses, and ballads turned to various ends. Sometimes songwriters abandoned subtlety to openly mock the Revolution:

Ne plus boire, ne plus chanter,	No more drinking, no more singing,
Toujours gémir et s'attrister,	Always moaning and sad,
Ma foi! c'est un martyre:	Good god! what a martyrdom:
La politique et ses débats	Politics and its debates
Ont remplacé dans nos repas	Have, at our suppers, replaced
Le petit mot pour rire.[16]	Little morcels of wit.

Or, like the name of the paper, they might present songs as part of an exercise in clever misstatement and innuendo clothed in revolutionary garb: "We know well that people made up songs under the Old Regime, and we admit that this argument carries great force; however, in our defense we must point out that people also ate bread under that gothic regime."[17]

While the editors of *Les Actes des Apôtres* used individual songs to make particular points, they represented the mere introduction of songs into their pages as a grand joke in itself, for it allowed the editors to play upon the frivolous and plebeian associations of singing as they used the form of the song to subvert the content of the lyrics. A satirist who recorded the details of a revolutionary event in a popular song implied that the event was petty and base: "One sings of what doesn't deserve to be read."[18] Other satirists made the same point by turning National Assembly debates and even the articles of the Constitution into song.[19] Royalists underscored the significance of these uses by pointed silence: events that they took seriously were spared the debasing association with song. Thus, of the murder of Delaunay after the fall of the Bastille,

Trop sombre est pour mes rimes,	Too somber for my rhymes,
La peinture des crimes,	Is the painting of the crimes,
Et je tais les victimes,	Not to speak of the victims,
Dont le sang a coulé.[20]	Whose blood flowed.

Unlike informative papers, which printed songs for singing in the streets and theaters, the editors of *Les Actes des Apôtres* and their compatriots made their point simply by making up songs about revolutionary events, ideas, and figures—whether or not those songs were actually sung was of decidedly secondary importance.

Turning an event into a song was the minimum required to make it a point of ridicule, but the choice of tune offered still greater opportunity for sarcasm and innuendo. For example, the author of a song about the history of the Revolution explained: "Convinced that we won't long be singing *Ah! ça ira* [things will work out] because it is impossible that *ça aille* [things shall work out], I found it necessary to choose another tune and other principles. All Paris remembers the vogue of twenty years ago for the song *La Bourbonnaise* . . . That is the tempo that I have adopted and tried to follow."[21] Those who remembered the fashion for *La Bourbonnaise* were also likely to remember that it was "a satiric vaudeville about a certain nobody, who climbed up from the most vile status to play an important role and make some kind of impression at Court."[22] Similarly, the *Journal en vaudevilles*, which rendered National Assembly sittings into popular song, set the business of 4 August to the tune *Upside-down and Inside-out.*[23] Satirists occasionally abandoned sarcasm and mockery to print a serious chant of royalism, and the tunes that they chose for such songs were as markedly different from the usual fare as the tone and message of the lyrics. Here, they often printed musical notation or, if choosing a popular tune, composers preferred slower, sadder melodies like *Pauvre Jacques* or *Comment goûter quelque repos?*[24]

Les Actes des Apôtres was by no means the only royalist satire that gave songs pride of place. The *Journal en vaudevilles* was almost entirely devoted to shaping the debates of the National Assembly into songs. The *Rocambole des journaux* had a format similar to that of the *Les Actes* but a lighter touch; its editors maintained their sense of the frivolous long after the *Les Actes* had been reduced to bitter and childish broadsides.[25] They maintained it even after the declaration of war:

Oui je suis soldat, moi;	Yes, I'm a soldier, I am;
Oui; pour ma Patrie,	Yes; for my homeland,
Pour ma Reine et pour mon Roi	For my queen and for my king

Je donnerais ma vie	I'd give my life
Du démagogue important.	As a puffed up demagogue.
Quand la fureur éclate,	When lightening strikes,
Je n'en vais pas moins chantant:	I won't sing any less:
Vive un aristocrate.[26]	Long live the aristocrat.

There were also the productions of François Marchant, the shadowy figure who produced one journal after another before publishing *Constitution française en vaudevilles* in 1792. This publication was so successful with revolutionaries and royalists alike that even *Révolutions de Paris* was forced to acknowledge its popularity.[27] This is only a partial list of the royalist satires that churned out songs between 1789 and 1792, but whether these songs were a product of the virulent and ultimately bitter royalism of *Les Actes des Apôtres* or of the more moderately aristocratic *Rocambole des journaux,* they made their point without ever having been sung.[28]

Satiric songs did not go uncontested. Like royalists who fought *Ça ira* by singing *O Richard,* some revolutionaries tried to meet the royalist satirists on their own ground.[29] *Le disciple des apôtres,* whose prospectus appeared in the spring of 1790, represented the first sustained attempt at response. Founded with the object of fighting *Les Actes des Apôtres* on its own terms, *Le disciple* used many of its enemy's most familiar stylistic weapons. But the paper was short-lived, disappearing after only six numbers.[30] In February 1791 another editor attempted a similar project, founding *La légende d'orée,* to "prove to the aristocrats that all the jokers are not on their side, and that one can also laugh in a revolutionary way."[31] This paper issued twenty-six numbers over the next three months, but it too was unable to sustain the longevity that characterized *Les Actes* or *Rocambole des journaux.*[32] Admittedly, *Les Actes* was a singularly clever journal, but the difference between revolutionary and royalist papers was greater than simple wit and longevity. For while *Le disciple* and *La légende d'orée* stood almost alone as revolutionary satires, *Les Actes* and *Rocambole* were simply two of the most visible within a much larger crowd of royalist journals. There were clear reasons why satire was, above all, a weapon of counterrevolution.

Revolutionary ideology and politics were believed to rest on the twin bases of transparency and virtue. Transparency was the ideal of political relations in a new society in which there would be neither factions nor misrepresentation. Each citizen would speak the truth from his or her heart, and no artificial manners or traditional conventions would hinder direct communication.[33] Transparency was the central feature of revolutionary political life, and virtue was its safeguard. *Le peuple* were naturally virtuous, hence they would protect the progress of Revolution.[34] Furthermore, a productive circularity was at work here: moral rectitude was thought to arise from the Revolution's continued progress. Aristocrats were held to be fighting bitterly against both natural virtue and progress, using every means at their disposal—political and cultural—to maintain old and corrupt ways.[35]

Satire, whose humor rests on the audience's ability to disentangle subterfuge and find a truth that is never stated directly, and ridicule, which is undaunted by any sacred principles, could not have been more foreign to such a way of thinking. Long before the Revolution, the *Encyclopédie* had warned its readers that ridicule "extends its empire over merit, honor, talents, consideration, and virtues; its caustic imprint is indelible; it serves as a means to root out the respect owed to virtue from the very depths of the heart and finally to extinguish the love of it: thus one is ashamed to be modest and becomes impudent through fear of ridicule; this vicious fear corrupts more honest hearts than do evil propensities."[36] Satire and ridicule, because of their reliance on double entendre, their iconoclasm, and their rejection of the ideals of revolutionary behavior, became primarily the humor of aristocrats.

This did not mean that satire was entirely absent from the pages of revolutionary journals, but it had a more narrowly circumscribed place there. The success of authors and editors who were skilled satirists, men like Camille Desmoulins and A.-J. Gorsas, did not depend on their satire alone; they mixed satire with the kinds of news items and editorials that were more common to revolutionary papers. More serious editors would not go even that far: they fought royalist satires by editorializing against them, warning Parisians of the machinations of certain editors and their complicitous booksellers. And, as an account in *Revolutions de Paris* made clear, such editorializing sometimes excited violence: "Some citizens condemned a ream of *Les Actes des Apôtres* to fire. . . . The next day they offered to save the bookseller Gattey from the huge stacks of aristocratic pamphlets that blocked the way to his shop, but the police seized them."[37]

Unable to fight satiric songs on their own terms, revolutionary newspapers vilified them while revolutionaries in the streets turned to violence. Even if these songs were not written to be sung, news of them spread beyond the confines of newspaper pages to excite reaction and dispute elsewhere. Nor was it violence alone that these songs excited. As we saw earlier, revolutionary elites distrusted popular songs, considering them the playthings of the aristocracy. While this attitude arose, in part, from Old Regime associations, the royalist use of satiric songs reinforced it. For royalists did not only turn songs against the Revolution, they played on traditional associations and manipulated songs in ways that revolutionaries found wholly foreign and were incapable of adopting.

THEATRICAL SINGING AND THE VAUDEVILLE

Theatrical songs followed a different trajectory during the early years of the Revolution, for several reasons. Songs in theaters, unlike those in newspapers, were actually performed, and audiences offered interpretations and opinions that influenced their reception. Furthermore, theaters were commercial enterprises. Rather than using songs to editorialize on the Revolution's progress, most produced timely or clever political songs to attract audiences and to distinguish themselves within a market that was increasingly crowded.[38] Such conditions shaped the relationship between theatrical songs and the course of the Revolution; as well, they helped to determine the choices available to one theater in particular, the théâtre du Vaudeville, when politics began to close in on its repertoire.

Theaters, unlike newspapers, were freed slowly and in piecemeal fashion: the critical legislation permitting anyone with resources and interest to open one was only passed in January 1791. Prior to the Revolution, Parisian theaters had fallen into two groups: the privileged Opéra, Comédie-Française, and Comédie-Italienne, and the unprivileged boulevard theaters, which catered to all Parisians but which were considered the purveyors of specifically "popular" entertainment. Although privileged and unprivileged theaters were legally distinct, audiences in both arenas had traditionally been disruptive, expressing opinions with applause or hoots during performances.[39] These expressions of opinion were not confined to aesthetic judgment: audiences called attention to songs or arias that seemed to allude to current events by applauding loudly or by demanding encores.[40] It was here, in the volatile relationship between stage and audience, that the Revolution made its most significant initial impact on the theater.

Sunday night the théâtre de Monsieur performed *Le souper d'Henri IV* [*Henry IV's Supper*]. The women of the markets and the "brigands" who went in search of the king [on October 5] were invited. . . . During the supper, our ladies jumped onto the stage and took part in the festivities: they were given glasses, or rather they drank indiscriminately from those at hand. . . . These ladies sang and drank to the health of the king, whom they kissed in the person of the actor portraying Henry.[41]

This was an exaggerated case—market women climbing onto the stage to kiss the king in the person of an actor—but even when audience members remained in their seats, they sustained an active relationship with the stage as they searched for suggestive lyrics and signaled them loudly.

The people never miss an opportunity to demonstrate their love and tender solicitude for their king. Yesterday, *Rodogune* was performed at the Théâtre français, and the verse *One cannot be too careful of a king's security* was applauded for several encores.[42]

Audiences were not alone in bringing the Revolution into the theaters. Even before playwrights had time to incorporate revolutionary events and sentiments into new productions, theaters were presenting pieces with unmistakable allusions to current circumstances. During a performance of *La mort de César* at the théâtre de la Nation, "all the verses exuding hatred of tyranny, love of the fatherland and of liberty" were applauded loudly.[43] And the celebrity of Marie-Joseph Chenier's *Charles IX*, a poorly written tragedy about royal corruption and the St. Bartholomew's Day massacre, owed much of its popularity to its perceived relevance to current events.[44] By the summer of 1790, theatergoers were watching plays that commented directly upon the Revolution or were intentionally allusive.[45]

Songs had traditionally played an important role in boulevard theater. Initially used as means to circumvent the Comédie-Française's monopoly on spoken dialogue, they become enormously popular in their own right.[46] With the opening of the Revolution, songs came to play an important part in the revolutionary dialogue between stage and audience. At their simplest, they helped to bring the Revolution into the theater because they served as an easy means by which a piece could be made explicitly relevant:

Saturday 9 July, after Oedipus, the *Réveil d'Epéminide à Paris* was performed for the 17th time. The author had added . . . verses about the federation, which were enthusiastically applauded and an encore was demanded.[47]

As well, they provided a means by which the audience could seize allusions and participate in the play without actually clambering onto the stage as the market women had done:

The English Spectator once wrote about us: "This desire to sing in concert with the actors is so dominant in France that, in the case of a *well-known song*, I have occasionally seen the musician on stage play practically the same role as a cantor in one of our parishes, who serves only to strike up the song before his voice is covered by that of the entire audience.[48]

But all initiative did not come from the stage. Audience members brought verses and songs into the theater and threw them onto the stage for the actors to read or sing. Sometimes they climbed onto the stage at the end of a performance to sing a song themselves. And the birth of *Ça ira* provided audiences with a song that allowed them to signal approval or disapproval of a play in avowedly political terms.

Like newspapers, theaters sustained dialogue and creative exchange with their audiences. But there was a reassuring distance between newspaper and audience that did not exist in theaters, where performance and interpretation took place in a single arena. The immediate presence of the audience had a profound impact on the piece being performed. The audience suggested allusions or conclusions that might not otherwise be apparent and signaled their opinions with applause or catcalls. The heterogeneity of the audience—split between expensive loges and cheap parterre seats, divided by political affiliations—made the process of interpretation all the more volatile. So even when all audience members agreed on the interpretation of a particular line or allusion, which was not always the case, they might still heatedly debate its political import.

The last time that *Iphigenia at Aulis* was performed at the Opéra, universal applause shook the hall; as soon as the sublime chorus, "Sing, celebrate our Queen, etc." began, the soldiers, who adorned the amphitheater, set the tone, which all followed except for a couple of grimy *enragés* in the parterre, who bellowed out . . . "peace, silence."[49]

There were evenings when it must have seemed as though all the hopes and tensions of the Revolution had been enclosed within the four walls of a single theater.

The abolition of preliminary censorship for boulevard plays in 1789 gave the little theaters greater freedom of production, but the decree of January 1791, which struck down all remaining theatrical privileges, threw the field open. Henceforth, anyone might establish a theater; theatrical supervision was transferred from the Opéra to the municipality of Paris, and it would be forbidden to arbitrarily suppress plays. The ownership of plays changed as well. Plays written by any author dead for more than five years fell into the public domain, while plays of living authors became their personal property to be performed only with their express approval.[50] The field was now open to all who sought to entertain or to interpret the Revolution on their stages, and it was beseiged: twenty new theaters were founded in Paris in 1791.[51] After increasing from fifteen to thirty-five, the number of Parisian theaters leveled off; this was already more than the market could bear. Old and new theaters entered into vigorous competition and, in 1792 alone, a dozen failed, only to be replaced by those of other entrepreneurs eager to try their hands at the project. Among the theaters created in 1792 was the théâtre du Vaudeville, which immediately distinguished itself by its devotion to the song form from which it took its name.

The *vaudeville* is an old genre, composed of simple, catchy tunes with consistent rhythms and repeated refrains that make the songs easy to learn and remember. A vaudevillist usually rhymed lyrics to a popular tune that reinforced or humorously opposed their content. So, for example, a song about the difficulties of joining a select group was set to the tune *I was born neither king nor prince*, while a prologue was sung to *Messieurs, pay attention*.[52] Because the tunes were familiar, the author could be reasonably certain that his or her audience would catch the joke suggested by the original title. Vaudevilles, like pont-neufs, were ideal vehicles for responding to current events because they were so easily composed; they differed from pont-neufs in their association with the theater, where they had once been used to circumvent theatrical privilege. In addition to being associated with the theater and subversion of privilege, the vaudeville's other essential characteristic, without which it could hardly be considered a vaudeville, was its affinity for satire.

> If a vaudeville is not seasoned and even a bit loaded with the spicy wit of
> the epigram, it is bland and scarcely interesting; so also, if the epigram is
> not animated by the wit of satire, it does not delight: rarely does one find
> a good couplet amongst those that are not laden with satire; and rarely
> does one find a bad one amongst those that are satirical.[53]

The *Encyclopédie* added: "the vaudeville was, to some extent, an outgrowth of satire; it is a caustic and clever taunt, pleasantly enveloped in a certain number of small verses."[54] This satiric element would become vitally important.

While other theaters incorporated single vaudevilles into their programs to celebrate the Revolution, or included *pièces en vaudevilles* (plays composed entirely of vaudevilles) in repertoires that were also composed of comedies and melodramas, only the théâtre du Vaudeville performed these songs and plays to the exclusion of all else.[55] It was this exclusiveness of repertoire that would allow the theater to have a profound impact on the revolutionary career of the vaudeville, as it shaped and reshaped the genre for commercial and political reasons. But the struggle that would develop over vaudevilles was not determined only by the activities of the vaudevillists and the political exigencies of the Revolution; the character of vaudeville itself would play an important part in the conflict.

The théâtre du Vaudeville was the creative offspring of five men, most of them middle-aged and with solid theatrical careers forged under the Old Regime. The formal director was Yves Barré, a former lawyer and parlementary clerk whose brother was in active service to the queen.[56] During the Old Regime, Barré had established his reputation as a playwright in collaboration with Antoine Piis, and the two had produced numerous comedies for the Comédie-Italienne.[57] Piis was the most illustrious and prolific of the Vaudeville's associates: his extraordinary career stretched without break from the Old Regime through the Revolution, Empire, and Restoration. Born into a well-placed Parisian family, Piis had written songs under the Old Regime while enjoying the patronage of the Comte d'Artois. However, his father's death and the loss of his patronage, coupled with a broken contract with the Comédie-Italienne, ruined his financial prospects by 1790. It was then that he began to discuss the project of a theater with Barré.

The other three Vaudeville associates did not enjoy the persistent fame of Barré and Piis, but their roles in the theater were of equal importance. Guillaume Desfontaines, fifty-six at the Revolution's opening, had produced light theatrical comedies under the Old Regime, as did Jean-Baptiste Radet, who moved from boulevard theaters to the Comédie-Italienne in the eighties. Like their compatriots, neither of these men had been required to support himself on theatrical earnings alone; both had enjoyed illustrious patronages. Finally, François Léger was, at twenty-four, the youngest and least-known of the associates. Having briefly supported himself as a tutor, Léger debuted as actor and playwright at the théâtre du Vaudeville and would go on to found his own theater under the Directory.

The Vaudeville's inaugural performance, in January 1792, was no great success.[58] It was not until February and the production of a new comedy by Desfontaines, *Les Mille et un théâtres*, that the theater's career began in earnest. *Les Mille et un théâtres* was a one-act *pièce en vaudevilles* that recounted the efforts of Momus, the god of satire, to reconcile with his wife Thalia, the muse of comedy. In the play, poor Thalia has been deprived of riches and realm by the suppression of theatrical privilege and, worse, she must face Momus's request that she recognize the illegitimate children he has fathered throughout the country. Only after sustained debate and much pleading does Thalia relent and allow Momus's bastards to remain in her realm. This resolution has been suggested by A Propos, a theater critic. He reminds Momus's children, as they scramble for a prize that Thalia holds beyond their reach, that

L'esprit qu'on veut avoir, gâte celui qu'on a;	The wit you want to have, ruins the one you've got;
Ou, si vous l'aimez mieux, mais n'allez l'oublier:	Or, if you prefer, but don't soon forget it:
Tel brille au second rang, qui s'éclipse au premier?	Who burns bright in second place, only to burn out in first?

Therefore,

Faut chanter l'amour et le vin,	You must sing of love and wine,
Plus de souci, plus de chagrin,	No more worries or woes,
Ricdon, ricdin,	Ricdon, ricdin,
Couplet badin,	Playful verse,
Joyeux refrain,	Happy chorus,
Digue, din, din, din	Ding, dong, dong, dong
Faut chanter, le verre à la main.[59]	You must sing, glass in hand.

The théâtre du Vaudeville may have been announcing its own project, to present comic vaudevilles that entertained in their own right without striving for the status of classical comedy; but in so doing it mocked the Revolution. More problematic still was the ambiguity of the play's satire, which alternated between gibes at privilege and gibes at its abolition. In reviewing the piece, the *Chronique de Paris* praised the gaiety and charm of the songs, but it highlighted only one side of the play's equivocal joking by criticizing the satiric representation of Thalia: "We believe . . . that the liberty of the theaters would seem a favor rather than an injustice to Thalia, and that this Muse would have more complaints than praise for exclusive privilege." Furthermore, the paper's editors argued, "However much people think they glimpse in this trifle the marked intent to take revenge on the [January] decree on behalf of the formerly privileged theaters, it is undeniable that this is not properly the provenance of the vaudeville."[60]

If *Les Mille et un théâtres* was slightly provocative, then François Léger's *L'Auteur d'un moment*, which opened two days later, was extraordinarily so. This play told the story of Mme. de Volnange, a young widow who sets out to humble M. Damis, the conceited playwright who is courting her, and of Damis's double humiliation. As the play begins, Damis comes to court the wealthy Mme. de Volnange, knowing that her fortune will help him to build his reputation. While he and his friend, Baliveau, await the widow, they see that a new pedestal has been placed in her garden. Since other pedestals bear the busts of great French *hommes de lettres*, Baliveau is convinced that a bust of Damis is intended for the new one. He engraves a quatrain upon it:

Aveugle en sa fureur, en vain la sombre envie,	Blind in its passion, vainly will dismal envy,
De traits envenimés attaqua son génie,	With poisonous strokes, attack his genius,
Dictés par la raison, ses sublimes écrits,	Dictated by reason, his sublime writings,
Seront de tous les temps et de tous les pays.	Will be for all times and all countries.

By the play's end, double humiliations have been played out: Mme. de Volnange publicly reveals that she has no intention of marrying Damis, and Baliveau's inflated verse is discovered as celebrants arrive bearing a bust of Rousseau.

After the play's premiere, rumors began to circulate in Paris that Damis and Baliveau were thinly disguised parodies of the playwright Marie-Joseph Chenier and the poet Charles Palissot. These rumors easily drew evidence from the text of the play itself. Of Damis:

Ses sublimes écrits étincellent de traits,	His sublime writings sparkle with qualities,
Que jusques à nos jours on ne connut jamais.	That were hitherto unknown.
Mais, Paris fatigué du style académique,	But Paris, tired of the academic style,
Siffle avec nous l'idole et le panégyrique.	With us hissed the idol and the panegyric.
Et rit de ses pédants, qui pensent à la fois,	And laughed at the pedantry, which hoped all at once,
Eclairer l'univers et régenter les rois.[61]	To enlighten the universe and instruct kings.

Palissot was believed to be the model for Baliveau because of his close friendship with Chenier and, as well, because the verse on the pedestal evoked a satire he had written at Rousseau's expense some thirty-seven years earlier.[62] Finally, Léger's lengthy public denial, printed in the monarchist *Logographe* after a troubled fourth performance, heightened public curiosity and the force of rumor. Few seemed to give credence to the claim that the play was intended only as a tribute to Rousseau.[63]

The fifth performance of *L'Auteur d'un moment* sold out. When the play began, loges and parterre remained silent until Mme. de Volnange's companion sang the song that was the real source of controversy, because it reputedly alluded to Chenier's celebrated *Charles IX*:

Il faut que ce fat à nos yeux	This peacock in our eyes, must
De honte et de fureur expire. . . .	Expire of shame and anger. . . .
Se voire berné par un pédant,	To see oneself fooled by a pedant,
Est bien fâcheux sur ma parole;	Is, on my word, very tiring;
Des rois quoiqu'il soit le régent,	He may be the regent of kings,
Sans respect pour son rudiment	But without respect for his funda-mentals,
Il faut l'envoyer, à l'école.	He must be sent to school.

Then hoots and competing shouts of "Bravo!" "Down with the Jacobins!" and "Down with the curtain!" brought the play to a stop. Someone in the parterre was accused of Jacobinism and dragged from the theater, beaten up, and pitched against a wall. The theater's guards restored order and allowed the play to continue, but news of the fracas circulated in the streets and, at the play's end, the well-dressed inhabitants of the loges found that they could leave the theater only by passing through a gauntlet of angry patriots.[64] In the face of such violence and revolutionary censure, Barré agreed to withdraw the play, but he did so in a very provocative way: he announced that the next evening's performance would include a play entitled, *La revanche forcée*. Again there were crowds, now dominated by revolutionaries, and again there were disruptions, and the evening's program was not allowed to continue until a copy of *L'Auteur d'un moment* had been burned onstage as the orchestra played *Ça ira*.[65]

In detailing the contest the following week, *Révolutions de Paris* attributed the worst possible motives to the owners and authors of the Vaudeville. The paper reminded its readers of the queen's hostility to Chenier's *Charles IX* and then pointed out that Barré's brother was a member of her household staff. Those who could not draw their own conclusions were treated to an imagined conversation in which the two brothers cooked up the project for *L'Auteur d'un moment*. Finally, the editor detailed the events of the play's last performance and explained the lessons to be drawn from them. To sustain a free theater, and ultimately a free society, the public was responsible for determining the political and moral value of all plays and expressing their opinions. But absenting oneself from a theater was not an adequate expression of opinion. Patriots "should come to the theater to exercise the right of censure that belongs to them alone, and to declare the proscription of plays that are contrary to the laws and of those that shock morals." As he had explained elsewhere, the result was that "Theatrical programs will be tumultuous perhaps, but the citizenry will be free."[66]

Neither the *Courrier* nor the *Chronique de Paris* wanted to openly accuse the owners and authors of the Vaudeville of royalist motivation: "We are certain that M. Barré is sadly affected by such a horrible scene," avowed the *Courier*. "We would like to believe that he never foresaw that the glorification of Rousseau would be the cause of it [and] we do justice to his intentions."[67] Both papers did, however, emphasize audience reaction. Of Barré's efforts to defend the piece before the National Assembly, the *Courrier* asked, "What does it matter that this play is not opposed to the Constitution, if it provoked trouble by making allusions which revolted patriots who love the Constitution . . . ?"[68]

Regardless of what motivation revolutionaries attributed to the Vaudeville, the audience's reaction was always the central issue. The audience at the first four performances of *L'Auteur d'un moment* fixed the play's meaning, which was then advertised by Léger's denial and by the subsequent newspaper articles about the events at the Vaudeville. Although it is undeniable that the text of the play could support such an interpretation, the audience might have ignored those allusions and emphasized instead the play's celebration of Rousseau. But the vaudeville form helped to shape the interpretation. Because of the vaudeville's association with satire and satire's with royalism, it was reasonable for audiences to emphasize *L'Auteur d'un moment*'s royalist allusions just as the *Chronique de Paris* had stressed the counterrevolutionary overtones of *Les Mille et un théâtres*.

The situation was all the more unstable because of the audience's habit of expressing itself audibly during performances. Although the *Révolutions de Paris* was willing to accept the possibility that such expression would lead to scenes in the theaters, such scenes were considered crucial to a process whose end was the suppression of "corrupt" plays, which would contribute to the improved health of the body politic. That an audience's interpretations of and reactions to performances was the critical issue was underscored by the fact that, a week after *L'Auteur d'un moment* had been pulled from the stage, *Rocambole des journaux* was still telling readers where they might purchase copies of it, and the theater itself continued to advertise printed copies of *Les Mille et un théâtres* at the very height of the Terror.[69]

Finally, just as the *Chronique* had raised the issue of the appropriateness of vaudevilles for serious subjects in its review of *Les Mille et un théâtres*, the *Courrier* did so now in regard to *L'Auteur d'un moment*.

> The théâtre du Vaudeville should be forever closed to these plays with satirical allusions that shock nimble and playful muses. . . . M. Barré ought to recall Boileau's verse and, in his theater, the vaudeville should only be a *pleasant chatterbox*, a *child of delightful witticism*, at which the aristocrat, the patriot, the Feuillant, and the Jacobin cannot help but smile and vie with one another in applauding.[70]

Unlike street songs, which were scorned early in the Revolution for their lack of seriousness, theatrical vaudevilles were admonished if they lacked frivolity. Their characterization by Boileau was taken as a formal definition to which vaudevilles must hew.

The Vaudevillists bowed before audience and critics. They pulled *L'Auteur d'un moment* from their repertoire, but only after a performance of that play had filled the theater to capacity and the controversy it excited had fixed the Vaudeville's name indelibly in the public memory. What had very nearly been a complete political fiasco was a commercial success and a brief *cause célèbre* that served to distinguish the Vaudeville from other theaters in the overcrowded market that the January decree had created.

The immediate conflict had been resolved, but larger issues remained. The Vaudeville had been urged to remain outside of politics at a time when all cultural forms and public relations were being invested with political overtones and implications. But this paradoxical situation would not be addressed for another year and a half, when audiences and newspapers again called attention to the ambiguity of the vaudeville's allusions and forced the Vaudevillists to find a new solution.

SILENCING OPPOSITION AND FIXING REVOLUTIONARY MEANING

Six months after the first round had been fought between the satire of the Vaudeville and the politics of the Revolution, the status of newspapers once more changed dramatically. Since 1789 occasional acts of popular violence had infringed on the freedom of the press without driving royalist newspapers from print. Then, during the revolution of 10 August, "the people made off with all the aristocratic newspapers without exception; a few authors escaped popular vengeance, but their publications paid for them and were pitilessly burned to the last page. Even presses and type, nothing was spared."[71] This violence was more widespread and systematic than at any previous time, and it was now backed by legislation. What the people did not lay their hands upon on 10 August was abolished by the Paris municipal government on the 12th, when the authors and editors of counterrevolutionary newspapers, those "poisoners of public opinion," were declared outside of the law and their presses were confiscated.[72]

The municipal government dramatically narrowed the field of political debate by driving counterrevolutionary arguments, rhetoric, and satire from the public arena. A few royalist works managed to slip through—François Marchant's last songbooks against the Revolution were published in 1793—but, for the most part, satire would henceforth be the property of Revolutionaries.[73] Among the few who continued to produce it was A.-J. Gorsas, deputy to the Convention for Seine-et-Oise and editor of the *Courrier des départements.*

Antoine-Joseph Gorsas, the son of cobblers in Limoges, had supported himself during the Old Regime by running a boys' school, but he had early shown his predilection for invective. In 1787 he had been imprisoned briefly at Bicêtre, ostensibly for the corruption of the minors in his charge but more probably for his satires against Loménie de Brienne and others.[74] When the National Assembly established itself, Gorsas did not wait for the declaration of a free press to begin to publish: on 5 July 1789 he issued the first number of the *Courrier de Versailles à Paris et de Paris à Versailles.* His paper appeared throughout the summer, detailing the attack on the Bastille and the king's subsequent visit to Paris, but it was only in October, when he published an eyewitness account of the "orgy" of the king's guards at Versailles, that the *Courrier* really gained notoriety. Gorsas's account was popularly considered to be most important in helping to mobilize the Parisian market women's march to Versailles, and for this he received the congratulations of the Paris districts. When the center of political activity shifted from Versailles to Paris, Gorsas followed, changing the title of his paper to the *Courrier de Paris dans les provinces et des provinces à Paris,* and continuing to publish, with only one interruption, for the next three and one-half years.

The *Courrier* was an excellent and respected source of revolutionary information.[75] Gorsas was sympathetic to the popular movement, and accordingly the *Courrier* included ample information about events in the provinces and anecdotes of Parisian popular activity as well as news of the court and the Assembly. And, less concerned than were the radicals to his left to raise up and remake the popular classes, he soon included accounts of popular singing and song lyrics in the pages of his newspaper. As he became accustomed to the role of editor, his stiff rhetoric loosened up and acquired the distinctive satirical tone for which he had already shown talent. His targets before the revolution of 10 August were unsurprising, but his satire was laden with idiosyncratic wit, such as when he pretended to have fed the ears of a prominent monarchist to his cat. After the king's flight to Varennes, he rhymed:

Après avoir pillé la France,	After having pillaged France,
Et tout le peuple dépouillé,	And stripped the shirts from people's backs,
N'est-ce pas belle pénitence,	Is it not a lovely penitance,
De se couvrir d'un sac mouillé?[76]	To cover yourself with a wet sack?

Even when the satire was not his own, Gorsas's usurpation of others' material had a distinct style. In 1791 he so cleverly appropriated a hostile song against him that when an entire *pièce en vaudevilles* was based on it, the original songwriter complained that he had become the victim.[77]

Because royalists and counterrevolutionaries were his targets, their silencing by the August revolution might well have silenced Gorsas's satire. But other political divisions had emerged and, as they became more pressing, the *Courrier* directed fire in new directions. When the National Convention was convened on 21 September 1792, it was already divided between Girondins and Montagnards. Although these factions agreed on the social objectives of the Revolution—abolition of privilege, anticlericalism, and economic liberalism tempered by a measure of social welfare—they were increasingly divided over the means by which those objectives could be reached.[78] As their struggles for power intensified, each faction came to be characterized by the position ascribed by its opponent. As the Girondins came to be suspected of royalism, an accusation born the preceding winter when their desire for war coincided with that of the king, Montagnards were attacked as the party of anarchy, accused of having encouraged the September massacres and playing into the hands of the Paris "mob."[79]

Gorsas had long held Girondin sympathies and so, scarcely a month after the August revolution and the silencing of royalism, he turned on the Girondins' enemies. On 26 September, he printed a lengthy editorial against the Jacobins, charging them with sowing division and discord that could only weaken the nation. Ten days later, he targeted Marat to accuse him, with some justice, of demagoguery and incendiarism. However, so quick and bitter were these attacks that even a close political ally publicly reproached Gorsas for fostering discord and dividing the nation on behalf of Brissot and the Girondins.[80]

Having entered into bitter opposition against the Jacobins, Gorsas did not confine himself to editorials; he used the same satirical weapons that he had mobilized against royalists. He printed a song that he claimed had been sung at the Jacobin Club:

Air de Nina

Quand les Marseillais reviendront	When the Marseilleans return
Près de la société mère,	To the mother club,
Nos plaisirs alors renaîtront,	Then our happiness will be born again,
Nous verrons régner Robespierre;	We'll see Robespierre reign;
• • • • • • • • • • •	• • • • • • • • • • •
Tu seras permanente alors,	Then you will be here for good,
Aimable et chère guillotine;	Lovable and beloved guillotine;
Tu dépêcheras chez les morts,	You'll speed along to the dead,
Toute la clique Brissotine.[81]	The whole lot of Brissotines.

In combating royalism, Gorsas had not relied wholly, nor even primarily, on songs and satire, nor did he do so now. He mingled this material with more serious articles and editorials, alternating serious criticism with attempts to undermine through ridicule. The *Courrier* included mocking accounts of Jacobin Club meetings, speeches by Robespierre footnoted with Gorsas's commentary, parodies of articles by Marat, and songs.[82] There was a "Christmas carol" against the Jacobins and a bitter parody of the *Marseillaise*:

Allons enfants de l'anarchie,	Forward children of anarchy,
Le jour de honte est arrivé . . .	The shameful day is upon us . . .
Du peuple aveugle en sa furie,	The people blinded by their rage,
Le couteau sanglant est levé.	Raise the bloody knife.
Dans ce temps d'horreur et de crimes,	In this time of horror and crimes,
Pour servir d'infâmes projets,	To serve iniquitous designs,
Il ne compte ni ses forfaits,	They count neither their infamies,
Ni le nombre des victimes.[83]	Nor the number of their prey.

The Montagnards and their allies reacted much as revolutionaries had reacted earlier to royalist attacks. Gorsas was denounced in *L'Ami du pe-*

uple and from the podium of the Jacobin Club, and in March 1793 his presses were sacked by a mob.[84] But his public voice was not effectively silenced until two months later.

The eight months that the Girondins and Montagnards spent fighting for dominance in the Convention witnessed mounting crises in the Republic, as it confronted inflation, war, and counterrevolution. The Girondin attempt to slow the trial and execution of the king heightened fears of their royalist sympathies, and their attacks on Montagnard alliances with Parisian sans-culottes ruined any possibility of their finding popular support in Paris. Finally, between 31 May and 2 June, Parisian radicals rebelled, surrounded the Convention, and demanded the expulsion of the Girondins. Gorsas was among the twenty-nine deputies declared under house arrest. He immediately fled Paris and took refuge in Calvados, where he tried to raise an armed force against the government. The project failed but not before news of it reached the Convention, which declared him outside of the law.[85] He returned to Paris in early October, where he was arrested, tried, and guillotined in the space of two days.

Gorsas was not proscribed or beheaded because he had written satiric songs but because he was a journalist who advertised his political criticism, because he was a deputy who lost one of the most important power struggles of the Revolution, and because he finally sought to undermine the government by force. Gorsas, like the royalists banned before him, used satiric songs as a weapon in a larger political struggle. As revolutionary governments and populace circumscribed ever more closely the limits of opposition and political debate, such songs declined in number. It was not simply a matter of forbidding oppositional songs but of suppressing the opposition itself. But abandoning debate was something that neither the royalists nor the Girondins would do. When they were finally driven from the public arena, the songs that served them were silenced as well.

Robespierre detested satire: "[It is the calumny] that has raised a barrier between the Revolution and the other peoples of Europe, by ceaselessly representing the French nation to them as a horde of cannibals."[86] Whether satire was the source of dissension between France and the rest of Europe is debatable, but fears about the impact of satire within France were not wholly groundless. The counterrevolutionary *Actes des Apôtres* and *Rocambole des journaux* sustained themselves far longer than did many a serious revolutionary publication. And satirists of all stripes played upon well-known associations drawn from revolutionary and Old Regime culture alike. If the success of François Marchant's *Constitution française en vaudevilles* is any indication, counterrevolutionaries were not the only readers of such material.

But the final months of Gorsas's *Courrier* revealed the other face of satire, as that journal traced the same trajectory that royalists had followed one and two years earlier. As Gorsas' opposition intensified and he saw himself outflanked and outnumbered, his satire became flatter and more bitter. His parodied *Marseillaise*—"Le couteau sanglant est levé"—was hardly more sophisticated or subtle than the scatological diatribes of the last issues of *Les Actes des Apôtres*. Revolutionaries like Robespierre may have had little room for the double entendre of satire, but the satirists demonstrated that a delicate balance of linguistic and political possibilities was necessary to sustain a truly effective lampoon. Shrill representations of the French as a "horde of cannibals" were signs of impending defeat, not victory.

Explicitly political satiric songs were silenced when open opposition ceased to be possible. Political debate had broadened beyond questions of what the Revolution ought to achieve to encompass, as well, how revolutionaries should express and entertain themselves. And one of the arenas in which this issue was fought was the commercial theater, where audiences and government moved to strip the vaudeville of its ambiguous resonances. Yves Barré and company would fare better than had Antoine Gorsas because they were willing to accommodate the Revolution at the critical moment. For, although the songs written for the théâtre du Vaudeville flirted with political opinion and played upon revolutionary rhetoric, they were written first and foremost to attract customers. When the Revolution demanded submission, the vaudevillists gave way. In so doing they had a profound impact on the revolutionary reshaping of the vaudeville genre.

After the uproar over *L'Auteur d'un moment*, performances at the theater continued peacefully throughout the next year as the Vaudeville presented thoroughly irrelevant comedies interspersed with a few unabashedly patriotic plays. In the wake of the August revolution, the vaudevillists made visible efforts to demonstrate their sympathy to the new order by announcing regular benefit performances for the widows and orphans of those "who perished during the day of 10 August while defending the cause of liberty."[87] They also asked the Tuileries section, where the Vaudeville was located, to place the theater under its surveillance—a direct request for the equivalent of preliminary censorship—perhaps because they feared the consequences of unintentional allusions.[88]

Whether or not surveillance was exercised, none of the Vaudeville's plays offended revolutionary sensibilities for months. Then, on 7 January 1793, the *Journal de Paris* reviewed a new production: "Gaiety, couplets that are racy, even a little impudent; that is the essential type of the vaudeville. It is all too dangerous to move away from this style, because the vaudeville lends itself poorly to touching situations, and because a popular tune and lively chorus ill accord with expressions of sadness and fear; this is, nonetheless, the risk chosen by the author of *La Chaste Suzanne*, performed yesterday for the first time, and success crowned all his efforts."[89]

La Chaste Suzanne recycled an Old Testament tale of virtue maligned but triumphant. As the play begins, Accaron and Barzabas, two old and respected judges, wait for the beautiful Suzanne to come to her bath so they may declare their love to her. When Suzanne first hears their declarations she believes that the old men are testing her fidelity while her husband fights at the frontier; finally, recognizing their sincerity, she refuses in horror. In revenge, Accaron and Barzabas claim that they discovered Suzanne in the arms of a young man, and they accuse her of adultery. As Suzanne awaits execution, Daniel comes forward to question the accusers separately and so reveal, through differences in their testimony, that they are lying. This was an unusual plot for a vaudeville; apart from an early scene when the judges vie comically for the role of declarant before Suzanne, there was little that was funny in the piece. But even though there was no hint of satire, audiences did as they had done with *L'Auteur d'un moment*: they found evidence of an implicit counterrevolutionary message.

The sources of contention in *La Chaste Suzanne* were a single line in the second act and one verse of the play's closing vaudeville. Debuting at the time of the king's trial, the play included a line in which Accaron and Barzabas were told that they could not hear Suzanne's case because "you are accusers, you cannot be judges." This line excited prolonged applause from many parts of the theater, causing the *Journal de Paris* to warn: "It is not difficult to see that the author wanted to make . . . allusions to the present situation; but when making allusions, one must be certain that they are just; because if there is no justice in their application, the author completely misses the mark."[90] The contested couplet was later claimed to be a comparison between a prostitute and a chaste woman, but audiences interpreted it as a comparison between old and revolutionary regimes:

Affecter candeur et tendresse,	Feign candor and affection,
Du plus offrant que l'amour presse,	From the highest bidder who love inspires,

Recevoir argent et présent,	Receive money and gift,
C'est ce que l'on fait à présent.	That's the way it's done in the present.
Refuser plaisir et richesse,	Refuse pleasure and riches,
Pour conserver gloire et sagesse,	To preserve glory and wisdom,
De la mort souffrir le tourment,	Suffer death's torment,
Oh! c'est de l'ancien testament.[91]	Oh! that's the way of the Old Testament.

The *Chronique de Paris* tried to downplay the whole matter. Its review made brief mention of the play's allusions to the king's trial but emphasized aesthetics above all, complaining that the play was too serious and "much inferior to the first three [by Radet, Desfontaines, and Barré]; the costumes and decor are new, tasteless, and without knowledge of the period, its customs and its locales."[92] Given the circumstances that had surrounded performances of *L'Auteur d'un moment* the preceding year, the *Chronique* was understandably cautious. But the theatrical public's attention was directed elsewhere throughout January, as the Municipal Council and National Convention debated whether to suppress *L'Ami des lois*, a play at the théâtre de la Nation that pointedly attacked the Jacobins in the name of democracy. The Municipal Council was victorious: performances of *L'Ami des lois* were forbidden because they were likely to "stir people up" during the king's trial, and the owners of all Parisian theaters were urged to avoid the production of any plays that had excited or would excite trouble.[93]

The Vaudeville did not heed the warning, nor would it give way before rumors that popular action would be taken to stop performances of *La Chaste Suzanne*. And yet, the actor Delpêche seemed surprised when a fight broke out in the theater over audience reactions to the play's controversial verse. On 29 January he appeared before the Paris Municipal Council to complain of troubles that he claimed were excited by Jacobins and to ask for the council's assistance in keeping order in the theater. The council complied but also ordered that *La Chaste Suzanne* be examined for its capacity to corrupt public opinion.[94] By mid-February, the Vaudeville was performing a "corrected" version of the play, from which offending lines had been struck.[95] The modified *Suzanne* remained a part of the Vaudeville's repertoire for the next several months.

In mid-September 1793, the National Convention passed the Law on Suspects, which defined counterrevolutionary suspects in the broadest possible terms. Five days later all the prominent vaudevillists except Piis were arrested as suspects, and they seemed convinced that *La Chaste Suzanne* had been the cause. Desfontaines, Radet, and Barré immediately sent a petition to the National Convention which tried to establish their revolutionary intent. Against imputed aristocratic references, the authors cited line after line that referred to "the people," "just and good," or "the people's law," and they contested royalist interpretations of the closing verse: "Since this couplet addresses no other issue than that of one woman who sells her honor and another who faces death to preserve it, any malicious interpretation is false and ridiculous."[96]

But experience had already shown these men that authorial intention was not adequate justification, so they also described favorable audience reaction founded on revolutionary interpretations of their play, and they reminded the Convention of the revolutionary services that the Vaudeville had performed since 10 August.[97] The three men, joined by Léger and another imprisoned associate, also sent a petition to the Committee of General Security, which reminded its members of the patriotic couplets that the Vaudevillists had included in their plays, of their having "enacted" the *Marseillaise*, and of the hymns that they had written for a local celebration of the Martyrs of Revolution.[98] Finally, the Tuileries section sent testimonials of the patriotism of the incarcerated vaudevillists: they verified Léger's participation in the revolution of 31 May and argued that aristocratic interpretations of *La Chaste Suzanne*, or of any other Vaudeville production, revealed the counterrevolutionary sentiments of "malicious people" in the audience, not the Vaudeville's directors.[99]

Barré and Léger were released fairly quickly, but Radet and Desfontaines remained in prison in spite of repeated requests for their liberty from the Tuileries section, including one that bore the signature of the recently released Léger as secretary.[100] Finally, the two prisoners tried a new strategy: they wrote a patriotic song that they sent to the Paris Municipal Council and to the revolutionary council of the LePelletier section, where Desfontaines lived. Desfontaines explained to the sectional council that he and Radet had written the song "in spite of the horrors of captivity and among the forty people who fill the room in which we live, only patriotism can overcome such difficulties."[101] The song itself bore visible signs of these conditions: it was extremely simple, and did no more than reiterate the sentiments of the letters that the authors had already sent to all committees concerned with their case.

Air: On doit 60 mille francs

L'aristocrate incarcéré	The imprisoned aristocrat
Par ses remords est déchiré	Is wracked by his remorse

C'est ce qui le désole;	That is his desolation;
Mais le patriote arrêté,	But the arrested patriot,
De l'âme a la tranquillité	Has peace of mind
C'est ce qui le console.	That is his consolation.
Des mesures de sûreté	Measures of security
Nous ont ravi la liberté,	Have despoiled us of liberty,
C'est ce qui nous désole;	That is our desolation;
Mais dans nos fers nous l'adorons	But in our irons we love it
Dans nos chants nous la célébrons	In our songs we celebrate it
C'est ce qui nous console.[102]	That is our consolation.

This, with a final appeal from the LePelletier section, won the men's freedom.

The gift of a revolutionary song was one of several strategies to win the liberty of the vaudevillists, but the gift had an important figurative meaning. It was an offering of the vaudeville genre to revolutionary politics. Within days of his release from La Force, Yves Barré wrote to the Committee of General Security to propose the formation of a society of authors to work at his theater:

> Convinced that this genre is more appropriate than any other to disseminate republican spirit among the people, because everyone knows what the vaudeville is capable of, "pleasant chatterbox which guides with a song / flies from mouth to mouth, growing as it goes" (Boileau); Barré promises to stage a patriotic play every fourteen days, and because he is not prompted by self-interest but wants only to serve the public good, as soon as a patriotic play has succeeded in his theater, all theaters in Paris and the other cities of the Republic may request copies and stage it without any recompense to the author.[103]

The proposed association would include, not surprisingly, Radet, Desfontaines, Piis, and Léger.

Satire, once the most essential characteristic of the vaudeville, had been stripped from the genre. Meanwhile, the satiric vaudevilles remembered from the Old Regime were claimed to have played a very different role from that of "pleasant chatterbox," which had been attributed scarcely years before. The *Journal des Spectacles* was not alone in claiming that "The vaudeville spoke the truth to tyrants when Melpomene, Thalia, and Polymnia were degrading themselves with the most servile flattery. . . . The vaudeville conducted an eternal war against abuse, in all its forms; and through the liberty of verses, the people tacitly prepared themselves to shake off the yoke of their oppressors."[104]

The vaudevillists now suggested that the defeat of tyranny meant that the vaudeville might rid itself of its satiric and oppositional character, to continue its work in a positive way. In Piis' play, *Le Mariage du vaudeville et de la morale*, performed in the year II, Vaudeville wins the hand of the much sought but distant Morale because he can teach lessons to citizens of all ages by making people happy. In chasing away his English rival, Vaudeville tells him:

Le Français par caractère	The Frenchman, by character,
Tient toujours a sa gaîté,	Holds tight to his gaiety,
Le vaudeville	The vaudeville,
Orné de fleurs,	Adorned with bouquets,
Est plus utile	Is more useful
Aux bonnes moeurs.[105]	To good mores.

Audiences still wanted a light song form, but political exigencies and commercial success required the Vaudeville to produce an explicitly revolutionary frivolity.

The Vaudeville continued to produce entirely apolitical comedies, *Arlequin afficheur*, for example, and *Colombine mannequin*, but the theater's most successful production—in fact one of the most successful productions in all of Paris during the Terror—was *L'Heureuse Décade*, an extremely simple piece in which a good, simple republican family sings of all its good, simple republican virtues, and everything ends happily.[106] Like *Ça ira*, vaudevilles had become straightforward and univocal, capable only of expressing enthusiastic support of the Revolution. Unlike *Ça ira*, the vaudeville was shaped by dissension among revolutionaries rather than agreement. This genre had been shaped by politics not because it was a part of any larger political struggle but because the primary purpose of the vaudeville—at least in so far as Radet, Piis, Barré, and Desfontaines were concerned—was to make money. Acquiescence to the demands of the Paris Municipal Government turned out to be a sure way to do just that.

And yet, the vaudeville bore at least one similarity to the explicitly political satires of royalists and Girondins in that both fell prey to the revolutionary need for simplification: while the opposition's satiric songs were silenced altogether, vaudevilles were stripped of their ambiguity. But there was more at issue than simple silencing. Once revolutionaries had achieved some apparent consensus about the content of songs and the purposes of singing, revolutionary song culture flourished. During the year II, song production would reach its peak, as hundreds of new songs were produced and published, performed, or offered to the Convention. Having become a simple declaration of revolutionary enthusiasm, songs would serve a myriad of purposes and become inextricably linked to the radical revolutionary movement.

Part II

◆

The Republican Crisis

Interlude

✦

From *Chant de Guerre* to *La Marseillaise*

✦ THE YEAR 1792 opened with a declaration of war already under debate in the Legislative Assembly. The preceding August, the emperor of Austria and the king of Prussia had declared that "[they] consider the King of France's current situation as a matter of common concern to all European sovereigns," and the émigré community on France's eastern border grew increasingly threatening. Inside the Assembly, Brissot and the Girondins led the war party, arguing that prompt military action would eliminate foreign threats and force a domestic taking of sides, which would expose counterrevolutionaries. Robespierre and his allies kept up a gradually weakening opposition against these arguments. Matters became more pressing in March, when the young and aggressive Francis II succeeded to the Austrian throne and refused to negotiate with the French. Now the question of war moved beyond Assembly walls to occupy public attention: endlessly debated in the political clubs, the issue appeared under many guises in private conversations and newspapers alike. In early April the Girondist newspapers, the *Chronique de Paris* and the *Courrier*, drafted song culture to the cause by generating enthusiasm for war songs. The *Chronique* raised the issue by printing an article about a battalion in the Dauphiné that had asked for "battle songs." "They express themselves with such enthusiasm, that we cannot doubt the effect that such songs would have on warrior's souls."[1] The *Courrier* immediately announced a competition on behalf of the Dauphiné battalion, offering three hundred livres for the best *chanson de guerre des soldats français*. The contest continued for weeks, as the *Courrier* promised an imminent decision; even the radical *Révolutions de Paris* joined in.[2]

93

But when France declared war against Austria on 20 April 1792, the nation still had no battle hymn. Clearly, song culture had made significant advances; lyrics intended to stir patriotism and combativeness were penned and published. Since nothing came along to truly replace the cheery *Ça ira*, however, this tune was drafted to the cause. Described as the "song of patriotism" that would animate the French "when it is time to fight the enemies of liberty," *Ça ira*'s title was claimed to be a souvenir from the American Revolutionary War.[3] Eventually a genuine war song would inherit *Ça ira*'s exalted place in revolutionary culture, acquiring its special status not simply because it was good but because of the particular conditions and timing of its appearance in Paris. Brought to the capital by radical revolutionaries from southern France, the song that would come to be known as *La Marseillaise* arrived only a few weeks before the republican revolution of 10 August 1792.

As all French schoolchildren know, *La Marseillaise*—originally the *Chant de guerre pour l'armée du Rhin*—was written by Joseph Rouget de Lisle, an army officer stationed in Strasbourg in 1792.[4] A constitutional monarchist and amateur composer who was exalted by war fever and an evening's champagne, Rouget reputedly produced his hymn in a single night after hearing Strasbourg's Mayor Dietrich and other local elites complain that *Ça ira* and *La carmagnole* were vulgar songs unfit for proper soldiers.[5]

Chant de guerre pour l'armée du Rhin[6]

Allons enfants de la patrie!	Forward children of the homeland!
Le jour de gloire est arrivé;	The day of glory is upon us;
Contre nous de la tyrannie	Against us, the bloody standard
L'étendard sanglant est levé.	Of tyranny is raised.
Entendez-vous dans les campagnes	Do you hear these ferocious soldiers
Mugir ces féroces soldats?	Bellowing in the fields?
Ils viennent jusque dans vos bras	They come into your very midst
Egorger vos fils, vos compagnes!	To slaughter your sons, your wives!
Aux armes, citoyens, formez vos bataillons,	To arms, citizens, form your battalions,
Marchez, marchez, qu'un sang impur abreuve nos sillons.	March on, march on, that impure blood will water our furrows.
Que veut cet horde d'esclaves,	What do they want, this hord of slaves,
De traîtres, de rois conjurés?	Of traitors, of conspiratorial kings?
Pour qui ces ignobles entraves,	For whom are these vile fetters,
Ces fers dès longtemps préparés?	These irons so long prepared?

Français! Pour nous, ah quel
  outrage!
Quels transports il doit exciter!
C'est nous qu'on ose méditer
De rendre à l'antique esclavage?
Aux armes . . . [etc.]

French people! For us, ah what out-
  rage!
What transports they should excite!
Is it us that they dare to consider
Returning to ancient slavery?
To arms . . . [etc.]

Quoi! des cohortes étrangères
Feraient la loi dans nos foyers!

What! these foreign troops
Would lay down the law in our
  homes!

Quoi! les phalanges mercénaires
Terrasseraient nos fiers guerriers!

What! these mercenary phalanxes
Would bring down our proud
  warriors!

Grand Dieu! par des mains
  enchaînées
Nos fronts sous le joug se
  ploîraient!
De vils despotes deviendraient
Les maîtres de nos destinées!
Aux armes . . . [etc.]

Great God! by means of shackled
  hands
Our heads would bend beneath the
  yoke!
Vile despots would become
The masters of our destinies!
To arms . . . [etc.]

Tremblez tyrans! et vous perfides,
L'opprobre de tous les partis;
Tremblez! vos projets parricides
Vont enfin recevoir leur prix,
Tout est soldat pour vous com-
  battre;
S'ils tombent nos jeunes héros,
La terre en produit de nouveaux
Contre vous tout prêts à se battre.
Aux armes . . . [etc.]

Quake tyrants! and you traitors
The disgrace of all parties;
Quake! your patricidal projects
Will at last receive their due,
All are soldiers to battle you;
If they fall, our young heros,
The earth will produce new ones
Ready to fight against you.
To arms . . . [etc.]

Français! en guerriers mag-
  nanimes
Portez ou retenez vos coups;
Epargnez ces tristes victimes,
A regret s'arment contre nous.

French people! as magnanimous
  warriors
Hold or rein in your blows;
Spare these sad victims
Who regretfully arm themselves
  against us.

Mais ces despotes sanguinaires!
Mais les complices de Bouillé,
Tous ces tigres qui sans pitié
Déchirent le sein de leur mère!
Aux armes . . . [etc.]

But these bloodthirsty despots!
But the accomplices of Bouillé,
All these pitiless tigers
Rending their mother's breast!
To arms . . . [etc.]

Amour sacré de la patrie,
Conduis, soutiens nos bras
  vengeurs
Liberté, Liberté chérie!

Sacred love of the homeland,
Guide us, sustain our avenging arms

Liberty, beloved Liberty!

Combats avec tes défenseurs	Fight alongside your defenders
Sous nos drapeaux que la Victoire	Beneath our banners to which Victory
Accourt à tes mâles accents:	Runs in answer to your manly tone:
Que tes ennemis expirants	That your expiring enemies
Voient ton triomphe et notre gloire.	Will see your triumph and our glory.
Aux armes . . . [etc.]	To arms . . . [etc.]

If Dietrich was hoping for a song that was dramatically different from *Ça ira*, then Rouget de Lisle answered his wish with the *Chant de guerre*. Lyrically, the two songs describe very different visions of the Revolution and the obstacles that it faced. All versions of *Ça ira*, whether written in 1790 or 1793, reflect the easy hopefulness of the title: things will work out because things are already working out. *Ça ira* places revolutionary actors at center stage and represents obstacles tumbling before them: in 1790 "L'aristocrate dit mea culpa" (The aristocrat says *mea culpa*); in the year II "Le brigand Prussien tombera / L'esclave Autrichien le suivra" (The Prussian brigand will fall / The Austrian slave will follow him).[7] The sense of accomplishment that was so pervasive in the summer of 1790 never ceased to inform the song's lyrics: the Revolution was advancing and singers of *Ça ira* envisaged no great difficulties in accomplishing it. In contrast, the *Chant de guerre*, written within days of the declaration of war, focuses on powerful and threatening enemies. Although the song begins by declaring that "the day of glory is upon us," it immediately continues with a fierce reminder of the real subject: "against us, the bloody standard of tyranny is raised." The lyrics conjure up an invading horde that will not simply overrun the countryside but "come into your very midst," killing sons and wives before enslaving the nation. In the end, the song does promise victory, but a victory that may be achieved only at great cost: "All are soldiers to battle you. If they fall, our young heros, the earth will produce new ones."

The songs are musically distinct as well. Like its lyrics, the bright, jiglike tune of *Ça ira* suggests an easy forward progression. The *Chant de guerre*'s rhythm is slower, closer to the pace of marching. Obviously a more formal composition, the tune is more complicated than the simple, repetitious melody of its predecessor; its steady rhythm and swelling notes ameliorate the fearful images conjured by the lyrics. This music lends greater sensibility to a song whose learned lyrics are difficult and likely to be confusing when heard in performance: the brief pause before the chorus and the swelling of the voice as the singer declaims "To arms, citizens, form your battalions" make absolutely clear the song's central message.

Rouget de Lisle, monarchist army officer, wrote his *Chant de guerre* for the king's soldiers. But there was nothing decisively monarchist about the song: performed in a different context, it would acquire republican associations and interpretations. Having been copied and distributed among soldiers in Strasbourg, the *Chant de guerre* was carried south by traveling merchants or perhaps a newspaper, changing context, as Michel Vovelle has pointed out, and taking on a broader meaning as it went.[8] In the East, it had been the war song of a formal army, composed by and for constitutional monarchists who, within months, would refuse to swear allegiance to the new Republic. In the south, the song was adopted as the anthem of the *fédérés* of Montpellier and Marseilles, men who had been radicalized by their confrontations with hostile royalists and who were prepared to extend the Revolution to defend it. These were the singers who would teach the *Chant de guerre* to Parisians, in the process lending it a new name and helping to fix a new set of political associations.

The southern *fédérés* headed toward Paris in midsummer, intending to join other provincials who had gathered there to protect the city and attempt to force the king's hand in a more aggressive prosecution of the war. Although contingents had been arriving from throughout France since early July, the volunteers from the south were awaited with a particularly keen combination of hope and apprehension.

> For the past several days, the arrival of the Marseilleans has been ostentatiously announced. Their numbers are enlarged upon; they are made a bogey for the court; their intentions are spoken of in various ways. On the one hand, they are represented as a bunch of villains. . . . On the other hand, to the contrary, they are proclaimed as devoted patriots . . . who intend to restore the public spirit of tired Parisians, and deliver the final crushing blow against the monarchy.[9]

Arriving in a city in which political tensions were already high, the Marseille volunteers quickly added to the ferment. On their first night in Paris, they insured their reputation as hot-headed Revolutionaries by fighting with a regiment that was singing, "Long live the king, long live the queen, long live Lafayette!" The volunteers then marched along the Champs Elysées singing *Ça ira* and shouting, "Long live the nation!"[10] Ten days later, they joined Parisians and other *fédérés* to take the Tuileries Palace and help overthrow the monarchy.

It was not until the end of August that newspapers began to publish accounts of popular performances of the *fédérés*' hymn. Then the stories came fast and furious, describing a song that had swept the city. On the 29th, the *Chronique de Paris* told its readers: "People in all of the theaters now request the song: *Allons, enfants de la patrie*. The words are by M. Rougez [sic], a captain of genius garrisoned at Huningue. . . . The *fédérés* brought the song from Marseille, where it was very popular."[11] The article closed with the song's six verses. The next day the *Courrier* reported that a patriotic printer in Compiègne had reproduced and distributed the "warlike song" to his brothers at arms; this article, too, closed with the song's lyrics.[12] Even the radical *Révolutions de Paris* joined in: "The people's spirits are still extremely good . . . ; one must see them, one must hear them repeating in chorus the refrain of the war song of the Marseilleans, which the singers in front of the statue of Liberty in the Tuileries gardens are teaching them every day with renewed success.[13]

These reports clustered together in the late summer, but it is unlikely that the southern volunteers had waited that long to sing "their" song publicly. In fact, the *Chant de guerre* had appeared in Paris even before their arrival: the *Courrier* reported its performance at a local civic banquet in late July, printing five verses of the song without mentioning title, tune, or author, and the same lyrics appeared in the *Trompette du Père Duchesne* at about the same time.[14] But the *Chant de guerre* had yet to acquire specific revolutionary associations; like *Ça ira* before it, this song achieved its peculiar emblematic status through a combination of political resonance and advertisement.

The *Chant de guerre*'s rousing tune and fiery lyrics had not been enough to distinguish it; had that been adequate, it might have become popular after its first Parisian performance in July. But the song was also associated with the radical Marseille *fédérés*, and its first flush of popularity followed closely upon the revolution of 10 August. These revolutionary associations helped the career of the song now known by a variety of popular titles: *Allons enfans de la patrie, Aux armes, citoyens*; or simply, the *Hymne des Marseillais* (The *Hymne of the Marseilleans*). The *Hymne*'s circulation by the radical Southerners and its appearance in Paris within weeks of the revolution of 10 August had bestowed upon it particularly republican associations. And once again, newspapers helped to broaden this popularity. Having searched for a successful war song for months, they celebrated performances of the newly popular *Chant de guerre*, thereby advertising and reinforcing the unofficial practice of the streets.

What had been written as a battle cry against Austrian enemies and hostile émigrés became a wholesale republican attack on despotism at home and abroad. This transformation was facilitated by the song's lyrics, which artfully marry evocative power and vagueness. *La Marseillaise* leaves unnamed France's enemies even as it describes them in terms that are graphic and highly provocative—they are "foreign troops," "mercenaries," "tyrants," "pitiless tigers." By evoking qualities without naming specific enemies, Rouget de Lisle's lyrics heighten general fears but permit individual singers (or auditors) to personalize their enemy, alternately envisioning Francis of Austria or George of England or any nameless foreign soldier. This same vagueness would also favor the song's republican appropriation, because it unwittingly allowed singers to add the faces of Louis XVI and Marie-Antoinette, domestic "aristocrats," and counterrevolutionaries to those of foreign soldiers and despots.

The *Marseillaise* completed the lyrical trajectory initially traced by *Ça ira*. As the Revolution progressed, the flexibility and nuance of *Ça ira* dwindled; as political opinions polarized, the number of song versions declined. Now *Ça ira* was replaced altogether by a song that described a politics of binary opposition, a Manichean struggle to the death. This polarizing vision of the Revolution paralleled the print history of the two songs. *Ça ira* was, above all, a song of oral invention that permitted singers to express their particular opinions about the Revolution; the *Marseillaise* had, from its very outset, a single, definitive version that was fixed in print. Early reports of the song's performances included all, or nearly all, of its verses, and during the next two years it would be reprinted repeatedly in all kinds of formats—with or without printed music, on single songsheets, or in small song books—with essentially the same lyrics.[15] The song's lyrical stability did not prevent other songwriters from using its tune or writing new verses that preserved the original choruses or rhyme scheme; but, after one final verse was added in the autumn of 1792, there were no alternate versions, only imitations and parodies.[16]

After the hymn's appearance in Paris, its popularity grew steadily. For more than two years, it would broaden the role of revolutionary anthem originated by *Ça ira*: performed at local and national festivals and sung in public gardens and fraternal dinners, its tune would be appropriated for the creation of more than two hundred new songs.[17] It was heard in moments of victory and defeat alike: *fédérés* sang it under the windows of the royal family after the August revolution of 1792, just as, in September 1793, "a fairly large number of people . . . sang the marseilloise very heartily, in spite of the bad news that is circulating . . . about the Vendée."[18]

But the *Hymne des Marseillais* was not only a popular civilian song; it had originally been written for the army of the Rhine, and it was already circulating among enlisted military men as the Marseille volunteers carried it to Paris. Copies of the song had been distributed to the Strasbourg regiments in April, and by September the hymn was so popular among soldiers at the front that they were said to have sung it at Valmy, where the revolutionary army won its first battle.[19] The song was adopted in the upper ranks as well. Less than a week after Valmy, the Minister of War wrote to General Kellerman: "The fashion for *Te Deums* has passed, we must substitute something more useful and in greater conformity with the public's mood [*esprit public*], thus, I authorize you general, if you believe you require authorization, to have *The hymn of the Marseillais* sung solemnly and with the same pomp that you would give to the *Te Deum*; I attach a copy of it to that end."[20] The following month, the *Moniteur universel* claimed that the "warlike sounds of the *national hymn*" had been the only song heard in the streets of Chambéry after the "liberation" of Savoy. In Paris, the *Hymne* again replaced the *Te Deum* at a public celebration of the same event.[21]

As the *Hymne des Marseillais* was being sung informally and officially, by civilians and by soldiers, entrepreneurs joined in too. The song was published in several dozen editions, profiting the publishers rather than the author, while Parisian theaters used their own means to celebrate the new tune. In mid-October, the *Chronique de Paris* reported that "the federal and revolutionary tune of *Ça ira* has given way to the warlike chant of the Marseillais, which is so much in harmony with the character of republican valor, and which rings through our theaters every night." The théâtres Italien, Feydeau, du Marais, and du Vaudeville expressed their patriotism and drew a crowd at the same time by performing the song during intermissions, "each with the props appropriate to its genre."[22] The Opera, more ambitious still, staged an entire piece by Gossec, *L'offrande à la liberté*, whose primary object was a grand finale in which men, women, and children crowded onto the stage to sing the *Hymne des Marseillais*.[23]

The formal elements and broad popularity of the *Hymne des Marseillais* combined with the cultural impact of war and republican revolution to galvanize the slow transformation of song culture that had been taking place since the appearance of *Ça ira*. The hymn's poetic and learned lyrics and its almost classical tune lent "higher" cultural associations to the genre of popular song, which had slowly been acquiring revolutionary respectability; its associations with the revolution of 10 August and the Republic's victorious armies solidified a growing faith in the capacity

of songs to rouse and unify enthusiasm. Meanwhile, war and the republican revolution made the manipulation of songs and singing a particularly pressing issue. At the official level, the government was increasingly
concerned with propaganda, searching for the means to instill republican values in an unlettered populace and sustain enthusiasm for the war
in a popular army. Unofficially, Parisians sang songs to express their
commitment to the Republic and to celebrate its victories. As government and populace alike sought to remake the French nation, there was
a growing concern that culture should express radically new political
and social alignments: language, popular and official iconography, even
costume, were all subject to reinterpretation and refashioning.[24] Increasingly deputies, journalists, and publishers would point to singing's revolutionary potential, explore its implications, and suggest means to
harness and implement it.

Historically, the *Marseillaise* galvanized the development of revolutionary song culture; figuratively, the song's career may be taken as a vantage
point from which to consider the broader milieu of which it was a part.
This song would become a critically important emblem between 1792 and
1796, setting a standard for popular song culture and yet remaining
unique. Its career highlights some of the dominant characteristics of the
larger culture that it helped to create, and of which it was an integral part.

The advertised search that preceded the *Hymne*'s appearance and the
specific circumstances surrounding its emerging popularity suggest both
a growing self-consciousness about song culture and, paradoxically, the
difficulty of creating popular songs by fiat. As singing came to be more
widely recognized as a revolutionary activity, those journalists who regarded songs most favorably attempted to draft them to particular political purposes; above all, they hoped to use the search for a battle song to
generate popular enthusiasm for war. But these men quickly found that
it was impossible to simply summon an anthem into existence. They
might publish new songs, but they could not single-handedly make them
truly popular. As the case of *Ça ira* suggested, and as the emergence of
the *Marseillaise* underscored, broad and meaningful popularity emerged
out of a lively and complex interaction between lyrics, singing practices,
and particular revolutionary events. This is one of the reasons that, in
the years to come, however much legislative deputies would try to direct
and even dictate popular song culture, they would repeatedly find themselves dependent upon and finally foiled by outside initiative and independent song production.

The *Hymne* was also significant in that it almost immediately came to
play a double role as a patriotic instrument and a source of profits. Its

marketability reflected, in part, the traditional marketability of *nouveautés*—here was the song that everyone was talking about, and so it sold well—but it also represented a first step toward the increasingly close relationship that would develop between songs as political emblems and songs as commodities. This relationship would prove equally beneficial to republican politics and republican commerce: political criteria would be used to judge the market value of republican songs, while entrepreneurs broadened republican culture by celebrating it in order to sell songsheets, songbooks, and theatrical tunes.

Above all, the *Hymne des Marseillais* represented the consensus that revolutionaries had temporarily achieved around song culture. For this song temporarily resolved persisting tensions between widespread practices and cultivated representations of them. In the *Marseillaise*, journalists, politicians, musicians, and composers found a song that was both wildly popular and respectable. With its complex tune and learned lyrics, this was a song that cultivated men and women could praise as a national and revolutionary anthem without embarrassment or hesitation.

The sudden and remarkable success of the *Marseillaise* was laden with irony, however. The *Hymne*'s adoption by the army and the Convention, as well as in the streets of Paris and throughout the countryside, pointed to new possibilities for the movement of songs between official and unofficial arenas. Belief in such a movement would encourage members of the National Convention to fund the National Institute of Music and, in company with other government officials, to patronize independent song production, thereby contributing to the extraordinary flourishing of song culture that France would witness in 1793 and 1794. But however much the ideal of a uniform, national song culture was celebrated in succeeding years, the *Hymne des Marseillais* would prove to be unique. Moreover, the multiple associations that favored the song's popularity in 1792 and 1793 would have opposing effects when consensus broke down, quite dramatically, in 1795. The song's affiliation with radical republicanism would almost prove to be its undoing during the Thermidorian reaction, as revolutionaries learned the difficulty of breaking down the univocality that they had so painstakingly created. Ultimately, however, the *Hymne*'s militarism would save it, pointing the way toward a new set of priorities during the final years of the Revolution.

For the moment, however, this song drew revolutionaries together, simultaneously revealing the coherence—both achieved and imposed—and the heterogeneity of republican song culture. Like the fixed lyrics of the *Hymne*, the multitude of songs produced during the next two years would reflect the rigid and radical nature of political life. Song production was about to reach its revolutionary zenith as songwriters celebrated republican principles, military victories, and revolutionary martyrs. But the immutability of the *Hymne*'s lyrics and the apparent homogeneity of republican song culture are equally misleading. The *Hymne* had already been shaped to a variety of ends in the first six months of its existence, when it was sung in informal celebrations by private citizens, incorporated into public festivals by government officials, and capitalized upon by entrepreneurs. So, too, would hundreds of seemingly similar republican songs be shaped to vastly different needs during the next two and one-half years, serving the distinct and sometimes opposed objectives of sans-culottes and Jacobins, amateurs and entrepreneurs alike.

Chapter Four

✦

The Revolutionary Song
(April 1792–Pluviose Year III)

✦ THE APPEARANCE of the *Marseillaise* coincided with the opening of a period of crisis that would persist until the election of the Directory in late 1795. The effort to wage foreign and civil wars while provisioning cities and seeking equilibrium between the competing constituents of the new Republic would create considerable material and psychological insecurity, which the National Convention and the Parisian populace sought to conquer with draconian legal measures backed by violence. Censorship was practiced with increasing rigor after the August revolution of 1792, and the Terror was formalized in the fall of 1793 with the wide-ranging "Law on Suspects." Henceforth, Paris prisons filled steadily as citizens became subject to arrest for a broad range of vaguely defined activities.

But republicans were not simply meeting crises, they were simultaneously trying to fashion a new political culture. So these were also years of feverish creativity. In the National Convention, deputies initiated and examined projects for public instruction, for the creation of a new calendar and the unification of the language, and for the establishment of republican cultural institutions. From beyond legislative walls, citizens from Paris and the provinces volunteered proposals that touched on almost every aspect of public instruction, suggesting projects for the regeneration of education, public monuments, and civic rituals. Meanwhile, the streets and sectional assemblies of the city were alive with discussion and debate: What is the proper means to express love of Liberty? In what terms should one celebrate the Republic? How should despotism be represented?

This complex combination of repression and creativity did not affect all forms of cultural production equally. Some kinds of media suffered badly: newspapers and pamphlets were hard hit by crowd action and judicial restraints, and their numbers declined precipitously in 1793 and 1794. In the theatrical world, Opéra and Comédie-Française saw their actors and directors imprisoned, as did the théâtre du Vaudeville.[1] Song culture was a much different case, however. For, even as particular kinds of songs were silenced, revolutionary song production soared well beyond anything yet seen. Twice as many songs were written in 1792 as in 1791, and the number of new compositions doubled again in 1793; almost a thousand revolutionary songs are known to have been composed in the year II of the Revolution.[2] Meanwhile, song culture took on a variety of seemingly contradictory faces. For even as the members of an apparently homogeneous revolutionary society came to share common singing practices and lyrical tropes, they simultaneously explored the broad range of possibilities offered by performance, publication, and interpretation.

Song production and singing practices had been slowly expanding and gaining respectability since 1789, and they were galvanized by the combined impact of war, republican revolution, and the brilliant career of the *Marseillaise*. The war effort encouraged singing and song writing by fanning the flames of a patriotism that amateurs and professionals alike were eager to express and reinforce musically. Republicanism encouraged widespread cultural experimentation at the same time that it explicitly raised the status of working people's culture, thus ameliorating some of the traditionally negative associations of singing. Meanwhile, radicals—above all, Jacobins—who continued to express doubts about singing were mollified by the popularity of the *Marseillaise*. Here they found an anthem that evoked the seriousness and respectability they sought.

But song culture was not simply growing; it was taking off at the very moment that print media was shrinking in the face of republican repression.[3] This singular trajectory was, in part, the product of the revolutionary development of the genre. After 1789, changing practices and vigorous, sometimes violent debate gradually stripped songs and singing of their ambiguity and associated them ever more closely with revolutionary enthusiasm. Then, what began as a gradual transformation was catalyzed by events between 1792 and 1795 to produce a singularly rich and prolific republican song culture.

Three factors were particularly important in these years.[4] Above all, singing became an integral element of sans-culottes' political culture. In the years to come, song culture would benefit from the republican celebration of common people's culture and from singing's unique capacity to express the enthusiasm and fraternity that were essential to a vigorous, radical politics. No longer cheap entertainment nor an ephemeral expression of political passion, unofficial singing would become inextricably linked with sans-culottes' activism. Simultaneously, the market would come to play an increasingly important role during these years. Entrepreneurs would not only help to expand song production; they would broaden the revolutionary credibility of singing by celebrating and elaborating its political pedigrees as part of their marketing strategies. Finally, administrators and legislators would come to recognize the revolutionary potential of song. They would praise and periodically subsidize certain kinds of song writing with genuine if haphazard enthusiasm.

But as song culture reached its revolutionary zenith, a new critique would emerge. In the winter of 1793–94 official uneasiness about the scope and force of the popular movement would find expression in a new wariness of singing. Equally concerned by the relationship between popular activism and singing, Robespierrists and Dantonists would disagree about how to respond to it. In the short term, the Robespierrist policy of channeling popular singing practices for official celebration would triumph over the Dantonist desire simply to impose silence. In the long term, however, post-Thermidorian governments would find compatibility between the two policies as they successfully married official appropriation with outright repression.

SANS-CULOTTES' SINGING

With the republican revolution of August 1792, sans-culottes moved to the center-stage of French song culture. Songwriters composed *nouveautés* that celebrated their initiative in the creation, constitution, and future of the Republic. Describing the August insurrection as the work of sans-culottes and *fédérés* alone, they went further still and dismissed legislators altogether, to assert that *le peuple* were the principal movers of the new Republic.

Si l'on ne voit plus à Paris	If you no longer see in Paris
Des insolents petits marquis,	Those insolent little marquis,
Ni tyrans à calottes:	Nor tyrants in skullcaps:
En brisant ce joug infernal,	If by smashing this infernal yoke,
Si le pauvre au riche est égal,	The rich and poor are equal,
C'est grâce aux sans-culottes.[5]	It's thanks to the sans-culottes.

When legislators do appear in song, they are peripheral or sub-servient figures. Relegated to a final verse or a single line, they are sketched as servants of the people without independent initiative. While this subordinate relationship is implicit in the structure and claims of particular songs, it is explicated in lyrics themselves, like the song title that describes Louis XVI as "brought to the bar of the National Convention and already judged by public opinion while awaiting the law to pronounce on his fate."[6]

The lyrical centrality of the sans-culottes is hardly surprising, given the importance of singing to sans-culottes' political culture. Near the end of the Revolution and later, in the nineteenth century, chroniclers and historians would look back at the Terror and marvel at the efflorescence of singing during years remembered for the revolutionary tribunal and the guillotine.[7] And it was remarkable: all varieties of unofficial political activity were interspersed with singing. Members of sectional assemblies heard songs about revolutionary martyrs and the Supreme Being, they sang together to celebrate the décade, and they closed General Assembly meetings with a chorus of the *Marseillaise*.[8] Deputations to the Paris Commune, and even the National Convention, performed songs there.[9] And such performances were recorded as rousing and wildly successful.[10]

More striking still was the popular singing that flourished in Parisian parks, theaters, and cafés, ordinary spaces that these collective expressions of republicanism transformed wholly.

> Five thirty in the evening at the café de Lattre . . . a group of good citizens gathered together and began to sing patriotic hymns. This seemed to bring enormous pleasure to all the spectators who, with a unanimous voice, began to shout Long live the Republic! Long live liberty! Down with the monarchy![11]

Citizens sang together in spite of bad news from the Vendée and because of the good news of the recapture of Toulon.[12] There were macabre performances of songs: "The conspirators were guillotined to shouts of Long live the Republic! . . . During this ceremony, the people sang, danced, and were very much satisfied." There were disruptive performances as well: "People have found a means to prolong theatrical performances. The last piece has scarcely been played before couplets rain down on the stage from all sides, which the actors are obliged to sing. If this mania of a few rhymesters is tolerated, the theaters will not close until midnight."[13] What is perhaps most surprising is that, given this propensity for singing, there were not more of both.

Why this particular means of celebration? It would be absurd to deny the most obvious explanations: singing was enjoyable, inspiring, and an easy means of instruction. Readily available in bars and cafés, it was cheap and patriotic entertainment. During moments of crisis, it relieved tension and drew singers together against threatening enemies. In neighborhood assemblies and at popular gatherings, it helped to disseminate the new principles among children and the illiterate. But songs had always served such functions; these reasons fail to explain why popular choruses multiplied to become almost omnipresent after 1792. The cause of this explosion lay in the development of republicanism and in the political culture of the sans-culottes.

Republicans did not simply extend the vote to all male citizens, regardless of income. Many of them actively celebrated the status, language, and culture of working people. This celebration of working people was most marked within sans-culotism, the extralegislative variety of radical republicanism that began to emerge in Paris and throughout France in 1791. Although historians once narrowly defined sans-culotism as a movement of artisans and shopkeepers who briefly exercised political power through Parisian sectional assemblies, it was in fact more broadly based.[14] Sans-culotism extended beyond militantly activist artisans and shopkeepers to include wealthier and better-educated radicals. At the same time, it appealed to working people who gave no evidence of political participation.[15] After the August revolution, sans-culotism designated a political ideology that advocated universal male suffrage and direct democracy, price controls, and a vigorous defense of the Revolution against foreign and domestic enemies. Even as a political ideology, however, it is significant that sans-culotism labeled itself a social movement and that it vociferously claimed to represent the interests and celebrate the condition of the working people. Regardless of the true social composition of the movement, the ideal sans-culotte would continue to be the working man who "lives quite simply with his wife and children, if he has any, on the fourth or fifth floor."[16]

As the early years of the Republic witnessed the formal recognition of working people as political actors and the valorization of their culture and means of expression, singing acquired an unheard-of respectability. The very quality that had once been its greatest liability, commonness, now became a source of strength. While popular songs gained respectability because of their commonness, they also won acclaim because they helped to celebrate and reinforce the essential values of radical republicanism. Above all, singing was uniquely suited to the republican effort to create a new politics that would draw the national community together, destroying barriers between citizens and encouraging all in a sustained revolutionary effort.

The republican ideal of transparency—the absence of artifice or barriers between citizens—was wholly congruent with contemporary singing practices. Radical republicans aspired to an energetic transparency rooted in an enthusiasm that proclaimed, advertised, and enacted revolutionary sentiments. In theory, this enthusiasm reinforced transparent politics by eliminating distance between citizens; in very practical terms, it served radical politics by countering the "moderationism" that threatened to cool the energy necessary to accomplish the Revolution and prosecute the war.[17] Through their enthusiasm, revolutionaries expressed their commitment to the Revolution and encouraged others to make sacrifices; it militated against delinquent citizens, not because they attacked liberty but simply because they failed to act on its behalf.[18] Thus, to proclaim attachment to the Revolution was both the expression of a patriotic desire and obedience to a political imperative.

Singing was consistent with these ideals because songs have a singular capacity to arouse and reinforce enthusiasm. Lyrics aside, the act of singing itself serves as a rallying cry that invigorates political ardor. A good orator was acknowledged to be one who spoke "energetically and as a true republican," and the enthusiastic singer was more republican still: songs produced "a saintly enthusiasm" and "electrified" auditors.[19] A song in the first person further underscored the singer's proclamation of his or her republicanism and call to action:

Partons, mes amis, pour la gloire	Let's go my friends, in search of glory
Accourons tous au champ d'honneur,	Let's all rush to the field of honor,
Nous sommes sûrs de la victoire,	We are certain of victory,
Et de la mort n'ayons pas peur.[20]	And of death let us have no fear.

While republican populism and enthusiasm nourished singing of all sorts, the cult of fraternity encouraged the increasingly widespread practice of singing in groups. Among intellectuals and politicians, fraternity had very specific meanings that could be traced to the Enlightenment, but in the streets and popular societies of Paris it had more quotidian resonance as it encouraged unity in a fragile polity.[21] Fraternity served as a necessary counterweight to republican equality by encouraging the development of new social bonds to replace the social hierarchies which the Revolution was sweeping away.[22] But even as fraternity offered a means to exert pressure on one's fellow citizens, it was celebrated as a positive force that drew the political community together and reinforced solidarity in the face of the Revolution's enemies.

Singing reinforced fraternity as perhaps no other means of expression could because of its ability to excite emotion and draw singers together in common chorus. A fraternal dinner was not complete without singing. In the section des Piques, for example, the "patriotic songs" "sung by a few young citizennesses and echoed by the citizens enhanced still further the love of liberty and equality," while toasts drunk to the Mountain and the sans-culottes "gave proof of friendship and fraternity."[23] Thus the sans-culotte Chaumette could choose singing as the principal representation of fraternity when he accepted the new Constitution on behalf of the Paris Commune: "Frenchmen, let us gather together in fraternal groups around these saintly laws that we have given ourselves. Let us preserve them from the unhealthy breath of fierce ambition, from partisan anger . . . ; let us join together in striking up a hymn to saintly fraternity; let shouts of elation, songs of liberty and friendship replace the bitter sound of the trumpets of discord."[24]

The cult of fraternity also encouraged singing in sectional societies, where meetings were often reported to have closed with collective performances of "the hymn of the marseillais." In particular, energetic choruses punctuated the episodes of fraternization between sections that guaranteed the dominance of radicals in the spring of 1793.

> The president of the section of Cité . . . explains that they belong to the same city and are neighbors of the Pont Neuf section, and that they will always be ready to aid their oppressed brothers, and they march through the hall singing the hymn to liberty.[25]

And even after that movement had ended, sections continued to send deputations to the Paris Commune and even to the National Convention, to offer songs as a sign of patriotism and fraternity with their representatives.[26]

From well beyond Paris, private citizens and members of provincial popular societies sent songs to the Convention for the same reasons.[27] Their songs, often with accompanying notes, suggest half of a dialogue between the populace and the government, a testimony of private citizens' patriotism, fraternity, and faith in the Convention. Each victory and every decree that reshaped civic life elicited a flurry of songs in which men and women attested to the power exerted over them by the creation of the republican calendar, the reconquest of Toulon, or the Convention's recognition of a Supreme Being. Sometimes poorly rhymed or badly misspelled, these compositions were moving expressions of faith in, and commitment to the Revolution.

> Always passionate to contribute, as a member of the republic, all that might be of use to it, I believe it my duty to share a patriotic song about the victorious reconquest of Toulon. . . . I want very much . . . to prove [to the Convention] the sincere and inviolable emotions by which I will live and die a true French republican.[28]

These were the most positive and creative dimensions of popular singing. But transparency, enthusiasm, and fraternity did not draw the community together in a wholly benign way; they drew it together against a crowd of hostile adversaries and, in the process, enforced conformity on its own members. Song lyrics forcefully expressed republican fear and exclusiveness. By 1792, simple disdain of defeated "aristocrats" and "oppositional parties" was giving way to increasingly detailed, fearful, and angry descriptions of enemies.[29] As we have already seen, the *Marseillaise* was one of the earliest and most important songs to elaborate this vision, and by 1793 many Parisian songwriters had appropriated Rouget de Lisle's lyrical conceits, and often his melody, to produce songs that balanced precariously between exploiting popular fears through vivid and violent imagery and reinforcing confidence by celebrating recent or impending victory.

Like the *Marseillaise*, the republican songs of 1793 and 1794 described the—typically male—republican's enemies on all sides, even at home.

Ma femme souvent me désole,
    j'm'en f——
	My wife often pesters me, I don't
	    give a shit

En fréquentant mauvaise école,
    j'm'en f——
	By frequenting bad company, I
	    don't give a shit

Elle me prône la charité	To me she extols charity

Moi je prêche la liberté; j'm'en
    f——.[30]
	Me, I preach liberty; I don't give a
	    shit.

As descriptions of the nation's foes grew lengthier, they were rendered in an increasingly violent language; enemies became "wolves," "vile hellhounds" (vils suppôts de l'enfer), "monsters vomited from hell" (monstres vomis de l'enfer), and "cannibals," who, in their rage, would strike out and spill blood until the cries of mothers, sisters, brothers filled the air.[31] As detail became more vivid, songwriters began to identify these hostile figures. By 1793, Rouget de Lisle's generic "tyrants" and "traitors" had been given specific names, faces, and actions. Foreign enemies were listed systematically—Frédéric, Pitt, Cobourg, the duke of Brunswick, and King George of England—and domestic foes received more attention still, as lyrical confessions were placed in their mouths.

Ne sachant que répondre,	Not knowing how to respond,
Brissot, d'un air troublé,	Brissot, with a troubled air,
Dit "Mon hôtel à Londres	Says, "My villa in London
N'est pas encore meublé.	Is not yet furnished.
Quoi, du fédéralisme on chasse ici l'apôtre?	What, you banish the apostle of federalism?
Si j'ai mis un Roi de côté,	If I brought down one king,
Cela n'était, en vérité,	It was only, to tell the truth,
Que pour en faire un autre."[32]	To raise up another."

Like vivid detail, naming made adversaries recognizable, transforming them from shadowy figures to specific individuals who carried out precise actions. But even as it heightened the sense of an enemy's presence, such naming also mollified fears by identifying the counterrevolutionaries and assuring that their plotting had been uncovered.

Ciel, que d'espèces d'intrigants,	Great God, what a bunch of schemers,
Roturiers, Nobles, et Calottes,	Commoners, nobles, and clergymen,
Pour dire mieux, que de brigands,	Or better yet, what highwaymen,
Vrais fléaux des vrais sans-culottes,	True scourges of true sans-culottes,
Mais, leur règne enfin est passé,	But their reign is finally done,
Leur fier orgueil est terrassé,	Their haughty arrogance is brought down,
Pour jamais tout est éclipsé,	All is vanished forever,
Grâce à la Montagne.[33]	Thanks to the Mountain.

Song lyrics like these, all printed on the cheap octavo sheets that were the medium of truly common songs, rendered the political world in stark black and white, naming friends and foes. This vision was characteristic of sans-culottes' ideology, and these lyrics favored rousing performances of republican enthusiasm.[34] But in spite of undeniably radical lyrics and rousing performances, songs continued to excite questions and occasional discomfort among some revolutionaries. Certainly, French men and women had to confront questions of signification and interpretation throughout the 1790s, but these matters became particularly acute in the years immediately following the August revolution, as republicans set out to redefine objects and gestures at the same time that they attempted to found a radically new, but absolutely stable system of signification. Songs, whose lyrics or performative impact could be changed in a single moment, continued to be subject to scrutiny. Who would be permitted to sing? What matters were appropriate to musical treatment?

Some people complained about obscene songs, and others expressed reservations similar to those that Jacobins had voiced. A man in a café feared that a versified Rights of Man was insulting rather than instructive; readers of the *Observateur sans-culotte* along with the newspaper's editor questioned whether street performers should sing as lightly of executions as they did of victories.[35] Although revolutionaries were unable to control all performances or song variations, many found that group singing permitted songs to be discussed, their performance or message corrected if necessary, and ambiguities conjured away.

> At the former church of St. Laurent . . . a young man of 10 years old sang a song about the conquest of Toulon; a verse of the song praised Robespierre. A member named Thibaut . . . said: citizens, I love and esteem Robespierre; but the living must never be flattered. They must not be raised onto altars until after they are dead; . . . otherwise liberty and equality will always be in danger. . . . The verse of which I spoke was stricken.[36]

Sans-culottes dealt with their lingering doubts about the malleability of songs by singing in groups, thereby policing lyrics and singing practices at the same time. This seemed a natural way to confront the problem, for singing was already intimately associated with a broad range of sans-culottes' activities, including fraternal dinners, sectional meetings, and appearances before the council of the Commune. But even as government administrators and legislators sought to co-opt and direct this energetic song culture, it remained a source of some discomfort for many of them. In particular, the Dantonists became increasingly uneasy about the close association between singing and sans-culottes' activism. This issue would not, however, emerge until the winter of 1793–94. But before considering it, we must consider the other force that most actively exploited and expanded republican song culture: the market.

SELLING REPUBLICANISM

As singing became a more esteemed means of republican entertainment and expression, songs acquired new status as commodities, and the market for songs that had begun to take root early in 1792 grew stronger. Entrepreneurs both exploited that reputation and helped to rewrite the history of popular songs by ascribing sound political purposes and pedigrees that they hoped would attract customers.

The song market that flourished in 1793 and 1794 emerged gradually during the early years of the Revolution, the product of shifting consumer habits and the deregulation of the publishing world. During the Old Regime and throughout the early Revolution, much of the market had been driven by the desire for *nouveautés*. This predilection for novel and sensationalist songs would persist into the nineteenth century. The long careers of *Ça ira* and the *Marseillaise* underscore the brief popularity—hence brief marketability—of most popular songs. While the desire for *nouveautés* remained constant, the song market witnessed other developments as well. As the newly found respectability of revolutionary songs attracted new customers, the growing popularity of singing played to the desire to purchase what was *à la mode*. The end result was a market that was both lively and politically sound.

As the desire for *nouveautés* and the growing fashionability of singing broadened the market for songs, the dramatic reshaping of the publishing world by revolutionary governments encouraged printers and publishers to fully exploit it. The calling of the Assembly of Notables in 1787 had begun the flood of ephemeral literature that would inundate France in the next decade, serving readers who were eager for news and opinions of current political events. After 1789, the steady dismantling of censorship and privilege forced printers and publishers to abandon the increasingly uncertain business of book publication for the more competitive world of ephemera: newspapers, pamphlets, sheet music, plays, and eventually, songs.[37]

And yet, politics also brought about the decline of certain kinds of publications. Royalists who managed to continue publishing until the summer of 1792 were driven from the scene by the August revolution; Girondins were the next to go, after their expulsion from the Convention in June 1793. Other writers and publishers were silenced by the strict press laws of 1792–93, and by the disturbingly broad Law on Suspects of September 1793. As a consequence, newspaper and pamphlet publication declined, and counterrevolutionary songs gradually disappeared from print.

Revolutionary songs, however, remained lucrative ephemera. Easy to produce and increasingly easy to sell, songs possessed sound republican resonances that publishers found elsewhere only with difficulty. Unlike newspapers and pamphlets, which critiqued, debated, and polemicized, revolutionary song lyrics rarely expressed contrary or even nuanced visions of the Revolution. Simple and enthusiastic proclamations, they were ideal commodities for publishers who were seeking to make their livelihoods under the strictures of the Terror. As publishers produced a growing number of songsheets and songbooks, editors included a growing number of songs in the pages of their newspapers, replacing editorials with the only items that were as politically secure as the *procès-verbaux* of the National Convention.

The period from 1792 through 1794 witnessed the diversification and the expansion of the market. At the beginning of the decade, revolutionary songbooks continued to appear in the cheapest of Old Regime formats. Tiny twelve- to fifteen-page pamphlets that contained a few topical songs and a romance or two, they were hawked in the streets by streetsingers or colporteurs.[38] Early in 1792, however, the Jacobin Thomas Rousseau introduced a new method of formating and marketing popular songs. Although his project would fail within a month of the August revolution, his example would provoke successful emulation.

Rousseau began to publish the periodical *Les chants du patriotisme* in the winter of 1792, announcing in the first issue that his central purpose was to "celebrate the most interesting periods of the Revolution, and engrave the memory of them in the hearts of our youth." Furthermore, "to add a new dimension of interest to words and tunes, I have enhanced the text with instructive or interesting notes." In an effort to outwit counterfeiters, he offered his songs in the form of a twice-weekly periodical; to insure that the songs reached as wide an audience as possible, he set the subscription rate at the "meager price" of 10 sous per month.[39] *Les chants du patriotisme* was a model of revolutionary pedagogy. Each issue contained a single song that celebrated what Rousseau believed were the most important events of the Revolution—the taking of the Bastille, the abolition of privilege on August 4, the creation of a *caisse patriotique*—and included lengthy footnotes that explained particular lyrics and allusions to classical figures or which developed the author's reflections on different aspects of the Revolution. When, at the end of his twenty-fourth number, Rousseau paused to remind subscribers to renew for the second trimester, he urged them on not by praising the quality of his compositions but by stressing the patriotism of the project.

Under the easy guise of the song, I offer instruction to all classes of citizens; instruction which is all the more precious because, far from distracting citizens from their respective tasks, it animates them all the more with songs that are pure, easy and everywhere repeated with civic-mindedness [civisme] and patriotism. . . . I hope that all good citizens . . . will make it . . . a duty to contribute, through their meager subscription, to the success of an enterprise that should produce such great advantages for all classes of people in general.[40]

Apparently, not enough citizens acknowledged this duty because, two months later, Rousseau was berating the public for its apathetic response to his work. Unless he tripled subscription rates beyond the current 150, he threatened "I break my lyre and silence myself."[41] But the crowds of new subscribers were not forthcoming and so, the next month, Rousseau announced that he was suspending publication.

Rousseau published only original compositions and the most properly revolutionary of songs. And yet his project failed. Perhaps it was because, in his eagerness to educate, he too often neglected to entertain. In celebrating the Revolution's history, he included a great many songs that must have been of dubious popular resonance in 1792: singers might be eager to recall the taking of the Bastille, but could they find equally moving the "Decree concerning a new edition of Voltaire's works"? Or the song celebrating the "Establishment of a *patriotic treasury* on 12 September 1789, to receive all the gifts and free tributes of the people"? Finally, there was the difficult matter of footnotes: taking up at least as many pages as the songs themselves, the notes, no matter how informative (or pedantic), undermined all pretense that this publication was a good buy. Better to learn the entertaining compositions from a friend and save one's sous for a booklet that devoted every page to songs.

Rousseau's case, however personally frustrating, set an important example. In promoting a lengthier format for popular songs, this committed Jacobin justified his novel marketing strategy by calling upon revolutionary principles. Rather than presenting himself as an entertaining composer or enterprising publisher, he sought to capitalize on his status as a good republican.[42] But his failure served as a potent reminder that no matter how revolutionary the product, it had to obey certain commercial principles. *Les chants du patriotisme* suggested lucrative publishing possibilities that other composers and publishers would improve on. Wedding the commercial and the patriotic more successfully, Rousseau's successors produced a wealth of revolutionary songbooks over the next three years. Aiming for the broadest possible audience, publishers would unite professionally trained composers with amateurs, actors, and authors of vaudevilles, to produce a new kind of publication that combined sober and learned hymns with lively but patriotic couplets. Unlike Rousseau, these publishers printed only songs that were devoted to the most illustrious and popular of past events, and they kept them free of lengthy footnotes.[43] On the other hand, while their prefaces and forewords praised the songs' traditional qualities of gaiety and entertainment, they imitated Rousseau by emphasizing the republican dimension of singing, thereby rendering even gaiety and entertainment into republican virtues.

> The vaudeville is to the French what moral lessons are to other peoples: there are neither events nor remarkable actions that have not been set in verse. . . . Most astonishingly, we will carry the precepts of the healthiest reason among our neighbors with the baubles of Momus. The silent Englishmen, the grave Spaniard, the speculating Dutchman, the thick German, will one day smile at the witticisms of our songs, and soon Truth, accompanied by the charms of lovable Folly, will introduce itself among these peoples by the means of pleasure.[44]

Compelled to disseminate revolutionary principles, editors and publishers wielded "patriotism" and "republicanism" as marketing slogans at the same time that they set out to redefine the traditional appeal to *nouveautés*.[45] Songsheets—cheap and ephemeral—provided songs for immediate celebration or commentary; songbooks were founded on commemoration. Admittedly, by the year II, publishers only celebrated events that had taken place since the August revolution, but even their celebrations of the most recent events had a commemorative dimension. If one sang about the taking of Toulon or the assassination of Marat, this was not because these events were current and newsworthy but because they represented decisive stages in the progress and development of the Republic. Publishers promised that such songs would not go out of vogue. And editors quite plausibly argued that commemorating the Revolution, tracing its history and celebrating its imagery, was a patriotic act: "There is no collection that brings together the best patriotic songs that have appeared since the Revolution; we believed that we would render a service to liberty and her friends in launching one."[46] Buying and selling revolutionary songbooks had become patriotic.

Theatrical entrepreneurs also brought politics to the service of their enterprises. As we have already seen, some theaters exploited the popularity of the *Marseillaise* by performing it during intermissions. Others produced patriotic plays and vaudevilles that described the war effort or treated republican themes, marrying the politically sound with the desire for *nouveautés*. Journalists who praised such productions and printed the best revolutionary couplets provided theaters with free advertising.[47] The most striking alliance between commercial theater and revolutionary politics was visible in the association of the general assembly of the Tuileries section with those masters of profitable politics, the owners and authors of the théâtre du Vaudeville. Here politics and commercial production became so intermingled as to be virtually indistinguishable.

As noted earlier, members of the Tuileries section were instrumental in winning the vaudevillists' freedom from prison early in the fall of 1793, and a working relationship developed between the two organizations over subsequent months. Piis and several actors from the Vaudeville began to write songs for celebrations of the *décade* in the Tuileries section, perhaps to ensure that they would have no more trouble with the authorities. Performances of the songs in sectional assemblies received newspaper coverage almost as regularly as did the theater, and the original lyrics appeared in songbooks published by the section's presses and by the Imprimerie Nationale.[48] Newspaper accounts reminded readers that the couplets they printed had been "sung at the Tuileries section and at the théâtre du Vaudeville"; songbooks repeated this claim or recalled the association between the section and the theater by identifying one of its principal songwriters as an "actor at the théâtre du Vaudeville."[49] These associations provided political and commercial benefits to both arenas. Those who could not afford a theater ticket could come to the Tuileries section to hear the latest compositions of one of the city's most popular theaters, perhaps receiving some republican instruction in the process. Meanwhile, the Vaudeville received incomparable advertising, which kept the theater's name perpetually in the public eye and suggested that patronizing it was truly a patriotic act.

But publishers and theater owners went further still. Not content to capitalize on the current status of revolutionary songs, they rewrote the history of singing.

All ancient peoples had poets in the fore who fired their courage and urged them into combat with war songs. More than once, the fierce Spartans owed the defeat of their enemies to the male accents of Tyrtée. The Gaulois had their bards [too.][50]

While the editor of the *Chansonnier de la Montagne* harked back to Old
Regime memorialists with this reference to the ancients, publicists for
the théâtre du Vaudeville were even more inventive, imagining a new
history of prerevolutionary singing.

> Everything ended with songs because everything could not yet be finished
> off by a spirited resistance to oppression; men were not yet mature
> enough to land powerful blows; but these songs more than once proved to
> the monsters who devoured the people's marrow, that the people recog-
> nized their infamy.[51]

This emphasis on patriotism made its way into critiques of published
and theatrical songs as well. Beyond asking whether a song was simply
pretty or clever, critics now analyzed its patriotic flair. Thus the songs in
the *Chansonnier patriote* were "in good taste, of the right pitch, and suit-
able for fortifying patriotism," while a rather flat song at the Vaudeville
was criticized with the assertion that "such nonchalance would seem less
reprehensible if it were applied only to subjects of no import. . . . But
that which represents liberty ought, even when singing, to respect its
work."[52] Critical judgments had certainly become infused with politics,
but this is hardly surprising in light of the active exchange that had developed between politics and commerce.

Traditionally, historians of the arts have complained that the Revolution disfigured cultural production by imposing political criteria upon
it.[53] Although this complaint has died away in the past decade, some
contemporary historians continue to regard the politicization of certain
cultural forms as the product of restraints imposed externally by the National Convention or zealous sans-culottes.[54] And yet, while the songwriters and theatrical entrepreneurs we have considered here were subject
to the same political constraints that weighed upon all Parisians during
the Terror, they were also intent on turning a profit. They were therefore eager to capitalize and expand on current fashions. Such men and
women did not simply bow their heads before political constraints; they
actively exploited them.

In the face of such entrepreneurial exploitation, we must also revise
traditional notions about the song culture of the early Republic. Historians have, accurately, represented early republican song culture as
healthy and flourishing. In so doing, however, they have implied that all
revolutionaries celebrated songs with equal enthusiasm.[55] In particular,
Thomas Rousseau's sloganeering might be taken as significant evidence
for the universal popularity of singing. But that sloganeering was not a

simple political pronouncement; it was also a means of commercial advertisement. Entrepreneurs developed an image of an unquestionably revolutionary song culture because it was in their interests to do so. But other members of republican society were less sure. In the National Convention, in government bureaus, and among the police of Paris, administrators and legislators considered songs more cautiously, weighing their extraordinary pedagogic potential against their association with sans-culottes' activism.

REPUBLICAN AUTHORITIES CONSIDER SONG CULTURE

As unofficial and commercial song cultures flourished, journalists, professional musicians, administrators, and legislators assessed singing practices and proposed specific policies for shaping them. These men did not always agree on policy, nor did they share the same attitudes toward songs, but they all defined themselves as members of a political and cultural elite with a responsibility not only to fight counterrevolution but to educate and contain their popular allies, whom they regarded with a mixture of paternalist concern and apprehension.

Inside the National Convention, deputies demonstrated an abiding concern with public instruction in many forms. But despite an active interest that was made manifest in speeches and decrees alike, the Convention was haphazard in its encouragement of the arts and cultural institutions, since it had to juggle political and economic crises with its desire to reshape French culture.[56] Singing fell prey to this haphazardness as much as did other means of expression. In January 1793, the deputy J. B. Leclerc was the first member of the Convention to explicitly raise the issue of using songs as a revolutionary instrument. He did so in the course of a speech on the importance of *poésie*—a category that he took to include hymns as well as lyric poems.[57] Leclerc began with the standard prejudice, acknowledging that *poésie* had been corrupted under the Old Regime because it was used to flatter the powerful and circulate the lies of religion. Such corruption was not, he argued, inherent in the genre itself; *poésie* was a sublime form, which had been turned to bad ends by dishonest men. "Once it has been regenerated, it can restore the courage of citizens, sustain in them the love of virtue, and serve the Fatherland, as much by its regular influence as by the authority that it exerts upon souls in moments of difficulty." Not surprisingly, to prove this point, "I call upon the example of the immortal hymn of the Marseillais."

Leclerc's voice was at first alone, however. Other deputies rarely addressed the pedagogic benefits of songs, and although music was central to the conduct and success of all festivals, ceremonial hymns continued to be solicited on a case by case basis as they had been since the opening of the Revolution.[58] Increasingly sympathetic to the revolutionary benefits of music and singing, the Convention nonetheless remained almost wholly dependent on outside initiative for song production until the year II. As the printing presses of the Paris Commune, local popular societies, and sectional assemblies churned out songs by members and admirers, the Convention mimicked the practices of the Assemblies that preceded it by contracting festival hymns from individual composers and occasionally printing a song that had been performed at its bar.[59]

Official song production began to grow more regular in the fall of 1793. Thomas Rousseau, who abandoned the commercial public to try his hand at winning government subsidies, secured an order from the minister of war for 100,000 copies of his *L'âme du peuple et du soldat*, to be distributed in the army.[60] More important still was the proposal that Bernard Sarette and the musicians of the Paris National Guard made to the Convention, requesting that they be subsidized and authorized to form a music institute.[61] The Convention decreed the establishment of the National Institute of Music in Brumaire year II (November 1793).[62] The Committees of Public Instruction and Public Safety were slow in supervising formal organization, but the men of the Institute acted quickly: they requested and received a depot for musical instruments and a printing press to publish festival music, and they began to compile songbooks for the provinces and the military.[63] In the end, the Institute would be given complete responsibility for the composition and performance of festival music.[64]

The cases of Thomas Rousseau and the National Institute of Music are instructive and exemplary: the Convention's nascent efforts to encourage pedagogic singing emphasized the composition of festival hymns and military songs. Festival songs and hymns served several purposes. Technically, they amplified rhetoric that might instruct and explain.[65] Unable to magnify a single voice throughout the enormous crowds that Parisian festivals assembled, directors could at least embed lessons in songs that could then be performed by a choir or, as in the case of the festival of the Supreme Being, sung by all participants. More generally, singing played the same unifying role here that it played in cafés and sectional assemblies, bringing together participants and spectators and underscoring the sense of national community that festivals were designed to impart and reinforce. Finally, it was hoped that songs would serve as a vehicle to carry the festival's lessons beyond their spatial and temporal boundaries.[66] In the military, songs were expected to educate the quickly expanding armed forces. Concerned about the loyalty and discipline of its soldiers, particularly after the treason and desertion of Generals Lafayette and Dumouriez, the Convention undertook to inform those at the front of the Revolution's progress and, above all, to remind them that their first loyalty was to the nation rather than to specific commanding officers.

The printed songs that the Convention sent to soldiers and sailors promoted republican principles. Unlike their ephemeral Parisian counterparts, however, the lyrics bore few traces of the independence, undisciplined anger, or vulgarity of the sans-culottes. Here one found no "je m'en foutre" (I don't give a shit) or gleeful celebrations of the guillotine. Unlike the Parisian songs that occasionally threatened—"Je suis un des vrais sans-culottes . . . je fais caca sur les despotes" (I am one of the true sans-culottes . . . I shit on despots)—official military songs favored classical imagery and formal language.[67] They characterized sans-culottes as "dignes émules d'Achille" (worthy equals of Achilles), and warned enemies in exalted terms:

Tremblez, ennemis de la France,	Quake, enemies of France,
Rois ivres de sang et d'orgueil;	Kings drunken with blood and arrogance;
Le peuple souverain s'avance;	The sovereign people advance;
Tyrans descendez au cercueil.[68]	Tryants descend to the tomb.

The most striking difference between military songs and many of those hawked in Paris was the proximity or distance of the Revolution that they conveyed. Parisian songs painted a vivid picture of events and personalities: they attacked Louis XVI, then Brissot, and finally Marie-Antoinette, "the Austrian tigress," with endless detail. French soldiers were far from all this, and the songs that the government distributed brought them no closer: official lyrics fixed their eyes on war and Austrian enemies, or praised the abstract principles of the Revolution: liberty, dignity, human rights. If the government hoped to use songs to educate and contain, their best hope lay with their captive audience of soldiers and sailors at the front.

Technically, songs were well suited to the government's objectives. Cheap to produce, they circulated still more cheaply once they left the printed page. Thomas Rousseau complained bitterly of lost profits— "[my songs] have flown, each day they continue to fly from mouth to mouth"—but ease of transmission was undoubtedly one of the benefits that the government sought.[69] Songs played the same unifying role amongst soldiers that they played in festivals and then went further still, easing the weariness of marching, encouraging soldiers when they attacked, and providing signals of advance or retreat.[70]

Songs were useful to festivals and the army for other reasons. The men of the newly founded National Institute of Music concurred with others who reflected on the pedagogic capacity of songs, arguing that music was singularly appropriate to bringing order to a society and "instilling in hearts the fires of patriotism and the enthusiasm of liberty."[71] Songs did not simply instruct and inspire; they organized.

> The marvels that [music] accomplished among the free peoples of antiquity are well known. . . . [The ancients] made it one of the bases of their social institutions. . . . Between the hands of the wisest legislators, music served as a powerful means to enlighten men, . . . fortify public spirit [esprit public], inspire love of the Fatherland and respect for laws, sustain patience, rouse the courage of their warriors, and nourish the seeds of useful and generous actions in all hearts.[72]

Like the commercial publishers and amateur songwriters who offered proposals to the Convention, deputies and professional musicians shared a common enthusiasm for revolutionary songs, which they justified by looking to the ancients. But these men found a different moral among the ancients. Rather than defining songs as an instrument equally available to all, they considered them to be a tool with which the few might gently guide the many: "in every period, there has been no more seductive means to encourage, seduce and lead a people than with music."[73]

And yet, even as powerful instruments for "encouraging," "seducing," and "leading" the people, songs were most often celebrated within the specific and controlled contexts of festivals and the military. Singing, like other forms of public instruction and celebration, was promoted as a community activity. Certainly, group singing promoted feelings of unity that strengthened the Republic, but we know as well that the group provided a potent means of controlling what images circulated and how those images would be represented and interpreted.

Beyond the confines of festivals and military life, songs made a somewhat more ambiguous contribution to the Revolution, and Jacobins continued to be those most likely to voice concerns about their potentially disruptive effects. Uncertain of their popular allies, many Jacobins feared that the mass of the citizenry was so unenlightened and buried in daily affairs that they had little time to develop rational political ideas. In their eyes, the polity's best hope lay with a small, educated elite endowed with the capacity to think and argue. Such an elite might win and keep the allegiance of the ignorant and undifferentiated mass.[74]

Jacobin editorials accused the Nation's enemies of using every means at their disposal to agitate the spirits of the people: "exaggerating terrible news; enfeebling all that is appropriate to raising national hopes; entering into the people's suffering."[75] Journalists reminded revolutionaries that "evil words incite evil actions; their presence must not be tolerated at the cradle of the Republic," at the same time that the revolutionary tribunal acted on the belief that songs were capable of exciting monarchism or dissuading youth from joining the army.[76] Like good oratory, singing might be turned against the Revolution for exactly the same reasons that it could be used so effectively on its behalf: songs stirred the emotions and shaped public opinion.[77]

Certainly, some of these fears were overblown. As a direct and noisy means to proclaim political sentiment, songs were a grossly inappropriate means to express counterrevolutionary opinion given the close scrutiny characteristic of the Terror. Few dared to sing such songs or even keep copies of them. The occasional man or woman arrested for counterrevolutionary singing usually claimed drunkenness; the more common attitude was quite likely that of the citizeness Rudeuil who, having heard that her tenant had found and kept a counterrevolutionary song, "scarcely slept the whole night. . . ."[78] But many radical republicans were concerned with more than counterrevolutionary singing. Some attacked songs that seemed to make light of revolutionary hardship or, worse still, obscene songs that they feared would threaten the very foundations of the Republic.[79] For if one believed, like Robespierre, that "immorality is the foundation of despotism, just as virtue is the essence of the Republic," then obscene songs did not simply overheat the imaginations of republican maidens (no one worried about the overheated imaginations of young men); they endangered the sound morals upon which the Republic must be founded, and so threatened to bring the whole political order crashing down.

In truth, such fears seemed old-fashioned and merely habitual by this point—of course, popular songs might be obscene or frivolous—and they were more than counterbalanced by the praise raised by these same men. The *Feuille de la République* ran bucolic accounts of spontaneous song performances, and police spies repeatedly measured the patriotic fervor of private assemblies by the singing done there: "The cafés on the boule-

vards . . . were full of people, but they sang only patriotic tunes . . ."[80]
Within the National Convention, however, a new critique of popular
singing emerged in the winter of 1793–94, which very explicitly responded to the singing practices that had developed since the August
revolution. Although this critique would briefly die with its exponents,
the Dantonists, it would return to shape government policy in later years.

A legislative movement to silence some kinds of revolutionary singing
emerged as Danton and his political allies began to agitate for a demobilization of the Terror. Persuaded that the Revolution's crisis was past, the
Dantonists urged the Convention to dismantle the extraordinary measures of the Terror and loosen its ties of alliance with radical sans-culottes.
Initially favored by Robespierre, the Dantonists seized all opportunities to
promote their position: Camille Desmoulins published increasingly explicit polemics against radical and popular government, while Danton
and even Robespierre made careful speeches at the Jacobin Club and
traded barbs with the sans-culottes' spokesman, Hébert, when he called
for intensification of the Terror. Inside the Convention, Danton made few
overtly moderate speeches, but he promoted the restoration of a more
businesslike politics by repeatedly urging that decrees be sent to committee rather than debated on the floor of the Convention.[81] And, at the end
of January, as the moderate campaign reached its first climax, he insisted
that the Convention take a more critical view of singing.

A deputation from the Piques section arrived to ask the deputies to
attend their celebration of the "martyrs of liberty" several days hence.
One of their members sang a "patriotic song of his composition," and
the deputy Laloi moved that the deputation's speech and song be included in the Convention's bulletin. Danton objected, "The Bulletin of
the Convention is in no way meant to carry verse throughout the Republic, but rather good laws written in good prose. Moreover, a decree
requires the Committee of Public Instruction to give preliminary consideration to all that concerns the arts and education." Laloi responded
with common republican praise of song, but Danton was not to be dis-
suaded. "One must not invoke principles we all recognize in order to
reach false conclusions. Certainly, patriotic hymns are useful . . . for elec-
trifying republican energy; but who among you is in any condition to
pass judgment on the song performed at the bar? Did you truly hear its
words and its meaning? Because I myself cannot judge them."[82] The
song was sent to the Committee without further debate.

It may quite plausibly be argued that at this point Danton was simply
urging that songs be treated with the same circumspection he promoted
for legislative decrees. But having regularized the Convention's proce-

dures for publishing songs, Danton went still further and attacked popular singing itself. Shortly after the arrest of the Hébertistes, which was quite clearly an overt attack on the extralegislative activism of the sans-culottes, a deputation from the Mont-Blanc section appeared at the bar to congratulate the legislature on its victory. Danton interrupted their singer in midverse.

> The halls and the bar of the Convention are meant to hear the solemn and serious expression of the citizens' wishes; none may allow himself to express these wishes with sideshow singing. . . . Here we must coolly, calmly, and with dignity sustain the great interests of the Fatherland, discuss them, sound the charge against tyrants, point out and strike down traitors, and raise the alarm against impostors. I acknowledge the civic-mindedness of the petitioners; but I request that henceforth we hear nothing at the bar but reason in prose.[83]

The proposal was adopted without discussion and popular singing was banished from the legislative halls.

Coming as they did at the height of the struggle for moderation and against popular radicalism, these brief speeches spoke volumes about the Dantonists' view of sans-culottes' singing. Danton himself recognized that the sans-culottes meant to express their fraternity and alliance with the Convention by means of their performances, and there could be no more evocative way of repudiating that alliance than by silencing popular singing. But this was more than an isolated critique developed within the context of a specific political battle. One of the distinctive features of early republican political culture had been its celebration of the laboring poor and its valorization of common people's means of expression, including singing. Now, one of the principal spokesman of the Convention had begun to criticize singing and drive it from the Convention, which amounted to arguing that sans-culottes had no legitimate place there. But by the time he made his second speech against singing, Danton was losing his political battle. Within three weeks, he and Camille Desmoulins would be arrested, tried, and executed. Yet Danton's critique of singing was only temporarily silenced; it would lie dormant for almost a year, only to return victorious.

Having eliminated their political opponents on the Left and the Right, the members of the Committee of Public Safety embarked on a frenzy of activity to regenerate and renew France. As the number of accused and executed rose dramatically, the National Convention passed decrees intended to set the foundations of a truly republican culture by creating monuments, reforming the language, and organizing education.[84] Now Montagnards turned their attention to actively shaping song culture, attempting to assimilate the popular to the official.

The Convention and the Committee of Public Safety issued decrees which requested the submission of hymns and songs that treated specific themes. On 18 Floréal (7 May 1794), for example, the Convention's decree recognizing a Supreme Being and organizing a national calendar of festivals included an article which "calls all talents worthy of serving the cause of humanity to the honor of contributing to its establishment with hymns and civic songs."[85] Two months later the Committee of Public Instruction issued an invitation that called upon republican poets to contribute to the celebration of the memory of Barra and Viala, youthful "martyrs" who reputedly chose death rather than renounce their republican principles.[86] True to the Convention's goals, these requests solicited songs that might be used within the controlled context of the Festival.[87] And, not content with simply harnessing popular initiative, legislators sought to broaden and reinforce festival singing. Thus, when plans were laid for the great festival of the Supreme Being, the Institute of Music sent its members to each Paris section, to teach locals the words and tune of the hymn that had been officially adopted.[88]

While they actively set about shaping popular song production and singing practices, the Jacobins also shaped publishing practices. For, at the same time that they complained about obscene or irreverent songs and promoted more elevated compositions for festivals and the army, a number of such songs and hymns were making their way into revolutionary songbooks. By the year III (1794–95), the informal and entertaining songs that had dotted and even filled songbooks had given way almost entirely to more formal republican hymns composed by learned poets or musicians, thus insuring that festival songs would stand a better chance of making their way to the streets. Ironically, even as reactionary newspapers began to blossom in Paris, booksellers were advertising their most republican publications yet:

> The citizen Chemin . . . has put a collection of almanacs on sale. The choice of songs and other pieces of which they are composed, do honor to his taste and prove his patriotism.
>
> 1. Poor Richard's almanac
>
> 2. New Republican songbook, with calendar of the decade
>
> 3. Almanac of the national festivals
>
> 4. Almanac of the sans-culottes[89]

The early years of the Republic witnessed the flourishing of the song culture that we most commonly associate with the French Revolution, one in which abundant compositions and performances received praise from all sides for their revolutionary and pedagogic power. During these years revolutionary song culture reached its zenith. Not only did production and performance flourish, compositional and singing practices unified a number of seemingly disparate arenas—commercial and amateur, legislative and popular, high-brow and common. For once, cultivated representations of singing accorded with practice, if only briefly. It is no coincidence, of course, that song culture came to flourish at the very moment that the Revolution claimed most forcefully to represent the interests of working people. Songs flourished now, as other cultural forms began to decline, partly because they were the poor person's means of expression *par excellence.*

But, as this chapter has meant to suggest, we would be missing a great deal if we contented ourselves with a simple picture of republican enthusiasm and homogeneity. For, in the first place, the homogeneity that was to be found among compositions and singing practices was enforced as much as it was achieved: Parisians sang soundly republican songs because, after the fall of 1793, no one dared to sing anything else. Secondly, and perhaps most significantly, much of this homogeneity was only apparent: different fractions of the population drew upon a common culture to achieve very different ends. The most ironic example of this was, of course, that sans-culottes used singing to encourage and celebrate the very qualities that enabled them to compete and negotiate with the Convention, even as deputies and bureaucrats hoped to draft songs to the task of disciplining and indoctrinating the populace.

Given these diverse motives, it is not surprising that tensions persisted concerning the significance of singing. Even in the streets, some were concerned by the unpredictability of this very fluid form of expression. While deputies and bureaucrats actively drew upon songs to encourage republican commitment, others were disturbed by the occasionally rough language of songs or, like Danton and his allies, by the alarmingly close association between singing and extralegislative activism. Many undoubtedly would have preferred that singing take place under controlled circumstances—at festivals, in local gatherings, in the army—and most hoped to create a song culture dominated by songs which, like the *Marseillaise,* brought together exalted language, formal composition, and wild popularity. While such tensions and diversity underscore the complexity of song culture even at the moment of its greatest uniformity, they also suggest quite pointedly the difficulties inherent in making assertions about republican culture that are based on the activities or statements of a single party. Even at its most homogeneous, republican culture remained an uncertain compromise between a diversity of practices, aspirations, and ideologies. However much they tried, neither the government nor any part of the populace could achieve uniformity without—as the final months of the Terror remind us—a staggering level of coercion.

Finally, 9 Thermidor was not the signal for a sudden, seismic change in this culture. Rather, Robespierre's fall initiated a slow and steady mutation which gradually solidified into a self-conscious culture of Reaction. Contemporaries at first believed that they had simply witnessed another republican victory over tyranny: "the day of 10 Thermidor enhances the glory of 10 August, of which it serves as a kind of anniversary."[90] The slow change that followed was as much the product of political considerations as it was of the peculiarities of cultural innovation: Thermidor swept away only the most powerful and vocal clique of the Convention, leaving behind a great many deputies who were themselves implicated in the Terror and none too eager for a sudden rush to vengeance and the settling of accounts.

The Convention acted slowly and hesitantly in dismantling the Terror, and the transformation of early republican culture was gradual, progressing slowly from Republican denials of Robespierre to debate to reaction. And as the reaction gained momentum and adherents inside of the Convention and out, its voice acquired an impressive volume and—need we be surprised?—became associated with a song. On 30 Nivôse, year III, in the Guillaume Tell section, the actor Pierre Gaveaux performed a song whose lyrics he had written. The *Réveil du peuple* would quickly become the anthem of reaction as well as the source of an ongoing cultural struggle within the populace, and between populace and government, for the next two years. This song, and not 9 Thermidor, marked another crucial shift in Republican song culture.

Chapter Five

✦

The Reactionary Song (Brumaire
Year III–Ventôse Year IV)

✦ JUST AS THE CULTURAL moment of the Terror did not come to an abrupt stop on 10 Thermidor, neither did the political convulsions of the early Republic end quickly or easily. Although there was talk of a return to the economic and political liberalism of 1789–90, the Thermidorian reaction did not signal a new beginning for the Republic.[1] Rather, it witnessed the continuation of struggles that had plagued the Republic from its declaration. As political parties fought for dominance in the National Convention and allied themselves with different fractions of the Parisian populace, politicians and private citizens alike struggled to reconcile political differences and national unity. Now, however, the "terrorist" replaced the "aristocrat" as the Revolution's most potent domestic enemy, and competing definitions of the Republic were once again discussed publicly, to the point of becoming the subject of violent debate.

Above all, revolutionaries debated the relationship between the pre- and post-Thermidorian Republics and, consequently, the limits of reaction. Many of the Convention's deputies had been implicated in the Terror and therefore feared the consequences of an extensive political reaction. Meanwhile, those who were eager to speed its pace sought and found extralegislative allies among the dandified *jeunesse dorée* (gilded youth), who roamed the streets of Paris "purging" them of sans-culotism. These were the young men who, with their journalistic allies, would popularize the anthem of reaction: *Le Réveil du peuple.*

The *Réveil du peuple* is commonly remembered as the song that was pitted against the *Marseillaise* in a series of battles that stretched through much of the Thermidorian reaction. The republican historian, Alphonse Aulard, called attention to these battles at the beginning of this century, describing their rhythm and scope.[2] But Aulard argued that the proponents of the *Réveil du peuple* were royalists who hoped only to undermine the Republic; in so doing, he badly misrepresented the song's significance. For the *Réveil du peuple* was only able to sustain its lengthy and visible career because the song and its tune were, in the spring and summer of 1795, adopted by a wide variety of republicans who used them as means to engage in debate about the future of France. The song was so bitterly contested at the time, and is so well remembered now, precisely because for a brief moment its seemed about to become the successor to the *Marseillaise*.

The essence of the political and cultural debates that would haunt the Thermidorian and early directorial periods would lie in determining how much of its earlier self the Republic might jettison and still remain a Republic, and how much it would be able to preserve and still dissociate itself from the Terror. From January 1795 until March 1796, a large part of this debate would focus on the principles associated with the *Marseillaise*, the *Réveil du peuple*, and with episodes of their performance. Songs and singing had become intimately linked with the apparent homogeneity that had dominated political life since the summer of 1793. So now, as reactionaries, moderates, and radical republicans began to debate how to regard the political culture from which they had just emerged and how to rebuild it, their relationships to song culture became increasingly complicated.

Simultaneously struggling for and against pluralism, citizens continued to use singing to act out political opinions, just as they had done during the Terror. The questions they raised about what an anthem meant and who it represented were often applied to the Republic itself. As singers struggled over these issues, they began to forge a more pluralist song culture, and in so doing they inadvertently amplified one of the lessons of the Terror. The battles between singers of the *Réveil du peuple* and the *Marseillaise* encouraged legislators to believe that singing was not simply associated with popular activism but with open disorder. Ultimately, the government would set about dictating the nation's anthems itself, simultaneously trying to quell popular disturbance and seize the cultural initiative: it alone would determine the representation of the Republic.

THE EMERGENCE OF REACTION AND THE RISE OF THE
RÉVEIL DU PEUPLE

Ever ready for *nouveautés*, "a singer in place Egalité had some verses against the tyrant Robespierre" only two days after his execution.[3] A second despotism had been overthrown, and the Republic could return to its true course. The description in the *Gazette française* of the celebration of the revolution of 10 August was barely distinguishable from descriptions of other festivals celebrated in the year II. It was, in fact, unique only in its acknowledgment of the recent change in the government: "This festival was even more dazzling than that of 14 July . . . ; during the last festival, it was popular to recall the memorable period of the seizure of the Bastille, but we still saw a new tyranny raising itself upon the ruins of despotism. . . ."[4] However, the popular and legislative movement that would come to be known as the Thermidorian reaction would spread steadily if fitfully through Parisian society. As private citizens and deputies to the Convention struggled for political initiative, factions began to appear. Within a few months of Robespierre's fall, the apparent political homogeneity of the preceding year would give way to a clamor of competing definitions of the Republic.

Having ceased to acquiesce in Terror, the members of the National Convention moved quickly to correct the most egregious faults of the "new tyranny": within days of 9 Thermidor they voted to restrict the power of the Committees of Public Safety and General Security and authorized the release of prisoners who were not properly subject to the Law on Suspects.[5] Beyond this, however, the deputies were badly divided between the remaining members of the Mountain and a growing faction of reactionaries. Meanwhile, the broad and moderate Plain hoped to play the Left off against the Right as a means to promote its own brand of politics.[6] Unable to resolve differences among themselves, many of these legislators sustained the practices of the Terror by turning to allies in the streets and exploiting the factions emerging there.

In the streets of Paris, political and civil society changed slowly but steadily. The press sprang back to life and, in less than two months, periodicals were flourishing. Meanwhile, a blossoming ephemeral literature embroidered on the theme of Robespierre's criminality. More significantly, a new and highly visible reactionary force was gathering. "Muscadins" and "Merveilleuses" were decadent and relatively wealthy young men and women who pursued cultural and political reaction by cultivating a highly stylized way of life meant to mock and undermine early republican sobriety. Thus Muscadins (male reactionaries) not only dressed well, they cultivated effeminate wardrobes and hairstyles that stood in sharp contrast to the rough masculinity cherished by sans-culottes. Together, Muscadins and Merveilleuses created their version of Old Regime society by holding salons, attending the theater regularly, and being careful to speak with exaggerated affectation and rigorous avoidance of *tutoiement*.[7] From this group of highly visible young dandies would come the shock troops of the Paris reaction: young men who called themselves *jeunesse dorée* (gilded youth).

Loudly proclaiming their loyalty to the Republic, the *jeunesse dorée* stepped into the breach created by divisions within the Convention and set themselves the task of initiating a reaction that they believed the government was too slow in pursuing. They began their careers by laying siege to the Jacobin Club in the fall of 1794, after its members had been disgraced by the revelation of atrocities committed in the Vendée. Benefiting from the encouragement of reactionary deputies and journalists, the youth progressed from breaking the building's windows to battling its inhabitants. Their efforts were successful. The Convention only broke its silence about the uproar to blame the Jacobins for it before closing and sealing the hall in which the Club met.[8]

Having defeated the Jacobins, the *jeunesse* turned their attention to other dimensions of public life. They visited cafés whose names had been changed during the Terror, where they "invited different café owners . . . to consider themselves free beings, and to give up the signs of slavery. This invitation has had its proper effect and already several have restored [the] former names [of their cafés]."[9] Regulars at the café de Chartres, a favored meeting place of these young men, argued that the *bonnet rouge* be replaced by a *bonnet tricolore* and that the proprietors of all the local cafés be "invited" to refuse service to Jacobins.[10] Most dramatically, and as part of the political project to have his remains removed from the Pantheon, the *jeunesse dorée* systematically destroyed busts of Marat until the Convention acquiesced again and "depantheonized" the spokesman of the sans-culottes.[11]

By January 1795, the *jeunesse dorée* had become a visible and highly recognizable force in Parisian society, and it was at this point that the *Réveil du peuple* was first performed. The song was composed by two men of the Paris theaters: J. M. Souriguières and Pierre Gaveaux. Souriguières, the author of the lyrics, was a dramatist of little note with dubious revolutionary credentials: he would be sentenced to deportation for royalism in 1797. Although a few of his plays had been performed during the Revolution, his most memorable production was the song that would become the rallying cry of the *jeunesse dorée*. Pierre Gaveaux was by far the more successful of the two. Born in Beziers in 1761, he began to prepare for an ecclesiastical career and then left the church to study musical composition in Bordeaux. Arriving in Paris shortly before the opening of the Revolution, Gaveaux moved from theater to theater before becoming a steady actor at the théâtre de la rue Feydeau in 1793, where he remained until 1801. After leaving the Feydeau, he continued to write popular vaudevilles until he went mad in 1812.

It was Gaveaux who gave the first public performance of the *Réveil du peuple,* at the William Tell sectional assembly. The assembly had been dominated by reactionaries for several months, and it provided an appreciative audience for the song.[12]

Réveil du peuple

Peuple français, peuple de frères,	French people, people of brothers,
Peux-tu voir sans frémir d'horreur,	Can you see without a shudder of horror,
Le crime arborer les bannières	Crime unfurling its banners
Du carnage et de la Terreur?	Of carnage and Terror?
Tu souffres qu'une horde atroce,	You suffer that an abominable horde,
Et d'assassins et de brigands,	Of assassins and brigands,
Souille par son souffle féroce,	Soils with its ferocious breath,
Les territoires des vivants!	The lands of the living!
Quoi! cette horde anthropophage,	What! this cannibalistic hord,
Que l'enfer vomit de son flanc,	Vomited up from the depths of hell,
Prêche le meurtre et le carnage!	Preaches murder and carnage!
Elle est couverte de ton sang!	It is covered with your blood!
Devant tes yeux, de la patrie,	Before your eyes, before those of the fatherland,
Elle assassine les enfants,	It murders children,
Et médite une boucherie	And contemplates a slaughter
De tes dignes représentants.	Of your dignified legislators.
Quelle est cette lenteur barbare?	What is this barbaric langour?
Hâte-toi peuple souverain,	Make haste sovereign people,
De rendre aux monstres du Ténare	To return to the monsters of Tenairon
Tous ces buveurs de sang humaine.	All these drinkers of human blood.
Guerre à tous les agents du crime!	War against all emissaries of crime!
Poursuivons-les jusqu'au trépas;	Hound them unto death;
Partage l'horreur qui m'anime,	Share the horror that impels me,
Il ne nous échapperont pas.	They will not escape us.
Ah! qu'ils périssent ces infâmes,	Ah! they will perish, these malefactors,

Et ces égorgeurs dévorants,	And these raging murderers,
Qui portent au fond de leurs âmes,	Who carry in the depths of their souls,
Le crime et l'amour des tyrans!	Crime and the love of tyrants!
Mânes plaintifs de l'innocence,	Plaintive shades of innocence,
Apaissez-vous dans vos tombeaux,	Soothe yourselves in your tombs,
Le jour tardif de la vengeance	The belated day of vengeance
Fait enfin pâlir vos bourreaux.	Will at last blanche your executioner.
Voyez déjà comme ils frémissent;	See already how they tremble;
Ils n'osent fuir les scélérats!	They don't dare flee the scoundrels!
Les traces du sang qu'ils vomissent	The traces of blood that they vomit
Décèleraient bientôt leurs pas.	Will soon slow their steps.
Oui, nous jurons sur votre tombe,	Yes, we swear upon your tomb,
Par notre pays malheureux,	By our unhappy land,
De ne faire qu'une hécatombe	To do nothing other than massacre
De ces cannibales affreux.	These horrible cannibals.
Représentants d'un peuple juste,	Representatives of a just people,
O vous législateurs humains,	O you humane legislators,
De qui la contenance auguste	Whose august countenances
Fait trembler nos vils assassins,	Make our vile assassins tremble,
Suivez le cours de votre gloire,	Follow the path of your glory,
Vos noms chers à l'humanité,	Your names, beloved by humanity,
Volent au temple de mémoire,	Fly to the temple of remembrance,
Au sein de l'immortalité.	In the bosom of immortality.

Musically, the *Réveil du peuple* lacks either the staccato gaiety of *Ça ira* or the measured majesty of the *Marseillaise*. Composed by two theatrical writers, it is hardly surprising that the tune is like that of most vaudevilles: simple and repetitive, it is neither vocally challenging nor particularly decorative. Rather, the music does little more than underscore the meaning of each word and facilitate their memorization. Stylistically, the *Réveil*'s lyrics are similar to those of most songs sold in the streets during the Terror. Focusing on enemies of "the people," it describes them in a violent and cruelly vivid language: "The traces of blood that they vomit already slow their steps." The song is most innovative in its perspective. Instead of casting the singer in the first person and permitting him or her to speak for the nation, the *Réveil du peuple* adopts an omniscient voice that describes the condition of the "French people" and urges them to take action. It is not until the second half of the fifth verse that the singer truly joins his voice with that of the "sovereign people" to swear revenge for massacred innocents: "Yes, we swear upon your tomb . . . to do nothing other than massacre these horrible cannibals."

Certainly, some of the *Réveil du peuple*'s effectiveness derives from its perspective. An outsider at first, the singer seems to offer an external description of reality rather than an individual opinion. Then, by joining his voice with that of "the people," he implies that the audience has adopted his perspective. Now, the newly unified citizenry demands action from its legislators: "O you humane legislators . . . make our vile assassins tremble." But the shift from third to first person, common to other songs of the period, also reveals a confusion about who exactly constitutes "the people" and who is demanding revenge for the events of the year II.[13] Is the singer himself one of the people? Having suggested the proper road for post-Thermidorian politics, will he join in and henceforth describe "our" project? Or does the use of the third person suggest that the citizenry is divided? The context of the song's performances would alternately favor both interpretations.

On the day after the *Réveil*'s first public performance, the reactionary *Messager du soir* reported its success and added that "the citizen Gaveaux was unanimously encouraged to bring the pleasure of hearing . . . this patriotic hymn from his own mouth to the citizens who meet regularly at the café de Chartres, a hymn whose tune will undoubtedly be rung out by all the friends of liberty, justice, and the Convention on the anniversary of the execution of our last king. That day should be consecrated to expressing the horror of tyranny and the love of independence; thus, it should be equally deadly . . . to Capet's accomplices and Robespierre's servants."[14] Two days later, the same paper suggested a link between reactionary sentiment and a more familiar variety of republicanism by claiming that the *Réveil* had been sung in concert with the *Marseillaise* and another republican song as Jacobins were burned in effigy at the Palais Egalité. Meanwhile the *Courrier républicain*, still further to the Right, reported that Gaveaux had performed his song with great success at the café de Chartres.[15]

These first performances of the *Réveil du peuple* took place just as the reactionary movement of the *jeunesse dorée* was gaining momentum and visibility. Well aware of the importance of possessing an anthem, right-wing newspapers immediately advertised the song's performances, promoting it among the young and suggesting that it represented the current mood of all French men and women. But the song could not easily play the part of successor to *Ça ira* or the *Marseillaise*. Unlike its predecessors, the *Réveil* suggested no constructive notion of the Revolution or the Republic. Having effectively called for the punishment of "terrorists," the song did not describe positive sources of domestic unity or a vision of the future. Without some notion of a united or forward-looking nation, it would become the most temporally restricted of all revolutionary anthems, exhausting its "analogousness" when the National Convention was finally dismantled. As well, the conditions of its first performances further complicated its adoption. The song appeared at a moment of extraordinary division and political uncertainty amongst revolutionaries, and it was performed in a context marked by the violent activism of the *jeunesse dorée* and their illegal brawling with radical republicans. Initially, the *Réveil* did not seem to be anything more than the song of a party. This impression was reinforced by Jacobins and sans-culottes who, still a visible presence in Paris, used print and performance alike to contest the song and call attention to its divisiveness. But as the desire to break decisively with the Terror gained ground, and as the song's radical opponents were silenced, the *Réveil*'s popularity spread.

The *Réveil du peuple* began its career as a signal for dissension and disorder among the *jeunesse dorée*. Because sectional assemblies had already been purged of sans-culottes and other radicals, the youth turned their attention to places where they were most likely to meet their political opponents: cafés and theaters. Just as these young men had agitated to "purge" those arenas of the old symbols of radical republicanism, so now they performed their anthem to announce their presence and enforce their dominance. And as long as radicals continued to identify and defend themselves, performances of the *Réveil du peuple* were the signal for public battles. At the théâtre de la République, for example, the reactionary audience demanded that the actor Fusil, accused of Jacobinism, make amends for his past by reading the copy of *Réveil du peuple* that had been tossed onto the stage:

> Fusil arrived and began to read; he acquitted himself very poorly. "He has no feeling for what he reads," said a voice. When he reached the verse,
>
> What is this barbaric langour?
> Make haste sovereign people,
> To return to the monsters of Tenairon
> All these drinkers of human blood.
>
> Someone shouted: *Listen up reader!* This rude shout was welcomed with the liveliest applause.[16]

Witnesses differed in their descriptions of these performances. Some blamed the the sectarian image of the *Réveil du peuple* on the continuing and visible presence of old radicals who inspired the *jeunesse dorée* to song and then fought over its performance.

The people's representative Armonville, who regularly wears a liberty cap, was insulted for his attire at the café Payen by the young people who meet there, and sing the *Réveil du peuple* with great vehemence, repeating several times: *down with drinkers of blood, with liberty caps, with the Mountain!*[17]

Radical Republicans, however, criticized the song because they feared that it was the expression of a party that did not simply reject the ills of the year II but sought to overturn the Republic altogether. Thus the *Journal des hommes libres* described a performance of the *Réveil du peuple* for the orphans of "those who, on the night of 9 Thermidor, gave proof of their republican virtue by marching against Robespierre": "Frightened by the new dangers which, they have learned, threaten the fatherland, these young republicans, rather than lavishing vain applause on the singer . . . occupy themselves, during the deep silence that follows, with suggesting a remedy for these ills. Scarcely had the hymn finished before their musicians struck up the tune: *Veillons au salut de l'empire.*"[18]

However, while the *jeunesse dorée* promoted a highly visible and often violent reaction, they were by no means alone in rejecting the Terror. A more moderate and peaceful reaction was visible in editorials that promoted the free expression of opinion, in the popular *Almanach des prisons*, which commemorated victims of the Terror by recounting tales of bravery in the face of imminent death, and in numerous songs that alternated between anger and melancholy.[19] Song preferences were shifting: "Because of its cheerful character, the vaudeville has long been the preferred song of the French. Today, and for a long time to come, it will be the romance, because our bruised hearts need soothing before once again ascending to gaiety."[20]

As the desire to disavow the Terror broadened and gained ground, moderates began slowly to adopt the *Réveil du peuple*. Increasingly, reports suggested that the song was being sung to celebrate recent events, and without encountering vocal opposition. By early March, newspapers across the political spectrum were carrying such reports. The reactionary *Courrier républicain* announced that the song was sung in the tribunes of the Convention when it decreed the arrest of Collot d'Herbois and his associates, while the republican *Annales patriotiques* reported that "the Parisian public uneasily watches the slow, awkward pace of the trial begun against the *décemvirs* [Collot d'Herbois and others]; in all of the theaters, when they hear this alarm of the people [ce réveil du peuple] *Quelle est cette lenteur barbare?* all the spectators express the sentiments that animate them with the most prolonged applause."[21]

These descriptions coexisted with more sectarian representations of the song until the popular insurrection against the Convention of

12–13 Germinal (1–2 April 1795). But after working people staged a new insurrection and invaded the Convention to demand bread, the Thermidorian reaction gained strength and coherence. Montagnard deputies were arrested and common people disarmed.[22] Radical republicans were driven from public view and a more homogeneous politics dominated, with moderate opinion hardening in the face of the threat of another radical Revolution. The months between March and August saw a uniform swing to the Right: reactionary rhetoric dominated the streets, while *émigrés*, many of them royalists in disguise, were allowed to return to their homes under the protection of legislative decrees.[23] In the theaters "the *Réveil du peuple* continued to be requested, sung, and loudly applauded; all that aims to attack and unmask the furies of terrorism is received with enthusiasm."[24] The *Réveil* became almost uniformly the song of the hour; factionalists were no longer those who demanded the song but those who opposed it.[25]

The critical condition of working people had not, however, been addressed. And so, desperate for some improvement in their condition, they once again invaded the Convention during the Prairial uprising in mid-May 1795.[26] After several days of negotiation, the Convention seized the initiative and used the insurrection as a justification for the final and decisive suppression of the popular movement. Troops accompanied by *jeunesse dorée* entered the faubourg Saint Antoine to repress further activity, and a military tribunal was created to judge suspected insurgents. By mid-June, radicals had been silenced or purged from official and popular milieus alike.[27]

Having defeated the threat from the Left, the Convention could now reconsider its dependence on the extralegislative activism of the *jeunesse dorée* and take aim at the newly flourishing signs of royalism. But before it could act, a detachment of émigrés landed in Brittany to recruit local counterrevolutionaries for a new insurrection. The populace did not rise, but almost a month passed before republican forces could defeat the invaders.[28] Apparently, there was nothing like the threat of invasion and counterrevolution to shake up Parisian political life. Several new republican newspapers were founded as the Convention resurrected symbols of republicanism, certain now that it could determine their limits. This was the context that encouraged the deputy Jean de Bry to propose a decree, which the Convention passed on the sixth anniversary of the taking of the Bastille:

The National Convention, desiring . . . to sustain the energy of true republicans, by solemnly affirming the sacred principles that overthrew the

Bastille, on 14 July, and the monarchy, on 10 August, decrees the following: The patriotic hymn titled *Hymn des Marseillais*, composed by the citizen Rouget de Lisle, and the *chorus of Liberty* . . . performed today . . . in
the meeting hall, will be published in their entirety in the proceedings.
The civic tunes and songs that have contributed to the success of the Revolution, will be performed by the musicians of the National Guard and
the troops of the line.[29]

This was the first official performance of the *Marseillaise* in almost a
year, and the song's first public performance since the closing of the Jacobin Club. The decree proved, however, to be the opening shot in a
new series of popular battles that would rage through Paris for the next
week. Even before the day was over, Parisian youth began to respond:
they quarreled in the gardens of the Palais Egalité and raised noisy complaints in the cafés de Chartres and de Valois, where most of them "pretended that the decree had been revoked, because the song recalled the
massacres of the first days of September 1792, and favored the terrorists." Some of the customers at the café du Caveau sang the *Marseillaise*
while a group of young people stood outside and shouted that the *Réveil
du peuple* was a worthier song.[30]

Matters became still more serious the following morning, when the
National Guard turned out to play the "civic songs" ordered by the Convention. A large crowd, "mostly *jeunes gens*," was awaiting them in the
place du Carousel, and when the guard appeared they began to shout
that they wanted to hear the *Réveil du peuple* and not the *Marseillaise*;
"this hymn," the agitators argued, "was dishonored when it was adopted
by the Jacobins and the drinkers of blood . . . do they want to reestablish
the Terror?"[31] The commandant replied that the Convention had already ordered this performance of the hymn, but, faced with such persistent ferment, he agreed to send a messenger for confirmation. The
messenger returned an hour later; then "drums sounded the march and
the public sang out the song of the *Réveil du peuple*. . . . The music repeated the chorus three different times, amid bravos and shouts of
down with terrorists, down with the drinkers of blood."[32]

The *Gazette française* reported that the Convention had rescinded its
decree concerning the *Marseillaise*, presumably because of the opposition shown at the mounting of the guard. What had, in fact, happened
was that Jean de Bry had offered to "explain the proposal," moderating
its terms in the process. However, although the Convention had very indirectly sustained the decree, the guard made no effort to perform the
Marseillaise on the next or subsequent mornings.[33] It must have seemed

to many that the Convention had simply backed down at the first sign of opposition.

Although the guard had not played the *Marseillaise*, the Convention's decree sparked an uproar in Parisian theaters that lasted several nights. On the same day that the National Guard musicians were shouted down, audiences at the theaters of the rue Feydeau and Montansier gladly heard a performance of the *Réveil du peuple* but refused to listen to the last verse, which praised the deputies of the Convention. At the théâtre de la République, attempts to sing the hymn caused a "great commotion," while an actor at the Opéra who tried to sing *Veillons au salut de l'Empire* was drowned out by shouts of "Here is the Terror returning! Down with the Jacobins, the murderers! The *Réveil du peuple!* The *Réveil du peuple!*" Another actor finally came forward to sing the *Réveil.*[34]

Within days of Jean de Bry's motion, the Committees of Public Safety and of General Security decreed that songs could not be played in any Parisian theater during or between pieces, unless they were already part of the plays being performed. But this did not bring an end to the disturbances: audiences pretended that the decree applied only to theater personnel and left them free to continue their singing of the *Réveil du peuple.*[35] Nor did the youth confine their singing to theaters: on 18 July a crowd of *jeunesse dorée* who were angry with the deputy Louvet gathered outside his home to bellow the *Réveil du peuple* and shout "Down with the Jacobins!" The next evening, after a fight over a performance of the *Réveil* at the Opéra which resulted in several arrests, the *jeunesse* continued their singing and marched to the Committee of General Security to demand the release of their fellows.[36]

The skirmishing died out quickly; within a week, Paris police spies could report that the *Réveil du peuple* had been performed at the théâtre de la rue Feydeau without exciting a tumult.[37] It was, however, the celebration of the anniversary of 9 Thermidor (27 July 1795) that formally closed this episode when, in a speech before the Convention, Boissy d'Anglas raised the *Réveil du peuple* to a stature equal to that of *Ça ira* and the *Marseillaise*. Having listened to a performance of the latter two songs by the National Institute of Music, Boissy addressed his colleagues: "The hymn [des Marseillais], to whose tune our soldiers march to victory, is sacred; it should not be proscribed because cannibals desecrated it by singing it in the wake of carts that took victims to the scaffold. . . . There is another song that accomplished the victory of 9 Thermidor and which insured all the successes which that day promised us, by this I mean the *Réveil du peuple*. . . . If other cannibals committed murders in prisons while singing this air, nevertheless it rendered great service to the Republic."[38]

Boissy may have been a radical reactionary, even a potential royalist, but his colleagues did not silence him, nor did they attempt to counter his remarks. His last comments only excited "violent murmurs" from the remaining members of the Mountain, and before these men could express their dissatisfaction at greater length, the National Institute of Music struck up the *Réveil du peuple*, "which was loudly applauded."

The debate over the singing of the *Marseillaise* and the *Réveil du peuple* was not only over which songs would receive official recognition, but over which political positions would be accorded a place in the national discourse and what the nature of French republicanism would be. Almost every political position of the Thermidorian period was rooted in fear—fear of a return to the Terror, of Restoration, of complete anarchy—and these fears gave the contest its particular intensity. But while political fears and aspirations determined the tone of the battle, it had been created in the first place by the vagueness of the Convention's language and the evolution of song culture since 1789.

The decree of 26 Messidor (14 July), which opened the controversy, claimed that the Convention wanted to maintain the vitality of true republicanism by celebrating the principles that had overturned the Bastille on 14 July and the throne on 10 August. The decree closed with the order that "the civic tunes and songs which contributed to the Revolution's success" would be played by the National Guard. Many Parisians believed, however, that true republicanism had only been realized on 9 Thermidor, with the defeat of the second French tyranny. Therefore, a celebration of Republicanism should include reference to 9 Thermidor and a performance of the other song that had contributed to the "Revolution's success": the *Réveil du peuple*.

One of the most striking aspects of the rivalry over the two songs was the relative absence of an explicit defense of the *Marseillaise*. The National Convention had declared that the hymn was uniquely revolutionary because of its role in the defense of the new nation; by decreeing that the song would be performed daily by the National Guard, the Convention was attempting to give the hymn a special position within Thermidorian culture, and trying to resurrect its original mystique. But the Convention backed away from such advocacy as soon as public criticism was voiced, and few outside commentators were willing to step into the fray and mount a positive campaign on the song's behalf.

When the hymn's most vehement critics argued that the song's primary associations were the September massacres and the revolutionary tribunals of the year II, its defenders did not deny it; they could only offer the song's more positive associations in juxtaposition. They agreed that the *Marseillaise* and *Ça ira* were "songs, in truth sublime, but which have been too much those of brigandage, of desolation and of death," but they believed this was mitigated by the fact that "*the hymn of the Marseillais . . . wounds the rotten ear of the royalist.*"[39] In conclusion, such "defenders" did not argue that the hymn alone should be played by the National Guard or in Parisian theaters, nor did they even suggest that it should be played in concert with the *Réveil*. Rather, commentators offered as a compromise that each song be played on alternate days, as though musical performances should reflect the careening between Left and Right that characterized Thermidorian political life.

Just as the Convention and newspapers muted their defense of the hymn, few Parisians, whether in the streets or the theaters, were willing to champion the song either. Few of the scenes that took place during the week following the decree were actually excited by attempts to perform the *Marseillaise*; the performances of republican songs that did take place were rarely spontaneous; rather, they were given by the National Guard or by actors.[40]

The relative absence of defenses of the hymn had several causes. The song had ceased to excite popular enthusiasm because it no longer seemed relevant to the dominant cultural and political mood—it had receded from the foreground with the change of times, just as *Ça ira* had earlier—and because there was some truth to the argument that the negative associations of the Terror now dominated popular perceptions of the song. As well, the nature of revolutionary song culture worked against an unambiguous resurrection of the *Marseillaise*. For several years now, revolutionaries had regarded their anthems as coherent expressions of a single point of view. This belief had worked to the advantage of song culture throughout the Terror, as it insured that songs would be regarded as a badge of committed republicanism. Now, however, revolutionaries were finding that they had to break down that notion of songs in order to reform the *Marseillaise*: how else might they successfully claim that the song should now be remembered only as the hymn of republican armies and not also as the chant of the Terror's guillotines? Or that the song might equally represent the interests of radical republicans and reactionaries?

In very practical terms, the hymn had few public advocates: moderates were unlikely to expend themselves defending the song, and radicals were in no position to do so. Jacobins had been banished from public life, and poor sans-culottes were too busy keeping themselves and their families alive during a harsh winter of high prices and food shortage to attend the theater or to conduct battles over republican songs. In the theaters, the *jeunesse dorée* invariably outnumbered their enemies, and in the street they did not hesitate to resort to their own brand of terrorism when provoked, as when they crowded outside the home of the deputy Louvet to roar out the *Réveil*. Only soldiers could truly protect themselves; they were the ones who defended the singing of the hymn at the mounting of the National Guard and who opposed the singing of the *Réveil* at the Opéra by drawing their swords, only to find that they were outnumbered anyway.[41]

And yet, whether motivated by indifference or by fear, all Republicans knew that the *Marseillaise* served as a baseline of Republican symbolism: *tutoiement*, Marat, and the phrygian cap had all been driven from public view, but the hymn's association with the nation's armies and the Convention's formal acknowledgment of its importance kept it from complete annihilation. Thus, a young man arrested for participating in some of the public disturbances admitted to demanding the *Réveil du peuple* and even to expressing surprise over the Convention's decree regarding the hymn, but he nonetheless "absolutely denied that he ever opposed singing *the hymn of the Marseillais*."[42] In short, he was debating what kind of republic France ought to have and how far the reaction should go; he was not suggesting that the republic should be abolished.

Defenders of the *Réveil du peuple* described it as the song that had confirmed the victory of 9 Thermidor and which "makes vile and infamous terrorists quake."[43] Like the proponents of the *Marseillaise*, they recognized that some negative associations attached to their song; in this case, because it had accompanied reactionary violence and assassinations in the south. But, like their opponents, they argued that this meant only that one should acknowledge both the positive and negative associations of the *Réveil* and end by performing both songs. Defenders might try to play down the southern reaction and its relationship to the *Réveil*—"the villains you despise most certainly adopted the letter and not the spirit of these admirable verses."[44] But they shared a common ground with their critics when they claimed that the song was an important symbol of 9 Thermidor.

Ultimately, the arguments of both sides revealed weaknesses within revolutionary song culture and revolutionary political culture alike. Unable to imagine a polysemous anthem that meant many things to many people, singers could only try to balance uniformly good images against uniformly bad ones. In another context, it might have been possible to abandon the common assumption that an anthem expresses a single sentiment or a single set of associations; it might have been possible to create a set of symbols that meant many things to many people. But the debate was being conducted in a society in which few citizens could imagine a plurality of political opinions. The vehemence of this and other debates arose from the fact that radical republicans and reactionaries alike believed that the Republic must live or die by their particular political project. Even moderates were unable to imagine a genuine compromise; hence the suggestions that republican musicians simply alternate between the two songs.

Criticism of the *Réveil du peuple* was invariably moderate, and editorialists hesitated to mount charges against it of the same vituperative weight as the worst attacks upon the *Marseillaise*. Even critics who deplored the violence and disruption that was excited by performances of the *Réveil* were careful to begin by excusing the *jeunesse dorée*. After all, during the Germinal uprising, these youth, "used [their] nimble and sturdy bodies to create an unassailable rampart for the national representatives [and] during those same days, they offered a calm, prudent, and imposing defense against the crowd of citizens who, exasperated by needs that are too real, and seduced by the agents of anarchy, came to ask for bread in the sanctuary of the laws."[45] The *jeunesse dorée* were the friends of liberty and its defenders; if they acted badly, it was because of the heat of the moment or because they had been led astray by a few royalists in disguise.

Journalists and deputies were not so much concerned with the *jeunesse dorée*'s demand for official recognition of the *Réveil du peuple*, nor even with the song's content: *Ça ira*, too, had called down vengeance upon other Frenchmen, and the *Marseillaise*'s lyrics had helped to set a standard of bloodthirstiness. The principal issue was the public disorder that accompanied performances of the song, because the shadow of anarchy, the threat of invasion, and the fear of a return to the Terror hung over the heads of all commentators. A poster that appeared overnight on the walls of Paris—and advertised itself as "A young man's advice to his brothers, the young folk"—warned its readers: "Citizens, believe a friend whose interests are intermingled with your own and who speaks to you from the bottom of his heart. The day when the Senate, suddenly stricken with impotence, saw one of its decrees ignored and violated under its very eyes, was the day that restored hope to your vicious enemies."[46] At the other end of the political spectrum was the *Courrier républicain,* a proponent of radical reaction and crypto-royalism, which warned of the internal threat of a new dictatorship. Describing a fight at the Opéra between *jeunesse dorée* and soldiers, the *Courrier* concluded: "this is how civil war is ignited; how hatreds, divisions, and discords are sown; how revenge is excited between men made to listen to and esteem one another; how preparations are made for the military regime, that hardest of all governments toward which we march with great strides."[47]

Police interrogations, too, were less concerned with whether or not suspects had sung the *Réveil* than with whether the young men had given signs of royalism by trying to prevent the singing of the *Marseillaise* or trying to suppress the last verse of the *Réveil,* and whether they had contributed to public disorder by fighting with those around them.[48] During the Terror, Danton had been critical of singing because it seemed too closely allied with sans-culottes' activism. Now singing and activism was feeding a similar fear. Although this singing was directed toward a different political goal, it seemed all the more threatening to the Republic.

The song debate quieted down after the anniversary of 9 Thermidor, when the Convention heard performances of both songs.[49] The *Journal de Perlet* even went so far as to claim that "the *Marseillaise* and the *Réveil du peuple* have been completely reconciled . . . One and then the other were played today at the mounting of the guard and equally applauded."[50] This may have been a rather optimistic account, but public disorder over the songs had diminished noticeably. The *Réveil* was sung with relative calm in the streets and theaters of Paris, and its tune flourished briefly in the press, much like any popular song; it appeared at the top of songs printed on half-sheets and in newspapers which celebrated a range of events and political opinions. The citizen Abril used the tune to praise the acceptance of the new constitution:

Peuple français, te voilà libre;	French people, here you are, free;
De toi dépend tout ton bonheur:	All your happiness depends on you alone:
De tes chaînes tu te délivre,	You deliver yourself from your shackles,
En agissant d'après ton coeur.	By following your heart's desires.
Sois sourd aux cris du réfractaire,	Close your ears to the cries of the dissenter,
Qui dans l'abîme te plongea;	Who will pitch you into the abyss;

146

N'écoute que le mandataire,	Listen only to the legislator,
Qui de l'abîme te tira.[51]	Who will pull you from the abyss.

At almost the same time, the royalist songwriter, Ange Pitou, used it to castigate the grain speculators who starved the people, and the legislature which allowed them to do so:

Ne pas enchaîner ces furies	Not to enchain these furies
Trop impuissants législateurs;	Too feeble legislators;
De ces dévorantes harpies,	Of these devouring harpies
C'est vous montrer les pro-	Is to show yourselves the protectors.
tecteurs.[52]	

While the *Courrier de Paris* used the *Réveil du peuple* to sing the praises of compromise, the republican *Journal du Bonhomme Richard* vacillated between using the tune for bitter attacks on the *jeunesse dorée* and songs that preached reconciliation.[53]

In Vendémiaire (September–October 1795), a new political crisis emerged as a consequence of the ratification of a constitutional requirement that two-thirds of the new directorial legislature be chosen from the members of the National Convention. The measure passed, but it was extremely unpopular in Paris and the *jeunesse dorée* began to spread through the sections and prepare an insurrection, activity that was accompanied by a renewal of partisan singing of the *Marseillaise* and the *Réveil du peuple*.[54] On 2 October, seven sections declared themselves in insurrection and, three days later, the insurgents were met by troops under the command of General Bonaparte. The battle was brief and left some three hundred dead, but the subsequent repression was moderate. The city's gates remained open, allowing those who were most seriously implicated in the insurrection to flee; only thirty convictions were returned by the military commission that tried the rebels, and of the seven death sentences handed down, five were *in absentia*.

The immediate threat of a royalist insurrection had been checked, but a great many royalists remained in Paris, to become a compelling political presence throughout the directorial period. In the aftermath of the Vendémiaire insurrection, however, Parisians, having faced this latest threat from the Right, once more displayed their fickle patriotism and rallied to the old symbols of the Republic.

After a performance of [*Oedipus at Colonnus*] the citizen Chéron announced that the Committee of General Security had withdrawn its decree concerning the singing of tunes in theaters, but only for the hymn of the Marseilleans and the Chant du départ. . . . Republicans received this news with applause and repeated shouts of long live the republic. The offering to liberty and the sacred hymns, *veillons au salut de l'empire, allons enfants de la patrie,* excited in all hearts this noble and lively enthusiasm that the royalists tried vainly to destroy.[55]

THE DECLINE OF THE *RÉVEIL DU PEUPLE*

The National Convention was replaced by the Directory in late October 1795, an uneventful transition. For the next few months Parisian police spies were concerned primarily with popular complaints about provisioning and with small gatherings of Jacobins and royalists. The Vendémiaire uprising had led to the nearly complete eclipse of the *Réveil du peuple.* So long the source of contention, the song's affiliation with an uprising labeled as counterrevolutionary wholly undermined its republican associations; the insurrectionists' performances seemed to confirm critics' worst accusations. With the decline of the *Réveil du peuple,* the song battles appeared to be dying out of their own accord when, on 8 January 1796, the Directory decreed that "all the directors, entrepreneurs, and proprietors of Parisian theaters are held individually responsible for having their orchestras play the tunes beloved of republicans each day before the raising of the curtain, tunes such as *La Marseillaise, Ça ira, Veillons au salut de l'Empire,* and *Chant du départ.* During the intermission between two plays, the hymn of the Marseillais or some other patriotic song will always be sung. . . . It is expressly forbidden to sing or to have sung the murderous tune called *le Réveil du peuple.*"[56] Anyone in a Parisian theater who called for a return of the monarchy or for the abolition of the current executive, or who in any way troubled good order and public tranquillity, would be arrested.

The Directors offered no explanation for this rather surprising piece of legislation, but the *Moniteur universel* suggested that the decree was part of an official project to regenerate public spirit and fight the persistent factionalism of Vendémiaire.[57] For even after the suppression of the Vendémiaire insurrection, royalists continued to live openly in Paris and to constitute an increasingly compelling political force throughout the country. The Directors may have intended their latest decree as a clear message of their commitment to republicanism, but the new law was a red flag waved before local factions: fights and public disturbances multiplied immediately. This time the foci of the song battles were strictly republican songs; singing the *Réveil du peuple* had become clear grounds for arrest and, since the song had been out of fashion for several months, few seemed interested in taking up its cause. Now opposition took the form of mockery and highly ironic performances of the *Marseillaise*. The théâtre du Vaudeville and the théâtre de la rue Feydeau, with which Pierre Gaveaux was associated, were already popular with royalists, and they became the principal sites of disturbance, as young men responded to performances of republican songs with shouts and whistles.[58] On 13 January, the proprietors of the théâtre de la rue Feydeau sent Gaveaux onstage to sing the required songs.

> On one side, the patriots strenuously opposed Gaveaux singing the sacred hymn of Liberty, calling him the cut-throat's singer. On the other side [were] all of the royalist party, in large part composed of musicians [and] the so-called honest people of the loges, supported by a few volunteers who were fooled by not knowing Gaveaux as one of the authors and howlers of the réveil du peuple . . . this mass, which was much superior in number, called for, supported, and applauded Gaveaux.[59]

A few days later a police spy at the Vaudeville remarked that its orchestra played the songs gracelessly and without feeling, while the actor appointed to sing appeared in royalist green and was enthusiastically applauded when he reached "Vile despots would become / The engines of our destinies!" These lines had apparently become, for royalists, a reference to the Directors, while "What! these mercenary phalanxes / Would bring down our proud warriors!" was celebrated as a description of the role of the police during the royalist revolts of Vendémiaire.[60]

These were only two incidents among the many that stretched on for the next two months, as opponents of the *Marseillaise* developed new ways to exhibit their disdain for the song and for the Executive Directory's decree concerning it. Sometimes hostile actors omitted the verse that condemned the marquis de Bouillé, one of the masterminds of the flight to Varennes.[61] Or they appeared on stage badly dressed, to sing the song flatly, or with an air of obvious embarrassment.[62] Royalists applauded loudly for "Quake tyrants! and you traitors / The disgrace of all parties," which they meant to turn back on the Directors. They treated the verse of *Ça ira* which commanded auditors to "Hang the aristocrats," ironically "pretending, with many republicans, that there is no longer any sort of aristocracy."[63] At the théâtre de la rue Feydeau, an army commandant attending the performances decided to cut short equivocal interpretations of "Quake tyrants!" by replacing it with "Quake *chouans*."

But royalists were only temporarily disconcerted for, within a few days, they were applauding that version ironically and using *chouan* as a familiar greeting in the street.[64]

Just as they had done before the revolution of 10 August, royalists once again turned to satire and irony to battle the Revolution, using form to subvert content and walking the fine line of political possibilities from which they had strayed in 1792. In mocking the *Marseillaise*, they mocked the regime itself, attempting to undermine respect for one of its central symbols and barely hiding their own political opinions. Royalists did not openly attack the *Marseillaise*, nor did they attempt to replace it with the another song, as the *jeunesse dorée* had done during the previous year; but the political stakes in this battle were far higher than they had been during the reaction. During the Thermidorian reaction, the majority of the *Réveil*'s supporters used that song to debate republican political life and to suggest how the nation ought to interpret recent history. They demanded that the government openly repudiate the Terror and confer upon 9 Thermidor a symbolic importance equal to that of 10 August. By 1796, however, there was no possible compromise, because the enemies of the hymn were also enemies of the Republic: they did not offer another interpretation of the Republic's history or another kind of symbol to represent it; rather, they attacked the symbols offered them because they hoped for a whole new system of representation.

A few police spies harked back to Jacobin ideas common in 1793 when they argued that the best means of dealing with this opposition was to place large numbers of patriots in predominantly royalist theaters, where they could counter attacks upon the hymn and perhaps even force the royalists to "retreat shamefully."[65] The actual response was simply to arrest and interrogate audience members who were believed to be exciting trouble. Many young men were arrested in the two months that followed the January decree, but negative responses to songs were as fleeting and ephemeral as singing itself, and so the police were often reduced to doing no more than detaining suspected troublemakers and verifying that their papers were in order.[66] When the dispute finally came to an end it was not because a compromise had been reached, as during the preceding summer, but, according to police agents, because audiences had simply become bored with the affair and bored with the songs that the government forced upon them.

During the intermission, the *chouans* deserted the parterre so as not to listen to the singing of the Marseillaise.

. . . the patriotic songs are generally heard with indifference.

A coolness toward the patriotic hymns is visible in the theaters. A couple of verses hastily sung seems sufficient to the actors.[67]

Directors and police had gained the upper hand through sheer force and perseverance. The government maintained the decree for several months longer and then, sure of its position, withdrew it to return to the former policy of prohibiting the performance of any songs that were not already part of the theater pieces.[68]

At the heart of the song debates of 1795 and 1796 were, in the first place, the question of what the Republic's official songs would be and what that signified about the government's policies and, second, whether the government had any right at all to decree what songs would be popular. The Thermidorian Convention resurrected the *Marseillaise* in the face of resurgent royalism, but only after it had eliminated the possibility of renewed radical republicanism. The reaction had swung as far to the Right as the government was willing to let it go, and it was necessary to give some public sign of unequivocal attachment to the Republic; hence, the *Marseillaise*. But political life during this period was saturated with fears of a new dictatorship and Terror. These fears did have some basis in fact because of the simple existence of "la queue de Robespierre" (Robespierre's tail): the majority of the Convention's members who were implicated in the Terror. Under such circumstances, the resurrection of the *Marseillaise*, in eclipse for almost a year, sent a frightening signal to radical reactionaries and moderates alike, many of whom believed that celebration of 10 August and the Republic could only be offset by an equivalent celebration of 9 Thermidor.

The *Réveil du peuple* began its career as the song of the radical reaction, but as the desire to disavow the Terror gained currency and as fears of another popular revolution spread in the wake of the Germinal and Prairial uprisings, the song gained a wider audience. When radical fears of a resurrection of the Terror no longer seemed excessive, proposals for visible and dramatic breaks with the early Republic acquired credibility. The need to repeatedly remind Revolutionaries of the lessons of 9 Thermidor became an urgent one, drowning out the voices of critics who feared that the *Réveil* was not simply an attack upon the tyrannical elements of the Republic but a call for its complete abolition. The *Réveil du peuple* may have appealed to royalists during the spring and summer of 1795, but at that point it was still a republican song, albeit one that celebrated divisiveness at a moment when the government was trying to create national unity. It was only after the song had been adopted by the insurgents of Vendémiaire, suggesting the true depth of its divisive message, that the balance of interpretation shifted and the song's associations became overtly antirepublican, leading to its public eclipse.

It was this development in the *Réveil*'s career that revealed most clearly its essential difference from the *Marseillaise*. The *Marseillaise* had negative associations, but they were counterbalanced by a positive and unifying association that no patriot could deny: this was the song that had accompanied French armies in the defense of the nation. The *Réveil du peuple*, on the other hand, had positive associations only to the extent that one was prepared to celebrate the need to purge Jacobins or that one believed the primary threat to the Republic came from the Left. And once radical reactionaries and royalists had threatened the Republic, while singing the *Réveil*, they could not even make that case for the song.

The battles over the *Marseillaise* and the *Réveil du peuple* also suggest just how fragile the Thermidorian political alliance was. Just as the polity strained between Left and Right, incapable of finding political compromise, so it was incapable of finding a cultural or symbolic compromise and creating a viable center. No single revolutionary song could be found because there was no set of associations that everyone could agree upon, and because no symbol could be found that might carry multiple positive associations. Of the *Marseillaise* the Right would only say that it had accompanied the executions of the Terror, while the Left came to see nothing but the bloodshed of the White reaction in the *Réveil du peuple*. The majority of citizens whose politics lay between those extremes tried to emphasize the positive dimensions of each song, but they were unwilling or unable to choose between them.

Under the Directory, many of the attacks upon the *Marseillaise* were made by royalists who, profoundly dissatisfied with the number of regicides who sat in the legislature, carried out by other means the opposition that they had begun by violence in Vendémiaire. Royalists saw the Directory's endorsement of the *Marseillaise* as an open sign of their sympathy with the radicalism of the year II; by mocking the hymn they expressed their disapproval of Directors and Republic alike. In decreeing theatrical performances of republican songs, the Directory set the terms of the debate; when engaging in that debate, royalists returned to their old weapons, using satire and irony to undermine revolutionary symbols.

Moderates were angered by Thermidorian and directorial decrees because they smacked of despotism and were at odds with their belief in the principles of free expression and open debate. Nor did the government have any right to decree the performance of songs outside of national festivals or to try to affect their popularity. On this point, at least, there was nearly universal agreement: both song battles were initiated by government decrees. Within days of the Directory's decree, the *Annales patriotiques* reprinted the editorial of another republican newspaper, the *Censeur des journaux*:

> *Prohibiting the singing* of a tune that has become the cue for massacres in the south is wise. . . . But *to order singing*. . . . What do these words mean? . . . Is it more permissible for the government to order the singing of a certain tune than to command a liking for a particular song? . . . The government could say: You will not sing any song, because songs have become the subjects of quarrels and the torches of civil war. But *ordering* the singing of four songs that are privileged and avowedly those of a party that inspires just defiance, is this not to openly declare oneself the protector of that party?[69]

During the debates of 1795, the *Messager du soir*, at the other end of the political spectrum, had made a similar argument: the government might express its opinion about a particular song, but it had no right to prescribe them: "the fad of the day will pass on to the songs that it adopts, whether they are as sublime as the *Chant du départ*, or wretched and ridiculous verses like those of *Cadet Roussel*."[70] Since the beginning of the Revolution, a diffuse and unofficial public opinion had determined the adoption of songs, setting the fashion just as it had done during the Old Regime. In decreeing which songs would be performed, the Thermidorian Convention and the Executive Directory flew in the face of established practice: it was not possible to create a popular song by fiat.

The Directory endorsed the *Marseillaise* because it wanted to stress its republican associations and because, unwilling to make any real concessions to the radical republicans, it sought to win allegiance through the manipulation of once-popular symbols. But the public was not so easily duped, and once the royalists had tired of battling decreed performances of the *Marseillaise*, there was no popular response other than boredom and inertia. Just as the suppression of the Vendémiaire insurrection foreshadowed the Directory's growing dependence on the army to remain in power, so the *Marseillaise* decree foreshadowed its growing dependence on legislation to sustain and propagate the symbols of the Republic.

Finally, while these song battles were very closely tied to the shifting political objectives and alliances of the Thermidorian reaction, they had long-term consequences for revolutionary ideas about song culture. In the first place, by rousing activism that was both disruptive and in some cases even counterrevolutionary, these song battles rendered the relationship between singing and unofficial activism increasingly problematic. Secondly, as the song battles worked haphazardly to restore pluralism to song culture, they also helped to restore the indeterminacy of singing. Performances of the *Réveil du peuple* and of the *Marseillaise* reflected the tastes of their proponents and the constraints of the law by becoming highly stylized, incorporating heavy doses of irony and satire. As we shall see, fears about activism and indeterminacy alike would fuel government efforts to control and silence this explosive but evanescent means of expression.

Part III

✦

Ending the Revolution

Chapter Six

✦

The Song in Retreat (Messidor
Year III–Brumaire Year VIII)

✦ IN MESSIDOR YEAR III (July 1795), only two days after its controversial order that the National Guard play the *Marseillaise*, the National Convention decreed that Parisian theaters must not perform songs that were not already part of their advertised programs. In Frimaire year IV (November 1795), the Directory reiterated the Convention's position, incorporating the substance of the Messidor decree into a project for the regulation and maintenance of good order in *spectacles*.

> ARTICLE 7: No tune, song, or aria which is not already part of the play being performed will be played or sung in any theater, either on the stage or in any other part of the hall; offenders will be punished with 24 hours in prison.[1]

As we have already seen, these laws were part of the government's efforts to quell the popular disturbances that it had excited with its decrees concerning the *Marseillaise*. But beyond the very specific role that they played in the controvsery between the *Marseillaise* and the *Réveil du peuple*, these laws were also part of a larger project to seize political and cultural initiative and bring the ongoing ferment of the Revolution to an end.

In the years after 9 Thermidor, official efforts to shape song culture grew increasingly effective. Festival and entertainment song writing would be institutionalized and professionalized as popular singing practices were restricted by laws and ordinances that defined acceptable public behavior more narrowly and thus helped to sever remaining ties between revolutionary singing and revolutionary activism. Ironically, this movement to reshape and restrict singing occurred during the same period in which publishing and theatrical production, now freed from the legal and political constraints of the Terror, were experiencing new vitality. Why was this so?

Legislators and the Parisian police had not set out with the explicit desire to undermine popular song culture; rather, this was the effect of the particular ways in which they came to define revolutionary cultural production, popular singing practices, and political activism. The institutionalization and professionalization of song writing was rooted in a post-Thermidorian shift in educational priorities and in the movement to regularize a national system of festivals. During the Terror, when the National Institute of Music's potential monopoly on festival music was offset by public calls for hymns and individual contracts for songs, amateur and professional song writing alike had been both rewarded and publicized. By the fall of 1795, however, the National Institute was almost wholly responsible for festival compositions and performances. More significantly, during this same year, the government's educational and cultural priorities began to shift from promoting an egalitarian educational policy to sustaining and improving France's high cultural heritage. Awards that were not directed toward professional composers and "men of letters" were allowed to die out at the same time that the National Institute, reorganized into a National Conservatory, would shift its goals from civic education to sustaining and improving the "musical art." The result would be marginalization of streetsingers and occasional patriotic composers from the national system of education, recompense, and recognition.

Meanwhile street singing was restricted, not because it was defined as a cultural practice but because it was seen either as political activism or as a public nuisance. In inheriting the *Marseillaise / Réveil du peuple* debate, the Directory faced a controversy that transformed political singing from a sign of revolutionary fervor to a provocation to disorder and, potentially, sedition. The government's efforts to quell such singing coincided with its alternate blows against the Left and the Right as it worked to silence any and all activist critics who, it believed, threatened the government and the civil peace considered essential to the Republic's survival. In some cases, the Directory attacked singing quite specifically, treating it as a provocation to disorder, but in other cases, as we shall see in regard to the Babouvists and the royalist streetsinger Ange Pitou, singing would become a secondary casualty of larger political battles, just as it had been in 1792.

The Directory demanded allegiance from the citizenry, but it dissociated that allegiance from political activism. Henceforth, the government would expect public cooperation as it attempted to orchestrate political life and cultural production alike. However, while Directory and Paris police played an important part in reshaping song culture, their actions were neither isolated nor decisive. For, as we shall see in the next chapter, private citizens were also redirecting their efforts and their cultural priorities, reconstructing song culture and political culture alike.

THE PROFESSIONALIZATION OF SONG WRITING

The formalization and professionalization of song writing during the later years of the Republic was most clearly manifested in the activities of the National Institute of Music and its reshaping into a National Conservatory. Although the institute had been created by individuals who were outside of the government, these men began to encourage the centralization of song production and festival planning almost immediately upon the institute's establishment. At the end of Pluviose year II (February 1794), in response to proposals made repeatedly by the institute's directors, the Committee of Public Safety agreed to underwrite their production of song periodicals for a year: each month a songbook containing symphonies, hymns, military marches, and at least one song would be published and a copy sent to each of the 550 districts of France.[2] It was a modest beginning, but the project was expanded a few months later, when the committee agreed to pay the institute to produce 12,000 songbooks a month for the military.[3] The following month, the musicians were given housing in a confiscated Montmartre mansion of an émigré.[4]

In addition to producing songbooks, the institute became increasingly involved in the composition and performance of music for national festivals. The musicians of the National Guard had played at local festivals even before the establishment of the institute, but their participation in the planning and execution of festivals intensified during preparations for the celebration of the Supreme Being in Prairial year II (June 1794). Over the next four and one-half months, institute musicians played a central role in organizing nine festivals. They taught a hymn to the members of sectional assemblies in preparation for the festival of the Supreme Being, created fifteen new compositions, and hired additional theatrical musicians for their performances.[5]

Although the institute's role as an important producer of revolutionary songs and music dated from year II (1793–94), the extent of its activities and the context within which it acted changed considerably throughout 1795. In the year II, the institute had operated within a very broadly based cultural context: its songbooks were more than matched by commercial songs and by the compositions published by the Paris City Council and sectional assemblies, while its monopoly on festival composition was, at least in theory, offset by official requests for private contributions. But this environment did not long survive Thermidor. The official request for songs to celebrate the festival of Barra and Viala, published on the day that Robespierre was overthrown, was the last of its kind, and the number of festival songs composed by professionals independent of the institute dwindled steadily, to disappear altogether before another year passed.[6] During this same period, the number of revolutionary songs that made their way into print declined precipitously as the presses of sectional assemblies were stilled and as commercial publishers turned their attention to other kinds of literature and ephemera.

In July 1795, after almost two years of petitioning by its directors, the National Institute of Music was formally reorganized. Henceforth known as the Conservatory, it became a national institution with a regular budget. Although administrators would be responsible for internal policing and regulation, the Conservatory quickly became an integral part of the republican educational system, subject to the protection and surveillance of the government. Expenses were to be regulated by the national executive and paid out from the public treasury, and artists would be selected for the teaching staff through public competitions judged by the members of the National Institute of Sciences and Arts.

Many of the functions included in the Conservatory's charter had long been a part of the National Institute's regular business, and the Convention's decree merely gave them formal judicial status: "With respect to performance, [the Conservatory] is devoted to celebrating national festivals; with respect to teaching, it is charged with training students in all aspects of the musical arts."[7] The charter did, however, include some innovations: most notably, it expanded the size of the institution and centralized its functions. With the stroke of a pen, the number of students to be enrolled increased sevenfold, from 80 to 600, while the number of instructors increased from 22 to 115 as the Conservatory combined the members and functions of the Ecole Nationale de Musique, Chant, et Déclamation with those of the National Institute.[8] The National Institute had been devoted to composition and the training of musicians who played wind instruments, while the Ecole Nationale had instructed students in the dramatic and musical arts.[9] By incorporating the two specialized establishments into a single institution, the National Convention insured that the Conservatory would have complete supervision over all elements necessary to the celebration of festivals and the teaching of music.

The administrators of the National Institute had been asking for formal organization since the fall of 1793, but the creation of the Conservatory was not simply the Convention's answer to that request. Rather, the establishment of the Conservatory served as part of the government's larger effort to rationalize and centralize the production of republican culture. Since the opening of the Revolution, legislators had been trying to realize the project of the Enlightenment by instituting a new and rational system of education. The desire for democratization motivated the projects proposed during the first two years of the Republic, but legislators began to retreat from their democratic aspirations in 1795. Increasingly fearful of popular activism after the Germinal and Prairial insurrections, and receptive to Idéologues who proposed educating an enlightened elite to lead the nation, deputies scaled back their commitment to primary education in favor of creating institutions that might restore and sustain the cultural heritage of France.[10] Only two months after the organization of the Conservatory, the deputy P.-C.-F. Daunou presented a decree to the Convention that paid scant attention to primary education before developing a plan for a National Institute and a series of special schools devoted to the arts and sciences.[11] The newly organized Conservatory meshed well with this projected educational system and with the new set of educational priorities being elaborated in the Convention.

Beyond proposing and creating new institutes of specialized study, the Convention underscored its growing commitment to the high arts by redirecting encouragement for extrainstitutional production. In 1791, and again in 1793, the government had set aside large sums of money with which to reward artists, *savants*, and "men of letters" whose work was useful to the nation.[12] As the contours of song culture changed after Thermidor, the importance of these monetary prizes grew. With the decline of honorable mentions and subsidies for song publication by sectional assemblies, prizes became the dominant form of official encouragement for artistic production. The awards themselves were generous if not extravagant, offering a few hundred livres to artists at a time when bread cost about twelve sous a loaf.[13] The shift from publication and honorable mention for single songs to government prizes for individual artists represented an important shift from the encouragement of amateur song production to the encouragement of professionals. Letters of nomination and application for the prizes described a candidate's circumstances and credentials in order to explain why he or she merited such an award. These conditions favored the composer or songwriter who could boast a body of patriotically and aesthetically successful compositions over the amateur who, moved by a particular event, wrote a single song and then returned to relative obscurity.[14]

Government encouragement of songwriters did not just favor professionals. The wording of the decrees that set aside special funds made clear that they were intended for "men of letters" and "artists," in other words, those who had a recognizable place in an artistic and commercial hierarchy and whose work could be judged on the basis of established aesthetic principles. So, for example, between September 1794 and January 1795, the Committee of Public Instruction considered awards for Champein, a professor of music and the author of operas and comic operas; Chapelle, a musician at the Opéra Comique and the Old Regime's Concert Spirituel, as well as an author of operas and concertos; Desfontaines, the associate at the théâtre du Vaudeville, whose comic operas had been popular at the Comédie-Italienne and the Opéra during the Old Regime; and Rigade, an instructor of music who had been raised in the Conservatory at Naples "under the greatest masters" and who, as well, wrote opera and oratorios.[15]

The names of the professional streetsingers who had advertised the events of the Revolution and proclaimed the principles of the Republic from the streets and bridges of the city were almost completely absent from these same files. Perhaps it is not surprising that "Bellerose," a *chansonnier* who had been performing on the pont Neuf in 1792, was not included; he may have died or left Paris; or perhaps the obscenities of some of his songs placed him beneath the notice of the Committee of Public Instruction.[16] The prolific singer and songwriter Leveau, "called Beauchant, republican singer," was not included either, perhaps because of his radicalism, which would result in his arrest in Prairial.[17]

In fact, the only popular streetsinger whose name did appear among the Committee's papers was Ladré, reputedly the author of *Ça ira*. His request for assistance was remarkable both because his qualifications were of a singularly low artistic order and because his tale of hardship rang painfully true, even in light of the hardship tales that were tropes in such letters. "I am . . . this Ladré whose name you see written at the top of more than five hundred revolutionary songs . . . , the *Ça ira* issued from my pen, dictated by my patriotic soul like all the others. But this one has had a greater influence on the people's spirit than all the others . . . my style is truly popular and more understandable for the mass of

people than are certain polished and sublime songs . . . which not everyone understands." Ladré explained that he was writing to the government only after having been told that he was already being considered
for recompense and after discussing the matter with the committee
member Harmon. Such consideration for recompense "could not come
at a better time because winter is an absolutely ludicrous season for
those occupied as public singers. . . . Citizen Harmon told me that he
would not forget me; now two months have gone by and I have had no
news. A few days ago, I waited until 8:30 in the evening to talk to Citizen
Harmon . . . I returned there the next morning, but they would not let
me talk to him for, seeing that I was in great need, they feared that I
would become too demanding."[18] Ladré's pleas were forwarded to the
Committee of Public Instruction, but they must have fallen upon deaf
ears because his name did not appear in the list of awards that was published three months later.[19]

Although the Thermidorian Convention and, later, the Directory
gave the lion's share of their efforts to restoring French culture, they did
not neglect common people altogether. However unwilling they were to
underwrite the costs of promoting basic literacy, legislators believed that
all citizens must have a civic education, which they considered essential
to promoting domestic peace and loyalty to the Republic.[20] To this end,
Daunou's proposed legislation for national education included a clause
that organized a series of festivals to be supervised by the legislature of
the Executive Directory. Mona Ozouf has already described the government's desire to supervise and homogenize festivals throughout the nation in the years after Thermidor, and this ambition for unity reinforced
the need to organize musical training.[21] Only through centralization
could the government be wholly certain of the nature and force of republican pedagogy; and centralization reinforced professionalization because it required the ready availability of trained and reliable musicians
and composers. If this was implicit in the legislation, it was made quite
explicit by some of the government's own members.

In 1795, J.-B. Leclerc, the Convention's key advocate of pedagogic
song writing, proposed to the Committee of Public Instruction that it seriously consider implementing a national song policy. This was the second time that Leclerc had spoken to his colleagues about revolutionary
songs, and this proposal stood in sharp contrast to his earlier celebration
of "poetry" in January 1793. The 1793 speech had stressed the importance of local and independent initiative in producing songs; even when
offering a poem of his own, he insisted that, "this is just a sketch that I
offer, not . . . a model of poetry." His central point was that songs and

poetry could serve as instruments of revolution, and he went on to suggest that romances celebrating the lives of exemplary local figures might be produced in villages throughout France. In closing, Leclerc assured his colleagues that all the Convention needed do was institute universal education and a sufficient number of poets would emerge.[22]

In his new proposal to the Committee of Public Instruction, which was published in the late spring of 1796, Leclerc placed extraordinary stress upon the need for centralization.[23] While he still had a high opinion of music's capacity to excite patriotism, his ideas about encouraging it had progressed well beyond the simple advocacy of national education. He now envisioned a system directed entirely from Paris: the legislature would establish a universal method for teaching music and would determine, by law, which and how many musical instruments should be distributed to every canton. The Conservatory would choose music for festivals, public games, and all local detachments of the National Guard, which the legislature would approve and distribute. "No tune will be admitted if it is not composed according to the principles decreed, and measured to lyrics that have also been judged worthy of admission."

To supervise musical training and performance in the provinces, music schools would be established in large towns to provide instruction and to supervise the distribution of instruments, musicians, and patriotic music throughout the canton. These local schools would be supervised by four "master schools," which would correspond with a central bureau in Paris. "A code will be drawn up for all offenses resulting from infractions of the laws concerning the choice of musical compositions, the number of instruments, and their type; in other words, for all innovations of any sort. The Directory will see to the execution of the code, and anyone may denounce its negligence to the Legislative Corps."[24] Obviously, strict adherence to such a plan would mean that the kinds of local festival songs that had once won praise and honorable mention from the National Convention would now earn their authors nothing more than arrest.[25]

The government's direct and indirect encouragement of professionalization helped to restore a more formal aesthetics for judging music and songs. This development was visible in the shift from rewarding individual songs to rewarding worthy composers, but it became increasingly explicit, as well, in ideas being expressed about the nature and function of the Conservatory. Early proposals for the organization of the National Institute had stressed pedagogy and the educational value of ornamenting festivals: "All the arts should enrich public festivals, but music alone animates them; its power is attested to by the use that the legislators of antiquity made of it, and by the service it has rendered throughout the French Revolution."[26] The concern with pedagogy did not disappear, but by the time that Bernard Sarrette came to preside over the official opening of the Conservatory in October 1796, his comments were almost wholly confined to the aesthetic merits of the institution. In contrasting the new regime with the old, he stressed methods of teaching: singing was taught better, wind instruments were given more attention, students of composition were provided with a broader experience of styles and harmonic possibilities. The new productions of the Conservatory would encourage young composers to emulate their elders and develop their genius. "And thus will enlightened Europe, appreciating the achievements of this school, impartially give it the place that it deserves alongside the schools of Germany and Italy; and thus will the artists whose works have contributed to this triumph, which is as useful as it is glorious for the Fatherland and for the arts, enjoy the sweet recompense of seeing their talents reproduced in those of their students."[27] Once again, what was explicitly stated by government officials found institutional reflection: the Magasin de Musique stopped printing periodicals for provincial festivals and the military and expanded its publication of sheet music for études, exercises, sonatas, and concertos.[28]

Although the centralization and professionalization of song writing was initiated during a particularly conservative period of the Revolution, the brief return to more democratic principles after the coup of Fructidor year V (September 1797) did not signal a retreat from this movement. In fact professionalization seemed to be outstripping centralization, to the point that legislators slighted revolutionary songs and hymns. J.-B. Leclerc later criticized the men who created the system of *fêtes décadaires*, supposedly the hallmark of democratization, without giving consideration to music:

> If, when the decadal festivals were declared, their celebration had been enhanced by the composition of appropriate hymns; if, following the example of the Greeks, they had been joined with songs for the different professions and the different stages of life . . . ; if, in one word, the legislator had inspired new habits rather than prescribing them by law, the French Republic would have a very different appearance than it presently does![29]

But Leclerc himself did not mean to return to the old republican program of encouragement and education; instead, his defense of patriotic compositions revealed just how important aesthetic concerns had become. Even in 1795, when he was backing away from a democratic song culture, Leclerc had celebrated "the people [who] remember, without the aid of notes, tunes that are sometimes very difficult." Now, as the Revolution was winding down at the end of 1798, he envisioned schools of music that would not simply provide patriotic songs for village celebrations but would "carry good taste and purity of execution even into the cantons."[30]

SINGING AND THE REPRESSION OF DISSENT

As centralization and professionalization marginalized amateur songwriters, the government's efforts to restore public order and eliminate its critics helped to silence singing in the streets. The authorities had become obsessed with the threat of popular insurrection in the wake of the Germinal and Prairial riots in year III, while the Vendémiaire insurrection encouraged the belief that enemies on the Right bore as much watching as those on the Left. These fears did not dissipate with the disbanding of the National Convention. Within weeks of the Directory's sitting, the minister of the interior was bitterly stirring the police to action: "I have not found a single piece of information that permits me to explain the source of the force's inertia."[31] Police spies became attentive to all possible means of exciting insurrection, and their reports were filled with notices of seditious posters, libelous newspapers, and suspicious gatherings.

Given such concerns, it is not surprising that singing was watched closely as a potential means of insurrection; but it was also quite clear that official attitudes toward popular songs had changed dramatically in the preceding year. In 1793 and 1794, police spies' reports had acknowledged performances of counterrevolutionary songs, but they stressed that popular singing was, first and foremost, a powerful expression of allegiance to the Revolution: "Ah! sing, women, and your spouses, your husbands, will fly into combat; that is the true method of enlistment."[32] By the fall of 1795 these positive descriptions had almost entirely disappeared from police reports and government correspondence. There were several reasons for this.

In 1793–94 singing had been intimately associated with sans-culottes' activism. This association alone might have been enough to render singing a suspect activity in the increasingly conservative environment of the Thermidorian reaction, but the debate over the *Marseillaise* and the

Réveil du peuple did still greater damage. The performances of these songs, which had become open provocations to public disorder, suggested that singing was associated with political activism of all stripes—activism that the government increasingly understood as opposition. By the end of 1795, the radical and popular associations of singing were matched by associations at the other end of the political spectrum to such a degree that the Executive Director, Reubell, could say of the Vendémiaire insurrection, "songs were one of the conspirators' principal means . . . to corrupt public spirit."[33]

So it was that the government balanced two seemingly contradictory goals. Even as it encouraged the formation of a professional corps of musicians to provide music for festivals, it continued to police street singing on the assumption that songs were the tools of factions who intended to corrupt public opinion and undermine the Republic. "It seems, citizens," wrote the minister of interior, "that the enemies of the public good, who agitate in every possible way to provoke counterrevolutionary movements, include songs and streetsingers among their guilty methods; by this means, they openly proclaim the monarchy or they prepare public opinion for the corruption of its principles."[34] And, in truth, one did not need to scratch the surface very hard to discover that the two policies were compatible, for they were based on the same assumption: songs were powerful political instruments that were safe only in the hands of the chosen few.

Factions had always been considered dangerous to the Revolution, but the police, with the memory of recent insurrections fresh in their minds, did not confine themselves to reporting on the "agents" of factionalism; they also observed their audiences. Take, for example, the royalist singer who appeared at the rues de Clery and de Poissonière on Sunday mornings to catch those who visited a chapel nearby: "after each verse, this man stops and quite cleverly tells little stories that mock the government and the legislative corps; if a few patriots show their indignation, they are pushed from the audience . . . in a single morning [the singer] sold more than two hundred songbooks at ten francs apiece; finally, his audience is so large that it obstructs the public passageway."[35] The following month, the police and the Directory became concerned with manifestations by the Left, and the minister of police urged his subordinates to arrest the singers of a song that was "criminally anarchic" and of which he believed some 40,000 copies had been made. Only two days later, he warned the police of still more incendiary material: this time, a poster containing the Babouvist song, *Chanson nouvelle à l'usage des faubourgs* (New song for the suburbs).[36]

But the "factions" with which the police were so concerned were just that: factions. The larger populace complained of food prices, occasionally remembered the Old Regime with fondness, or believed that the Directors were corrupt, but it was not inclined to take political action to redress its grievances. The suppression of the Prairial uprising had squashed the popular movement, and the government's relatively casual response to the Vendémiaire insurrection suggested that even they did not believe royalists to be a serious threat.[37] Even police spies, among the most paranoid of government officials, sometimes admitted the truth of this: "Opinions among the groups offer nothing worth reporting or following up; sometimes there are curses against certain deputies and against the government, which must, they say, be overturned; a few minutes later, it is no longer the same: people hope only for bread and say that if they have enough, they will be happy."[38]

Political and cultural activism alike was becoming marginalized, and the government's object seemed to be to drive it from the public arena altogether. To this end, the Directory passed several laws in 1795 and 1796 that had the ostensible purpose of preserving good order, but which also contributed to the dramatic reshaping of popular singing practices. The earliest such law was the one with which this chapter began: the Frimaire decree concerning the regulation of Parisian theaters.

At first glance, the Frimaire legislation (passed in November 1795) seems intended only to regulate the daily business of the theaters—its first five articles deal with such details as the conditions of ticket sales and hours of performances—but the subsequent articles have much broader ramifications. Article six warns that all artists in every theater must comport themselves with the respect owed to an assembly of patriots: "Every artist whose actions trouble public tranquillity . . . will be punished with a minimum of 24 hours and a maximum of three days in prison." Article seven, as we have already seen, establishes what songs may and may not legally be played in the theaters: "No tune, song, or aria which is not already part of the play being performed will be played or sung." Finally, article eight orders all patrons to behave properly in the seats, corridors, and foyers. Those who fail to do so will be asked to leave; any persons refusing to leave will be arrested by the armed force that, henceforth, is to be stationed regularly in all theaters.[39]

Clearly, the specific objective of the legislation was to put an end to the disorder regularly excited by performances of the *Marseillaise* and the *Réveil du peuple*, but it had more long-range consequences as well. In the future, the government alone would be permitted to determine when and if additional songs would be performed in the theaters, as it did in January 1796 when it commanded performances of the *Marseillaise* and a few other republican songs, only to cancel them in June. Not only had editorializing against the government been legally banished from theaters, so had all spontaneous demonstrations of enthusiasm as well. Henceforth, couplets added to a vaudeville to announce a military victory, applause or singing to celebrate a recent event, even a spontaneous chorus of *Ça ira* or the *Marseillaise* would be illegal. The Directory alone would determine the form and locale of popular expressions of patriotism.

The decree was, of course, only partially successful. The disputes over the *Marseillaise* did not immediately cease, and even when almost all spontaneous singing had been silenced, patriots and royalists alike continued to prolong applause for especially pointed bits of song or dialogue. The police ignored much of this activity and used the Frimaire decree as a weapon against theaters that attracted royalists who were repeatedly and excessively disruptive. But the decree was a double-edged sword, because those most likely to obey it were those most loyal to the government. Thus, when news of the capitulation of Mantua to Bonaparte's troops reached Paris, "an intermission was nicely filled for the spectators by the announcement of a new victory." But rather than respond to that announcement with a hearty chorus of songs, as they most certainly would have done in 1793, the audience could only express approval with applause which was "quite lengthy."[40]

Having established the boundaries of good behavior in the theaters, the government did the same in the streets. In June 1796 the central bureau of the police, observing that public passageways and the circulation of traffic were being obstructed by independent entertainers, decreed that "tumblers, singers, jugglers, and those who show curiosities and foreign animals, may not stop in the streets and squares, nor on the bridges and quays of this city."[41] The decree closed with a list of thirty locales that would be open only to those singers and acrobats who had been issued police permits and assigned places in which to perform. The permits, not easy to come by, were issued only to holders of "a certificate of good conduct delivered to them by the Commission of police of the division in which they live, and stamped by the Municipal Administration of the Arrondissement"; nor were the places easily held, because a performer was forbidden to appear anywhere regularly and required instead to divide his or her time between several different sites.

Under the guise of freeing local roads and passageways, the police had given themselves a powerful means of supervising the most irregular of professions. In distributing locales, they controlled the kinds of neighborhoods in which a singer could appear and were thus able to prevent radical singers from finding sympathetic audiences. Forbidding regular appearances undermined potentially seditious gatherings of like-minded individuals around a singer whose political opinions corresponded to their own, like those that had taken place around a royalist singer at the rue de Clery. Finally, by requiring that all singers hold a permit from the central bureau, as well as a certificate of good conduct from the police of their own arrondissement, the police could scrutinize the lives of streetsingers and silence those whose opinions or conduct suggested disagreement with the current political order.

To say that the police provided themselves with a sweeping ordinance for the supervision and regulation of streetsingers is not, of course, to say that they were wholly successful. Streetsingers had been ducking police regulation for centuries, and they would continue to do so. But the legislation was significant for two reasons. In the first place, its phrasing lacked any suggestion of a particular political agenda, so it enabled the authorities to strike in all directions at once, suggesting that the Directory was less concerned with Jacobinism or royalism *per se* than with the simple repression of disorder and dissent. Secondly, this was a novel effort to control street singing that was far more extensive than censorship, because police were concerned not simply with the specific content of the songs being sung or sold but with the singer's overall social and political conduct.

Just as the Directory limited popular singing practices directly by means of laws that regulated public behavior in the streets and in theaters, it limited them indirectly by eliminating radicals on the Left and the Right in 1796 and 1797. Singing was a sign of the continuing political engagement of many of these radicals, who quite self-consciously used songs to circulate their message. But the Directory set about restraining, silencing, or expelling its critics with the passage of a new law in Germinal year IV (April 1796).

ARTICLE I: Considered guilty of a crime against the internal security of the Republic and against the individual safety of citizens, and to be punished by the death penalty . . . all those who by means of speech or printed writings, whether distributed or posted, urge the dissolution of the national representation or the Executive Directory, or the murder of all or any members who constitute it, or the re-establishment of the monarchy or the constitution of 1793 or the constitution of 1791, or of any government other than that established by the Constitution of the year III.[42]

Nor was this law confined strictly to the content of political expression: "Any assembly in which provocations of the sort described in the first article are made, becomes a *seditious mob*."

The Germinal legislation allowed Directors and police free rein in determining the forms and boundaries of the seditious. Under its terms, sedition included more than planning or executing an insurrection; an editorial criticizing directorial policy could be seditious, as could a simple gathering of Jacobins or royalists in a Paris garden. But however broad the language and later uses of this legislation, it was initially passed as a means of silencing and prosecuting a single group, the Babouvists, who had been disseminating insurrectionary posters, newspapers, and songs throughout Paris for weeks.

The Babouvists have been described as early communists and, more realistically, as forerunners of the nineteenth-century utopian socialists, but they play a more idiosyncratic role here. The Babouvists were the last activists on the Left who tried to resurrect the popular movement and force the Revolution back onto a more radical path. In their efforts to do so, and in their defense of these efforts during their trial; they made free use of songs, quite straightforwardly as propaganda and, more subtly, by playing upon republican associations to suggest the nature of their opposition and by manipulating Old Regime associations to deny the activist implications of their political ideology. Their trial and its outcome encapsulated the changing nature of revolutionary song culture as activism became increasingly marginalized.

The Conspiracy of Equals, as the Babouvists called themselves, was born early in 1796 after the Directory suppressed the democratic Pantheon Club. Gracchus Babeuf, a journalist from Picardy and the nominal leader of the group, had spent almost the entirety of the Revolution in Paris. Imprisoned during the Terror, he at first celebrated Robespierre's fall as the beginning of a popular victory, but soon came to see that the reaction of the sectional assemblies was directed against sans-culottes and Jacobins alike. The famine of 1794–95, for which the Convention's freeing of the grain trade was partially responsible, completed his radicalization and confirmed his disillusionment with the reaction. By the time that the conspiracy was formed the following year, Babeuf had already been arrested and imprisoned by the Thermidorian Convention for attempting to provoke rebellion.

Babeuf himself had not been a member of the Pantheon Club, he only propagandized on its behalf through his newspaper, the *Tribun du peuple*; but he was joined by other activists who had belonged to the club and who were radicalized by its suppression. These men included the

Italian revolutionary Filippo Buonarotti; a former soldier, Charles Germain; the poet Sylvain Maréchal; and the Jacobin and one-time public accuser of Arras, Augustin Darthé. This group constituted themselves into a "secret executive," which took as its program incitement to insurrection, the circulation of a message of radical social equality among Parisians, the restoration of confidence to the poor, and the winning of converts. To accomplish their project, the Babouvists worked to establish a network of agents within the military, among the ranks of the Paris police, and in the neighborhoods of the city.[43]

The Equals had a keen sense of the value of gathering information and disseminating propaganda, and they used every means at their disposal. In addition to Babeuf's critiques of the government, which appeared regularly in the *Tribun du peuple*, and the insurrectionary posters plastered on the walls of Paris and in several provincial towns, the "secret executive" instructed its local agents on the means to prepare an insurrection. In its first directive, it urged agents to organize patriotic meetings and keep notes on the tone of popular opinion, which they hoped to shape by distributing popular newspapers.[44] Soon afterward, the executive issued a second list of instructions which suggested that agents search for local depots of food and munitions, organize teams to paste up clandestine posters containing "free writings," and create companies of activists to visit popular gathering spots and "speak always in the sense of the most recent issues of the popular newspapers, which is to say, neither too high nor too low."[45]

Given such a lively sense of the need for good propaganda in common language, it is hardly surprising that the Equals relied upon songs as well. It was most likely Sylvain Maréchal, the poet in their midst, who produced the best-known of the Babouvist songs, the *Chanson nouvelle à l'usage des faubourgs* (New song for the suburbs). The song spoke directly to the experience of the Parisian poor at the end of two murderous winters.

Air: C'est ce qui me désole

Mourant de faim, mourant de froid	Dying of hunger, dying of cold
Peuple dépouillé de tout droit	People stripped of every right
Tout bas, tu te désole.	You smother your dejection.
Cependant le riche effronté	Meanwhile, the impudent rich
Qu'epargna jadis ta bonté	Whom your bounty once spared
Tout haut il se console.	Make public their satisfaction.
Gorgés d'or, des hommes nouveaux	Engorged with gold, these new men

Sans peine, ni sans travaux	Without trouble or work
S'emparant de la ruche,	Seize hold of the hive,
Et toi, peuple laborieux	And you, laboring people
Mange et digère si tu peux	Suck in your stomachs
Du fer comme l'autruche.[46]	And take it as you can.

More hopeful were the lyrics of the *Nouvelle carmagnole* which, matching the cheerfulness and vigor of the tune, reminded audiences of the year II and popular political activism:

Sans-culottes, rassurez-vous	Sans-culottes be reassured
La victoire sera pour nous.	Victory will be ours.
Oui, certes, ça ira	Yes, certainly, things will work out
Toujours l'on chantera;	Forever we'll sing;
Chantons la carmagnole,	Sing the carmagnole,
Vive le son,	Long live the sound,
Vive le son;	Long live the sound;
Dansons la carmagnole,	Danse the carmagnole,
Vive le son,	Long live the sound,
du canon![47]	of the cannon!

The Equals bring to mind the practices of the year II in their use of songs to circulate information, stimulate political activism, and reinforce group solidarity—a kind of singing that would become one of the distinctive, and contested, points of their trial.

The Directors hesitated to respond to the Babouvists for some time because the moderates among them feared that repression would only reinforce the royalism that had been nourished by the Thermidorian reaction. By April 1796, however, matters passed beyond any possibility of reconciliation: the Babouvists' refusal to collaborate with the government ruined the moderates' credibility, and the proponents of force gained the upper hand. On the 14th, the Executive Directory published an attack upon any and all individuals who menaced property or threatened to bring a return to anarchy. Two days later, the legislature approved the law of 27 Germinal and made all attacks on the Constitution of 1795 punishable by death. The Babouvists responded with a poster entitled "Doit-on obéissance à la Constitution de 1795?" (Do we owe obedience to the Constitution of 1795?).[48]

Babeuf and the other members of the "secret executive" were arrested almost a month later, and all of their papers were seized. The Directory used the arrest of the Equals as an excuse for a sweeping suppression of democrats throughout the country. To reinforce the impression that an enormous conspiracy had been uncovered, warrants were issued against some two hundred people in Paris alone.[49] After a brief blaze of publicity, the Equals spent almost ten months in prison waiting to be tried. Sixty accused Babouvists were finally brought to trial before a high court in the provincial town of Vendôme in February 1797. The trial was scheduled for a high court because one of the accused, Drouet, was a member of the legislature and his case legally required such procedure. However, after Drouet escaped, or was allowed to escape, the Directory did nothing to change the venue, probably preferring to have the trial conducted by a court whose verdict could not be appealed.[50]

Before their trial, the Babouvists decided that in order to save the lives of as many defendants as possible, they would present themselves as political theorists and critics rather than as actual conspirators against the regime.[51] Such a decision did not, however, prevent them from using the trial as a forum in which to attack the legality of police and court procedures, and from which to criticize the Directory for its betrayal of the Republic. On the very first day, Babeuf himself took the offensive when asked his name by the presiding judge: "Citizen, you question me about my name . . . under the apparent pretense that the tribunal is presently within the terms and circumstances established by article 341 of the legal code. . . . Apart from all other motives for refusing to respond, I will, for the moment, restrict myself to simply pointing out that this matter is not of the proper legality to be brought before a jury for judgment."[52]

The defendants seized every opportunity to put the prosecution on trial. They pointed out that it was relying on police spies for much of its evidence; they charged that some of the witnesses had been émigrés until quite recently and, consequently, should have been disqualified; and they repeatedly demanded the right to cross-examine the witnesses against them.[53] When not taking issue with the functioning of the court, they advertised their criticism of the Directory, which they believed was committed to corrupting revolutionary principles and effacing republican symbols.[54] Then, ten days into the trial, the defendants began to sing.

On 1 March, after the judge had refused to hear the defendant Blondeau's complaint that at least one of his accusers was an émigré, the defendants left the courtroom singing the *Marseillaise*.[55] Five days later Sophie Lapierre, a singer from the café Bains Chinois and a former militant from the Society of Republican Revolutionary Women, led the group in a chorus of a hymn to liberty that dated from the year II; again, on the following evening, the group repeated the song's refrain, "Chantons, chantons avec courage" (Let us sing, sing courageously).[56] A few days later, Madame Lapierre and her chorus of defendants changed songs and sang *Goujon's Lament* for several days, in celebration of the deputy executed in 1795 for his association with the Germinal insurrection.[57] Five days more and the defendants began to sing *Veillons au salut de l'Empire,* which they sang for several days before returning to the *Marseillaise.*[58]

The confrontational attitude of the defendants and the activist stance of their singing rang powerfully through even the ostensibly neutral language of the officially approved transcripts. On 25 March, for example, the prosecution brought in the witness Meunier, whom they expected to give testimony against the Babouvists. When the judge asked his name, Meunier responded with a verse from *Goujon's Lament,* "Raise yourselves, illustrious victims." When the judge admonished, "It is forbidden to sing; you did not come here to sing," Meunier replied, "You should love this song as I do; it is patriotic: it is for the friends of liberty and saintly equality." Having finally gotten name and status from Meunier, the judge asked him what knowledge he had of the issues in question. The witness answered, "I will tell you nothing but the truth. Sworn citizens, what do you ask of me? What do you want from me? Is it to pay homage to humiliated virtues, to oppressed innocence, to the courage of the people's friends? I cherish them all, and I despise their oppressors. My youth is frank and incapable of deception. May my tongue dry up in my mouth and cleave to its roof before I would accuse the friends of their cause, of my own, which is that of all French republican people." The judge never received the testimony he sought, and the young man was finally taken from the courtroom, singing yet another song "that could not be heard."[59] This bit of impudence would cost Meunier a trial of his own and a sentence of twenty years in irons.[60]

Even as the judge demanded silence in his courtroom, it was clear that both sides understood that the singing was not simply disruptive; it was a sign of political activism and opposition. This meaning was most clear when Meunier sang rather than testified against the Babouvists, but the other episodes of singing were of a piece with the continuing oppositional strategies of the defendants. The songs that the Babouvists chose to sing underscored the critical nature of their singing. Rather than sing their own songs—the *Chanson nouvelle* or any of the others found among Babeuf's and Charles Germain's papers—they sang songs that had broader associations and expressed their political beliefs and affiliations.[61] They sang songs that evoked popular radicalism and the

democratic principles of the Republic: *Goujon's lament* recalled the Germinal insurrection, while *Veillons au salut de l'Empire* and the *Marseillaise*
were so closely associated with the Republic's victories that even the Directory at its most reactionary could not attempt to silence them; a
hymn to liberty was self-explanatory. All of these songs implied the critique of current circumstances that Buonarotti made explicit before the
court. After Vendémiaire, he said, "the order subverting popular sovereignty was established; the proxies, traitors to the nation, unfaithful to
all parties, kept power; and those who had defended them for the
preservation of the Republic, saw the Republic lost, and themselves disarmed, reviled and proscribed."[62]

The activism of Babouvist singing was not only visible in courtroom
performances; its meaning was debated by parties to the trial as well. At
the trial's opening, Veillart, a high court official, explained the case
against the Equals. He accused them of wanting to "disorganize all,
rouse all, maintain popular agitation, and so arrange everything for a
general insurrection." And by what means? By means of newspapers,
posters, rumors, and local agents who had been instructed to find out
who was friendly, who was hostile, and who was armed. Veillart continued, "It might seem that this would be the place to begin by analyzing
this heap of newspapers, writings, pamphlets, posters, and songs . . .
which incited disobedience of the law, abolition of the constitution, the
massacre of constituted authorities. But recall that the issue here is not
one of the crime of the writings themselves. We want only to treat these
writings as means employed to execute a project of insurrection, which
was the first goal of the conspiracy under consideration."[63]

The Directory was undeniably less authoritarian than the Convention
had been during the Terror: the crime against the state lay not in the
simple act of penning an attack upon it but in advertising that attack.
Under the conditions of the law of 27 Germinal, once one advertised a
criticism—taught the *Chanson nouvelle* to a few friends and acquain-
tances, for example—one became a traitor. Such a deed was a means to
rouse the populace, involve it politically, and urge it to take action. What
had been vital to the Revolution at its opening had become anathema to
the Directory, which sought to suppress activism, restore public calm,
and keep political and cultural initiative for itself. It was for this reason
that singing had become associated with opposition: if one did not sing
on behalf of the government, through the Conservatory, then one could
only sing against it. Song culture had come full circle, from the oppositional singing of the Old Regime to oppositional singing under the Directory.

It was this notion of singing as a call to action that Charles Germain tried rather disingenuously to undermine when he answered the testimony of Grisel, the state's key witness. Grisel described a meal he had taken with the Babouvists at the café Bains Chinois, where they discussed insurrection and sang.[64] Three days later, Germain replied, "The Bains Chinois is a café open to all comers, but one which patriots are most likely to frequent . . . It is not surprising that on the last day of each *décade* patriots gather there in greater numbers. Regardless of austerity or the harshness of the season, the worker celebrates a festival every ten days: his songs and his plain drunkenness are not dangerous. 'What do the people do?' the crafty Mazarin asked when demanding a new tax— 'They sing, monseigneur' [was the reply] 'They sing: well good! They'll pay.' "[65]

Once again, as though the Revolution were turning back on itself, this old tale about political activism and singing had been resurrected. In the early years, radicals used it against the popular classes to claim that their singing was a substitute for true political activity, and subsequent experience had given the lie to that belief. Obviously Charles Germain was making the defense that the Equals had agreed upon, that they had only criticized the government, not actively tried to topple it, but he was speaking during an important moment of transition. The singing of most Parisians was, in fact, no longer either an encouragement to political activism or an expression of it. But this was not true of the Babouvists, and their use of songs and singing proved that. They were on trial because they were activists, and their singing was an integral element of that activism. The experience of the Revolution, to which their singing alluded, and the experience of the trial itself gave the lie to Germain's hyperbole.

In the end, the high court punished only those who were most directly responsible for the opposition to the government: Babeuf and Augustin Darthé, a Jacobin, were sentenced to death; Buonarotti, Germain, Blondeau, and three others were sentenced to deportation. The remaining thirty-nine defendants, the *chanteuse* Sophie Lapierre among them, were acquitted. The Babouvists were not, of course, convicted because they had written songs, nor because they had sung a great many of them, even in the courtroom; they were convicted because of their opposition to the government and their faith in the capacity of popular politics to overcome that government. It was the association between popular politics and songs that made the songs dangerous, and if the government could succeed in dissociating the two, it would rest more easily.

STRIKING AGAINST THE RIGHT

With the arrest of the Babouvists and the sweeping away of Jacobin authorities that accompanied it, the threat that the Directory saw to its left was eradicated, but there remained a powerful coalition of royalists to the right.[66] Remaining free in public, and occupying administrative positions vacated by Jacobins, the royalists' position in public opinion was strengthened by the Babouvists' attempted insurrection at the camp de Grenelle and by their subsequent trial. Even before the trial began, a police spy wrote that "the government is torn to pieces everywhere, and more than ever one sees the royalist show himself boldly confident and without any difficulties in the cafés of the Palais Egalité. They seek every means to divert republican opinion . . . The most royalist songs are even sung publicly."[67]

The royalist press was reasserting itself as well. The *Rapsodies du jour*, established in Prairial year IV (May–June 1796), took up the mantle of the pre-Republican satires against the Revolution and used the dependable method of setting the government's business to music.

On a deux fois par semaine	There will be, twice each week,
Les arrêtés, les décrets,	Orders, decrees,
Une nouvelle certaine	News that is sure
Des rapports menteurs ou vrais;	Reports, lying or true;
Pour les retenir sans peine,	To remember them easily,
D'après l'esprit du Français,	As is the French way,
On les arrange en couplets.[68]	They will be put in verse.

Like the earlier newspapers, the *Rapsodies du jour* served as a notice board for complaints and mockery: the editors printed letters from readers, ridiculed the government's business, and pretended that the epithet "royalist" was mere calumny circulated by those who were offended by the publishers' desire to "speak the truth" about the deputies of the Directory.[69] The *Courrier républicain* chimed in as well, printing songs that matched the counterrevolutionary messages of its scurrilous editorials and reportage:

Français, réunissez vos voix	French people, unite your voices
Pour implorer la providence;	To beg providence;
Bientôt, pour gouverner la France,	Soon, to govern France,
Au sort on va tirer les Rois.	By lottery they'll choose kings.
Protège-nous bonté divine	Protect us divine munificence
Quel bonheur, s'il sortait un quine![70]	What bliss, if they draw five at once!

The law that restricted street singing aided the police in their efforts to clear the streets of the government's critics, but that same law embarrassed the police when they failed to catch all of its critics. A customer at the café Procope was overheard saying that "all the royalists know how to make counterrevolutions with songs; the minister of police even allowed someone to appear at the place du Louvre who did more ill by himself than all the others together, and whose songs were applauded by the royalists."[71]

One of these noisy and noticeable royalists was Louis-Ange Pitou, who had taken to the streets as a singer in 1796. Pitou was a thorn in the side of the Paris police: appearing regularly near the Eglise Saint-Germain l'Auxerrois, he drew a faithful crowd which blocked public passageways and edged out hostile audience members or suspected police agents. For these reasons alone, Pitou's career would be worth considering as exemplifying the difficulties and successes of the enforced supervision of street singing. But he was not just a singer of verses critical of the Directory; he waged a long battle with the police, which came to a close with his deportation following the coup of 18 Fructidor year V (4 September 1797) and the ensuing attack upon royalists. As a "Fructidor deportee," Pitou may stand as a representative of the last activist voices to be driven from the public arena of the Revolution.

Ange Pitou was raised and educated in the Aube by an aunt who insisted that he follow a career in the church. Chafing under his aunt's dictatorial tendencies, and too preoccupied by the charms of both *philosophes* and girls to seriously consider becoming a priest, Pitou ran away to Paris in October of 1789. When he arrived in Paris, however, his first sight was of an angry crowd carrying the head of a baker they had just hanged on suspicion of grain hoarding.[72] The experience soured Pitou on the Revolution, and his disillusion was reinforced as he wandered Paris, admiring the Tuileries and the Louvre, taking their beauty as a sure sign of the magnificence of the French royalty.

Having abandoned his enlightened ideas and become an ardent royalist in a single day, Pitou vigorously devoted himself to the cause for the remainder of the Revolution. During his first years in Paris, he divided his time between working as a correspondent for the monarchist *Journal de la cour et de la ville* and writing pamphlets on behalf of the queen, to whom he had been introduced and who paid for his services. The revolution of 10 August did little to dampen his ardor for the royal family, and he continued to serve their cause for another year, corresponding for the *Journal historique et politique* and helping to run guns to the Vendée until he was arrested and imprisoned.[73]

Ironically, considering the scope of his counterrevolutionary activities, Pitou was arrested for having sung a complaint against the Jacobins. At a small private dinner, he had entertained guests by singing an attack set to the popular theatrical tune, *Réveil d'Epiménide*:

Je voudrais bien voir le repaire	I would certainly like to see the lair
Où tous ces brigands font des lois;	Where all these crooks make the laws;
Ils occupent le sanctuaire	They inhabit the sanctuary
Et de nos dieux et de nos rois.	Of our gods and of our kings.
Aujourd'hui tout change de place,	Today everything changes place,
Au gré du sort tout est soumis,	To the whims of fate all is subject,
Et je ne fais plus la grimace	And I no longer grimace
De voir l'enfer en paradis.[74]	To see hell in paradise.

He was denounced by one of the guests, an Austrian deserter named Hirchtmann, and spent several months in prison before appearing before the revolutionary tribunal. Ever the clever one, or so he would have us believe, Pitou evaded the guillotine by claiming that the foreigner Hirchtmann had been duped by his difficulties with a new language and then by singing the *Réveil d'Epiménide*, this time with its true lyrics. Hirchtmann, recognizing the tune, volunteered that this was the song he had heard. Pitou was released, only to demand, and receive, an indemnity from the government for the months that he had spent in prison.[75]

Having spent the first half of the Revolution as a journalist, Ange Pitou backed into the singer's career after Robespierre's fall. He achieved his first success as a songwriter late in the year II, when he jumped on the bandwagon set in motion by Mehée de la Touche and published a nasty little song about "Robespierre's tail."[76] But the step from song writing to street singing was not necessarily a natural one, particularly for a man like Pitou who pursued the reasonably respectable occupation of a journalist: like many of his colleagues, he saw street singing as lowly and irregular work.[77]

By the spring of 1795, however, Pitou had found that inflation and shortages were so severe that he could barely live on what he earned writing for the *Annales patriotiques et litteraires*. "Singing cheers the soul, I told myself . . . : why should I be more embarrassed to sell my songs than a bookseller who sells a volume he did not make? . . . But don't proprieties and prejudices oppose this resolution which, however wise in itself, is at odds with the opinion that others ought to hold of you? However, my first duty is to earn a living by the sweat of my brow. And I cannot live on two ounces of bread."[78] His first effort, singing his own couplets against grain hoarding, was so successful that he bought bread enough to feed himself and the journalists with whom he shared a loge at the Assembly—and who shared his bread despite their caustic remarks about his new means of employment.[79] In a short time, Pitou gave up on the *Annales patriotiques* altogether and began to live on his earnings as a singer alone.

Ange Pitou was not long in attracting the attention of the police. He was arrested several times for singing and for a pamphlet he wrote concerning the events of Vendémiaire,[80] and his case represents a fine example of the difficulty of maintaining surveillance on street singers. In January 1797, for example, a police spy reported that he had several times seen Pitou singing near the old place Saint-Germain l'Auxerrois. Pitou's songs, "are composed with wit and delicacy, he sings them in a way that does not always benefit the Republic and the government; he places words between the verses that could well turn public sentiment against the republican regime . . . , at least, I believe that this is the case, but I might be mistaken . . . it would be helpful to have him closely surveyed by others, who might better expand upon his intentions."[81]

This report was followed by another several days later, which complained of denunciations against this singer who sold songs that "tend to make fun of the government." When the administrator of the police finally acquired a copy of the songbook, he claimed that, "none [of these songs] appeared to us to require surveillance." This did not, however, put the matter to rest because the administrator added that "[some] commissioners of police and some observers heard the ideas of this singer which, judging from their report, are reprehensible."[82] Pitou was brought in for questioning shortly afterward and informed that if he sang or spoke anything that was not printed in his songbook, his permission would be revoked and he would be brought before the tribunal. He promised to be more careful in the future.

Pitou did not keep his word; he was neither more careful nor more discreet in his criticism. The following summer, a police spy who noticed the sizable crowd that Pitou's singing had drawn, asked to see his permission. When the singer could provide only a merchant's patent he was taken to the police commissioner, who asked why he broke the law by appearing without permission. Pitou explained that the members of the central bureau had arrested and then freed him, only to withdraw his permission "against all right"; he concluded by noting that "they were rogues."[83] These games of cat and mouse, arrest and release, continued through the next year. Having retracted his permission, the police harried Pitou for months without charging him with graver crimes. Then in the fall of 1797, Pitou was caught in the purge of royalists that followed the coup of 18 Fructidor.

As we have already seen, the arrest and trial of the Babouvists had exactly the effect the moderates feared by strengthening the position of the royalists publicly and politically. Royalist sentiment and symbols were displayed openly, with little decisive response from the government. The impact of this resurgence became most clear in the results of the Germinal elections, held to replace one-third of the legislature's deputies. The departments returned a rightist majority, and for several months, the government inclined sharply toward reaction: émigrés and refractory priests began to return in significant numbers as the laws against their participation in public life were suppressed.

The republicans and moderates who remained in the government hesitated temporarily and then began to negotiate with the army. On the night before 18 Fructidor, troops were brought into Paris and, the following morning, it was announced that all proponents of monarchism or of the Constitution of 1793 would be summarily shot. Two directors, 42 legislative deputies, and 11 deputies of the Council of the Ancients were expelled from the government and condemned to deportation; 42 opposition newspapers were suppressed and their editors condemned to deportation as well; and the election results of 49 departments were declared invalid. Finally, émigrés were given two weeks to leave France, and refractory priests were once more declared outside of the law.[84]

It was in this environment that Ange Pitou was arrested for the last time. As he explained most disingenuously, almost a decade later: "A . . . vaudeville . . . was one of the principal causes of my deportation. Since I often happened to put my hand in my pocket, they pretended that I made indecent and counterrevolutionary gestures, a crime foreseen by the law of 27 Germinal and carrying the death penalty."[85] The song in question began:

Républicains, aristocrates,	Republicans, aristocrats,
Terroristes, buveurs de sang,	Terrorists, blood suckers,
Vous serez parfaits démocrates	You will be perfect democrats
Si vous nous comptez votre argent.	If you hand over your money to us.
Et comme la crise est urgent,	And since the crisis is urgent,
Il faut vous conformer au temps,	You must keep up with the times,
Et prendre tous une patente	And all take a license
Pour devenir honnêtes gens.	To become honest folk.

Having sided with those who benefited from the arrest and trial of the Babouvists, Pitou was finally brought down by the same law that had been the cause of their undoing. The director of the jury before which he was tried declared that "the accused Pitou has, for several years, involved himself in singing and distributing songs in public squares, most of which he has composed and which contain diatribes against the Republic and the current government. . . . In all the squares and locales where he appears, he is quickly surrounded by a large circle of auditors without end, who, receptive to enthusiasm and to what the singer insinuates with his gestures, soon drowns his voice with applause."[86] Pitou was found guilty of all charges and deported to Guyana, where he remained for the next four years.

It is ironic that popular song culture was subjected to new constraints and restrictions at the very moment that other cultural forms were experiencing renewed freedom and dynamism. But this was in part a question of definition; neither the police nor legislators treated popular songs as a cultural form deserving of the consideration shown, in varying degrees, to newspapers, theater, or painting. Having taken charge of patriotic hymns, the government regarded unofficial song culture as a series of incitements to political activism which had to be silenced, or as cheap entertainment which was beneath its notice.

As had been the case in 1792–93, political singing and song writing fell prey to larger political battles because it was associated with opposition. The Thermidorian Convention and the Directory were, above all, concerned to impose order and eliminate radicals; it was of little import to them if, in so doing, they circumscribed popular singing. Having done their best to contribute to the preservation and improvement of music deemed aesthetically or patriotically worthy, they had little interest in the rest. What made these years distinct from the period of 1792–93 was the absence of a positive tradition of revolutionary singing to counterbalance the one that was being silenced. While government and police struck left and right, the civil populace withdrew from revolutionary singing practices. Turning to art songs, drinking songs, and war songs, they were laying the foundations of the song culture of the nineteenth century.

Chapter Seven

✦

Songs Silenced and Changed
(from Ventôse Year IV into
the Nineteenth Century)

✦ AS THE GOVERNMENT centralized song production and encouraged
professionalization, and as the police harried, chased, and prosecuted
radicals and critics, Parisians retreated from public and revolutionary activism. The battles that they fought in 1795 and 1796 over performances
of the *Hymne des Marseillais* and the *Réveil du peuple* were the last gasps of
a mobilized populace. When that movement subsided, civil peace became the order of the day. Like the early years of the Revolution, when
new practices of singing and song writing evolved slowly from Old
Regime customs, so now the directorial period witnessed the emergence
of cultural practices that would persist beyond Brumaire and well into
the Empire.

These final years of the Revolution are the ones of which we know
least; historians of the Revolution or of nineteenth-century republicanism pay scant attention to the Directory. This is due, in part, to the fact
that the key elements of revolutionary political culture—language, symbols, festivals—had already been elaborated during the more volatile,
pre-Thermidorian years, and in part because the Directory has traditionally been considered a period of widespread political apathy, a
steady and rather unremarkable decline into the Empire.[1] But such assertions obscure what was important and historically specific about the
directorial period. For although republican language, iconography, and
festivals were already in place, their meanings changed significantly after
1795 as they were deployed and interpreted in an increasingly unique
political context. The political culture of contraction and conservatism
that characterized the Directory did not simply represent the dying out

of what had come earlier; it was also the site of invention of political and cultural practices that would contribute to the emergence of the Empire and to the Revolution's legacy. What was true of the political culture in general was true of song culture in particular. New singing practices emerged after 1795 that were distinctly and sometimes quite self-consciously different from those that preceded. While these new singing practices expressed the conservative mood of the last half of the decade, they would also come to serve as a foundation for new, even activist singing practices that would emerge in the next century.

Certainly the most important development after 1795 was the reemergence of social hierarchy as a significant means of classifying the population. Although French citizens had never ceased belonging to particular social and economic groups, social place had been conflated with political opinion between 1790 and 1795: one was either "revolutionary and third estate," later "sans-culotte," or one was "counterrevolutionary and aristocrat." With the progress of the reaction and the development of directorial society, however, social place and political affiliation were redefined as discreet categories that did not necessarily mirror one another. Social difference, already well defined economically, was given new cultural and political expression, a process in which directorial song culture played an important part.

Under the Directory the cultural practices and representations of common people and of elites diverged sharply. Working people's presence in the shared public spaces of Paris had begun to diminish at the very height of the Terror. Simultaneously retreating and excluded from local and national politics, common people ceased singing publicly in parks and squares and took refuge in bars and cafés around the central markets and in the faubourgs Antoine and Marceau. This political and geographic retreat was matched by gradual exclusion from print culture, as descriptions of plebeian songs and singing practices—in fact, news of any activity common to the working quarters of the city—vanished from printed memoirs and from the pages of the daily papers. At the opposite end of the social scale, revolutionaries and royalists constituted an increasingly homogeneous cultural elite that devoted itself to forming intimate groups for socializing, philosophical speculation, and cultural projects. These were the men and women whose activity dominated directorial culture. They published educational treatises, literature, songbooks, and almanacs, and they received copious and admiring attention from the press. If any single characteristic was common to these two fractions of French society, it was that each was turning in on itself.

Meanwhile, political life was changing too. Others have demonstrated that although the notables of the Directory wanted a liberal Republic, they were as incapable of accepting the emergence of parties as had been the Jacobins of 1792.[2] These men did not simply fear the dominance of the Left or the Right, which they avoided by cynically suppressing the results of one election after another; they also feared the level of political discussion that elections and political parties excited. Both inside and outside the government, a great many men and women were tired or fearful of the presence of politics in daily life, and they hoped for its silencing, or at least its privatization.

This rejection of public activism would affect song culture in several ways. Intensely fearful of divisiveness and debate, citizens turned away from political and politicized singing. This shift was manifest among common people in the form of changed singing practices. Customers in local bars and cafés continued to sing songs with revolutionary lyrics, but strictly for entertainment. The songs that truly engaged them treated the one issue upon which all French men and women were certain to agree: the nation's military efforts abroad. Among elites, song lyrics changed in tandem with singing practices. Private citizens and small singing societies condemned revolutionary songs and set about reviving an idealized "traditional" song culture that they believed had been badly damaged by the "storms of Revolution." Claiming to reject politics, these men and women created a song culture that they hoped would foster a new kind of political order: songs would calm sectarian passions and distract the citizenry from political action, which would become strictly an affair of the polls. In short, Parisian society was characterized throughout by caution and conservatism. When Napoleon Bonaparte seized power in 1799, he would find that his way had been prepared culturally as well as institutionally.

SINGING IN THE FAUBOURGS

When Sebastien Mercier described the festival of 10 Thermidor year IV, he alluded to the social cleavages that were fragmenting Parisian society by describing two distinct groups which celebrated the fall of Robespierre on opposite sides of the Seine. Gathered around the arena at the Champ de Mars were the most glamorous members of Parisian society. Here the wealthiest citizens of the city—moderates, Jacobins, and royalists alike—showed off their best as they jostled for a view of the official games. On the other side of the river, at the Champs

Elysées, "there was another kind of show: . . . here were no more of those women glittering with charms and finery, nor English horses, nor dandies . . . : here was bourgeois simplicity, here were the working people, the people of small incomes, the people *par excellence*." And here, Mercier implied, was the real festival. Situated well away from the government's exclusive arena, and far from high society primping and posing, crowds of common people had spread out picnic dinners and were wiling away the day as they waited for Ruggieri's fireworks to light up the night sky. Amongst such simple citizens might be found the camaraderie and plain virtue that could guarantee the future of France. "The obscurity of the night, the sweetness of the air, the mingling of groups, the popular mood, the sound of dances, the magic of the trees, all combined to favor gentle discussions as it seemed to encourage effusiveness and gaiety."[3]

What is striking about Mercier's description of this "other kind of show" is the absence of any mention of politics: taken out of context, the scene at the Champs Elysées might have been a gathering for almost any sunny holiday of the Old Regime or Empire. In fact, it was most likely the weather and the promise of fireworks, not the commemoration of 9–10 Thermidor, that brought this happy and peaceful crowd to the Champs Elysées; such successful festivity was not the rule under the Directory. Far more common was the mood described in a police report written only six weeks later, following the festival of 1 Vendémiaire year V (22 September 1796): "There was a lot of grumbling against the festival today. Every national celebration provokes the same comments: the government would do better to find the means to pay bondholders rather than undertaking foolish expenses; they ought to put off all of these festivals until we have peace, which they should hasten to conclude."[4] Rather than drawing together a revolutionary citizenry and reinvigorating its common sense of purpose, the Directory's festivals were more likely to provoke expressions of bitterness and censure. The complaint that the government should pay its debts before throwing away money on public celebrations was voiced repeatedly during the last years of the Revolution; with each new festival, new complaints were appended.[5]

Parisians did not just criticize festivals, they avoided them. Whether the government encouraged participation, chastised disaffection, or simply set up public platforms and proceeded with celebration, police and deputies alike complained that the number of spectators was insufficient and their participation disappointing: "some singer shouted *long live the republic* after the songs and no one shouted with him."[6] Although the press tended to blame festival organizers for "insufficient splendor,"[7] popular indifference could not simply be conjured away with more attractive festivals because it was a symptom of the cynicism that was taking hold throughout directorial society. As the Directors, ministers, and police scrutinized Jacobins and royalists, fearfully guarding against activism and party politics, the mass of common citizens drifted ever further from any sincere attachment to the regime.

Certainly the most common complaint of the period was against the dramatic extremes of wealth and poverty that had so visibly come to dominate Parisian life.[8] Such striking inequalities were, in part, the product of years of revolution and foreign war, but the government aggravated them further by creating new conditions for the sale of national lands, by allowing military contractors to amass huge fortunes, and by defaulting on its debt to state bondholders. Meanwhile, Directors and deputies themselves publicly indulged extravagant habits and styles of living.[9] Against such a backdrop, official festivals that appeared inordinately expensive were an added insult.

Extremes of wealth and poverty and the opulent spending of government officials were not the only sources of popular complaint. Even had the economy been sound—and harvests did improve in the later years—the political practices of the Directory inspired growing disdain, as the government annulled the results of legal elections, tampered with electoral lists, and deported political opponents. But rather than inciting activism, as had the conduct of previous revolutionary governments, the malfeasance of the Directory met with little resistance. Some people had simply become too cynical about the nature of the political process, like the workers in the faubourg Antoine who reminded themselves that "we should not get involved in anything . . . because all that we could do is futile," while others feared that activism of any kind could only bring a return to the "anarchy" of the early years of the Revolution.[10]

Common people had lost faith in the Revolution. No longer believing that the government represented them, they disparaged their representatives and stayed away from festivals, which could only mimic civic feeling without exciting it. These same sentiments were also at the root of dramatically changed singing practices. Gone were singers who hounded refractory priests from their churches or who proclaimed their loyalty to the Convention in assembly halls; gone too were crowds that used choruses of the *Marseillaise* and *Réveil du peuple* to represent competing notions of the Republic. Singing still bore traces of earlier political enthusiasm, but it was no longer capable of unifying crowds or inspiring action. By the end of 1796, revolutionary singing was more likely to serve as an occasion for expressions of bitterness, as the cause of skirmishes in the streets of Paris, or as a source of entertainment in the cafés and cabarets of working-class neighborhoods.

Newspapers rarely reported incidents of public singing after the *Marseillaise / Réveil du peuple* debates ended. When they did carry such stories, they used them to illustrate the patriotic myth that republicans continued to vigorously oppose the agents of counterrevolution, albeit in a law-abiding fashion.[11] In truth, apart from the handful of critics who seized upon the anonymity of the street to sing their complaints, those who were most likely to sing in the streets were the same figures who had once done so under the Old Regime: wandering streetsingers who hawked tunes through the city. No longer described in romantically republican terms as pedagogues of revolutionary principles, streetsingers were reinvested with an image that had been theirs before the Revolution. These men and women once again became outsiders who earned an uncertain living and who merited the suspicious surveillance of the police as potential agitators of opposition.

> On the quays and in public squares, they sing in such a way as to suggest the double meanings hidden in the lyrics; these professional singers take great care to add special qualities to their voices which they pretend not to hear.[12]

But the fears of the police in this matter, as in so many others, were out of proportion to the real possibility of danger. Whether revolutionary or royalist, these singers were entertainers trying to make a few sous on their republican hymns or counterrevolutionary satires; their complaints rarely drew more than an admiring laugh or an indifferent shrug, and the most political response that a singer received were the blows of an opponent, not a crowd primed for action.[13]

Away from bridges and public squares, in the working-class faubourgs Antoine and Marcel and around the central markets, were the cafés and cabarets where laboring men and women, soldiers, and prostitutes spent their evenings. These cafés and cabarets were important centers of sociability. Patronized even in the most economically difficult of times, they provided food and drink, entertainment, and warmth when one could no longer afford to heat one's home.[14] These were the settings in which common people sang together, but even when they sang republican and patriotic songs their singing was no longer a sign of revolutionary activism.

Men and women sang in local cafés to amuse themselves and others. The police spies who watched them repeatedly claimed that customers sang "but didn't say anything against anyone," or, that they "spoke of nothing . . . but drinking and eating."[15] Disassociated from revolutionary passion, the act of singing lost its capacity to incite committed action or hostile reaction. Even royalist songs failed to shock or elicit common opposition: when sung in cafés, they aroused little more than friendly concern that the singer not run afoul of the police.[16] And, on the rare occasions when café singers did come into direct opposition, hostilities were attenuated and contests quickly resolved. For example, in the spring of 1799 a few drinkers in a cabaret began to sing the *Réveil du peuple*, and several soldiers responded with the *Marseillaise* "and other hymns dedicated to liberty." Four years earlier, such activity had been capable of stopping theatrical performances, dividing audiences and café crowds, and leading to open violence. Now, "the innkeeper, and other citizens there, came to quiet both parties, telling them, if both of you do not stop this and remain calm, each at his table, then we will have to send for the guard to make peace between you."[17] The irritated response of cabaret host and customers, and their common anger with all parties to the conflict, suggests how mundane such singing had become: no longer a sign of partisanship, oppositional singing was little more than a disturbance of the peace. Even the police, who remained suspicious of anyone who sang counterrevolutionary songs, rarely showed the fervor like that with which they had pursued Ange Pitou.

Beyond political cynicism and simple fatigue, the desire to maintain public order was a potent incentive to refrain from engaged and activist singing. Even before the Fructidor coup, and certainly afterward, common people and government officials alike had begun to place an increasingly high value on "civil peace." With vivid memories of the personal and political violence of past years, many argued that the only means to preserve the Republic was to maintain a moderate, almost passive attitude that shunned all political passion or "factionalism." Even the police spies who wandered Paris acknowledged this change. "Most people agree in saying that no matter what happens, they will remain peacefully at home, because they know from experience that the parties that they served only maintained and restored themselves the better to destroy the people afterwards, and each said that he was tired of revolutionary movements."[18] And when disputes did arise, neither café owners nor regulars drew distinctions between the political opinions being expressed. All disturbances of the peace were the same: arguments had to be silenced before they could spread.

That revolutionary singing had become a simple act of entertainment could be no clearer than in the circumstances of a dispute that arose in 1797 between a café owner named Arnoud and two of his customers, Arbulot and Randon. Scarcely two weeks after the Director's coup of Fructidor year V, Arbulot and Randon left work together and stopped in at Arnoud's for a beer. "There, they felt the effects of the happy day of 18 Fructidor. Citizen Arbulot . . . , to better express his joy, began to sing the republican song *Chantons, chantons avec courage* (Let us sing, sing courageously)." Arnoud, known for verbally abusing his customers, told the men to stop singing and pay up. The two men did pay, but in the process they ordered another beer and, "not believing that the noisy demonstration of their happiness and patriotic songs could trouble public order . . . they continued with their singing." Arnoud responded by sending for the guard, who arrested Arbulot and Randon and held them overnight. The affair did not end there, however, because at the guard station the commander "took it into his head to forbid and prohibit the citizens to continue the songs that their patriotism inspired them to sing during their detention." At the same time Arbulot and Randon "were doubly encouraged by the applause of the citizens composing the guard, who expressed joy and a lively desire to hear and listen to the beloved tunes."[19]

The official account of this event was signed by Arbulot and Randon. In spite of the men's efforts to suggest the contrary, *Chantons, chantons avec courage* more closely resembled a drinking song sung to annoy a difficult barkeeper and amuse bored militia than a republican hymn inspired by fervent patriotism. And once *Chantons, chantons avec courage* was sung as a drinking song, its performance ceased to be a sign of commitment to the Revolution and became instead a civil offense. The fact that such singing was treated as essentially apolitical is underscored by the questionable reputation of the café owner Arnoud. Only a month earlier, Arnoud and his wife had been the object of a complaint filed by three local artisans and their wives. The Arnouds were charged with attacking the reputation of fellow citizens, because they were said to have called the men "crooks" and "scoundrels" and the women "sluts" and "whores"; furthermore, the wife of a barrel maker who carried the evocative name of Marat, was told that her husband was "a drinker of blood, a cutthroat, and a Jacobin." When threatened with a complaint to the police, Mme. Arnoud retorted, and later repeated before a judge, that she had already had police "on her ass."[20]

Certainly, these complaints suggest that there were grounds for assuming the Arnouds were counterrevolutionary. And yet the Arnouds did not fear calling the guard against two men who sang an ostensibly republican song on their premises, nor did the guard or even the singers try to use the song's patriotic subject to attack the Arnouds' complaint. Even the account of the events that was signed by Arbulot and Randon, which referred repeatedly to the patriotic allusions of *Chantons, chantons avec courage*, made no explicit criticism of Arnoud's politics, nor did it suggest that he might have had political reasons for silencing the singers. Complainant, defendants, and city guard all seemed to agree on the civil and apolitical nature of the offense; Arbulot and Randon held forth as their strongest defense that they had not been singing at an unseemly hour.

Apolitical, cynical, resigned: the only events capable of exciting enthusiastic, patriotic singing were military victories and peace treaties.

> I went to the faubourg Antoine [where] I went into several cabarets . . . Drink and sing. That seemed to me to be what occupied people the most. We are singing, they said, of our armies' victories and of the arrival of our Father, our savior Bonaparte.[21]

Hopeful and energetic, war songs not only excited a vigorous change of mood; they celebrated a new perspective and offered new descriptions of battle. Singers' identification with the government, so popular in 1793, had disappeared altogether by 1795 as images of a unified polity fragmented. Now, in the final years of the Revolution, they found a new source of identification in the army. As French citizens, singers claimed military victories as their own—"Mantoue est à *notre* pouvoir" (Mantua is under *our* power), "*nos* troupes vont à Rome" (*our* troops are going to Rome)—and they expressed a direct identification with the nation's armies that they had once found with the national representation:

De victoire en victoire	From victory to victory
Nous marchons pleins d'ardeur	We march filled with ardour
Et nous avons la gloire	And we have the glory
De forcer l'Empereur	Of forcing the Emperor
Devant la République	Before the Republic
De demander la paix.[22]	To request peace.

New descriptions of war emerged as well. The fearful and violent lyrics that dominated early republican songs, conjuring up visions of bloodthirsty foreigners and slaughtered children, were in decline. Now songwriters preferred to ridicule and mock foreign tyrants.

Mantoue est à notre pouvoir	Mantua is in our power
La chose est véritable;	This is true;
Mais l'Empereur, pour la ravoir,	But the Emperior, to have it back,
Se donnerait au diable,	Would give himself to the Devil,
Il veut armer, se nous dit-on,	He wants to arm, we are told,
La faridondaine, la faridondon;	Faridondaine, Faridondon;
Tous les femmes de Hongrie, biribi,	All the women of Hungary, biribi,
A la façon de barbari, mon ami.[23]	Like a Barbary pirate, my friend.

Or they belittled the nation's enemies by portraying them in foolish dialogues, elaborating vain projects against France, or worrying over the futility of resisting French armies.[24] These songs often reinforced their disdain for the enemies by giving them only a verse or two before turning the limelight on the fine soldiers of France. And, among these, no figure was more lauded than Bonaparte. Celebrated as "the model for our warriors" and compared to "the heroes of antiquity," he almost single-handedly took the place once occupied by philosophes, politicians, and revolutionary martyrs.[25]

Bonaparte was a dynamic popular hero who cultivated his own image, but he benefited as well from the fact that war excited enthusiasm as formal politics no longer could. Regardless of their differences over the conduct of domestic politics or their disdain for the current government, all citizens could agree on the need to protect the nation and check the overweening ambition of crowned heads of state by means of republican principles. In the face of a corrupt and indifferent government, enthusiasm for war replaced enthusiasm that had once been sung for domestic politics. "I went to Lefevre's . . . in the faubourg Antoine," writes one policeman. "There were a lot of workers there with their wives. . . . They sang republican songs, and everyone seemed quite content; they drank toasts to Bonaparte and to all the armies. . . . I would have expected to hear speeches for or against the primary assemblies in such a place, where all the heads seemed much heated by the wine, but everyone kept their silence."[26]

The government played upon war fever as well, hoping that this enthusiasm would fill a void that civic festivals could not conjure away. So, officials and civil service bureaus used announcements of peace or victory as occasions to hold small celebrations and civic banquets, which received an inordinate amount of coverage from the press. The republican press, still seeking to represent the citizenry as actively republican, seized upon these events as patriotic festivities that were otherwise absent from directorial society.

REVIVING ART AND ENTERTAINMENT

While descriptions of laboring and poor people disappeared from print, diminishing in rhythm with these people's dwindling capacity to affect legislative or communal politics, other members of Parisian society remained highly visible. Beyond the faubourgs Antoine and Marcel were legislative deputies and government bureaucrats, actors and actresses, dramatists, salonières, and poets. These men and women not only had more wealth and education than their fellow citizens, they received more publicity: their activities and creative productions filled the press and memoirs. Like their poorer counterparts, many of the singers and songwriters of this milieu were in the process of abandoning an explicitly revolutionary song culture. Rather than disappearing into obscurity, however, they remained very much in the public eye as they created a new song culture that replaced republican enthusiasm with taste, literary accomplishment, and wit.

Two songbooks emblematic of these trends appeared in the fall and winter of 1796–97. The *Journal des Muses* and the *Dîners du vaudeville*, which promoted literary and drinking songs respectively, shared the common purpose of promoting Old Regime models of song writing and isolating poetic and song culture from political interests and debates, which—the songbook editors claimed—had damaged such literature in recent years. This revival of more "traditional" and apolitical song forms was described by publishers, critics, and imitators alike as a simple effort to restore France's rich cultural heritage.

The *Journal des Muses*, a literary journal, announced that its project would be "to gather up the blossoms scattered through the great field of literature and assemble them together in a flower bed, where their choice, variety, and purity might attract the friends of sweet and peaceful pleasures. . . . It is by offering agreeable distractions to persons who are tired of their work or of their leisure that we hope to assist in restoring good spirits and simple tastes to our fellow citizens."[27] Appearing monthly, at the relatively high cost of 12 livres a year for subscribers, the *Journal* promised to print literature of all genres, and it kept that promise by publishing poetry, criticism, and translations of classical literature as well as songs.[28]

Beyond the immediate task of gathering the "scattered blossoms" of literature, the larger project of the journal's editors was to contribute to the restoration of the arts and letters in France. They believed that the arts had "languished" during the Revolution, the victim both of simple neglect and of "vandalism" and "anarchy." So the task of cultured men and women was to "bring the muses back to France."[29] The journal brought together writers of all political persuasions, republicans and royalists alike. These "friends" of culture believed that by restoring the arts and letters they could achieve several goals at once, helping to reestablish the glory of France among Europeans and set fine examples for future citizens. Perhaps the journal's most important contribution, its editors argued, would be the restoration of taste and the improvement of public instruction, for this would contribute to the stability of public order itself.[30]

Whereas the editors of the *Journal des Muses* looked to the literary traditions of the Old Regime, the authors of the *Dîners du vaudeville* aspired to revive middle-brow entertainment and sociability.

> If there is . . . a nation distinguished by [the] love of singing, it is certainly the French nation. . . . Collé, Pannard, Dufresny, Piron, you who . . . created the charm of the epoch in which you lived, what delicious verses you left us in your works, how greatly would French gaiety regret your loss . . . if the Republic did not count among the children worthy of it, successors who are worthy of you![31]

Collé, Pannard, Piron: taking as their predecessors Old Regime playwrights and members of the already famous singing society of the café du Caveau, the authors of the *Dîners* announced their devotion to reviving the gaiety and banter that, once so common among Parisians, had lain dormant in recent years.

But even as they declared their patrons to be Momus and Bacchus, the mythological representatives of satire and of drinking, the authors of the *Dîners* took great care in establishing their society. The thirteen members, almost all of them dramatists, drew up a constitution in verse that set rules for their meetings—each member would provide a new song and share the costs of food and drink whether he attended or not—and determined strict conditions for the acceptance of any future members: "Pour être admis, on sera père / De trois ouvrages en couplets, / Dont deux, au moins (clause sévère) / Auront esquivé les sifflets" (To be admitted, one must have fathered / Three works in verse, / Of which two, at least (a stern clause) / Have eluded hoots).[32] In short, only composers and lyricists of proven—professional—authorship would even be eligible for consideration. The songs that the diners produced would be published once a month and, at a cost of seven livres a year, they would be provided to subscribers along with an annual issue that supplied engraved music for new tunes.

Although concerned with reviving different kinds of Old Regime songs, the editors of the *Journal des Muses* and the *Dîners du vaudeville* shared a mutual and explicit disdain of politics. These were not the first journals of the Revolution to print apolitical songs and poetry—the *Almanach des Muses* and the *Almanach des grâces* had published a great many since 1789—but they were the first to state as a condition of publication that they would refuse any and all compositions that treated political subjects:

Champ libre au genre érotique,	Free rein to the erotic,
Moral, critique,	Morals, criticism,
Et bouffon;	And clowning;
Mais, jamais de politique,	But never politics,
Jamais de religion.[33]	Never religion.

The authors of the *Dîners du vaudeville* did not elaborate on this clause of their Constitution, but the objectives of their singing society suggested that they found politics and religion to be far too serious for artists seeking to revive French gaiety and wit. The editors of the *Journal des Muses* were not much more explicit, saying only that enterprises which seek to "generate the taste for letters . . . have no place for polemical discussions," implying that such concerns would be as deadly for determinations of taste as they were for the light entertainment of the vaudevillists.[34]

The desire to revive older cultural forms and practices and the explicitly apolitical nature of the *Journal des Muses* and the *Dîners du vaudeville* were complimentary: the rejection of politics allowed songwriters and their publishers to disassociate themselves from the politically motivated iconoclasm of the early Revolution and to reappropriate Old Regime culture. And, no longer divided by politics, well-educated and cultured men and women might now join together to renew and sustain a cultural heritage that was based on learning and shared notions of taste. Just how far writers and publishers might distance themselves from revolutionary conceptions of culture, politics, and history became apparent in yet another songbook that appeared in 1797 and which was loosely affiliated with the *Journal des Muses*.

The *Nouveaux troubadours* was founded by Jacques Lablée, also editor of the *Journal des Muses*, who intended to use this periodical to publish only songs, in particular, "[those] which, through expressions of feeling, of innocent and discerning judgments, or through the abandon of pure joy, best recall the style of the troubadours and the prosperous time of ancient chivalry." The announcement of the periodical's objectives and its conditions of publication was followed by a lengthy history of the troubadours whose compositions served as its model. Lablée himself wrote the *Notice sur les troubadours* and, although he began in a scholarly voice—"I will only say of them what seems to me to be incontestable"— his disquisition soon became a mournfully sentimental celebration of a lost age. "So glory, honors, voluptuousness everywhere accompanied the [troubadours]. So in the time that we call barbarous, people knew how to profit from the brief moments of life by placing above all else the pleasures of which feelings and spirit are an inexhaustible source; and we who believe ourselves civilized! . . . When I consider what our ancestors were, in the twelfth century, what we were ourselves . . . what we may yet be . . . I cannot stop the tears streaming from my eyes."[35]

Only two years earlier, such an introduction would have signaled quite decisively that this was the work of a counterrevolutionary who, beneath a thin veneer of literary history, sought to attack the barbarism of revolutionary culture and the anarchic innovations of its politics. But Lablée was by no means a counterrevolutionary: he had served the Revolution as a faithful moderate from its beginning, and he presented a copy of the first issue of the *Nouveaux troubadours* to the republican and Idéologue, Roederer.[36] Rather, Lablée was writing as a man of letters who, regardless of political sympathies, regretted the passing of more romantic days.

In spite of the apparent difference of their literary projects, there was considerable overlap between the songs of the *Journal des Muses* and the *Nouveaux troubadours*, on the one hand, and those of the *Dîners du vaudeville* on the other. The *Journal des Muses* and *Nouveaux troubadours* were more likely to print pastoral and romantic songs, whereas the *Dîners du vaudeville* showed a marked preference for comedy, but all songbooks shared a common appreciation for wordplay and, in keeping with their abhorrence of the too immediately relevant, they sustained a mutual propensity for the frivolous. The *Nouveaux troubadours* appeared only four times and, after it was incorporated into the *Journal des Muses*, the singularity of the individual songbooks declined still further, particularly given the tendency of the *Journal* to reprint the *Dîners*'s more successful songs.

The *Dîners du vaudeville* had begun its career by publishing verse that celebrated its authors and projects: almost half of the songs printed in the first issue were devoted to praising the vaudeville form and insisting upon the need for amusing parody. But once the vaudevillists had given sufficient voice to self-congratulation, they settled into celebrations of mundane objects. Songs with a banal and superfluous subject—*The Lamp, The Night Cap, The Fan*—gave authors more opportunity to demonstrate their sense of humor and facility with rhyme.[37] These men also published a number of songs which, like those in the *Journal des Muses*, paid tribute to flirtatiousness and the reemerging world of the salon. Absent from both journals were hardy republican mothers who sent their sons to war or solid citizens who celebrated equality or the patriotic mining of saltpeter in private cellars. Instead, the reader of the *Dîners du vaudeville* was entertained by *Kisses, erotic verses* and the subscriber to the *Journal des Muses* was likely to sing such pastoral couplets as

Le triste hiver de ses rigueurs	Sorrowful winter with its rigors
Ne désole plus la campagne.	No longer oppresses the country-side.
Le printemps vient, paré de fleurs;	Spring arrives, draped in flowers;
L'Amour sourit, et l'accompagne.[38]	Love smiles, and stands by his side.

In spite of their admonitions against political song writing, the editors of both journals were unable to resist an occasional sally into the world of factions and events. The *Journal des Muses* accused the *Dîners du vaudeville* of printing too many songs with "allusions to events and persons that recall nothing pleasant," but it was in fact the former that appealed most directly to the political world.[39] An exceptionally absent-minded reader, upon reading the fable about the "old cat" unable to change his murderous ways, might take at face value the admonition that "once a cat, always a cat"; but others must certainly have seen a veiled warning against the resurgence of Jacobinism. And there was no mistaking the subject of the mournful romance of "Adelaide," because the song's note explained quite clearly that "the woman named here was condemned to death at the end of Prairial. Her pregnancy won a reprieve: she was freed at the time of 9 Thermidor."[40] But references to old battles and persistent enemies declined quickly, and they disappeared almost entirely by the year VII.

Like the disenchanted singers in the faubourgs, literary editors did not always include war- and peace-making in the realm of the political. A few songbooks included songs or verse that celebrated military victories in a way that would have been inconceivable had legislative victory been at issue. And although he went unnamed, here too Bonaparte was clearly an object of reverence.

Salut au chef de nos Soldats,	Hail to our soldiers' leader,
Qui, brave autant que sage,	Who, courageous as well as wise,
Conduit les Français aux combats,	Leads the French into combat,
Ou retient leur courage.	Or restrains their bravery.
De l'Europe le Vainqueur,	Of Europe, the victor,
En est Pacificateur.	And the pacifier.
Gloire au Guerrier habile,	Glory to the able warrior,
Qui, n'ayant pas trente ans encore,	Who, not yet thirty years old,
Joint la valeur d'*Achille*,	Joins to the valour of Achilles,
Aux vertus de *Nestor*.[41]	The virtues of Nestor.

The *Journal des Muses* and the *Dîners du vaudeville* set examples of pub-lication that were taken up by a crowd of imitators in subsequent years: the *Bouquet de roses*, the *Chansonnier des grâces*, the *Etrennes des troubadours*, and the *Lyre d'Anacreon* all repeated this formula with some success. Like the periodicals that they imitated, these songbooks stipulated that new compositions be apolitical. While the *Journal des Muses* and the *Dîners du vaudeville* shared the honor of having set the standard, subsequent song-books perfected it; domestic events and "party hatreds" were wholly ab-sent from their pages. The editors and publishers had good reasons to disassociate song culture from politics. They were, after all, wooing an audience that had consciously abandoned politics and that would be re-membered by subsequent generations for its dizzily fashionable life spent in salons, public balls, theater, and opera. Nouveaux riches or weary nobles, these members of an elite singing public had turned their backs on the politicization of daily life, and they were eager for celebra-tions of the frivolous and the mundane.

Like painters, interior designers, and theatrical entrepreneurs, song-writers and their publishers were trying to efface the first half of the 1790s by resurrecting styles and models that had been developed in the last decades before the Revolution. But their efforts were in vain: the events of 1790–94 continued to shape the cultural life of the Directory as profoundly as they shaped its political life. Despite declarations to the contrary, literati and wits alike were fashioning a song culture that was as deeply imbued with the politics of the moment as it was with memories of the recent past. Above all, these men and women hoped to use culture to dispel political passions and prevent a revival of the maelstrom from which they had so recently emerged. By 1796, many French citizens looked upon their experiences of the years II and III with horror. Terrified of political divisiveness and forgetful of the im-pact of foreign and civil wars, commentators castigated the "factionalism" that they believed had been the sole cause of the violence of the Terror and the Thermidorian reaction. Unable to develop peaceful means to resolve public conflict, politicians and writers, too, sought not only to alleviate and eliminate political opposition, but to define political action so narrowly as to dramatically circumscribe political conflict, thus removing it from Parisian society.

To the widespread fear of the "anarchic" consequences of political opposition and activism, conservatives joined criticism of the Convention's alliances with sans-culottes during the Terror and argued for government by the propertied and the well educated. Only such men as these, they believed, could guarantee liberty for all within a stable nation in which progress occurred through gradual reform rather than revolution. And gradual reform could only be guaranteed if the propertied and educated were free from the interference and pressure of the common people.[42]

These concerns were not new in 1797 and 1798: they had already been raised, and addressed quite explicitly by the deputies of the Convention, who drafted the Constitution of 1795. The result was a lengthy and detailed document which restricted political activity in a number of ways.[43] Political action was narrowly defined by article 363, which declared that "citizens may exercise their political rights only in primary or communal Assemblies." In other words, the citizen was a political actor at the polls, and there alone. This cramped formulation was further circumscribed by the Convention's definition of the citizen as a man who paid at least three days' wages in taxes, and by its elaboration of complicated registration and electoral procedures that discouraged political participation in city and country alike. Finally, legislators sought to guarantee against future activism by forbidding popular societies and national networks of political clubs and by conferring the right to petition the government upon individual citizens alone.[44]

The Constitution's clauses restricting political activism and discouraging "factionalism" were inconsistently enforced, but the anxiety that gave rise to them was echoed throughout directorial political culture. We have already heard from café customers in the faubourgs; their fears were shared by bureaucrats and elites. Thus, when Le-Noir-La-Roche became minister of police in 1797, he reminded citizens that "the only frame of mind appropriate to Frenchmen at this time is a conservative one; the only means to repair the ills of the past and to prevent those that are still worse, are love of order, obedience to the laws, attachment to the Constitution of the year III [1795], enlightened patriotism, and peace and union among citizens."[45]

Le-Noir-La-Roche placed love of order and obedience to laws above attachment to the Constitution because, like many of his contemporaries, he believed that the latter could not exist without the former. Critics who spoke of the "anarchy" of the Terror rarely used the word figuratively; many had come to believe that anarchy was the inevitable consequence of political conflict. Hence, politics should be strictly contained while citizens worked to build a peaceful and coherent society. This attitude lay behind the claim—made by the editors of the *Veillées des Muses*, a literary journal—that the only way to direct the arts toward "a median of shared usefulness" was to sever their ties with *la politique.*

Certainly songbooks and literary journals could easily contribute to the political project of the Directory simply by refusing to treat political matters. But journalists and other writers across the political spectrum argued that the arts had a more active role to play in the new political life. Since at least 1792, the arts had been considered a crucial means to instill and reinforce republican principles; by 1796, however, the kinds of principles that they should instill had changed. Now, rather than exciting a vigorous and active patriotism, "men of letters [should] honor Liberty by proclaiming its maxims, by opposing instruction and enlightenment to error, fanaticism, and lies, and by giving the support of their talents to the reign of the law."[46] Revolutionary culture should no longer inspire republican passion; rather, the arts must calm the passions and distract those engaged in the hard work of politics from the pains of their labors. Only patience, compromise, and circumspection, all of which might be encouraged by a beneficent culture, would allow French citizens to leave the "revolutionary labyrinth."[47]

Revolutionary arts and culture were not, of course, supposed to serve the same purpose for all French citizens: the ideal of a shared revolutionary culture had gone the way of a universal, male politics. Common people were in greatest need of pedagogic arts because, unlike their more reflective social superiors, they did not have the education and inner force that naturally excited them "to the sacrifices and duties that the Fatherland and society imposes." Because common people were guided only by their senses, they were constantly in need of "emblems, symbols, spectacles, music . . . ; in short, all that speaks to the imagination, elevates the soul, and excites enthusiasm and the intoxication of courage, is necessary . . . to quench weak spirits and raise men to the heights of morality."[48] On the other hand, social elites, whose education and reflective capacity provided them with the patriotic energy that common people lacked, had their own cultural needs. Charged with governing the country and guiding the popular classes out of the labyrinth of their passions, these men and women needed not only the relaxation that culture offers but also culture's contribution to the elevation of taste and morals.[49]

Such theories of the arts are commonly associated with the Idéologues, who developed them to their fullest and used them to shape government policy for arts and education.[50] But the Idéologues possessed no monopoly on these ideas. Just as the songbooks of the directorial period brought together artists and songwriters of all political persuasions, so these ideas about the arts found expression in journals from both the Left and Right. Of course, political divisions did not simply vanish; writers commonly accused their political opponents of violating the ideals of aesthetically pleasing and politically disinterested culture—which they themselves promoted.[51] In practice, however, a cultural elite of heterogeneous political opinion was finding unity in a set of ideals that reserved cultural production and aesthetic judgment to itself.

It was within this new political and social context that the vaudeville, that faithful barometer of popular ideas about popular songs, was once again redefined.[52] Reshaped, during the early years of the Revolution from critical satire to amusing teacher of republican principles, the vaudeville became a witty and entertaining distraction that corresponded to the mood of many directorial elites.

> The vaudeville is a genre of poetry at which the French have achieved almost exclusive celebrity. It requires wit, gaiety, a light touch, a little pungency and charm; all qualities that have long distinguished the French nation.[53]

Like the editors of the *Journal de Paris*, other commentators praised the vaudeville, emphasizing its ability to lift spirits and make auditors forget the difficulties and drama of recent years; they claimed that the vaudeville served, with particular acuity, the task that was assigned to songs generally: that of lifting spirits and easing passions that threatened the citizenry.[54]

Authors and critics who redefined the vaudeville as strictly entertainment, both severed its association with politics and fixed its isolation by emphasizing formal rules for its composition. Gone were concerns with the political message of *pièces en vaudevilles*. Critics focused instead on the relationships between character and plot, the uses of songs and puns, or the clannishness of the authors at the théâtre du Vaudeville. The most that was asked of the vaudeville's essence was that it propagate that vague entity, *la morale*. And once the genre's specifically revolutionary content had been abandoned, the vaudevillists were free to reinstate its satiric dimension, but in a wholly harmless form. In the earliest editions of the *Dîners du vaudeville*, the song's satire was described as guaranteeing the quality and wit of theatrical performances. Looking back to *Les Mille et un théâtres*, the authors recalled Thalia's repugnance for the vaudeville and then reassured auditors:

Le vaudeville est votre appui;	The vaudeville is your support;
Pour embrasser votre défense,	To embrace your defense,
Vertus, talents, comptez sur lui;	Virtues, talents, count on him;
Chantre avoué de la nature,	Devoted bard of nature,
Tendre ami de la vérité	Tender friend of truth
Pour triompher de l'imposture,	To triumph over deceptiveness,
Il ne lui faut que sa gaîté.	He needs only his gaiety.
C'est du théâtre qu'il dirige	It's from the theater that he directs
Le trait qui pare son refrain;	The taunt that adorns his chorus;
C'est au théâtre qu'il corrige	It's in the theater that he corrects
L'auteur qui pille son voisin;	The actor who steals from his neighbor;
C'est au théâtre qu'il décèle	It's in the theater that he discerns
Les défauts à l'oeil échappés;	Faults that escape the eye;
C'est au théâtre qu'il appelle	It's in the theater that he calls upon
Des succès au Pinde usurpés.[55]	Pindare's usurped successes.

In later years, the authors of the *Dîners* became more willing to recall the vaudeville satires of the Old Regime, but no longer as a means to reveal the truth to kings; now they defined vaudeville only as an excess of gaiety that was sometimes taken too seriously by its targets.[56]

NINETEENTH-CENTURY SONG CULTURE

The rejection of revolutionary activism that was apparent in all dimensions of song culture by the late 1790s would become one of the Directory's legacies to Napoleon, part of the package of institutions, political practices, and political culture that the little general inherited and that seemed almost ready-made for Consul and Empire.[57] Certainly, Napoleon's seizure of power brought innovation in its wake as the censorship and supervision of press, theater, and songs became increasingly restrictive and as violations of personal and civil liberties increased, justified by allusions to the supreme importance of national stability. But such legislative and police activity was facilitated by the political and cultural climate that had taken root under the Directory. In many cases, legislators and bureaucrats merely ratified trends that had emerged well before the installation of the Consulate: thus, restrictions on political newspapers reinforced the already popular tendency to emphasize arts and literary debates over news and editorials, while censors' attacks on books, songs, or plays "which tend to recall hatreds" or "which might feed revenge and factionalism" encouraged the continued publication of authors and composers who stripped away all hints of political engagement from their work.[58]

Imperial authorities did not, of course, openly repudiate the Revolution; they claimed to protect its essence by violating its principles, ostensibly protecting the polity by harassing and imprisoning political opponents. Like the Directors before them, these men drew few distinctions between the Left and the Right as they hounded citizens at both ends of the political spectrum in an attempt to maintain civil order. Radicals who resisted the regime were dealt with harshly. The Jacobin songwriter Theodore Desorgues was among the more celebrated of the Empire's victims—confined to an insane asylum for writing a few verses against Napoleon—but police files included as well accounts of lesser-known citizens who were arrested, imprisoned, and even executed for singing, or merely possessing, "a song against the Emperor."[59]

Radicals were, however, the exceptional figures. The majority of citizens presented few problems of order. Many of the poets, composers, and publishers who had founded literary journals under the Directory were free to continue their enterprises with a minimum of interference. The *Dîners du vaudeville* ceased publication two years after Brumaire, but only because several of its leading members had won important government positions; the songwriters they left behind simply joined new singing societies with similar tendencies.[60] In fact, it was under the Empire that the efforts of such men to revive an apolitical, middle-brow song culture reached its zenith: in 1805 a handful of self-proclaimed epicureans, most of them artists and men of the theater, succeeded in reviving the much-celebrated Caveau singing society.

Like the original Caveau, and like the most popular singing societies of the directorial period, the new Caveau explicitly shunned politics to focus attention on celebrations of eating, drinking, and the antics of their chosen predecessors.[61] The Caveau occasionally published songs that celebrated notable events like the birth of Napoleon's heir or the return of the Grande Armée, but such songs were meant only to acknowledge current events rather than to suggest any particular political sympathies. The society disbanded in 1815, in disagreement over whether celebrations of Louis XVIII were political, but it was resurrected a decade later and continued with few interruptions until the eve of World War II. The Cavistes' popularity would prove to be rather more uneven than their longevity. Increasingly dominated by royalists, the society was considered politically conservative by midcentury, and by the end of the Second Empire its cultural conservatism led Pierre Larousse to warn that it threatened to come apart "like a worm-eaten Academy if it does not admit a few modern minds."[62] And yet, in spite of this, it nourished an important tradition within song culture, ensuring that the Caveau of the Old Regime and the popular song tunes of several generations would not be forgotten.

It would be a mistake, however, to see in directorial song culture only the seeds of conservative singing practices. In the retreat of working people to cafés and wineshops in the late nineties lay the roots of *goguettes*: singing societies that began to emerge early in the nineteenth century and which would become centers of politicized and class-conscious singing under the July Monarchy. Having grown up during the Empire, *goguettes* numbered perhaps several hundred by the early years of the Restoration.[63] Often located on the upper floors of local cafés scattered throughout Paris and its suburbs, they were modeled on elite singing societies like the Caveau. In them artisans and laborers would gather to eat and drink while singers performed their latest compositions under the supervision of a president. Although closely watched by the police, members of the *goguettes* often successfully interspersed patriotic and political songs with lighter tunes about drinking or love.[64]

Many *goguettes* became still more explicitly political after the Revolution of 1830. Among the most famous were the *Lice chansonnière* and the *Ménagerie*, both of which self-consciously opposed themselves to the rigorously apolitical stance of the Caveau by proclaiming their liberal and republican principles. The founder of the *Ménagerie* was reputed to open sessions with the statement, "Political songs are acceptable. Here you can say shit to the king."[65] Here, too, working people might listen to the compositions of some of the most well-known, activist songwriters of the period: Vinçard, the son of an artisan and a Saint-Simonian; Gustave Leroy, a brush maker; and Charles Gilles, a radical republican corset maker who founded the *Ménagerie*. These men did not see themselves simply as entertainers; rather, they adopted the early republican role of singers as pedagogues and used their songs to disseminate messages of hope, cooperation, or revolution to the laboring classes. Charles Gilles in particular was quite explicit about this role:

Courez donc à la goguette	Run then to the goguette
Joyeux faiseurs de chansons,	Happy writers of songs,
Dans un coin l'amour vous guette,	From a corner love looks on,
Le peuple attend vos leçons.	And the people await your lessons.
Mais faites qu'il utilise	But make sure the people use
Les instants qu'il y perdrait,	The moments they might lose,
Et que l'ouvrier s'instruise	And that the worker gain
Aux refrains du cabaret.[66]	From the cabaret refrain.

As arenas of political singing, the *goguettes* were harassed into oblivion by Napoleonic bureaucrats under the Second Empire, and the locus of song culture moved to *café-concerts*. These were crowded and smoky beer halls in which men and women of different social backgrounds gathered to listen to frivolous entertainment songs by professional singers. As examples of the new, commercial entertainment, *café-concerts* did not fail to excite nostalgia for *goguettes* among political activists who believed that the latter had been sites of authentic working-class culture. "Authentic" working-class culture is a dubious notion, but the comparison reveals something about contemporary attitudes toward *café-concerts*. For while *café-concerts* had their novelties—they drew a sharp distinction between the stage performer and a silent audience, and they played a pivotal role in the new world of commercial entertainment—they also evoked older traditions: they provoked the obsessive concern of authorities to control the political content of their songs, and, above all, they excited a typically ambivalent response from commentators, who fell into the well-worn habit of either praising French wit and gaiety or bemoaning the potential consequences of such tawdry forms of amusement.[67] And these complaints remind us that, while each epoch of French song culture was historically specific, there were as well certain continuities. To find those continuities, we must return to the Directory.

The steady abandonment of a public and activist political culture under the Directory helps to explain the ease with which Napoleon took and maintained power. Along with political institutions, he inherited a population that had self-consciously rejected political engagement and expression. Such disaffection, which was manifest at all levels of society and among citizens of every political position, was in part the result of a common desire for domestic peace and stability after more than half a decade of political turmoil. Fearful of divisiveness and uncertain about how to constitute an arena of public political discussion in which differences might be acknowledged and sustained without violence, many citizens turned to cultural practices that they believed were less explicitly political. But disaffection with an activist republicanism was also the often unintended by-product of government activity which, even as it sought to institutionalize revolutionary political culture, hastened its demobilization.

We have already seen, in preceding chapters, how bureaucrats and legislators of the National Convention and the Directory alike set out to monopolize revolutionary political culture and, in particular, song production. In so doing, they facilitated the decline of both. By monopolizing musical composition and performance for festivals, the government rendered still more distant a ceremony from which the populace had always been at considerable remove. But the Conservatory's monopoly on official music was not the only reason for an increasingly apathetic response to festivals. Official corruption and government indifference to the material needs of the citizenry gave the lie to the Directory's efforts to celebrate republican politics through festivals. This corruption and indifference helped to further undermine an already dispirited public confidence in political representation. In the end, common people and elites alike were neither moved to continue producing their own republican culture nor to embrace the culture that was ostensibly being produced for their benefit.

The transformation of political life and political culture under the Directory renders more problematic the Revolution's legacy to the nineteenth century. Historians tend to locate the origins of the republican tradition in the events and figures in 1793–94 and then skip immediately to Napoleon's coup in 1799. And yet, while the first half of the Revolution witnessed the expansion of political activism and the creation of a republican iconography, it was the second half that saw the first adaptations of that iconography to a nonrevolutionary society and the creation of cultural practices that would survive, even flourish, during the conservative decades to come. The popular retreat to bars, cafés, and singing societies represents one such kind of creation.

The retreat to neighborhood bars and elite singing societies reflected the privatization and circumscription of politics at all levels of society, and for this reason it must be counted among the Revolution's politically conservative legacies. But within two decades, cafés, bars, and some singing societies would become the sources of a newly class-conscious and explicitly politicized singing. Such a transformation could take place, at least in part, because singing had moved indoors: the suspicions and insecurities of authorities under the Empire, Restoration, and July Monarchy necessitated more private and restrained means of political expression. In the end, the retreat to bars and singing societies helped to create an arena in which revolutionary singing practices might be preserved and, eventually, nourished. Quite inadvertently, the conservative practices of the Directory contributed to the survival of the revolutionary tradition into the nineteenth century.

Criticism of *café-concerts* in the late nineteenth century evokes another continuity within French song culture: the persistent uneasiness that it provoked. As should be clear by now, song culture was by no means the unique possession of common people. With a few notable exceptions, however, it was repeatedly identified as a popular cultural form, probably because songs were and are among the most accessible forms of communication and expression. But the consequence was that concerns about the lower classes in general were conflated with critiques of songs and singing: so when Danton worked to demobilize sans-culottes, he also criticized the appropriateness of their public singing, just as Third Republicans would later express fears about class mixing and commercialization by questioning *café-concerts*. The same qualities of malleability and accessibility that made songs so popular also made them extraordinarily difficult to police, and so these qualities were also a source of fear. Thus, the intermingling of social tensions and cultural fears visible during the Revolution, and even before, would persist as members of all social groups used the means available to them to create, appropriate, and react to the society around them.

Conclusion

✦

The Impact and Legacy
of Revolutionary Culture

✦ THROUGHOUT THE revolutionary decade, French men and women noisily debated the political meaning of singing and the broader associations of particular songs. The gestures, words, and images with which they conducted this debate, and their inability to reach a lasting compromise, speak volumes about the contentiousness and uncertainty within revolutionary political culture and the fragility of the notion of republicanism. The changing definitions of singing as a form of popular culture point to the many social tensions at work within the revolutionary process and the ways in which those tensions intersected with and inflected political negotiations. In short, revolutionary singing practices reveal the degree to which the political culture of the French Revolution was contingent and contested.

This book has taken as a given one of the axiomatic principles of French Revolution scholarship: fundamental to the unfolding of the Revolution was the invention of a new language and a new iconography of politics. As Mona Ozouf, François Furet, Lynn Hunt, and others have demonstrated, what revolutionaries said about themselves and the particular ways in which they represented their aspirations were as important to the Revolution's progress and outcomes as was new legislation and revolutionary events. But historians' discovery (or perhaps invention) of revolutionary political culture has resulted in a strange bifurcation in our vision of the eighteenth century, which has led us to sorely underestimate the degree to which the Revolution was a contested event. Contemporary studies of political culture have generally been either investigations of prerevolutionary political culture that seek to explain how the Revolution became possible or analyses of the political culture of the Revolution which represent it as an interlocking system of symbols or as a coherent linguistic event.[1] Neither body of work explains precisely how revolutionary political culture came into existence or the particular ways in which it changed over time. Yet mastering these points is fundamental to explaining the Revolution, for as this book demonstrates, the Revolution was a fluid and changing event. The attitudes of 1792 were by no means present in the attitudes of 1789, nor can the culture of 1793 stand in for that of 1797. The French Revolution was a profoundly historical event: its politics and culture changed repeatedly throughout the decade of its occurrence. As the study of song culture suggests, revolutionary political culture was as much the haphazard product of negotiations for social, cultural, and political power as it was the offspring of Old Regime politics or the fruit of revolutionary legislation. In the end, French citizens' inability to resolve their differences and to forge a shared song culture reflect their more general failure to create a common republican culture.

SONG CULTURE AND POLITICAL CULTURE

Revolutionary political culture materialized slowly, for French men and women began the Revolution without a clear sense of how to describe themselves and their aspirations, or even what it meant to be revolutionary. The new singing practices that they elaborated and the changing wasy that they represented them were integral elements of revolutionary politics: practices and representations alike served as potent means to imagine politics. Songs made a particularly important contribution to the revolutionary process, for singing offered ordinary people a medium in which to express their political hopes and expectations and carry the Revolution into the most quotidian aspects of their, and their neighbors' lives. Because of its availability and pervasiveness, singing became tightly bound up with politics. Thus the gradual hardening into uniformity of revolutionary song culture between 1789 and 1793 was inseparable from the polarization of revolutionary politics in these same years.

The emergence and growing popularity of *Ça ira* was the first process by which revolutionaries began to define themselves through their elaboration of specifically revolutionary singing practices. After the song's appearance in the summer of 1790, revolutionary activists repeatedly sang *Ça ira* in explicitly political ways and so began to suggest the extent to which singing might be a revolutionary act. But these singers did not

act in isolation. Journalists and others described their gestures and ceremonies in revolutionary and royalist newspapers and pamphlets: they
broadened the activism by advertising it; they contributed to its political
respectability by giving it greater pride of place and by editorializing
about its significance. And as singing gained credibility, first in the
streets and then in the press, it came to be a matter of concern for revolutionary legislators.

Just as singers did not act in isolation, neither did revolutionaries sing
in solitude. They sang in literal and in figurative opposition to royalists
and, in so doing, they forged increasingly homogeneous representations
of who they were and what they aspired to. It was through this process of
opposition that revolutionary self-definition became more rigid and revolutionary politics polarized. Revolutionaries steadily imposed greater
uniformity on themselves, narrowing the parameters of debate and expression until, having silenced royalists in the wake of the republican
revolution of August 1792, they began to turn upon former allies, silencing loyal opposition and determining the very forms of expression that
might be considered revolutionary. Legislators and revolutionary crowds
closed opposition presses and struggled to purge ambiguity from all
genres, songs included. This trajectory of increasing rigidity began with
Ça ira and was completed by the *Marseillaise*, whose lyrics were decisively
fixed in print from the outset. The *Marseillaise* eloquently served a republicanism that the play of competing forces had rendered univocal;
during the next three years, singing came to be seen as a direct and unambiguous statement of revolutionary enthusiasm.

But even at the moment that singing appeared to be most univocal,
songs continued to serve a multiplicity of purposes. Most importantly,
they helped to express and sustain the extralegislative activism of the
sans-culottes, even as legislators and bureaucrats looked hopefully to
songs as a means to organize and guide the populace. The tension between singing as incitement to popular activism and songs as official
pedagogic instruments was one that both Dantonists and Robespierrists
tried to resolve in favor of government, albeit in very different ways. The
Dantonist effort to marginalize singing and the Robespierrist attempt to
draft popular song culture to the service of official festivals were both
motivated by the common desire to give order to the Revolution and
subordinate it to the guidance of the legislature and its institutions.

The desire to give order to the Revolution survived Thermidor, but
the radical aspiration to constitute a single set of political means and
goals did not. Having weathered the Republic's crisis and no longer willing to bear the costs of making uniform a society that was in steady re-

treat from its government, deputies to the National Convention restored civil liberties and the freedom of formal expression. The Republic remained bitterly divided, however, and French citizens remained too fearful of the consequences of political opposition to construct a peaceful and democratic arena of public discussion. This division and fearfulness were at the root of the battles over the *Marseillaise* and the *Réveil du peuple*. On the one hand, the *Marseillaise* represented a republican past that revolutionaries could neither put behind them nor rehabilitate. On the other, the *Réveil du peuple* stood for a political alternative that veered unsteadily between loyal opposition and counterrevolution; even some of the song's most sincere proponents were forced to admit that the implications of its performances were not always clear.

Believing themselves unable to achieve pluralism without anarchy but unwilling to resort to the violent enforcement of republican uniformity, private citizens began to seek other means to stabilize French society. These unofficial efforts to banish the difficulties raised by political and cultural pluralism coincided with an ongoing legislative desire to give decisive order and guidance to republican culture and to restrict the activist associations of singing. The Directory, following the lead of the National Convention, set out to monopolize cultural production and restrict political debate, so that it alone might determine the representation of the Republic. Meanwhile, private citizens retreated to the social and cultural hierarchies that had once ordered their lives, seeking a coherence and unity that eluded them in revolutionary politics. The well born and the well educated of all political opinions met on the common ground of aesthetic principles. Drawn together around particular kinds of cultural objects and practices, they engaged in implicitly political arguments about the value of abandoning explicitly political action. Working people, who were once again excluded from political institutions and from official and learned culture, found a sense of unity in their common celebration of Bonaparte and war. Here they believed they found a source of agreement that was as powerful and satisfying as revolutionary politics once had been, but without the potential for divisive conflict. This is not to say that any of these citizens—legislators, cultural elites, or working people—had abandoned politics: rather, they had come to conduct politics by more discreet means.

The evolution of song culture between 1789 and 1799 suggests that we revise our current notions of revolutionary political culture. Above all, we can no longer assert that republican culture was a coherent entity which meant roughly the same thing to all members of revolutionary society. The festivals, ideologies, and symbolism described by Ozouf, Furet,

Hunt, and others made up only a tiny fraction of the more general phenomenon that we call political culture. Compositions, singing practices, and changing attitudes toward songs indicate the degree to which song culture in particular, and revolutionary political culture more generally, emerged haphazardly, pieced together by a mobilized and heterogeneous populace whose members engaged in almost perpetual struggle among themselves as well as against their royalist opponents. The consensus that some revolutionaries forged during the first years of the Republic was temporary, more the product of political circumstances than a masterpiece fashioned by legislators.

Because revolutionary society was irretrievably fragmented, neither legislators nor even a broad cross-section of republican society was able to create a lasting and homogeneous republican culture. French society was divided by politics, by changing definitions of appropriate expression and behavior, and by ongoing tensions between an emerging bureaucratic state and an unruly populace. All these divisions favored the creation of a mobile and effervescent culture. Each fault line that traversed revolutionary society shaped not only the kinds of songs that citizens chose to write or sing but also how they sang and how they interpreted the performances, or silences, of others. At any given moment, songs and singing served multiple purposes. Even when all voices seemed to be united in a single chorus—as they were when they praised republican singing in 1793 and 1794—individual goals remained disparate or even diametrically opposed. The Revolution as a whole had scarcely any uniformity, for opinions, alliances, and aspirations shifted repeatedly, winning new partisans and evoking novel kinds of behavior as the years passed.

The fluidity that was visible within song culture suggests a great deal about political culture more generally. Certainly songs and singing were more accessible than almost any other expressive form during the Revolution, but song culture was not isolated. Rather, songs and singing throw into relief trends that were apparent elsewhere. The heterogeneity that characterized song culture, and revolutionary society more generally, suggests the limits of genres that were less accessible than singing and song writing. Such genres as newspapers, pamphlets, plays, novels, and paintings, all of which were more restricted at the level of production or consumption, tell us less about the Revolution than songs do precisely because they represented the hopes and aspirations of a smaller fraction of the population.

Besides suggesting the heterogeneity and conflict that characterized revolutionary political culture, the development of song culture also underscores the importance of the directorial period for song in the nineteenth century. Certainly 1793–94 marked the zenith of song culture and of the broader republican culture of which it was a part. These years witnessed an extraordinarily intense level of cultural activity and the production of many broadly shared symbols. But it was in the years after Thermidor that the government began to fix the content of revolutionary culture and institutionalize the symbols that it hoped to promote as signs of the Republic. It was also in the years after Thermidor that the vestiges of activist republican culture moved indoors to bars and cafés: protected arenas in which that culture would persist and, eventually, again flourish.

Finally, the ongoing conflicts and frictions that were inherent in the constitution of revolutionary song culture help explain not only the intensity with which revolutionaries treated cultural matters but also the failure of republican culture at the end of the eighteenth century, a failure that contributed to the slow, steady decline of French politics into the authoritarian regime of Napoleon Bonaparte. It was the revolutionaries' failure to create a successful and pluralistic republican political culture that contributed to the Revolution's decay after 1795. Unable to find homogeneity without coercion and believing themselves unable to sustain political pluralism without violence or instability, few protested the Directory's efforts to freeze republican culture and promote it from above in the same heavy-handed manner with which it orchestrated electoral life. At the same time, many private citizens sought new avenues of activity and worked to achieve a cultural consensus that they believed to be apolitical and nonrevolutionary. It was this abandonment of an activist and engaged republicanism that helps to explain the success of Napoleon's coup in 1799, for Napoleon was prepared to foster a culture in which the citizenry would find domestic peace and unity: a supply of frozen political icons, an entertainment culture emphasizing wit and style over substance, and foreign wars that would nourish national unity as domestic politics could not.

Song Culture as Popular Culture

Although revolutionary political culture may be said to have failed in the short term, it was a rousing success in the long run. Why was this so? Republican political culture survived and flourished in the nineteenth century in part because of its ability to incorporate forms of what had been, and would again be considered "popular culture." The visible adoption of the objects and practices of popular culture stands as one of the most radically novel dimensions of revolutionary political culture; it was the iconic equivalent of universal male suffrage. Furthermore, in drawing on the "popular," republicanism gave new life to the notion of popular culture itself. Just as republicanism might be represented as the property of all members of the polity, so particular forms of popular culture—songs among them—acquired a distinct political identity. This identity persisted throughout the nineteenth and into the twentieth centuries, as radical republicans and the proponents of a self-conscious working-class culture adopted and expanded it.

Songs had been a form of popular culture under the Old Regime because singing was commonly represented as lowly and frivolous and as a special expression of *le peuple*. These representations did not simply coexist with the broadly shared practices of song culture, they shaped them and gave them precise political meanings. Above all, learned representations drove home the idea that singing did not deserve serious political consideration. In this way, government officials and educated observers marginalized a means of expression that served those who were unable to produce more formal varieties of culture. Even during the pre-Revolution and the early Revolution, when singers composed new lyrics to celebrate increasingly radical events, singing continued to suffer representationally. Revolutionary journalists updated Old Regime prejudices by claiming that singing recalled a political impotence and frivolity that ought to remain a thing of the past. Royalists reinforced that prejudice by exploiting it, using songs to mock revolutionaries and suggesting that the form alone was sufficiently ridiculous to belittle all that it treated.

Ordinary citizens' ability to contest representation effectively gradually persuaded revolutionary journalists and their allies to abandon disparaging descriptions of singing. The emergence of *Ça ira* and *O Richard, ô mon Roi* as distinctive anthems was closely tied to this transformation. From the taking of the Bastille onward, common citizens gained status as political actors by participating in the revolutionary movement in a sustained way. Using riots, demonstrations, songs, and gestures, Parisians involved themselves on both sides in the movement to enforce the Civil Constitution of the Clergy, in the increasingly rancorous opposition between Revolution and royalism, and in the debate over the king's loyalty to France and the Constitution. Simultaneously, extralegislative activists began to contest the way they were represented. They engaged in noisy and effective demonstrations, sometimes going so far as to smash opposition presses and howl down the plays that they deemed counterrevolutionary. *Ça ira* and *O Richard* were associated with almost all of these activities, and it was through such associations that their performances came to signal political opinion with great clarity and force. As revolutionary journalists, pamphleteers, and legislators began to describe these new practices and acknowledge the political import of singing, the gap between practice and representation narrowed.

Increasingly positive representations of revolutionary singing did not, however, emerge only because of the particular ways in which singing practices were being elaborated in streets, theaters, and cafés. As republicanism flourished, songs also shed their marginal status, for republicans sought to construct a more inclusive polity and to give credibility to common cultural forms. We should not, however, take republican valorizations of singing as a sign that these men aspired to a truly democratic polity. Rather, the particular ways in which republican leaders—by which I mean journalists, club spokesmen, and legislators—gave credibility to singing reveals the tensions that were inherent within revolutionary republicanism. So, for example, it is both telling and ironic that the Jacobins did not lead the way in appropriating songs to the revolutionary project. Although Jacobins were increasingly regarded as the close political allies of working people, particularly after the August revolution, they were never interested in accepting working people or sansculottes on their own terms politically or culturally. Even before Montagnard deputies began to struggle to guide their extralegislative allies politically, Jacobin club members showed concern to initiate the revitalization of the common man by weaning him from traditional cultural forms which, they believed, reinforced slavish social relations and political practices. Jacobins began to praise singing only after witnessing concrete examples of the revolutionary uses to which it might be put. They became enthusiastic only after the appearance of the *Marseillaise*, a song that carried the seriousness and majesty that they hoped to impart to the whole revolutionary movement. Although they went on to celebrate singing and tried to recruit songs for pedagogic uses, their persistent uneasiness about the irreverence, disorder, and crudity of many songs hampered their efforts: hence the failure of festival hymns to make their way into the streets or the cafés. Hence, too, Thomas Rousseau's discovery that the popular market would never match government contracts in support of his song writing.

Moderate Republicans were far more receptive to popular songs, because they were more willing to work with the social and cultural hierarchies that they found in place. So it was Gorsas, at the *Courrier*, and the editors of the *Chronique de Paris* who turned their readers' sympathetic attention toward singing well before Desmoulins, Danton, or Robespierre took notice. We ought not, however, to infer from this that moderates were more democratically inclined than Jacobins, for they too believed that working people must be given firm political guidance. Moderates were simply more pessimistic about the possibility of reforming the common condition generally or popular culture in particular. And it was perhaps this pessimism about the possibility of abandoning the past that helps to explain the ease with which Girondins came to be labeled as royalists after the August revolution. For however radically different his aspirations for the future, a man like Gorsas did share with royalists a common willingness to continue to draw upon the cultural tools of the Old Regime. Ironically in both cases, then, the men who did the most to publicize revolutionary singing were precisely those with the lowest expectations of what it might accomplish.

By the end of 1792, the gap between practice and representation had almost closed: singing was widely practiced, and it was represented in word and image as an exemplary republican activity. But it is worth stressing again that this transformation did not come about because singing had been purged of its association with common people. With the growing political importance of the sans-culottes, all common people acquired greater political status. By 1793, all good republicans were sans-culottes, and all sans-culottes sang. And yet, the association of singing with common people became a liability once more. When the Montagnard deputies to the Convention began to urge the demobilization of the popular movement in the winter of 1794, they set out to distinguish republican singing practices that served the interests of the emerging state from those which contested it. Although the Robespierrist project of channeling popular song writing temporarily triumphed over the Dantonist desire to silence it, both projects were motivated by similar concerns and both would be fully realized by directorial legislators.

Like their predecessors in the Convention, many members of the Directory developed ideas about, and policies concerning singing that were shaped by the way their political goals intersected with changing singing practices. Directorial deputies were not simply more conservative than deputies to the Convention had been. By the time they came to sit, singing had been all the more damningly associated with unofficial activism. Now republican legislators and others could point to the competing performances of the *Marseillaise* and the *Réveil du peuple* that had characterized the Thermidorian reaction and continued beyond it, and quite plausibly describe singing as an activity that hindered the nation's progress by exciting violence and political chaos. Thus the universally republican associations of song culture, so slowly constituted during the early years of the Revolution, were undone as certain kinds of singing and song writing came again to be designated as "popular."

Concerned to demobilize a revolutionary nation after the winter of 1794, legislators alternately co-opted and marginalized the singing with which extralegislative activism had been associated. First the Thermidorian Convention and then the Directory regulated republican song culture by establishing a monopoly over the production of festival music and by more narrowly circumscribing the limits of public activity. Thus the revolutionary state, like its Old Regime predecessor, delegitimized unofficial singing by describing it as unworthy and by treating it as illegal. Simultaneously, many well-educated and well-born men and women turned away from revolutionary politics and set out to purge it from French culture by restoring aesthetic hierarchies. Although this resurrection of aesthetics was explicitly meant to revive French culture by freeing it of political constraints, it narrowed the field of what might be considered "legitimate" cultural or political expression, which again marginalized the common means of expression and artistic productions of those without formal educations. This movement progressed as quickly as it did because it met with a minimum of opposition. For, fearful of "anarchy" and subdued by the violence of the Terror and Thermidorian reaction and by the famine of 1795, most Parisians had ceased to contest representations of themselves or refused to become involved in extralegislative politics; they turned away from revolutionary singing because they had come to fear the consequences of revolutionary activism. Thus, the gap between a shared practice—singing—and its representation yawned anew, and songs once again seemed to become a form of "popular culture," not meant to be taken seriously as a means of political expression.

The transformation of song culture during the second half of the revolutionary decade underscores the degree to which aesthetics may serve political purposes. For here, in the post-Thermidorian world, the resurrection of taste and precise rules for appropriate expression dovetailed with police measures designed to impose order in the streets. Although less violent than measures imposed under the Terror, these strategies worked effectively to silence particular expressions of opinion and to marginalize a significant fraction of the population. Cultural elites and members of the Directory may have been less punitive of contestation than the sans-culottes and the legislators of the National Convention, but they nonetheless confirmed a normative language in which politics might be discussed and criticism voiced. Such normative language helped to narrow the range of discourse that might be considered legitimate by political authorities.

But the silence that grew up under the Directory proved to be only temporary, for a powerful tradition of revolutionary singing flourished in the nineteenth century. By the early years of the Restoration, the bars and cafés in which common people met to sing drinking and war songs had begun to give way to *goguettes*, in which explicitly political songs were once again popular. As the Saint-Simonian *chansonnier* Vinçard explained, "There people sang or recited all kinds of poetry, either serious or critical, and among the latter there was no shortage of attacks against the government and the Church. . . . It is clear that [these *goguettes*] were . . . potent schools of patriotic instruction. The workers of Paris came to these gatherings to nourish the love of our national glories and of public liberties."[2] Nor should we forget the vibrant tradition of the *Marseillaise* itself. Sung in France by the revolutionaries of 1830 and by the Communards of 1871, the hymn was shared throughout Europe during the revolutionary upheavals of 1848 and again in the twentieth century, when revolution seemed about to spread from Russia through central Europe.[3] And, in all cases, these traditions of singing played on the duality that had been at the heart of republican song culture in the year II, exalting common people as they claimed to defend the rights and liberties of all.

Nineteenth-century French and revolutionary song cultures were very much shaped by the experience and the knowledge of the French Revolution. Above all, conflicting definitions of songs and singing emerged from social tensions that were woven into revolutionary politics and revolutionary political culture from the outset. The French Revolution did not involve a simple change in the institutions and practices of politics; revolutionaries sought as well to give voice to new constituencies. Most radically, revolutionaries briefly gave legitimacy to those expressions and cultural forms that had traditionally been marginalized as "popular." That this legitimation of the popular came to be linked with universal male suffrage and radical social programs in 1793 and 1794 would not be forgotten by republicans in the nineteenth century. Here, for the first time in modern French history, popular culture was linked with concrete social and political alternatives and thus became capable of giving voice to new and radical aspirations. This was one of the reasons that singing served as a powerful revolutionary tradition, upon which working-class and bourgeois radicals actively drew throughout the nineteenth century.

For similar reasons, entertainment and politicized singing remained a source of uneasiness for monarchist, imperial, and republican authorities alike. Associated with a powerful political tradition, singing carried potent associations that were silenced only with great difficulty. Further-more, singing continued to be an unregulated and unregulable means of expression. Songs remained exceedingly difficult to police: ephemeral because so often oral, they were shaped by tones of voice and gestures that outsiders interpreted only with difficulty and found almost impossible to seize. Equally important, singing was unregulated and un-regulable because it continued to exist outside the normative categories of expression. Serving as a potent means of criticism—a means given new legitimacy by the Revolution—songs continued to be represented as frivolous and lowly by authorities who both disdained and feared them. Taken together, these qualities enabled songs to express criticism of po-litical, social, and cultural orders all at once. They implicitly described an alternative order on all planes.

In light of the important interpretive debates that have reshaped scholarship on the French Revolution in the last half-century, it is ironic that Marxists, revisionists, and postrevisionists share a common and striking failing. None seem to have given a sense of contingency to our understanding of the Revolution. Whether driven by class struggle or ideological struggle, united by paranoia or by political culture, the French Revolution that we know continues to be a revolution of extraor-dinary coherence in which interpretations of 1789 or 1793 shape con-ceptions of the whole period. And perhaps it is a natural human response to try to impose some kind of conceptual order on a moment of extraordinary, even chaotic disorder. One of my goals here, however, has been to restore some measure of chaos to our vision of the Revolu-tion, to call attention to the difficulties, social tensions, and uncertain-ties that were inherent in the production of revolutionary political culture. Here was a nation in movement as never before, its population fragmented in myriad ways over how politics, culture, and society could be reconstructed. It is not surprising that neither the government nor even the whole revolutionary cohort was able to determine single-handedly the content or reception of revolutionary symbols and an-thems. And even as the nation began to take some distance from the po-litical turmoil of the Revolution and sort out its principal values, it could not reach consensus over revolutionary culture. That took another cen-tury, and then some. And perhaps certain dimensions of the Revolution will never truly be over, for the struggle to construct a truly democratic and pluralist political culture may, in truth, be endless.

Notes

Introduction

[1] Louis Sebastien Mercier, *Paris pendant la Révolution (1789–1798), ou le nouveau Paris* (reimpr: Paris, 1862); J. Peltier, *Dernier tableau de Paris, ou récit historique de la Révolution du 10 août 1792* (London, 1794); Frédéric Jean Laurent Meyer, *Fragments sur Paris*, translated from German by Général Dumouriez (Hambourg, 1798).

[2] Constant Pierre, *Les hymnes et chansons de la Révolution française* (Paris, 1904); Cornwall B. Rogers, *The Spirit of Revolution in 1789* (Princeton, 1949); Pierre Barbier and France Vernillat, *Histoire de France par les chansons*, vol. 4: La Révolution (Paris, 1957); James Leith, "Music as an Ideological Weapon during the French Revolution," *Canadian Historical Association Report* (1966); Robert Brécy, "La chanson révolutionnaire de 1789 à 1799" and "La chanson babouviste," *Annales historiques de la Révolution française* 53 no. 244 (1981) and 54 no. 249 (1982); G. and G. Marty, *Dictionnaire des chansons de la Révolution, 1787–1799* (Paris, 1988); Herbert Schneider, "The Sung Constitutions of 1793," in Malcolm Boyd, ed., *Music and the French Revolution* (Cambridge, 1992).

[3] A notable exception is Alphonse Aulard, "La querelle de la *Marseillaise* et du *Réveil du peuple*," which examines competing performances of the two songs during the Thermidorian reaction. See Aulard, *Etudes et leçons sur la Révolution française*, 3d series (Paris, 1902). For a critique of Aulard, see Chapter 5.

[4] The notion of a single, inert, and authoritative text has given way before demonstrations of how translation, publishing apparatus, and performance can alter textual meaning. In such cases, however, the definitive shaping of the text remains in the hands of professional culture producers rather than being delivered into the hands of amateurs. On editorial strategies, see Henri-Jean Martin and Roger Chartier, general editors, *Histoire de l'Edition française* vol. 2, *Le livre triomphant, 1660–1830* (Paris, 1984); on performance, see Stephen Greenblatt, *Shakespearean Negotiations* (Berkeley and Los Angeles, 1988).

[5] A sizable body of literature attests to the accessibility and flexibility of songs across temporal and geographic boundaries. See, for example, Jacques Rancière on nineteenth-century French songs, "Good Times or Pleasure at the Barriers," in *Voices of the People: The Social Life of "La Sociale" at the End of the Second Empire*, ed. Adrian Rifkin and Roger Thomas, trans. John Moore (London, 1988); Lawrence W. Levine on African-American

songs, *Black Culture and Black Consciousness*, (New York, 1977); Vernon Lidtke on labor songs in Germany, *The Alternative Culture: Socialist Labor in Imperial Germany* (New York, 1985); John Collins and Paul Richards on highlife and *juju* songs in contemporary West Africa, "Popular Music in West Africa," in *World Music, Politics, and Social Change*, ed. Simon Frith (Manchester, U.K.,1989).

[6] Mona Ozouf, *Festivals and the French Revolution*, trans. Alan Sheridan (Cambridge, Mass., 1989); Lynn Hunt, *Politics, Culture, and Class in the French Revolution* (Berkeley, 1984); Maurice Agulhon, *Marianne into Battle: Republican Imagery and Symbolism in France*, trans. Janet Lloyd (Cambridge, 1981); François Furet, *Interpreting the French Revolution*, trans. Elborg Forster (Cambridge, 1981); *The French Revolution and the Creation of Modern Political Culture*, vol. 2, *The Revolution*, ed. Colin Lucas (Oxford and New York, 1987–1989).

[7] Hunt, *Politics, Culture, and Class*, p. 14.

[8] See Mona Ozouf's discussion of the competing festivals of Simonneau and Chateauvieux and Lynn Hunt's description of the distinctive representations of Hercules promoted by Girondins and Montagnards. Ozouf, *Festivals and the French Revolution*, pp. 66–79; Hunt, *Politics, Culture, and Class*, pp. 94–119.

[9] On the relationship between revolutionary and counterrevolutionary culture, see Amy Wiese Forbes, "Royalist Satire in the French Revolution, 1789–1790," Masters' Thesis, University of Georgia, 1992.

[10] William Sewell, *Work and Revolution in France: The Language of Labor from the Old Regime to 1848* (Cambridge, 1980); Morris Slavin, *The Making of an Insurrection: Parisian Sections and the Gironde* (Cambridge, Mass., 1986); Dominique Godineau, *Citoyennes tricoteuses: Les femmes du peuple à Paris pendant la Revolution française* (Paris, 1988); Michael Sonenscher, "Artisans, *sans-culottes*, and the French Revolution," in *Reshaping France: Town, Country, and Region during the French Revolution*, ed. Alan Forrest and Peter Jones (Manchester, U.K., 1991).

[11] Suzanne Desan makes this argument most explicitly in *Reclaiming the Sacred: Lay Religion and Popular Politics in Revolutionary France* (Ithaca, N.Y., 1990). See also, Bryant T. Ragan, Jr. and Elizabeth Williams, eds., *Re-creating Authority in Revolutionary France* (New Brunswick, N.J., 1992); Godineau, *Citoyennes tricoteuses;* Marcel David, *Fraternité et Révolution française* (Paris, 1987).

[12] Agulhon, *Marianne into Battle.*

[13] François Furet is by far the most explicit on this point, arguing that after 9 Thermidor the French nation returned to an atemporal and normative model of the relationship between politics and society. *Interpreting the French Revolution*, pp. 73–79. See also Lynn Hunt's critique of Furet's characterization of "[pre-Thermidorian] revolutionary government as in some sense pathological . . . because its politics do not represent social interests in the normal . . . fashion." *Politics, Culture, and Class*, pp. 11–12.

[14] Chandra Mukerji and Michael Schudson, eds., "Introduction," *Rethinking Popular Culture: Contemporary Perspectives in Cultural Studies* (Berkeley, 1991), pp. 3–4.

[15] Robert Isherwood, *Farce and Fantasy* (New York, 1986), p. 250.

[16] Pierre Bourdieu, *Distinction: A Social Critique of the Judgement of Taste*, trans. Richard Nice (Cambridge, Mass., 1984); Nicholas B. Dirks, Geoff Eley, and Sherry Ortner, eds., "Introduction," *Culture/Power/History: A Reader in Contemporary Social Theory* (Princeton, 1994).

[17] On the definition and significance of cultural authorities, see Sonya Rose, "Introduction," *Limited Livelihoods* (Berkeley, 1992).

[18] Jacques Revel, "Forms of Expertise: Intellectuals and 'Popular' Culture in France (1650–1800)," in *Understanding Popular Culture*, ed. Steven Kaplan (New York, 1984).

[19] Revel, "Forms of Expertise," p. 263. Revel argues that a more anthropological approach to popular culture emerged at mid-century which tended to relativize rather than

judge practices. As I suggest in Chapter 1, however, the normative approach persisted until the eve of the Revolution, at least in regard to songs.

[20] *Le dictionnaire universel d'Antoine Furetière* (1690; reprint, Paris, 1978); *Encyclopédie, ou dictionnaire raisonné des sciences, des arts et des metiers*, par une Société de Gens de Lettres (Neufchatel, 1765). See also *Dictionnaire historique de la langue française*, general ed. Alain Rey (Paris, 1994), which notes that the sense of *chanson* as a popular composition emerged in the sixteenth century.

[21] Mukerjee and Schudson, "Introduction," *Rethinking Popular Culture.* Mukerjee and Schudson choose classic and evocative examples by contrasting Natalie Davis's analysis of sixteenth-century carnival with E. P. Thompson's discussion of late eighteenth- and early nineteenth-century working-class culture. Davis, *Society and Culture in Early Modern France* (Stanford, Calif., 1965); Thompson, *The Making of the English Working Class* (New York, 1966). See also, Roger Chartier, "The World Turned Upside-down," in his *Cultural History*, trans. Lydia Cochrane (Ithaca, N.Y., 1988). Chartier points out that popular images of "the world turned upside-down" diminish and, in some cases, disappear altogether after the Revolution. He explains this change by arguing that, after the Revolution, such images ceased to be seen as a means to preserve the social order by releasing tension; in many cases, they came instead to be seen as provocative and potentially subversive.

[22] Yves-Marie Bercé, *Revolt and Revolution in Early Modern Europe*, trans. Joseph Bergin (New York, 1987), p. 218.

1. Songs under the Old Regime

[1] Edouard Fournier, *Histoire du Pont Neuf*, vol. 2 (Paris, 1862), pp. 410–13.

[2] At the bottom of many songsheets was the note: "Persons who would like to learn the tune will find Baptiste, 'called the Entertainer,' every night at the quai de la Ferraille, between seven and nine." Fournier, *Histoire du Pont Neuf*, vol. 2, p. 414.

[3] Isherwood, *Farce and Fantasy.*

[4] Most cultural studies of France under the Old Regime emphasize the emergence of print. Although these works are acutely sensitive to the ways in which print was appropriated in semi-literate cultures, they are concerned primarily with charting the expansion of print culture. I recommend turning that approach upside down and considering what remained beyond this expanding culture. A few key texts in the massive literature on print culture are: Natalie Z. Davis, "Printing and the People," *Society and Culture in Early Modern France* (Stanford, Calif., 1965); Elizabeth Eisenstein, *The Printing Press as an Agent of Change* (Cambridge, 1979); Roger Chartier, *The Cultural Uses of Print in Early Modern France*, trans. Lydia Cochrane (Princeton, 1987); Roger Chartier, ed., *Les usages de l'imprimé* (Paris, 1987). The literature concerned with the poor or with working people is most suggestive about the extent to which Parisian culture remained oral: Daniel Roche, *The People of Paris*, trans. Marie Evans (Berkeley, 1987); Arlette Farge and Jacques Revel, *The Vanishing Children of Paris*, trans. Claudia Miéville (Cambridge, Mass., 1991); Arlette Farge, *Fragile Lives*, trans. Carol Shelton (Cambridge, Mass., 1993); David Garrioch, *Neighborhood and Community in Paris, 1740–1790* (Cambridge, 1986).

[5] Even Jacques-Louis Ménétra, a glazier who wrote a personal memoir of several hundred pages—indicating a significant degree of literacy—has almost nothing to say of reading print (the sole instances of reading that he reports are private letters). Ménétra, *Journal of My Life*, trans. Arthur Goldhammer (New York, 1986).

[6] On the rumors about the death of the regent, see Arlette Farge, *Dire et mal-dire: L'opinion publique au XVIIIe siècle* (Paris, 1992), pp. 105–12; on the rumors surrounding Damiens's attack on the king, see Dale Van Kley, *The Damiens Affair and the Unraveling of the*

Old Regime (Princeton, 1984); on the exile of Parlement, Siméon Hardy, "*Mes loisirs*," BN MSS. ff, 6687.

[7] See, for example, Walter Ong, *Orality and Literacy: The Technologizing of the Word* (London, 1982), pp. 6–7.

[8] On the importance of visual detail and ritualized gesture, see David Garrioch, "The Primacy of Neighborhood and Local Community," *Neighborhood and Community in Paris.*

[9] On royal displays of power, particularly in regard to public executions, see Farge, *Fragile Lives.*

[10] Henri-Leonard Bordier, "Preface," *Le chansonnier huguenot au 16e siècle* (Paris, 1870), pp. 32–33.

[11] J.-M. Vaccaro, "Introduction," in J.-M. Vaccaro, ed., *La chanson à la Renaissance* (Tours, 1981), p. 9. In addition to the songs that they had composed themselves, Protestants also received published collections from Switzerland. See Bordier, "Preface," *Chansonnier huguenot* (Paris, 1870).

[12] Bordier, *Chansonnier huguenot*; Barbier and Vernillat, *Histoire de France par les chansons*, vol. 1, *Les Guerres de Religion* (Paris, 1956–1957).

[13] G. Pau, "De l'usage de la chanson spirituelle par les Jesuites au temps de la contre-réforme," in Vaccaro, *Chanson à la Renaissance*; Barbier and Vernillat, *Histoire de France*; Bordier, *Chansonnier huguenot*, pp. ix–x.

[14] During the Fronde, Parisian presses produced thousands of *mazarinades*, which included pamphlets and broadsheets as well as songs. Marie-Noelle Grand-Mesnil, *Mazarin, la Fronde, et la presse* (Paris, 1967); Christian Jouhaud, *Mazarinades: la Fronde des mots* (Paris, 1985).

[15] Grand-Mesnil, *Mazarin*, p. 199.

[16] Ordonnance de police (1651), BN MSS ff, 22087, folio 124.

[17] *Pont-neuf* referred to the compositional practice of rhyming new verses to popular tunes; *vaudevilles* were satiric *pont-neufs* that were associated above all with urban life and, later in the eighteenth century, with the theater. See entries "Chanson" and "Vaudeville," *Encyclopédie*; Claude Brossette, *Du vaudeville: Discours prononcé à l'Académie de Lyon en 1729* (Paris, 1846).

[18] *Anthologie française* (n.p., 1765), pp. 51–55; Edouard Fournier, *Histoire du Pont Neuf*, vol. 2 (Paris, 1862), pp. 211–18; Louis-Sebastien Mercier, *Tableau de Paris*, vol. 6 (Amsterdam, 1782), pp. 40–43; Nicolas Restif de la Bretonne, *Nuits de Paris*, vol. 4 (London, 1788), pp. 1817–19.

[19] Isherwood, "The Singing Culture of the Pont Neuf," *Farce and Fantasy.*

[20] Fournier, *Histoire du Pont Neuf*, 2:410–14; Isherwood, *Farce and Fantasy*, pp. 160–67; Dossier Roussel and Cligny, 1741, BA MSS, 11,501, nos. 337–58. Cafés must have been a lucrative arena: when Cligny was arrested again ten years later, it was once more for selling "coarse and licentious songs" there. Dossier J.-B. Cligny, "dit Michel le Musicien," July 1751, BA MSS, 11,741, nos. 330–418.

[21] Ménétra, *Journal*; Farge, *Fragile Lives.* Marivaux's novels, *La vie de Marianne* and *Le paysan parvenu*, also contain scenes in which seemingly personal events draw not only the attention of neighbors but actually bring a crowd to the hero's door to watch the goings-on.

[22] Mercier, *Tableau de Paris*, 5:67–68. Singing in the street to people in their homes still occurs in many neighborhoods of Paris today.

[23] Dossier Tavernier *et al.*, February 1717, BA MSS, 10,633, nos. 261–65.

[24] Dossier LaPlace (femme Heron), July 1739, BA MSS, 11, 428, nos. 70–77; Dossier Caillou, October-November 1717, BA 10,628, nos. 14–30.

[25] Dossier Roussel and Cligny, 1741, BA 11,501, nos. 337–58.

[26] On colporteurs, see Jacques Savary des Bruslons, *Dictionnaire universel de commerce*, vol. 1 (Paris, 1723), pp. 827–28. Admittedly, this was the written law only; in truth, there were

many illegal colporteurs. For streetsingers, see memo of 15 March 1773, BN MSS ff, 22116, no. 80, and *Chanson sur les réjouissances qui ont été faites à Paris à la naissance du Dauphin* (Paris, 1721), Bibliothèque de la Chambre des Deputés MSS 1421, fol. 255. Printers and libraires were subject to very stiff penalties for producing and selling songs without permission. See dossier Pecquet, September 1752, BN MSS ff, 22092, pp. 160–63; "Sentence de police," 20 August 1782, BN MSS ff, 22070, p. 142.

[27] François Lebas to Lieutenant General of Police, undated, BN MSS ff, 22116, no. 92.

[28] Restif de la Bretonne, *Nuits de Paris*, vol. 4 (London, 1788), pp. 1817–19; Marchands de chansons, BN MSS ff, 22116, no. 80, pp. 82–83; *Chansons nouvelles*, par LaJoye (1761), BN MSS ff, 22116, no. 86; "Arrêté de la Basoche en faveur des Avocats du Parlement de Paris," BN MSS ff, 25570, pp. 664bis-664ter; "Supplément au receuil alphabétique des questions sur les patentes" (1792), AN, H² 2106.

[29] "Vaudeville," *Encyclopédie*. The word *chansonnier* appears in neither the *Encyclopédie* nor in Rousseau's *Dictionary of Music*, and in both books the word *chanteur* signifies only those who sang in the Opéra.

[30] For approbation, see *Chanson sur les réjouissances*. For violations, see Dossier Pecquet, September 1752, BN MSS ff, 22092, pp. 160–63. Pecquet, a *libraire*, received an extremely harsh judgement and was banished from his guild for having printed a number of relatively harmless songs with a statement of permission that he did not have. The printers Frère and Levé and their compatriots were fined 20 livres for printing and selling obscene songs and warned that a second offense would be treated even more harshly. "Sentence de police," 20 August 1782, BN MSS ff, 22070, p. 142. Despite the severity with which false permissions could be punished, they were not a rare occurrence. Mercier, *Tableau de Paris*, 6:40–43; Dossier Caillou, October–November 1717, BA MSS, 10,628, no. 19.

[31] *Chanson nouvelle*, BN MSS ff, 22116, fol. 89; *Chanson nouvelle sur M. de Montempuys* (1726–1727), BA MSS, 10,319, fols. 124–31; songs in dossier Caillou, 1717, BA MSS, 10,628, nos. 14–30; songs in dossier J.-B. Cligny, BA MSS, 11,741, nos. 330–418.

[32] The price for one or two songs was two or three liards; for a very short song booklet, two or three sous. See Isherwood, *Farce and Fantasy*, p. 7; Mercier, "Chanteurs publics," *Tableau de Paris*; "Lettre de vendeurs de chansons à Sartine, Lt. Général de Police," 21 Mar. 1773, BN MSS ff, 22116, no. 82.

[33] LaJoye, *Sur l'entrée à la campagne* (n.p.,1761), BN MSS ff, 22116, no. 86.

[34] For illegal songs, see Barbier and Vernillat, *Histoire de France*, 1:352; Chansons anonymes, undated [1726–27?], BA MSS, 10,319, fols. 124–31; Siméon Hardy, "Mes Loisirs," BN MSS ff, 6686, fols. 36–38. For legal songs, see *Chansons nouvelles* (Paris, 1729), BN MSS ff, 21741, no. 294; *Chanson sur la naissance de Monseigneur le Dauphin* (Paris, 1729), BN MSS ff, 21741, no. 306; Fournier, *Histoire du Pont Neuf*, 2:366–68.

[35] Fournier, *Histoire du Pont Neuf*, 1:211–13.

[36] Joseph Mervesin, *Histoire de la poésie française* (Paris, 1706), pp. 283–85.

[37] Thus, in a dialogue printed a mere four months after the fall of the Bastille, Margotin complains about a song on this topic. "The Bastille, that's the cutting edge? We know all about that now." *Gazette de Paris*, 20 November 1789.

[38] In 1788 Hardy noted that the imprisonment of Sylvain Marechal for his *Almanach des honnêtes gens* boosted the Almanach's sales and price. Hardy, "Mes loisirs," 9 January 1788, BN MSS ff, 6686, p. 341. Condorcet explained the phenomenon in more general terms: because of the natural human desire to exercise liberty and exhibit bravery, forbidding a book almost always inspired the desire to buy or read it. M.-J.-A.-N. Condorcet, "Fragments sur la liberté de la Presse," *Oeuvres* (Paris, 1847), 11:287.

[39] "Chanson," *Encyclopédie*.

[40] "Vaudeville," *Encyclopédie*.

[41] "Avertissement," *Anthologie française* (n.p., 1765).

[42] In an effort to maintain its monopoly over theatrical entertainment, the Comédie fought for a decree at the beginning of the eighteenth century which forbade the smaller theaters to use dialogue. These theaters responded by adopting vaudevilles to tell stories on stage and by using mime and dialogues in nonsensical languages similar to pig Latin. See Isherwood, *Farce and Fantasy*, chap. 4; Michèle Root-Bernstein, *Boulevard Theater and Revolution* (Ann Arbor, 1984).

[43] Isherwood, *Farce and Fantasy*, chap. 5; Brigitte Level, *A travers deux siècles: Le caveau, société bachique et chantante, 1726–1939* (Paris, 1988).

[44] Fournier, *Histoire du Pont Neuf*, 2:374–79. The number of informative and aggressive songs preserved in journals and private manuscript collections attests to their popularity. See, for example, Emile Raunié, *Chansonnier historique au 18ème siècle* (Paris, 1879).

[45] "Contre Delainval et Gastellier," 1738, APP, Aa5, no. 568; "Contre de Mairobert," 1749, APP, no. 659.

[46] Hardy, "Mes loisirs," 3 February 1788, BN MSS ff, 6686, p. 364.

[47] Robert Isherwood, "Popular Musical Entertainment," *International Review of Aesthetics and Sociology of Music* 9, no. 2 (December 1978): 299.

[48] On the use of handbills during the Fronde, see Jouhaud, *Mazarinades*, chap. 3; for the eighteenth century, see Roche, *Le Peuple de Paris*, pp. 234–35; for handbills posted in response to the meeting of the Assembly of Notables, see Hardy, "Mes loisirs," BN MSS ff, 6686.

[49] *Chanson* "Sur l'air, du bas en haut," (Paris, 1744) BN Ye 17504.

[50] Siméon Hardy, "Mes loisirs," entry for 3 September 1774. BN MSS ff, 6681.

[51] Mercier added that the court was so concerned about Parisian opinion that the police sometimes planted individuals in various quarters to speak loudly and favorably on behalf of the crown. Mercier, *Tableau de Paris*, 1:62–63.

[52] Mercier, *Tableau de Paris*, 1:72–74.

[53] Joel Cornette, *Un révolutionnaire ordinaire* (Paris, 1986).

[54] Farge, *Fragile Lives*; Garrioch, *Neighborhood and Community*.

[55] Pierre Manuel, *La police de Paris dévoilée*, vol. 1 (Paris, an II), pp. 107–10.

[56] E. J. F. Barbier, *Journal historique et anecdotique du regne de Louis XIV*, vol. 1 (Paris, 1847), pp. 216–17.

[57] Although available evidence usually refers to sung attacks on members of high society, they were not confined to that arena. One need only remember Rousseau's assertion in his *Confessions* that the Provencaux exacted vengeance on their enemies by means of song. See also "Chanson," in *Encyclopédie*. Parisians undoubtedly did the same. Songs between neighbors or local enemies could be improvised, sung, and forgotten without pen ever having been set to paper.

[58] Manuel, *Police de Paris dévoilée*, 1:167–71, 192–94; Contre Pecquet, Sept. 1752, BN MSS ff, 22092, fols. 160–63.

[59] On the pursuit of rumor and gossip, see Van Kley, *The Damiens Affair*; Farge, *Dire et mal-dire*.

[60] On this dimension of language in oral cultures, see Ong, *Orality and Literacy*, pp. 43–45.

[61] Mervesin, *Histoire de la poésie française*, pp. 283–86.

[62] Siméon-Prosper Hardy, *Mes Loisirs*, vol. 1 (Paris, 1912), pp. 227–28.

[63] "The public in general disapproves of the procedure of the lawyers, who have not escaped being sung about this time." Barbier, *Journal historique et anecdotique*, 1:373.

[64] Hardy, "Mes loisirs," 20 August 1787, BN MSS ff, 6686, pp. 184–85.

[65] Restif de la Bretonne, *Nuits de Paris*, 6:2495–97.

[66] Contre Pecquet, September 1752, BN MSS ff, 22092, pp. 160–63; Dossier Caillou, October–November 1717, BA MSS 10,628, no. 19.

[67] Quoted by Barbier, *Journal historique et anecdotique*, 3:82.

[68] Mercier, *Tableau de Paris*, 7:281–83.

[69] Hardy, *Mes loisirs*, 1:230.

[70] Mercier, *Tableau de Paris*, 8:287–93.

[71] Hardy, *Mes loisirs*, 1:253–54.

[72] Particularly striking examples of such negotiation may be found in the work of Restif de la Bretonne, that great celebrant of rural virtues. Restif rejected that most urban representative of song culture—the *chansonnier*—only to celebrate young people singing on Saintmarcel as though they were at a *veillée*, far from the corrupting influence of the city.

[73] Popular songs were doubtless pulled down even further by the low cultural position given music generally. See William Weber, "Learned and General Musical Taste," *Past and Present*, no. 89 (November 1980).

[74] *Ibid.*, p. 67.

2. Songs in the Street (1787–July 1792)

[1] Hardy, "Mes loisirs," 28 Sept. 1787, BN MSS ff, 6686, pp. 246–47; *L'heureux retour de Parlement* (n.p., n.d.), Bibliothèque de l'Arsenal, Collection Rondel, Ro 14,008.

[2] Hardy, "Mes loisirs," 30 September 1787, BN MSS ff, 6686, p. 249.

[3] Hardy, "Mes loisirs," 30 September–1 October 1787, BN MSS ff, 6686, pp. 249–50.

[4] Farge, *Fragile Lives*, pp. 202–3.

[5] Hardy, "Mes loisirs," 14 September 1789, BN MSS ff, 6687, p. 475.

[6] On popular offerings to, and exchanges with the king, see Farge, *Fragile Lives*, pp. 171–77.

[7] In May 1789, for example, the electors of the third estate received a deputation of fishwives, who complimented them on their choice of deputies to the Estates General by reading a laudatory address and presenting the electors with a song that celebrated Necker and the third estate. Hardy, "Mes loisirs," 19 May 1789, BN MSS ff, 6687, pp. 325–36. Accounts of similar occasions appear in the *Journal de Paris*, 22 July 1789, and the *Chronique de Paris*, 21 June 1790.

[8] John Lough, *Paris Theater Audiences in the Seventeenth and Eighteenth Centuries* (London, 1957), pp. 185–206.

[9] *Moniteur universel*, 10 October 1789. Henri IV was remembered as an exemplary king. To compliment Louis XVI highly, one had only to compare him to Henri.

[10] *Courrier de Paris*, 20 April 1790. *Marlborough s'en vat en guerre* was a song that became popular in the 1770s. It parodies the death and burial of the Duke of Marlborough, an English general who was a powerful enemy of France in the early eighteenth century. Martine David and Anne-Marie Delrieu, *Aux sources des chansons populaires* (Paris, 1984), pp. 225–28.

[11] *Courrier de Paris*, 20 July 1789.

[12] This observation is based on an analysis of lyrics in songsheets and song booklets printed without music, since these were the most widely available forms.

[13] *L'Assemblée des Notables, Pot Pourri*, recorded in Hardy, "Mes loisirs," 9 Apr. 1787, BN MSS ff, 6686, fols. 46–48.

[14] *Récit historique de ce qui s'est passé dans la ville de Paris* (n.p., n.d.), BN Ye 35763(2).

[15] *La France régénérée* (n.p. n.d.), BN, Ye 55471(949).

[16] *Le désir du peuple accomplie* (n.p., n.d.), BN, Ye 35763(21).

[17] *Chronique de Paris*, 22 December 1789.

[18] *Chronique de Paris*, 20 October 1789.

Notes

[19] *Journal de Paris*, 19 May 1790.

[20] *Révolutions de France et de Brabant*, no. 8, p. 370.

[21] *Chronique de Paris*, 18 May 1790.

[22] See, for example, M.-J. Chenier, *De la liberté du théâtre en France* (n.p., 1789); Jack Censer, *Prelude to Power: The Parisian Radical Press, 1789–1791* (Baltimore, 1976).

[23] "Aux auteurs," *Chronique de Paris*, 26 October 1789.

[24] "Aux auteurs," *Chronique de Paris*, 8 July 1790.

[25] On the symbolic importance of the festival of Federation, see Ozouf, *Festivals and the French Revolution*, chap. 2.

[26] There is some debate on this issue. See Pierre, *Hymnes et chansons*, and Julien Tiersot, *Les fêtes et les chants de la Révolution française* (Paris, 1908), for summaries and treatments of the classic arguments.

[27] *Révolutions de France et de Brabant*, no. 34 (n.d.); *Révolutions de Paris*, no. 52, 3–10 July 1790.

[28] *Mercure de France*, July 1790, pp. 214–16.

[29] *Révolutions de France et de Brabant*, no. 34; "Juillet," *Almanach du Père Duchesne* (Paris, [1791]), pp. 65–77; Louis-Sebastien Mercier, "Travaux du Champ de Mars," *Paris pendant la Révolution*.

[30] *Courrier de Paris*, 9 July 1790.

[31] *Chronique de Paris*, 10 July 1790.

[32] *Révolutions de Paris*, no. 52, 3–10 July 1790, pp. 753–56; *Détails de la fête nationale du 14 juillet 1790* ([Paris], [1790]), BN, Lc39 3754; *Mercure de France*, July 1790, pp. 214–16.

[33] *Chronique de Paris*, 9 July 1790.

[34] Tiersot, *Fêtes et chants*, pp. 19–26.

[35] *Journal des Halles*, no. 1 [July 1790].

[36] *Fête nationale le 14 Juillet 1790* (n.p., n.d.), BN, Lb39 9115.

[37] *Ah! ça ira, dictom populaire* (n.p., n.d.), BHVP, 106901, no. 60.

[38] *Mercure de France*, July 1790, pp. 214–16. Constant Pierre's catalogue includes an entry for a variation on this version among the songs that he lists for 1790. However, the source for this entry is a manuscript transcription which probably dates from 1830 (BN MSS naf, 6620, no. 30). The lyrics given there correspond, for the most part, to a version of *Ça ira* that appeared under the title "Les voeux des républicains" in the *Nouveau chansonnier patriote* (Lille and Paris, an II).

[39] *Chronique de Paris*, 10 July 1790.

[40] In *La Chute de la monarchie, 1787–1792* (Paris, 1972), Michel Vovelle mentions a smaller celebration of the Tennis Court Oath on 20 June. Other legislative dates that might have served as anniversaries include the declaration of the National Assembly (9 July) and the vote on the Declaration of the Rights of Man (26 August).

[41] The first celebration of the taking of the Bastille, organized by market women and the Paris guard, had taken place a mere two months after the event. See *Chronique de Paris*, 15 September 1789.

[42] The need to participate, rather than just watch, is reported in Gorsas' *Courrier* (18 July 1790), which claimed that on the day after the Federation "the citizens of place Dauphine celebrated the festival of our good King Henry IV, they raised an altar in the middle of the square . . . they revived the oath taken at the Champ de Mars, the clergy of Saint Bartholomew's sang a *Te Deum*." On the exclusion of common people from the festival, see Ozouf, *Festivals and the French Revolution*, chap. 2.

[43] *Révolutions de Paris*, no. 54, 17–24 July 1790.

[44] George Rudé, *The Crowd in the French Revolution* (Oxford, 1959), chap. 5.

[45] See testimony of De Vuwersault, Lieutenant des Gardes du Roi, AN, BB3 222, no. 31.

[46] *Moniteur universel*, 9 October 1789.

[47] *Courrier de Versailles à Paris*, 3 October 1789.

[48] One correspondant to the *Courrier* claimed that it was not black but the Bourbon white that had replaced the tricolor cockade. The white cockade was part of the king's guards' uniform, however, and was already being worn by many revelers. Moreover, the widespread belief that Louis XVI was favorable to the Revolution meant that the white cockade, an emblem of service to the king, could not easily suggest antipathy toward the Revolution. See *Courrier de Versailles à Paris*, 5 October 1789. Black later came to be popularly considered the color of Marie-Antoinette's livery.

[49] Hardy, "Mes loisirs," 4 October 1789, BN MSS ff, 6687, p. 501.

[50] See testimony of Mounier, AN, BB3 222, nos. 23–25; *Révolutions de Paris*, no. 57, 7–14 August 1790.

[51] *Ami du Roi*, no. 134, 12 October 1790.

[52] *Courrier de Paris* and *Chronique de Paris*, 5 November 1790.

[53] *Journal du Palais Royal*, no. 3, [1790].

[54] *Chronique de Paris*, 3 November 1790.

[55] *Actes des Apôtres*, no. 145, [August–September 1790].

[56] *Ami du Roi*, no. 197, 14 December 1790.

[57] For a more detailed discussion of the reactions to and consequences of the oath to the constitution, see Timothy Tackett, *Religion, Revolution, and Regional Culture in Eighteenth-Century France* (Princeton, 1986).

[58] *Chronique de Paris*, 23 July 1791.

[59] Mercier, "Scène comique," *Paris pendant la Révolution*.

[60] Rudé, *Crowd in the French Revolution*, p. 89.

[61] The number of people actually killed by the guard is unclear. Mathiez, after reviewing the various claims—ranging from thirteen corpses (Bailly) to four hundred (Marat)—suggested that there were probably about fifty dead after the affair. George Rudé and Michel Vovelle accept this estimate. Albert Mathiez, *Le Club des Cordeliers pendant la crise de Varennes* (Paris, 1910), pp. 148–49.

[62] Dossier Destrumel Sauge, 21–22 July 1791, APP, Aa206, no. 386 (this carton contains a number of pieces detailing similar incidents during the last weeks of July 1791). See also Rapport de la Garde de la Halle, 25 July 1791, APP, Aa85, no. 132.

[63] *Impromptus* were songs that were supposedly composed on the spot (hence the name), and then thrown onto the stage in the hope that the actors would sing them.

[64] *Courrier des 83 départements*, 19 September 1791.

[65] *Courrier des 83 départements*, 21 September 1791. Another production of the opera did not occur until 1806; see David Charlton, *Grétry and the Growth of the Opéra-Comique* (Cambridge, 1986), p. 250.

[66] *Chronique de Paris*, 21 September 1791; *Courrier des 83 départements*, 23 September 1791.

[67] *Courrier des 83 départements*, 24 February 1792; *Chronique de Paris*, 27 February 1792.

[68] *Courrier des 83 départements*, 27 February 1792; *Chronique de Paris*, 29 February 1792.

[69] See, for example, notice on *spectacles* in *Chronique de Paris*, 29 February 1792; for "purifying" a café, see the same newspaper, 5 March 1792.

[70] *Courrier des 83 départements*, 21 August 1791.

[71] *Chronique de Paris*, 5 March 1792; *Courrier des 83 départements*, 20 March 1792.

[72] *Rocambole des journaux*, 26 April 1792. See AN, C168, dossier 415, which reports on a member of the king's guard who sang, "Ça ira, les trois couleurs à la lanterne" [Ça ira, string up the tricolor] and spoke of the need to rid the guards of Jacobins; also *A deux liards, à deux liards, mon journal*, 1ère mois, no. 29 [October 1791].

[73] "The events which took place at the café Herculanium, written in opposition to the insidious and slanderous account of the Gazette universelle," was the claim of *Courrier des 83 départements*, 29 February 1792.

[74] *Chronique de Paris*, 2 March 1792.

[75] *Chronique de Paris*, 2 August 1791.

[76] Barbier and Vernillat, *Histoire de France*, 1:129–30.

[77] *Courrier de Paris*, 16 September 1791.

[78] *A deux liards*, 5ème mois, no. 10 [February 1792].

[79] Charlton, *Grétry*, pp. 42–44.

[80] *Courrier de Paris*, 15 May 1790 and 13 March 1792.

[81] *Ami du Roi*, no. 184, 3 July 1791.

[82] J. M. Coupé, *Vues proposées dans l'Assemblée des Amis de la Constitution, séante aux Jacobins Saint-Honoré, pour éclairer le peuple de la campagne* ([Paris], 1791), BHVP, 676, no. 73.

[83] *Chronique de Paris*, 24 June 1791.

[84] *Chronique de Paris*, 10 April 1792.

3. Songs off the Street: Newspapers, Theaters, and Satire (1789–September 1793)

[1] *Declaration of the Rights of Man*, in *The French Revolution: The Fall of the Ancien Regime to the Thermidoran Reaction, 1785–1795*, ed. and trans. John Hardman (New York, 1982).

[2] On pamphlets, see Ralph Greenlaw, "Pamphlet Literature in France during the Period of Aristocratic Revolt, 1787–1788." *Journal of Modern History* 29, no. 4 (December 1957): 349–54.

[3] Jacques Godechot, "La presse française sous la Révolution et l'Empire," in *Histoire générale de la press française*, vol. 1, ed. Claude Bellanger (Paris, 1969), p. 436.

[4] For a detailed discussion of how journalists chose events in accordance with their political beliefs, see Censer, *Prelude to Power*, chap. 4.

[5] Although they expressed a slowly evolving set of political opinions, both the *Chronique de Paris* and the *Courrier* eventually came to sympathize with the Girondins. See below and Eugene Hatin, *Histoire politique et littéraire de la presse en France* (Paris, 1860).

[6] Censer, *Prelude to Power*, chap. 3.

[7] *Courrier de Paris*, 13 January 1791.

[8] *Révolutions de France et de Brabant*, no. 58 [3 January 1791].

[9] Similarly, when the *Chronique* and the *Courrier* were running accounts of performances of *Ça ira* that averted violence over the Civil Constitution of the Clergy, radicals still used accounts of singing to express their fears about a counterrevolution. In the winter and spring of 1791, the *Révolutions de Paris* printed nothing about singing except an account of a battle between two aristocrats and several members of the National Guard over the latter's refusal to stop singing that "maddening chorus," *ça ira*. *Révolutions de Paris*, no. 98, 21–28 May 1791. On the rare occasions that royalists described street singing sympathetically, they exploited its "popular" associations, by printing *poissardes* (songs in a comically broad, lower-class accent) or claiming that a song had been "sung publicly," to suggest that the simple people of Paris continued to be the king's loyal subjects. See, for example, *L'Ami du Roi*, 7 November 1791 and 1 February 1792; *Rocambole des journaux*, 19 February 1792.

[10] *Actes des Apôtres*, no. 145.

[11] This was not the first time that Gorsas was involved in such activity. His articles against the *Journal de la Cour et de la Ville* encouraged several members of the National

Guard to beat one of its editors. See *Courrier de Paris*, 13, 18, 19, 20 August 1791 and *Chronique de Paris*, 25 August 1791.

[12] *Le rambler*, no. 21 [November 1791]. This interaction between readers and newspapers was not limited to sharing songs and news of popular celebrations; readers sometimes wrote to one newspaper to defend themselves against their treatment in another. See, for example, *Révolutions de Paris*, no. 133, 21–28 January 1792

[13] William J. Murray, *The Right-Wing Press in the French Revolution: 1789–1792* (Suffolk, 1986), pp. 22–23; Marc Bouloiseau, "Robespierre vu par les journaux satiriques (1789–1791)," *Annales historiques de la Révolution française*, no. 152 (1958): 28–49.

[14] For background see Godechot, "La presse française," pp. 475–78; Murray, *Right-Wing Press*, pp. 52–60; and Jean-Paul Bertaud, *Les Amis du Roi: Journaux et journalistes royalistes en France de 1789 à 1792* (Paris, 1984), pp. 22–30.

[15] Bertaud develops this analysis in his treatment of a passage in which Suleau ridicules his loss of civil rights. The comic reading focuses on the simple absurdity of declaring someone "civilly dead," while the moralizing dimension asks the reader to reflect on the nature of a nation that declares itself egalitarian and yet distinguishes between "active" and "passive" citizens. See Bertaud, *Les Amis du Roi*, pp. 23–26.

[16] *Actes des Apôtres*, no. 77.

[17] *Actes des Apôtres*, no. 160.

[18] Frédéric Marchant, *La Constitution en vaudevilles* (Paris, 1792), pp. 33–34.

[19] *Journal en vaudevilles*, [January–April 1790], BN, 8° Lc² 271.

[20] "Epilogue," *Actes des Apôtres*, 7th version (n.d.).

[21] "Epilogue," *Actes des Apôtres*, 7th version (n.d.), p. 6.

[22] [Bachaumont], *Mémoires secrets*, entry for 15 Octobre 1768, as quoted in Fournier, *Histoire du Pont Neuf*, 2:377.

[23] Individual deputies were also mocked. For example, the editors claimed that they would set Mirabeau's speeches to the tune *Vive le vin* and Robespierre's to *Je suis un pauvre misérable. Journal en vaudevilles*, prospectus (n.d.).

[24] *Rocambole des journaux*, 29 July 1792; *Actes des Apôtres*, nos. 217–218. *Pauvre Jacques* became, after 1793, a favorite tune for laments of the king's trial and execution; see, for example, BN MSS ff, 12755, pp. 43, 65. For written music, see *Adieux de M. Favras à ses enfants* in *Actes des Apôtres*, no. 67.

[25] See, for example, the *Ronde patriotique* in *Actes des Apôtres*, no. 199.

[26] *Rocambole des journaux*, 3 June 1792.

[27] *Révolutions de Paris*, no. 138, 26 February–3 March 1792. On Marchant, see Murray, *Right-Wing Press*, pp. 63, 199. Marchant published *Chronique du manège*, *Sabats jacobites*, and *Grands sabats*. In the prospectus to *Sabats jacobites* he claimed to dislike extremists of all political persuasions, but he clearly favored the royalist cause.

[28] There were also *Le rambler*, *A deux liards*, and the *Journal du Palais-Royal*, to name a few that appeared more than once.

[29] See, for example, Camille Desmoulins' response to the *Journal en vaudevilles*, *Révolutions de France et de Brabant*, no. 9.

[30] *Le disciple des apôtres*, "Prospectus," nos. 1–6, [1790], BN, 8° Lc² 275.

[31] *Légende d'orée*, "Prospectus."

[32] *Les Actes des Apôtres* consisted of 311 issues published over a period of a year and a half, and *Rocambole des journaux* appeared for fourteen months.

[33] Hunt, *Politics, Culture, and Class*, pp. 44–46; Jean Starobinski, *Jean-Jacques Rousseau: Transparency and Obstruction*, trans. Arthur Goldhammer (Chicago, 1988).

[34] See Censer, *Prelude to Power*, chap. 3.

[35] See the attack on "libertine works and licentious engravings" in *Révolutions de Paris*, no. 67, 16–23 October 1790.

[36] "Ridicule," *Encyclopédie.*

[37] *Révolutions de Paris*, no. 46, 20–29 May 1790.

[38] On the effect of post-1791 competition on the repertoire of theaters, see Root-Bernstein, *Boulevard Theater and Revolution*, pp. 212–13.

[39] John Lough, *Paris Theater Audiences in the Seventeenth and Eighteenth Centuries* (London, 1957), pp. 185–206.

[40] Isherwood, *Farce and Fantasy*, pp. 91–94. H. Monin cites a passage from Hardy's journal for 1781: at a performance of *La partie de chasse d'Henri IV*, given shortly after Necker's first dismissal, the audience responded to "all allusions to a minister struck by an unjust disgrace and a king fooled by his courtesans." Hippolyte Monin, *L'Etat de Paris en 1789* (Paris, 1889), pp. 638–39.

[41] *Courrier de Paris*, 17 November 1789.

[42] *Chronique de Paris*, 15 October 1789. *Révolutions de Paris* took such activity so much for granted that it closed a note on performances of *Iphigénie en Aulide* and *La partie de chasse d'Henri IV* with the comment that "the public did not fail to seize upon all allusions that were analogous to the circumstances." *Révolutions de Paris*, no. 2, 18–25 July 1789.

[43] *Courrier de Paris*, 1 December 1790.

[44] This explanation of the play's success was a point upon which even the radical *Révolutions de Paris* and the royalist *Ami du Roi* agreed. *Révolutions de Paris*, no. 20, 21–28 November 1789; *Ami du Roi*, no. 134, 12 October 1790.

[45] See complaints about the many *pièces de circonstance* relevant to the festival of Federation, in *Révolutions de Paris*, no. 54, 17–24 July 1790, and a notice for *La Chêne patriotique, ou la matinée du 14 Juillet*, in *Courrier de Paris*, 26 July 1790. Cousin Jacques's *Réveil d'Epémenide* was enjoying some success at this time as well.

[46] Isherwood, *Farce and Fantasy*, pp. 96–97; Root-Bernstein, *Boulevard Theater and Revolution*, pp. 17–28.

[47] *Révolutions de Paris*, no. 53, 10–17 July 1790.

[48] *Chronique de Paris*, 19 October 1792.

[49] *Journal du Palais-Royal*, no. 5 (1790).

[50] For full text of the decree, see Maurice Albert, *Les théâtres des boulevards* (Paris, 1902), pp. 66–67.

[51] Root-Bernstein, *Boulevard Theater and Revolution*, p. 201.

[52] Claude Brossette, *Du Vaudeville: Discours prononcé à l'Académie de Lyon en 1729* (Paris, 1846); Dorothy Packer, " 'La Calotte' and the Eighteenth-Century French Vaudeville," *Journal of the American Musicological Society* 23 (1973): 61–83; Clifford Barnes, "Vocal Music at the Théâtres de la Foire," *Recherches sur la musique française classique* 8 (1968): pp. 141–60.

[53] Brossette, *Du Vaudeville*, pp. 45–46.

[54] "Vaudeville," *Encyclopédie.*

[55] Albert, *Les théâtres des boulevards*, p. 74.

[56] Bibliographic information on the owners and authors of the Vaudeville is taken from Michaud's *Biographie universelle*, nouvelle édition (Paris, 1843), and from the biographical notes in M. Lepeintre, ed., *Suite du répertoire du théâtre français: Vaudevilles* (Paris, 1823).

[57] A two-volume collection of their theater pieces was published in 1784: *Théâtre de Piis et Barré*. Michaud's *Biographie universelle* claims that Barré was responsible for plot, while Piis wrote couplets and dialogue.

[58] One historian of the theater even argued that it was a resounding failure. See "Notice historique sur le théâtre du Vaudeville," in N. Gallois, *Théâtres et artistes dramatiques de Paris* (Paris, n.d.), BN MSS naf, 3040, no. 102–3.

[59] G. F. F. D. Desfontaines de la Valée, *Les Mille et un théâtres* (Paris, 1792).

[60] *Chronique de Paris*, 16 February 1792.

[61] F. P. A. Léger, *L'Auteur d'un moment* (Paris, 1792).

62 "Des théâtres," *Chronique de Paris*, 27 February 1792; "Melanges: L'Auteur d'un moment," *Rocambole des journaux*, no. 9, 4 March 1792; Michaud, *Biographie universelle*, article on Charles Palissot.

63 The issue of the *Logographe* that carried Léger's letter was said to have circulated widely, and the text of the letter was reprinted in the *Courrier de 83 départements*, 26 February 1792.

64 *Courrier des 83 départements*, 26 February 1792; *Révolutions de Paris*, no. 138, 25 February–3 March 1792.

65 *Courrier des 83 départements*, 27 February 1792; Chronique de Paris, 29 February 1792.

66 *Révolutions de Paris*, no. 138, 25 February–3 March 1792; no. 74, 4–11 December 1790.

67 *Courrier des 83 départements*, 26 February 1792; see also *Chronique de Paris*, 27 February 1792.

68 *Courrier des 83 départements*, 1 March 1792.

69 *Rocambole des journaux*, no. 19, 4 March 1792. The paper, in the review which preceded the advertisement, underscored the allusions to Chenier. For the advertisement of *Les Mille et un théâtres*, see "Catalogue des pièces du théâtre du Vaudeville," in A. Piis, *La Nourrice républicaine* (Paris, an II), Princeton University Library, 3278.67.1780, vol. 3, no. 3.

70 *Courrier des 83 départements*, 26 February 1792.

71 *Révolutions de Paris*, no. 162, 11–18 August 1792.

72 Murray, *Right-Wing Press*, p. 193.

73 For the publication of Marchant's songbooks, see Murray, *Right-Wing Press*, p. 199.

74 Septime Gorceix, "Antoine-Joseph Gorsas, journaliste et conventionnel (1753–1793)," *L'Information historique* 15, no. 5 (November–December 1953): 179–83. The *Nouvelle biographie générale*, and Michaud's *Biographie universelle* have also served as sources of biographical information on Gorsas. On Gorsas's art criticism, much of which was enlivened by his sense of the comic, see Thomas Crow, *Painter and Public Life in Eighteenth-Century Paris* (New Haven, 1985) and Bernadette Fort, "Voice of the Public: The Carnivalization of Salon Art in Prerevolutionary France," *Eighteenth-Century Studies* 22, no. 3 (Spring 1989): 368–94.

75 When considering candidates for the National Convention, the editors of *Révolutions de Paris* would say of Gorsas and his editorship of the *Courrier*: "he will be more indispensable to the Convention outside [its walls] rather than within." *Révolutions de Paris*, no. 164, 25 August–1 September 1792.

76 *Courrier des 83 départements*, 1 July 1791. See also issue for 15 March 1791.

77 *Sabats jacobites*, nos. 4, 6 (n.d.); *Courrier des 83 départements*, 5 March 1791 and 24 March 1791; *Grands sabats*, no. 5 (n.d.).

78 Norman Hampson, *A Social History of the French Revolution* (London, 1963), pp. 157–58.

79 M. J. Sydenham, *The Girondins* (London, 1961). Sydenham provides important details on the opposition between Girondins and Montagnards before 31 May, but his conclusion that the Girondins did not constitute a party is questionable. Although it was a smaller party than that considered by Sydenham, the Girondins did form an alliance based on shared principles and common opposition to the Mountain.

80 *Courrier des 83 départements*, 26 September, 12 and 30 October 1792.

81 *Courrier des départements*, 25 April 1793.

82 *Courrier des départements*, 21 October 1792; 2 and 6 January 1793.

83 *Courrier des départements*, 12 and 13 January 1793.

84 Gorceix, "Antoine-Joseph Gorsas," p. 181.

85 Michaud, *Biographie universelle*.

Notes

86 Bouloiseau, "Robespierre," p. 28.

87 *Courrier des 83 départements*, 16 August 1792.

88 *Chronique de Paris*, 17 August 1792.

89 *Journal de Paris*, 7 January 1793.

90 Ibid.

91 Yves Barré, *La Chaste Suzanne* (Paris, 1793).

92 *Chronique de Paris*, 8 January 1793.

93 *Républicain française*, nos. 60, 61 (13, 14 January 1793). See Henri Welschinger, *Le théâtre de la Révolution* (Paris, 1880), pp. 381–408 for documents on the debates over *L'Ami des lois* in the Municipal Council and the National Convention.

94 *Chronique de Paris*, 31 January 1793.

95 *Chronique de Paris*, 15 February 1793; *Journal des spectacles*, 29 July 1793.

96 Petition from Desfontaines, Radet, and Barré to National Convention, and forwarded to Committee of Public Instruction (29 September 1793), AN, F^{17} 1004^a, dossier 2, no. 356.

97 Dossier Radet, AN, F^7 4774^{86}.

98 Letter to the Committee of General Security, dated 22 September [1793], dossier Radet.

99 Memos from the Tuileries section, 24 and 30 September 1793, dossier Radet.

100 Note from Tuileries section, 20 brumaire an II, dossier Radet.

101 Letter from Desfontaines to Section Le Pelletier, 9 Frimaire l'an II, dossier Desfontaines, AN, F^7 4672.

102 *Feuille du salut public*, 4 frimaire an II.

103 Letter from Barré to Comité du Sureté Générale, 29 du 1er mois [an II], dossier Radet.

104 *Journal des spectacles*, 19 September 1793.

105 A. Piis, *Le Mariage du vaudeville et de la morale*, comédie en un acte, en vers, mêlée de vaudevilles (Paris, an II).

106 On the popularity of *L'Heureuse Décade*, see Beatrice Hyslop, "The Theater during a Crisis: The Parisian Theater during the Reign of Terror," *Journal of Modern History* 17, no. 4 (December 1945): 332–55.

Interlude: *From* Chant de Guerre *to* La Marseillaise

1 *Chronique de Paris*, 6 April 1792.

2 *Courrier des 83 départements*, no. 7, 24 and 27 April 1792. *Révolutions de Paris* even printed a song that fit the specificied criteria in its no. 144, 7–14 April 1792.

3 *Courrier des 83 départements*, 27 June 1792; *Chronique de Paris*, 10 April and 4 May 1792.

4 The following discussion of the career of *La Marseillaise* before its arrival in Paris is drawn from Louis Fiaux, *La Marseillaise* (Paris, 1918); Jean-Louis Jam, "Fonction des hymnes révolutionnaires," in *Les fêtes de la Révolution*, ed. Jean Ehrard and Paul Villaneix (Paris, 1977); Hervé Luxardo, *Histoire de la Marseillaise* (Paris, 1989); Constant Pierre, "La Marseillaise," in his *Hymnes et chansons*; Julien Tiersot, *Rouget de Lisle: Son oeuvre, sa vie* (Paris, 1892); Michel Vovelle, "La Marseillaise: La guerre ou la paix," in *Les lieux de mémoire*, vol. 1: *La République*, ed. Pierre Nora (Paris, 1984).

5 F. J. L. Meyer and Désiré Monnier both claimed to have heard of this complaint from Rouget de Lisle himself. F. J. L. Meyer, *Fragments sur Paris*, translated from German by General Dumouriez (Hambourg, 1798), pp. 89–91; Désiré Monnier, "Rouget de L'Isle à Strasbourg," *Souvenirs d'un octogénaire de province*, (Lons-le-Saulnier, 1867).

[6] A facsimile of the first Strasbourg edition appears in A. Rouget de Lisle, *La vérité sur la paternité de la Marseillaise* (n.p., 1865). This corresponds to a number of subsequent versions, although a few leave out the fifth stanza.

[7] *Ah! ça ira: Dictom populaire* (n.p., 1790), BHVP, 106901, no. 60. "Les voeux des Républicains," air: ça ira. *Nouveau chansonnier patriote* (Lille and Paris, an II).

[8] Vovelle, "La Marseillaise." On the distribution of the *Chant de guerre* among soldiers in Strasbourg, see Fiaux, *La Marseillaise*, pp. 29–30.

[9] *Révolutions de Paris*, no. 160, 28 July–4 August 1792.

[10] *Chronique de Paris*, 31 July 1792; *Courrier des 83 départements*, 2 August 1792; *Journal de Paris*, 4 August 1792. That the *fédérés* were described as singing *Ça ira* rather than the *Chant de guerre* may tell us more about the newspaper report than about what the soldiers actually sang. The *Chant de guerre* had not yet acquired emblematic status, so its presence would carry no particular weight with readers. Singing *Ça ira*, on the other hand, was immediately recognizable as shorthand for the political convictions of the *fédérés*.

[11] This version differs somewhat from the version that was printed and sold by the publisher Frère.

[12] *Chronique de Paris*, 29 August 1792; *Courrier des 83 départements*, 30 August 1792.

[13] *Révolutions de Paris*, no. 167, 15–22 September 1792.

[14] *Courrier des 83 départements*, 28 July 1792; for the *Trompette du Père Duchesne*, see Pierre, *Hymnes et chansons*, p. 232.

[15] Constant Pierre catalogued about 65 separate printings of the *Marseillaise* in Parisian public collections. Pierre, *Hymnes et chansons*, pp. 223–26.

[16] The final verse was called the verse of the children.

[17] For uses of the tune of *La Marseillaise* for other songs, see entry for "Allons enfants de la patrie" in the index of airs, Pierre, *Hymnes et chansons*, pp. 999–1000.

[18] *Chronique de Paris*, 13 September 1792; Report of Rousseville for 11 September [1793], AN, F^7 3688^3, dossier 2. See also *Chronique de Paris*, 29 March 1793; Report of Perrières for 8 June 1793, AN, F^{1c}III Seine 27, dossier 1; *Moniteur universel*, 7 July 1793; Report of Bacon for 26 nivôse an II, AN, F^7 3688^3, dossier 6; Pierre, *Hymnes et chansons*.

[19] Fiaux, *La Marseillaise*, pp. 34–35.

[20] Quoted in Tiersot, *Rouget de Lisle*, appendix Q, pp. 415–16.

[21] *Moniteur universel*, 25 October 1792. In Paris, the celebration took place near the pedestal that had, until 10 August, held a statue of Louis XV. A statue of Liberty had already been erected in its place. *Courrier des départements*, 15 October 1792.

[22] *Chronique de Paris*, 19 October 1792.

[23] Meyer, *Fragments sur Paris*, vol. 1.

[24] Serge Bianchi, *La révolution culturelle de l'an II* (Paris, 1982); Hunt, *Politics, Culture, and Class*; Jean-Claude Bonnet, ed., *La carmagnole des Muses* (Paris, 1988); Emmett Kennedy, *A Cultural History of the French Revolution* (New Haven, 1989).

4. *The Revolutionary Song (April 1792–Pluviose Year III)*

[1] On newspaper production, see figures in Claude Bellanger, ed., *Histoire générale de la presse française*, vol. 1 (Paris, 1969), p. 436; Antoine de Baecque includes figures on pamphlet publication in "Pamphlets: Libel and Political Mythology," in *Revolution in Print: The Press in France, 1775–1800*, ed. Robert Darnton and Daniel Roche (Berkeley and Los Angeles, 1989). On Opéra and Comédie-Française, see Kennedy, *Cultural History*, pp. 176–79.

[2] These figures do not accord with the generally accepted figures for song production given by Pierre in his *Hymnes et chansons* because he lumps together revolutionary and

counterrevolutionary songs. When the counterrevolutionary songs are separated out, the growth of revolutionary production is striking: from 147 songs in 1791, to 270 in 1792, to perhaps 500 in 1793.

[3] Other forms of revolutionary culture also expanded at this point in the Revolution. For example, more paintings may have been produced, or perhaps more amateur works exhibited, as a result of the abolition of academic privilege. See Udolpho Van Sandt, "La peinture: situation et enjeu," in Bonnet, *La Carmagnole des Muses.*

[4] This chapter necessarily slights song production in the provinces. While provincial song production is beyond the scope of this book, much of it did make its way to Paris in the form of songs and poetry submitted to the National Convention. See AN, F[17] 1002–1009; AN, D XXXVIII 5.

[5] Beauchant, *La chanson des sans-culottes* (n.d.) BHVP, 18148(2). See also Ladré, *La Révolution de 10 août,* (Paris, n.d.), BN, fiche Ye 35763(28); *A tous les citoyens morts pour la patrie, à l'affaire des Thuilleries, du 10 août 1792* (Paris, 1792), BN, Ye 35763(15).

[6] *Chanson au sujet de Louis Capet, ci-devant Roi, traduit à la barre de la Convention Nationale* . . . (n.p., n.d.), BN, Ye 2230. Similarly, singers of the *Carmagnole du café Yon* confidently proclaimed: "[Louis] n'est que suspendu / mais il sera déchu," [Louis is only suspended, but he will be dethroned]; Déduit, *La Carmagnole du café Yon* (n.p., n.d.), BHVP, 10151(30).

[7] See, for example, Mercier, "Chansonniers gagés," *Paris pendant la Révolution,* 2:219–20; Fournier, *Histoire du Pont Neuf;* Fernand Engerand, *Ange Pitou: Agent royaliste et chanteur des rues* (Paris, 1899).

[8] *Feuille du salut public,* 28 frimaire an II; Minutes from section Molière et LaFontaine, floréal an II, Bibliothèque Victor Cousin MSS 118; report by Bacon for 28 nivôse an II, AN, F[7] 3688[3]; Procès-verbal de l'Assemblée Générale, Section du Contrat Social for 23 April 1793, in *Die Sansculotten von Paris,* ed. Albert Soboul and Walter Markov (Berlin, 1957), p. 10; songbooks published by section Tuileries, AN, AD VIII 35, nos. 52–58, 65, 71.

[9] For sections, see report by Leharivel for 29 September 1793 and the report by Bacon for 28 nivôse an II, AN, F[7] 3688[3]; register from section Molière et La Fontaine, floréal an II, Bibliothèque Victor Cousin MSS 118, p. 45; Soboul and Markov, *Die Sansculotten von Paris,* pp. 10, 32, 50, 146. For the Commune and Convention, see *Chronique de Paris,* 15 May and 6 July 1793.

[10] See, for example, accounts of the performance of the *Marseillaise* by singers from the Opéra and of the *Hymne dédié aux Jacobins de Paris* by Legall, both published in *Affiches de la Commune de Paris,* no. 90 and 95 (17 and 25 September 1793).

[11] Report by Mercier for 30 nivôse an II, AN, F[7] 3688[3]. For an outdoor performance, see Report by Perrière for 8 June 1793.

[12] Report by Rousseville for 11 September 1793; reports by Dugard for 4 nivôse an II, Monic for 5 nivôse an II, Courvoyers for 10 nivôse an II, AN, F[7] 3688[3].

[13] Reports by Bacon for 2 pluviose an II, Dugard for 11 nivôse an II, AN, F[7] 3688[3].

[14] The classic definition of the sans-culottes is, of course, that of Albert Soboul, *The Sans-Culottes: The Popular Movement and Revolutionary Government, 1793–1794,* trans. Remy Inglis Hall (Princeton, 1980). For critical discussion, see Gwyn A. Williams, *Artisans and Sans-Culottes: Popular Movements in France and Britain during the French Revolution* (London, 1968); Richard Andrews, "Social Structures, Political Elites and Ideology in Revolutionary Paris, 1792–1794," *Journal of Social History* 19 (Fall 1985); Michael Sonenscher, "The Sans-Culottes of the Year II: Rethinking the Language of Labor in Revolutionary France," *Social History* 9 (October 1984).

[15] See, for example, discussions about whether women should wear cockades (in September 1793) as well as debates over executions and the innocence of Hébert (nivôse an II) recorded by police spies in AN, F[7] 3688[3].

[16] Albert Soboul, *The Sans-Culottes*, p. 37.

[17] See comments on political "moderatisme" in Soboul and Markov, *Die Sansculotten von Paris*, p. 26.

[18] See article 8 of regulations concerning accordance or refusal of *certificats de civisme*, in Soboul and Markov, *Die Sansculotten von Paris*, p. 214.

[19] Procès verbal de la section Contrat Social, 21 avril 1793, AN, C 355; *Affiches de la Commune*, no. 21, 7 July 1792; *Feuille de la République*, 19 messidor an II.

[20] *Le courage martial de la jeunesse en réquisition*, by Ladré [slnd], BN, Ye 56375(184).

[21] On learned ideas of fraternity, see entry for "Fraternity," in François Furet and Mona Ozouf, eds., *The Critical Dictionary of the French Revolution*, trans. Arthur Goldhammer (Cambridge, Mass., 1989). See also Marcel David, *Fraternité et Révolution française* (Paris, 1987). David's book has the advantage of distinguishing between learned and popular ideas of fraternity: the former, he argues, was a theory that gave birth to practice whereas the latter idea emerged from practice. Although he examines the relationship between fraternity and sectional business, and between fraternity and violence, he does not examine its relationship to equality.

[22] When sans-culottes celebrated equality, they celebrated a world in which all social hierarchy was to be swept away. Just as all aspects of Old Regime public life had served to remind the king's subjects of their social status, so now every aspect of revolutionary society—from the use of the word "citizen" to the disorder of public processions—was taken as a reminder of the equality of all men. For discussion of the meaning of disorderly processions, see report by Latour-Lamontagne for 10 nivôse an II, AN, F^7 3688^3.

[23] Report by Bacon for 7 pluviose an II, AN, W191. For other accounts of singing at fraternal dinners, see reports by Bacon for 10, 16, and 26 nivôse an II, AN, F^7 3688^3.

[24] "Suite du discours prononcé par Chaumette au nom de la Commune de Paris, à la Convention nationale," *Affiches de la Commune*, no. 34, 21 July 1793.

[25] Procès verbal de la section du Pont Neuf, 4 September 1793, Soboul and Markov, *Die sansculotten von Paris*, p. 148.

[26] For presentations to the Commune, see Albert Soboul, ed., *Affiches de la Commune de Paris, 1793–1794* (reprint: Paris, n.d.), nos. 95 (25 September 1793); 99 (27 September 1793); 101 (30 September 1793); 109 (9 October 1793); 145 (28 brumaire an II). For presentations to Convention, see the sittings described in *Moniteur universel*, 7 July 1793; *Chronique de Paris*, 6 July 1793.

[27] Even before 1789, citizens corresponded with the government to offer inventions or projects that might benefit the realm. Such correspondence expanded with the opening of the Revolution, as citizens appeared before the bar of the Assembly to give speeches, make proposals, or simply to celebrate the Assembly. The Committee of Public Instruction, created by the Legislative Assembly, collected proposals that were concerned, in the broadest possible terms, with education and instruction; their papers bear witness to the reflections of private citizens on the means to reshape France. The archival cartons for the Committee of Public Instruction, primarily F^{17} 1001–1010, are filled with educational proposals, poetry, songs, and pedagogic tracts. Series C, the papers of sessions of the Assembly and the Convention, also include some statements and proposals made to both bodies.

[28] Letter and song from Massabiau to National Convention, 20 nivôse an II, AN, F^{17} 1009^a, no. 1811.

[29] For examples of early songs, see, *L'enterrement de Dame Aristocratie au Champ de Mars*, in *Recueil de chansons patriotiques*, no. 3 (n.p.,1790), Princeton University, Firestone Library, (Ex)DC141.C6 no. 431. See also, *Récit historique de ce qui s'est passé dans la ville de Paris* (n.p., n.d.), BN, fiche Ye 35763(2); Ladré, *Ah! com' ça va* (n.p., n.d.); *Complainte de notre très Sainte Père, le Pape* (n.p., n.d.), BN, Res. Ye 3171; *Chanson nouvelle: Les adieux aux curés aristocrates de Paris* (n.p., n.d.), BN, Ye 56375(86).

Notes

[30] Ladré, *Chanson burlesque* (n.p., 1793), BN, Ye 56375(78). See also *Hymne des Sans-Culottes*, par un citoyen de la Section du Panthéon Français (n.p., n.d.), BN, Ye 55471(1120).

[31] See, for example, *L'énergie de la Montagne, ou le triomphe de la République française*, par un Jacobin de la section régénérée de Beaurepaire (n.p., n.d.), BHVP, 18148(3); *Couplets pour l'inauguration des bustes de Marat et LePelletier* (n.p., n.d.), Bibliothèque de l'Arsenal, Collection Rondel, Ro 14,026; Ladré, *La liberté universel* (n.p., n.d.), BN, Ye 56375(223).

[32] "Les députés conspirateurs devant le Tribunal Criminel révolutionnaire," Le citoyen Sauvage, *Couplets* (n.p., n.d.), Bibliothèque du Senat: 5/155. See also, *La Fuite, ou le pas redoublé des Prussiens and Autrichiens* (n.p., n.d.), BN, Ye 56375(431); *Chanson d'un sans-culotte sur la prise de Toulon and d'autres, qui ont dansé l'même branle à la queululu, Affiches, annonces, et avis divers*, no. 391, *Supplément à la feuille du septidi 7 pluviose; Couplets faits par des citoyens, détenus comme suspects à la Maison d'arrêt de la Force, bâtiment de la Dette, à l'occasion de la prise de Toulon* (n.p., n.d.), BHVP, 8447(2); *Insurrection des Montagnards contre les Brissotins* (n.p., n.d.), Bibliothèque du Senat, 5/160. Against Louis XVI and Marie-Antoinette, see *Ho-la! Ho la!*, (n.p., n.d.), BN, Ye 46375(286); *Recueil d'ariettes*, by Bellerose (n.p., n.d.), BHVP, 18149(1); Leveau, *Extrait des crimes de Louis-le-dernier . . .* (Paris, n.d.), BN, Ye 35763(19).

[33] *L'énergie de la Montagne.*

[34] On sans-culottes' conception of friends and enemies, see Soboul, *Sans-Culottes;* David, *Fraternité et Révolution française.*

[35] Report by Latour-Lamontagne for 22 pluviose, an II, AN, W191; report by Charmont for 9 nivôse an II, AN, F⁷ 3688³. On obscene songs, see reports of Bolin for 1 ventôse an II and by Perrières for 16 ventôse an II, AN, W112; *Le Batave*, 16 brumaire an II.

[36] Report by Bacon for 20 pluviose an II, AN, W191.

[37] Carla Hesse, *Publishing and Cultural Politics in Revolutionary Paris, 1789–1810* (Berkeley, 1991).

[38] See, for example, *Recueil de chansons patriotiques*, no. III, (Paris, n.d.), Princeton Univeristy, Firestone Library, (Ex) DC141.C6 n° 431; *Le chansonnier patriote, ou recueil de chansons nationales, et autres, choisies, composées et chantées par Ladré, père, accompagné de son fils* (Paris, 1791), BN, fiche Ye 35763(5). Counterrevolutionary songbooks evolved more quickly: royalists produced a number of lengthy, sung satires against the Revolution. See, for example, the productions of Frédéric Marchant, *Etrennes au beau sexe* (Paris, 1792); *La Constitution en vaudevilles*; and *La République en vaudevilles* (Paris, n.d.).

[39] Thomas Rousseau, "Avertissement," *Les chants du patriotisme* (Paris, 1792).

[40] Thomas Rousseau, "Quelques observations sur les chants du patriotisme," *Chants du patriotisme*, no. 24.

[41] Thomas Rousseau, "Circulaire à mes abonnés des départements," *Chants du patriotisme*, no. 41.

[42] In one issue, Rousseau even went so far as to encourage subscriptions by quoting the minister of foreign affairs's praise of the republican advantages of his work. See Rousseau, *Chants du patriotisme*, no. 24.

[43] *Triomphe de la Liberté et de l'Egalité*, par la citoyenne Ferrand (Paris, 1793), BN, Ye 34121; *Chansonnier patriote* (Paris, "an I de la République"), BN, Ye 10659; *Chansonnier de la Montagne* (Paris, an II), BN, Ye 22156; *Chansons patriotes*, par le citoyen Piis (Paris, an II), BN, Ye 11287; *Chansonnier de la Montagne* (Paris, an III), BN, Ye 17630; *Lyre républicain* (Paris, an III), BN, Ye 26958.

[44] "Préface de l'éditeur," *Nouveau chansonnier patriote* (Paris and Lille, an II). See also "Avertissement," *Chansonnier de la Montagne* (Paris, an II).

[45] At least one bookseller went so far as to advertise his songbooks by associating them with specific republican ceremonies: "*Chansonnier décadaire*, or anthology of select hymns

... meant to be sung in our temples, in popular societies, in primary schools." "Annonce," *Courrier républicain*, 26 fructidor an II.

[46] "Avertissement," *Chansonnier patriote* (Paris, "an I de la République").

[47] *Journal des hommes libres*, 6 brumaire an II; *Feuille du salut public*, 16 brumaire, 9 frimaire an II.

[48] Songbooks for section des Tuileries, AN, AD VIII 35. nos. 52–58, 65, 71. *Journal des spectacles*, 26 September 1793; see also next note.

[49] *Annales patriotiques*, 25 germinal an II; *Feuille de la République*, 24 germinal and 5 floréal an II.

[50] "Avertissement," *Chansonnier de la Montagne*.

[51] "Théâtre du Vaudeville," *Spectacles de Paris* 1794, pp. 17–23. See also letter from Mentelle to National Convention, 6 floréal an II, AN, D XXXVIII 5, dossier 65.

[52] Notice for *Le chansonnier patriote, Chronique de Paris*, 11 January 1793; review of "La nourrice républicaine," *Feuille du Salut Public*, 12 germinal an II.

[53] See Bonnet, "Le chantier et la ruine," in his *La carmagnole des Muses*.

[54] See, for example, James Johnson, "Revolutionary Audiences and the Impossible Imperatives of Fraternity," in *Re-creating Authority in Revolutionary France*, ed. Bryant Ragan and Elizabeth Williams (New Brunswick, N.J., 1992).

[55] Brécy, "La chanson révolutionnaire"; Leith, "Music as an Ideological Weapon."

[56] On the Convention's cultural policies, see Roger Hahn, *The Anatomy of a Scientific Institution* (Berkeley, 1971), pp. 226–85; Kennedy, *Cultural History*, pp. 141–373; Carla Hesse, *Publishing and Cultural Politics*, pp. 125–44.

[57] J. B. Leclerc, *De la poésie, considerée dans ses rapports avec l'education nationale* (Paris, 1793). Leclerc claimed that his thoughts had turned to the matter after hearing Rabaut St.-Etienne's proposals for decrees on public education. Leclerc did not add that Rabaut had very little to say about the relationship of *poésie* to public instruction. See also "Opinion de Rabaut sur l'éducation national," *Républicain universel*, no. 23, December 1792.

[58] Dominique Julia, *Les trois couleurs du tableau noir* (Paris, 1981); Pierre, *Hymnes et chansons*.

[59] Pierre, *Hymnes et chansons*, pp. 30–34, 58–68.

[60] Letters from Rousseau, AN, F^{1c}III Seine 27, no. 3249. According to John Lynn, Minister of War Bouchotte recorded paying Rousseau 80,000 livres for songbooks. See Lynn, *The Bayonets of the Republic* (Urbana, 1984), pp. 143–44.

[61] Petition from Les Artistes de Musique de la Garde Nationale Parisienne, AN, F^{17} 1007, no. 1275. See also, Constant Pierre, *B. Sarette et les origines du Conservatoire national de musique* (Paris, 1895).

[62] "Loi qui ordonne la formation d'un Institut National de Musique à Paris," 18 brumaire an II, *Lois et actes du gouvernement*, vol. 8 (Paris, 1834–1835).

[63] Professors of the Music School of the Paris National Guard to Committee of Public Instruction, 27 frimaire an II, AN, F^{17} 1047, dossier 3; J. Guillaume, *Procès-verbaux du Comité d'Instruction publique* (Paris, 1891–1907), 180th session, 21 nivôse an II; "Extrait des délibérations du Comité d'Instruction publique," 29 ventôse an II, AN, AF II 67, p. 32.

[64] Tiersot, *Fêtes et chants*, pp. 132–33.

[65] Jam, "Fonction des hymnes révolutionnaires."

[66] Jam, "Fonction des hymnes révolutionnaires"; Ozouf, "The Future of the Festival: Festivals and Pedagogy," *Festivals and the French Revolution*.

[67] These lines are from Ladré, *Chanson burlesque* (n.p., n.d.), BN, Ye 56375(78).

[68] Thomas Rousseau, "A nos frères et amis des fauxbourgs Saint-Antoine et Saint-Marceau, dit les sans-culottes," *L'âme du peuple et du soldat* (n.p., n.d.), AN, F^{1c} III Seine 27, dossier 5; Marie-Joseph Chenier, *Chant du départ*, reprinted in *Chansonnier révolutionnaire*, ed. Paul-Edouard Levayer (Paris, 1989).

[69] Thomas Rousseau to National Convention, 11 March an II, AN, F^{17} 1004a, no. 395.

[70] John Lynn quotes a recruit in the Armée du Nord, "We marched without order, in profound silence, each man absorbed in his own thoughts. Suddenly the smallest man in the batallion began to sing. . . . The whole battalion repeated the chorus, and great joy replaced the sadness in our ranks." Lynn, *Bayonets of the Republic*, p. 143. See also, Jean-Paul Bertaud, *La révolution armée* (Paris, 1979), pp. 144–52.

[71] Société des Artistes Musiciens de la Garde-Nationale-Parisienne, *Prospectus de deux ouvrages periodiques de musique à l'usage des Fêtes Nationales*, AN, F^{17} 1013, no. 17.

[72] Ibid.

[73] "Plan d'institution d'une musique et education nationale," from Martini to Comité d'Instruction Publique, AN, F^{1c}I 84 no. 1873. See also, Leclerc, *De la poésie*.

[74] "Sadly, the people of the departments and even some of those in Paris are not as enlightened as the groups, or perhaps only the orators within the groups," report of Perrières for 6 June 1793, AN, F^{1c} III Seine 27, dossier 1.

[75] *Feuille du salut public*, 2 July 1793.

[76] *Feuille de la République*, 27 floréal an II. On the revolutionary tribunal, see interrogations of those accused of singing counterrevolutionary songs: dossier Desestangs and Mandavy, AN, W39, no. 2618; dossier Charles François Amée, AN, W51, no. 3325.

[77] Even an individual singer had the power to reach many people. "If one hears perhaps the same orators every day, [the audience] is not always composed of the same citizens; each goes there or stops by as his affairs permit or as chance leads him." *Feuille du salut public*, 2 July 1793.

[78] Interrogation of Durland, dossier Desestangs and Mandavy, AN, W39 no. 2618. Alexis Beaupré, "dit Tarras," was alone in openly stating that he had sung a counterrevolutionary song, but he was quite clearly insane and was declared so by physicians who visited him in prison. AN, W1 no. 59.

[79] See, for example, reports by Perrière for 16 and 19 ventôse an II, AN, W112.

[80] Report by Rousseville for 12 September 1793. See also, reports by Le Harivel for 8 September 1793, by Courvoyers for 7 nivôse an II, and by Bacon for 13, 26, and 28 nivôse an II, AN, F^7 3688^3; *Feuille de la République*, 13 and 19 messidor an II.

[81] See, for example, Danton's interventions at National Convention séances of 8, 9, and 18 nivôse, 5 pluviose, 7 ventôse an II, as reported in *Moniteur universel.*

[82] National Convention, sitting of 26 nivôse, as reported in *Moniteur universel*, 27 nivôse an II.

[83] Ibid.

[84] R. R. Palmer, *Twelve Who Ruled: The Year of the Terror in the French Revolution* (New York, 1966), pp. 317–34.

[85] Decree of the National Convention, 18 floréal an II AN, F^{1c}I 84, dossier 1.

[86] "La Commission d'Instruction publique aux poètes," published in *Journal de Paris* and *Feuille de la République*, 9 thermidor an II.

[87] These invitations were hardly necessary. Private compositions had been pouring into the Convention for months: citizens offered them as expressions of patriotism which, many hoped, would compensate for their meager talent. See AN, F^{17} 1002–1009, D I, sec. 2^1, D XXXVIII 5.

[88] Document from the Institut National de Musique, 19 prairial an II, BHVP 773, no. 256.

[89] "Annonce," *Feuille de la République*, 22 vendémiaire an III. Similar announcements appeared in the *Courrier républicain*, 25 and 26 fructidor an II; *Journal de Paris*, 5 and 29 vendémiaire an III.

[90] *Gazette française*, 25 thermidor an II.

5. The Reactionary Song (Brumaire Year III–Ventôse Year IV)

[1] See François Furet and Denis Richet, *La Révolution française* (Paris, 1965), pp. 258–59.

[2] Alphonse Aulard, "La Querelle de la *Marseillaise* et du *Réveil du peuple*," *Etudes et leçons.*

[3] Police report for 12 thermidor an II, in Alphonse Aulard, *Paris pendant la réaction thermidorienne et sous le Directoire*, vol. 1 (Paris, 1898), p. 9.

[4] *Gazette française*, 25 thermidor an II.

[5] In the three months following 9 thermidor 4,300 people were released. Furet and Richet, *Révolution française*, p. 277; François Gendron, *La jeunesse dorée* (Québec, 1979), p. 9.

[6] François Gendron, *Jeunesse dorée*, pp. 62–67.

[7] Kare Tønnesson, *La défaite des sans-culottes* (Oslo and Paris, 1959), pp. 115–16.

[8] Kare Tønnesson, *La défaite des sans-culottes*, p. 84.

[9] *Journal de Paris*, 29 nivôse an III.

[10] Police report for 26 nivôse an III, in Aulard, *Paris pendant la réaction*, 1:390–91.

[11] See police reports for 25–29 nivôse an III, in Aulard, *Paris pendant la réaction*, 1:387–403.

[12] *Messager du soir*, 1 pluviose an III.

[13] See, for example, *Couplets* (n.p., n.d.), BN, Ye 19197; *Invitation aux français*, (n.p., n.d.), BN, Ye 55471(1145).

[14] *Messager du soir*, 2 pluviose an IV; in Aulard, *Paris pendant la réaction*, 1:411–12.

[15] *Messager du soir*, 4 pluviose an III. See also, la Butte des Moulins section to the police commissioner for 3 pluviose an III, APP, Aᵃ 96, no. 15; *Feuille de la République*, 5 pluviose an III (neither source mentions specific songs). For Gaveaux's performance at the café de Chartres, see *Courrier républicain*, 4 pluviose an III, in Aulard, *Paris pendant la réaction*, 1:414–15.

[16] *Courrier républicain*, 5 pluviose an III, in Aulard, *Paris pendant la réaction*, 1:421.

[17] Report of Barbarin, Jacot for 16 ventôse an III, in Aulard, *Paris pendant la réaction*, 1:533–34.

[18] *Journal des hommes libres*, 13 ventôse an III. It was the representation of the *Réveil* as an anti-Republican song that the *Messager du soir*, sympathetic to the *jeunesse dorée*, fought when it twice reported that the *Réveil* had been sung in concert with the *Hymne des Marseillois*. Other Parisian papers did not report performances of the *Hymne*, but it was still clearly a powerful symbol of allegiance to the Republic.

[19] "Réflexions sur les opinions révolutionnaires," *Annales patriotiques*, 14 and 16 brumaire an III; letter and song printed in *Feuille de la République*, 22 pluviose an III; "L'infortunée Lyonnaise," *Feuille de la République*, 3 ventôse an III, and "Le chien victime de sa fidelité," *Feuille de la République*, 14 ventôse an III. See also, *Le Voeu du Peuple: Chanson à l'ordre du jour*, par le vieux sans-culotte, HERSY [slnd], BN, Ye 24135; *Le Cri de la Vengeance* [slnd], BN, Ye 19325.

[20] *Journal de Paris*, 2 ventôse an III. The note was followed by the lyrics to a song by Jauffret and Méhul, with information about where to purchase the sheet music. The same song was reprinted in the *Feuille de la République* the next day, 3 ventôse an III. Jauffret and Méhul must have found some success with this lugubrious romance because, only ten days later, the two newpapers announced that the composers had produced another, similar song. "Le chien victime de sa fidelité" commemorates a faithful dog who fell victim to a Jacobin prison guard while carrying messages between his imprisoned master and the master's young wife. *Feuille de la République*, 14 ventôse an III; *Journal de Paris*, 16 ventôse an III.

[21] *Courrier républicain*, 14 ventôse an III; *Annales patriotiques*, 7 germinal an III.

[22] Furet and Richet, *Révolution française*, p. 298.

[23] Furet and Richet, *Révolution française*, p. 307.

[24] Police report for 6 floréal an III, in Aulard, *Paris pendant la réaction*, 1:685.

Notes

²⁵ See police reports for 17 floréal and 24 floréal an III, in which the *Réveil* is described as the song favored by "the public." Aulard, *Paris pendant la réaction,* 1:704, 720.

²⁶ Rudé, *Crowd in the French Revolution,* pp. 152–59.

²⁷ Furet and Richet, *Révolution française,* pp. 301–2. The repression, while ending in the execution of only half of those convicted, otherwise bore a striking resemblance to repression in the year II: citizen Menier was disarmed because he was overheard singing a song in favor of the guillotine, while a certain Rouland was arrested because his neighbors claimed that he had "Pain et la Constitution de 1793" written on his hat and because he possessed a parody of the *Réveil du peuple* which was "a stranger to good morals." See dossier Menier, AN, F⁷ 4774⁴² and dossier Rouland, AN, F⁷ 4775¹.

²⁸ Georges Lefebvre, *The French Revolution,* trans. Elizabeth Moss Evanson, J. H. Stewart, and J. Friguglietti (New York, 1964), pp. 155–56.

²⁹ "Loi portant que les airs et chants civiques . . . seront executés par les corps de musiques des gardes nationales," *Lois de la République française,* no. 163. For newspapers, see Furet and Richet, *Révolution française,* pp. 309–10.

³⁰ Report of Rouchas, jeune, and Doillot for 26 messidor an III, in Aulard, *Paris pendant la réaction,* 2:77–79.

³¹ *Courrier républicain,* 29 messidor an III; *Courrier de Paris,* 27 messidor an III.

³² *Courrier républicain,* 29 messidor an III.

³³ For the *Gazette française* and discussion of Jean de Bry's speech before the Convention, see text and note in Aulard, *Paris pendant la réaction,* 2:85; *Courrier républicain,* 29 messidor an III.

³⁴ *Courrier de Paris,* 28 messidor an III. See also, *Courrier républicain,* 28 and 29 messidor an III.

³⁵ *Journal des hommes libres,* 30 messidor an III; *Annales patriotiques,* 3 thermidor an III.

³⁶ *Courrier républicain,* 1 and 2 thermidor an III; *Courrier de Paris,* 1 thermidor an III.

³⁷ Report of Léger and Rouchas, jeune, for 6 thermidor an III, in Aulard, *Paris pendant la réaction,* 2:109–10.

³⁸ *Moniteur universel,* 15 thermidor an III.

³⁹ *Courrier de Paris,* 29 messidor an III. For a similar kind of description, but one more heavily weighted against the *Hymne,* see *Messager du soir,* 28 messidor an III.

⁴⁰ *Courrier de Paris,* 28 and 29 messidor an III; *Courrier républicain,* 29 messidor an III. The only exception was on the evening that the decree was passed, when some of the customers at the café du Caveau sang the *Marseillaise.*

⁴¹ After the soldiers pulled their swords "the young people hurled themselves upon the sabres and repelled the soldiers." *Courrier républicain,* 2 thermidor; *Courrier de Paris,* 2 thermidor an III. In Vendémiaire, too, there was an incident in which several soldiers went to sing the *Marseillaise* in the gardens of the Palais Egalité, a known royalist enclave, and ended by fighting with the *jeunesse dorée,* who responded to the song by pitching chairs at them. "Declaration des citoyens Deneuilly, Blondel et Romain qu'ils ont été maltraités à la maison Egalité," APP, Aª, nos. 502–4.

⁴² Dossier Gavaudan, AN, F⁷ 4720. See also interrogations of Micalef and Gavaudan in dossier Micalef, AN, F⁷ 4774⁴⁴.

⁴³ *Courrier de Paris,* 29 messidor an III.

⁴⁴ Compare this to the same article's description of the *Marseillaise:* "the hymn of the *Marseillais* guided your victorious march against foreign enemies; but revolutionary assassins abused the enthusiasm that the song inspired in patriots." *Messager du soir,* 28 messidor an III.

⁴⁵ *Courrier de Paris,* 2 thermidor an III. See also "Discours prononcé . . . par Boissy d'Anglas," in *Courrier de Paris,* 4 thermidor an III.

⁴⁶ "Conseils d'un jeune homme à ses frères les jeunes gens," in *Courier de Paris,* 30 messidor an III.

[47] *Courrier républicain*, 2 thermidor an III.

[48] Dossier Gavaudan, AN, F[7] 4720; dossier Micalef, AN, F[7] 4774[44].

[49] Aulard, "La querelle entre la *Marseillaise* et le *Réveil du peuple*," *Etudes et leçons*, p. 255.

[50] *Journal de Perlet*, 16 thermidor an III, in Aulard, *Paris pendant la réaction*, 2:133.

[51] *Couplets au peuple français sur l'acceptation de la nouvelle constitution*, par le citoyen Abril (Paris, an III), AN, F[7] 3688[4], nos. 431–34.

[52] L.-A. Pitou, *Le désespoir du peuple contre les Agioteurs* (n.p., n.d.). See also the notice for the song in the review of a book by a writer named Saint-Aubin, *Courrier de Paris*, 8 thermidor an III.

[53] *Courrier de Paris*, 23 thermidor, 3 and 28 fructidor an III; *Journal du Bonhomme Richard*, no. 17 [n.d.]; *Journal du Bonhomme Richard*, 3 thermidor, 6 fructidor an III.

[54] *Courrier républicain*, 3 vendémiaire an IV; *Courrier de Paris*, 5 vendémiaire an IV; "Déclaration de Deneuilly, Blondel, Romain . . . ," APP, A[a] 98, nos. 502–4.

[55] *Journal des hommes libres*, 20 vendémiaire an IV. See also "Arrêté du Comité de Sureté Générale," APP, A[a] 98, no. 566.

[56] "Arrêté du Directoire executif concernant les spectacles. Du 18 nivôse . . . ," *Bulletin des lois de la République française*, no. 18 (Paris, an III).

[57] *Moniteur universel*, 28 nivôse an IV.

[58] Correspondence between police and the minister of interior on surveillance of théâtre du Vaudeville, brumaire–frimaire an IV, AN, F[7] 3688[4], no. 3026; *L'ami des lois*, 14 frimaire an IV; *L'anti-royaliste*, 30 pluviose an IV.

[59] Report of Champion for 24 nivôse an IV, AN, F[7] 3491, dossier 2.

[60] Report of Champion for 27 nivôse an IV, AN, F[7] 3492, dossier 4.

[61] The verse in question begins, "Français! en guerriers magnanimes . . ." See note from Ferizel to police générale, 3 pluviose an IV, AN, F[7] 3491, dossier 2; report of Maisoncelle for 21 ventôse an IV, AN, F[7] 3688[5], dossier 3.

[62] Anonymous note to minister of police, 13 pluviose an IV, AN, F[7] 3491, dossier 2; notes on théâtre du Vaudeville by Courrier, 21 floréal an IV, APP, A[a] 253, no. 348.

[63] *Annales patriotiques*, 4 pluviose an IV.

[64] "Chouans" were royalist peasants in upper Brittany who waged a lengthy guerilla war against the Revolution. *Courrier républicain*, 20 and 22 pluviose an IV; *L'anti-royaliste*, 23 pluviose an IV.

[65] Report of Champion for 23 nivôse an IV, AN, F[7] 3491, dossier 2; note to minister of police, 3 pluviose and 6 pluviose an IV, AN, F[7] 3492, dossier 4, nos. 15, 17.

[66] "Trois jeunes gens pour bruit au Vaudeville," 25 pluviose an IV, APP, A[a] 253, nos. 169–72; "Procès-verbal sur Vaudeville," 8 ventôse an IV, APP, A[a] 253, no. 197; "Dossier sur Crosnier," ventôse–floréal, AS, D1U[1] 35, dossier 4045; "Rapport de police," 1er jour complémentaire an IV, APP, A[a] 100, nos. 425–29.

[67] Report of [illegible], division du secret, 16 ventôse an IV, AN, F[7] 3688[7]; report of Maisoncelle, 14 and 17 ventôse an IV, AN, F[7] 3688[5].

[68] *Courrier de Paris*, 5 messidor an IV; *Courrier républicain*, 26 messidor an IV.

[69] *Annales patriotiques*, 22 nivôse an IV.

[70] *Messager du soir*, 28 messidor an III.

6. The Song in Retreat (Messidor Year III–Brumaire Year VIII)

[1] Letter and proposed regulation from administrative commissioners to minister of interior, 5 Brumaire an IV (issued 3 frimaire), AN, F[7] 3688[8], dossier 3380. For the Messidor decree, see *Journal des hommes libres*, 30 messidor an III.

[2] Notice from musicians of National Guard and arrêté du Comité du Salut Public, AN, AF II 67, dossier 493, pp. 15, 17.

[3] Association of Artistes-Musiciens to Committee of Public Safety (n.d.) and arrêté du Comité de Salut Public, 21 messidor an II, AN, AF II 67, dossier 493, pp. 65–66.

[4] Arrêté du Comité du Salut Public, 6 thermidor an II, AN, AF II 67, dossier 493, p. 68.

[5] Pierre, *B. Sarrette*, p. 96. See also papers of Committee of Public Safety, AN, AF II 67, dossier 493, pp. 60, 62.

[6] "Journal des mandats expédiés sur la Trésorerie Nationale en vertu des fonds mis à la disposition de la Commission de l'Instruction Publique," an III, AN, F^{4*} 363.

[7] "Loi portant établissement d'un Conservatoire de Musique à Paris pour l'enseignement de cet art," article II, 16 thermidor an III, in *Organisation du Conservatoire de Musique* (Paris, an V).

[8] Ibid.; report by administrators of the National Institute of Music for the Committee of Public Instruction (n.d.), AN, F^{17} 1069, dossier 1.

[9] "Ecole Nationale de Musique, Chant, et Déclamation au Comité d'Instruction Publique," 28 germinal an III, AN, AF II 67, dossier 494, p. 29.

[10] R. R. Palmer, *The Improvement of Humanity: Education and the French Revolution* (Princeton, 1985), pp. 221–36.

[11] P.-C.-F. Daunou, "Rapport sur l'instruction publique," in *Une éducation pour la démocratie: Textes et projets de l'époque révolutionnaire*, presented with notes and introduction by Bronislaw Baczko (Paris, 1982). See also Julia, *Les Trois Couleurs*; Hahn, *Anatomy of a Scientific Institution*; Pierre, *B. Sarrette*.

[12] The first decree was voted by the Constituent Assembly on 9 September 1791; it was extended on 3 September 1793. Jacques Guillaume, *Procès-verbaux du Comité d'Instruction Publique*, 54th sitting, 20 February 1793 (Paris, 1891–1907).

[13] For example, in Germinal year III a prize of 3,000 livres was divided among more than a dozen individuals. "Loi qui accorde des gratifications aux savants et artistes y dénommés," 27 germinal an III, AN, F^{17} 1021^b, dossier 6, no. 40. For the price of bread during that same period, see Rudé, *Crowd in the French Revolution*, pp. 142–44.

[14] This tendency would become still more marked at the end of the year III, when the Convention voted to allow individuals "who carry out several tasks related to public instruction" to accumulate prizes. Law no. 1063, 16 fructidor an III, *Lois de la République française* (Paris, an III).

[15] Champein to Committee of Public Instruction, 17 nivôse, AN, F^{17} 1210, no. 41; Chapelle to the committee, 19 nivôse, AN, F^{17} 1213, no. 43; Desfontaines to the committee, 30 vendémiaire, AN, F^{17} 1210, no. 63; Chapelain to Fourcroy, 20 nivôse an III, AN, F^{17} 1213, no. 57. The awards offered in the year VII were smaller, but the individuals being considered fit a similar professional profile; see AN, F^{17} 1021^a, dossier 7, nos. 2–4, 8–9.

[16] For a description of Bellerose, see letter to *Chronique de Paris*, 17 February 1792.

[17] Arrest of Duval, Leveau, and others, 6 prairial an III, AN, F^7 4699, dossier 1.

[18] Ladré to Committee of General Security, nivôse an III, AN, F^{17} 1210, nos. 89–90.

[19] "Loi qui accorde des gratifications . . . ," AN, F^{17} 1021^b, dossier 6, no. 40. In fact, the Germinal subsidies did not include any musicians or songwriters. Two other, undated, lists of subsidies among the papers of the Committee of Public Instruction did include the names of several musicians and composers whose status accorded with that of Champein, Desfontaines, and Rigade. Ladré's name did not appear on either of them. See "Troisième liste des hommes de lettres et artistes compris dans les recompenses . . . ," undated, and "Suite de la liste des artistes et gens de lettres demandant des secours" (n.d.), AN, F^{17} 1012, dossier 6.

[20] Palmer, *Improvement of Humanity*, pp. 222–25.

[21] Ozouf, *Festivals and the French Revolution*, pp. 118–25.

[22] Leclerc, *De la poésie.*

[23] Jean-Baptiste Leclerc, *Essai sur la propagation de la musique en France, sa conservation, et ses rapports avec le gouvernement* (Paris, an IV).

[24] Leclerc, *Essai sur la propagation,* p. 52.

[25] The proposal was not adopted, and in the year VII Leclerc was still suggesting new means of organizing national musical education. Jean-Baptiste Leclerc, *Rapport fait par Leclerc . . . sur l'établissement des écoles spéciales de musique* (Paris, an VII).

[26] Petition from Sarrette and Gossec, in the name of the National Institute, to the National Convention (n.d.), AN, DXXXVIII 2, dossier 24, no. 50. See also letter from National Institute to Committee of Public Safety (n.d.), AN, DXXXVIII 5, dossier 70; *Prospectus de deux ouvrages periodiques de musique à l'usage des fêtes nationales* (Paris, an II), AN, F^{17} 1013, no. 17; *Ouvrage periodique de musique à l'usage des fêtes nationales . . . : prospectus* (Paris, [an III?]), AN, AF II 67, dossier 494, p. 35.

[27] *Organisation du Conservatoire de Musique* (Paris, an V).

[28] Constant Pierre, *Magasin de Musique à l'usage des fêtes nationales* (Paris, 1895), app. A–F.

[29] Leclerc, *Rapport.*

[30] Leclerc, *Essai sur la propagation,* p. 16; Leclerc, *Rapport,* p. 12.

[31] Letter from minister of interior to administrative commissioner of police, 24 Brumaire an IV, AN, F^7 3688^4, no. 3074.

[32] Report of Perrières, 8 June 1793, AN, F^{lc} III Seine 27, dossier 1.

[33] Letter from Reubell to minister of interior, 24 frimaire an IV, AN, F^7 3688^8, no. 3406. The excessive concern shown by police for different kinds of counterrevolutionary singing was more a reflection of official concerns about sedition than of a marked change in the nature of street singing. Newspapers of the period described both kinds of songs and singing—the patriotic as well as the counterrevolutionary. See, for example, *L'ami des lois,* 28 frimaire an IV; *Courrier républicain,* 11 messidor an IV; *L'ami des lois,* 3 vendémiaire an V; *Clef du cabinet,* 9 thermidor an V.

[34] Letter from Minister of Interior to central bureau of police, 29 frimaire an IV, AN, F^7 3688^8, no. 3406.

[35] "Chansonnier dont les discours et les manières pervertissent l'esprit public," 27 nivôse [an IV], AN, F^7 3688^6, dossier C.

[36] Letters to minister of police from Maisoncelle, 27 ventôse an IV; letter from Amel, 29 ventôse an IV, AN, F^7 3688^7, dossier 3.

[37] After a pitched battle between insurgents and the army, in which some three hundred people were killed, the gates of the city were left open and those most seriously implicated were allowed to escape. Thirty insurrectionaries were tried and only seven sentenced to death, five of them *in absentia.* Denis Woronoff, *La République bourgeoise de thermidor à brumaire* (Paris, 1972), pp. 42–45. This stands in sharp contrast to the vigorous suppression of the popular movement after the Germinal and Prairial uprisings.

[38] Report of central bureau of police for 27 germinal an V, in Aulard, *Paris pendant la réaction,* 3:120.

[39] These articles are taken from the draft of the project for regulation, sent from administrative commissioners of police to the minister of interior, 5 brumaire an IV, AN, F^7 3688^8, no. 3380.

[40] Report of Bréon for 23 pluviose an V, in Aulard, *Paris pendant la réaction,* 3:744.

[41] "Bateleurs, chanteurs, faiseurs de tours, etc. Extrait des registres des délibérations du bureau central du canton de Paris . . . ," 3 messidor an IV, AN, F^7 3688^5, no. 12893.

[42] "Loi portant des peines contre toute espèce de provocation à la dissolution du Gouvernement républicain . . . ," 27 germinal an IV, *Bulletin des lois,* no. 40.

[43] Claude Mazauric, *Babeuf et la conspiration pour l'égalité* (Paris, 1962), pp. 188–90.

Notes

[44] From *Première instruction du Directoire secret adressée à chacun des agents révolutionnaires principaux*, summarized in Gerard Walter, *Babeuf et la Conjuration des Egaux* (Paris, 1937), p. 128.

[45] "Directoire secret . . . aux principaux agents révolutionnaires des arrondissements municipaux," in Haute Cour de Justice, *Copies des pièces saisies dans le local que Babeuf occupoit lors de son arrestation* (Paris, an V), 17th piece.

[46] *Chanson nouvelle à l'usage des faubourgs*, "Papiers trouvés chez Babeuf," AN, F^7 4278, dossier 2, no. 35.

[47] *La nouvelle carmagnole*, in *Copies des pièces saisies . . .*, 33d piece.

[48] Mazauric, *Babeuf*, pp. 197–99.

[49] Isser Woloch, *Jacobin Legacy: The Democratic Movement under the Directory* (Princeton, 1970), p. 49.

[50] Woloch, *Jacobin Legacy*, p. 53.

[51] Woloch, *Jacobin Legacy*, pp. 56–58; Mazauric, *Babeuf*, pp. 209–10.

[52] Session of 2 ventôse, an V, *Débats du procès instruit par la Haute Cour de Justice, contre Drouet, Babeuf, et autres; recueillis par des sténographes* (Paris, an VI), no. 1.

[53] See, for example, the session of 11 ventôse an V, *Débats du procès*, no. 17.

[54] See, for example, Buonarotti's explanation of his critical attitude toward the Constitution of 1795. Among the factors that drove him into opposition he included the closing of clubs, the freedom of which had been constitutionally guaranteed; the favor shown to returning émigrés; the protection given to grain hoarders and speculators; the violation of freedom of the press; and the proscription of republican words, symbols, and festivals. Session of 14 germinal an V, *Débats du procès*, no. 76.

[55] *Débat du procès*, no. 17

[56] Session of 16 and 17 ventôse an V, *Débats du procès*, nos. 21, 23. On Sophie Lapierre, see Mazauric, *Babeuf*, p. 210.

[57] Sessions of 21, 23, and 27 ventôse an V, *Débats du procès*, nos. 33, 38, 46.

[58] Sessions of 2 and 10 germinal an V, *Débats du procès*, nos. 54, 68; session of 30 ventôse, reported in *Clef du cabinet*, 5 germinal an V.

[59] *Débats du procès*, no. 61. For another episode of dramatically confrontational singing, see the debate that took place on 19 ventôse an V, which ended with the defendants singing the *Marseillaise* with raised fists.

[60] Mazauric, *Babeuf*, p. 216.

[61] For example, *Couplets de circonstance, Stances faites à l'anniversaire du tyran le 21 janvier*, in "Papiers trouvés chez Babeuf," or an untitled song to the air of *La tentation de St. Antoine*, among "Papiers trouvés chez Ch. Germain," AN, F^7 4278, dossiers 2, 3. See also *Copies des pièces saisies*, vol. 1, 33d piece; vol. 2, 2d–4th, 26th, and 45th pieces.

[62] Session of 14 germinal an V, *Débats du procès*, no. 76.

[63] *Exposé fait par les accusateurs nationaux près la Haut-Cour de Justice* (Paris, an V).

[64] Session of 22 ventôse an V, *Débats du procès*, no. 35. The testimony of another state's witness, Lidon, is similar. He described a generous lunch in a café followed by a discussion of insurrection and the singing of the *Marseillaise* and "several songs analogous to their scheme." See session of 5 germinal an V, *Débats du procès*, no. 61.

[65] *Débats du procès*, no. 40.

[66] Denis Woronoff, *République bourgeoise*, pp. 65–66.

[67] Report of agent 21, 13 frimaire an V, AN, F^7 3688^{11}, dossier "Rapports d'agents."

[68] *Rapsodies, ou Seances des deux conseils, en vaudevilles*, Prospectus? [n.d.].

[69] *Rapsodies du jour*, no. 2 (1796).

[70] *Courrier républicain*, 11 germinal an V.

[71] Report of agent 33, 18 frimaire an V, AN, F^7 3688^{11}, dossier "Rapports d'agents."

[72] Louis-Ange Pitou, "Ma vie et les causes de mon exil," preface to *Voyage à Cayenne* (Paris, 1807), p. xix.

[73] Fernand Engerand, *Ange Pitou, agent royaliste et chanteur des rues* (Paris, 1899), chap. 5.

[74] Reprinted in Engerand, *Ange Pitou*, p. 52.

[75] Engerand, *Ange Pitou*, chap. 6.

[76] "Robespierre's tail" refers to the radicals who remained in the National Convention after 9 Thermidor.

[77] "By singing in public squares, I found myself associated with most of those who are without status and without quality." Louis-Ange Pitou, *Les déportés de fructidor*, annotated by Albert Savine (Paris, 1909), p. 16.

[78] Pitou, *Voyage à Cayenne*, p. xlii.

[79] Ibid., p. xliv.

[80] Dossier Pitou, AN, BB^{18} 745, no. 4069D; Engerand, *Ange Pitou*, pp. 115–31.

[81] Observations of no. 40, 27 nivôse an V, AN, F^7 3688^{10}, dossier 1.

[82] Correspondence with central bureau of police, pluviose an V, AN, F^7 3688^{10}, dossier 1.

[83] From testimony given at Pitou's trial in Brumaire, year VI. Printed in Engerand, *Ange Pitou*, pp. 148–49.

[84] Lefebvre, *French Revolution*, 1:198–99; Woronoff, *République bourgeoise*, pp. 74–75.

[85] Pitou, *Déportés de fructidor*, p. 21.

[86] Ibid.

7. Songs Silenced and Changed (From Ventôse Year IV into the Nineteenth Century)

[1] Both Hunt, *Politics, Culture, and Class*, and Ozouf, *Festivals and the French Revolution*, describe directorial culture as simply representing a continuation of the symbols and practices elaborated during the early years of the Revolution. On continuities between Directory and Empire, see Georges Lefebvre, *Napoleon*, vol. 1, *From brumaire to Tilsit*, trans. Henry F. Stockhold (New York, 1969), chap. 4. For a critique of representations of the Directory as a period of political apathy, see Lynn Hunt, David Lansky, and Paul Hanson, "The Failure of the Liberal Republic in France, 1795–1799: The Road to Brumaire," *Journal of Modern History* 51, no. 4 (December 1984): pp. 734–59.

[2] Woloch, *Jacobin Legacy*; Hunt, Lansky, and Hanson, "Failure of the Liberal Republic."

[3] Mercier, "Fête du 10 thermidor an IV," *Paris pendant la Révolution*, vol. 2.

[4] Surveillance de Paris for 1 vendémiaire an V, AN, BB^3 85.

[5] See, for example, complaints included in undated report [Messidor?] from year V, AN, BB^3 86; report for 28 ventôse an VI, AN, F^7 3688^{13}; "Renseignement pour le ministre de police," AN, F^7 3688^{14}, dossier 2, no. 25. An article about the "fête du souveraineté du peuple" in the *Rédacteur*, 1 germinal an VI, is quite unintentionally funny when explaining that many people (presumably the same "people" whose sovereignty is being celebrated) could not take an active part in the festival because of the need to keep the audience small enough to hear the speeches.

[6] Report by agent 19 on esprit public, vendémiaire–germinal an VI, AN, F^7 3688^{13}. See also *Rédacteur*, 1 vendémiaire an VI; "Renseignements pour le ministre de police," thermidor an VI, AN, F^7 3688^{14}; report by agent 8 for 16 ventôse an VII, AN, F^7 3688^{17}, no. 184.

[7] See, for example, *Journal des hommes libres*, 27 messidor an VII.

[8] For an overview of the economic life of the Directory, see Martyn Lyons, *France under the Directory* (Cambridge, 1975).

[9] See complaints in police report for 3 vendémiaire an V, AN, BB^3 85; report for 10–11 thermidor an VI, AN, F^7 3688^{13}.

[10] Police report for 23 floréal an VI, AN, F^7 3688^{13}.

[11] "People traversed the park singing patriotic tunes while repeating a thousand times, *down with the thieves, long live the republic.* This music, these cheers displeased a few of the loudmouths of the night before, who had the imprudence to loudly proclaim their discontent. The people were content to arrest and hand [these malcontents] over to the guard." *Journal des hommes libres,* 26 messidor an VII; see also 25 messidor an VII and 28 messidor an V; *Clef du cabinet,* 9 thermidor an V.

[12] Report by agent 5 for 13–14 frimarie an VII, AN, F^7 3688[15].

[13] Dossier 4081 on chansonniers patriotes, thermidor an VII, AN, F^7 6218; *Clef du cabinet,* 9 thermidor an V; report to minister of police for 3 messidor [an VI], AN, F^7 3688[14]; report by agent 34 for 23 fructidor and report by agent 25 for 27 fructidor an VII, AN, F^7 3688[19]; report by agent 7 for 19 vendémiaire an VIII, AN, F^7 3688[20].

[14] Report for 12 vendémiaire an V, AN, BB^3 85; report for 27–28 frimaire an V, AN, F^7 3828; report by agent 27 for 18 pluviose an VII, AN, F^7 3688[16].

[15] Report by agent 1 for 24 brumaire an VII, AN, F^7 3688[15]; report by agent 27 for 30 germinal an VII, AN, F^7 3688[18]. See also, report by agent 5 for 9 pluviose and for 29 pluviose an VII, AN, F^7 3688[16]; report by agent 27 for 20 ventôse an VII, AN, F^7 3688[17]; report by agent 41 for 23 frimaire an V, AN, F^7 3688[11].

[16] Reports by agents 43 and 45 for 22 pluviose an VII, AN, F^7 3688[16]; report by same for 15 ventôse an VII, AN, F^7 3688[17].

[17] Report by agent 77 for 20 germinal an VII, AN, F^7 3688[18]. A similar dispute over the singing of songs relative to Ash Wednesday was resolved in a still more peaceful fashion, as the opposing parties ended by drinking together; see report by agent 5 for 18 pluviose an VII, AN, F^7 3688[16].

[18] Undated police report for floréal an VI, AN, F^7 3688[13]. Another police spy noted, "Perfect tranquility reigns over the public and all conversations and every opinion announces horror of any kind of agitation." Report for 26 germinal an V, AN, BB^3 86. Mercier's description of the festival of 9–10 thermidor an IV, discussed above, is a celebration of such moderation.

[19] Notes to minister of police re: Citizen Arnoud, AN, F^7 3688[12], dossier 2, no. 6.

[20] Ibid.

[21] Report by agent 13 for 22 vendémiaire an VIII, AN, F^7 3688[20].

[22] *Rondeau des armées d'Italie, de Sambre et Meuse, du Rhin et Moselle, forçant l'Empereur à demander la paix,* par Leveau, dit Beauchant (Paris, n.d.), BN, Ye 46543.

[23] *Détail de la prise de Mantoue,* par Perottin, BN, Ye 49215.

[24] See *Dialogue entre le prince Charles et l'Empereur, demandant la paix,* par Leveau, dit Beauchant (Paris, n.d.), BN, Ye 46543; *Le songe affreux du roi d'Angleterre* (Dieppe, n.d.), Princeton University, Firestone Library (Ex)DC141.C6, no. 412; *L'accomplissement du songe du roi d'Angleterre* (Paris, n.d.), BN, Ye 55471(16).

[25] *Idylle sur la paix,* "addressée aux braves armées de la République française, paroles du Cn. Moline," (Paris, n.d.), Bibliothèque du Sénat, 6/277; *A la gloire de l'Armée d'Italie et de son général en chef, Buonaparte,* par le C. Buard, fils (Paris, n.d.), Bibliothèque du Sénat, 6/180.

[26] Report by agent 5 for 21 ventôse an VII, AN, F^7 3688[17].

[27] "Avertissement," *Journal des muses,* no. 1 (Paris, 1797).

[28] Songs were, in fact, not a major feature of the *Journal des muses.* This publication is worth considering, however, because it explicitly developed literary principles that other song journals would adhere to, and because it published the poetry and songs of several prolific songwriters.

[29] "Avertissement des nouveaux editeurs," *Journal des muses,* no. 7 (an V).

[30] "[Men of letters] seem to have seized upon the idea that it is of great import, even to matters of public order, that minds be turned once again to taste and to the culture of-

fered by literature's most seductive genres." "Avertissement," *Journal des muses*, no. 3. See also *Clef du cabinet*, 28 fructidor an V; *Rédacteur*, 21 brumaire an VII.

[31] Notice for *Les dîners du vaudeville*, no. 21, in *Clef du cabinet*, 12 messidor an V.

[32] "Rapport des commissaires nommés par la société des Dîners du vaudeville," *Dîners du vaudeville*, no. 1 (Paris, vendémiaire an V).

[33] *Dîners du vaudeville*, no. 1 (vendémiaire an V). The *Journal des muses* was less explicit, but gave its editors more room for discretion by saying only that "we will admit nothing that could encourage or aggravate party hatreds." "Avertissement," *Journal des muses*, no. 1.

[34] "Avertissement," *Journal des muses*, no. 3 (an V). This was hardly a surprising regulation in light of the eighteenth-century notion that taste ought to be based on "pure disinterested satisfaction." Such a determination could hardly be accomplished if confused with the interests of the political world. See Peter Gay, "The Discovery of Taste," *The Enlightenment: An Interpretation* (London, 1973); entry for "Goût" in *Encyclopédie*.

[35] *Les nouveaux troubadours*, recueil lyrique, no. 1 (Paris, an V), BN, Ye 29070.

[36] Lablée was elected president of the Luxembourg section and then of the Gravilliers section before going on to serve as general administrator of military subsistance and as public prosecutor in the Loiret. Imprisoned for publicly criticizing the trial of the king, Lablée later took great pride in refusing to seek revenge on Jacobins when he served as a prosecutor after Thermidor. See *Biographie de Jacques Lablée* (Paris, 1838); entry for Jacques Lablée in M. le Dr. Hoeffer, *Nouvelle Biographie Générale* (Paris, n.d.). For the presentation to Roederer, see the manuscript note on the title page of the Bibliothèque Nationale's copy of *Nouveaux troubadours*, BN, Ye 29070.

[37] See, for example, subjects for songs in *Dîners du vaudeville*, no. 15 (frimaire an VI).

[38] "Les baisers et les roses," *Journal des muses*, no. 3 (an V); *Dîners du vaudeville*, no. 25 (vendémiaire an VII).

[39] "Notice des ouvrages nouveaux," *Journal des muses*, no. 4 (messidor an V).

[40] *Journal des muses*, no. 12 (an V), no. 4 (an VI).

[41] "La paix," *Dîners du vaudeville*, no. 13 (vendémiaire an VI). See also "Couplets chantés à la fête des arts," *Dîners du vaudeville*, no. 20 (thermidor an VI); "Les adieux d'une mère à son fils partant pour la réquisition," *Chansonnier des grâces*, (Paris, an VII); Verse to Buonaparte, *Journal des muses*, no. 4 (an V); "Couplets chantés à la fête des arts," *Journal des muses*, no. 4 (an VI).

[42] Woloch's *Jacobin Legacy* contains the most complete discussion of conservative critiques of popular politics and legislative attempts to circumscribe it.

[43] "Constitution de 1795 ou de l'an III," *Les constitutions de la France depuis 1789*, ed. Jacques Godechot (Paris,1970), pp. 93–141.

[44] See articles 361, 362, 364, "Constitution de 1795 ou de l'an III," *Constitutions de la France*. On the difficulties of electoral registration and the consequences of article 362, which forbade national networks of political clubs, see Woloch, *Jacobin Legacy*.

[45] *Rédacteur*, 4 thermidor an V.

[46] "Proclamation du directoire exécutif aux Français, du 23 fructidor an V," *Journal des hommes libres*, supplément to no. 118 (28 fructidor an V).

[47] See, for example, review of *Journal des muses*, in *Rédacteur*, 9 frimaire an VI.

[48] Letter from August Hus to *Rédacteur*, 10 thermidor an VI.

[49] Letter from Joseph Rosny to *Le Thé*, 10 thermidor an VII; letters 14 and 15, on Paris theaters, in Joseph Rosny, *Le Peruvien à Paris* (Paris, 1801).

[50] See Chapter 6. See also Lyons, *France Under the Directory*, pp. 116–45; Palmer, *Improvement of Humanity*, pp. 222–36; Joanna Kitchin, *Un Journal "philosophique": La Décade (1794–1807)* (Paris, 1965), pp. 193–234.

[51] See, for example, the editorial in *Journal des hommes libres*, 28 fructidor an V.

[52] Earlier definitions of the vaudeville had centered on productions by the théâtre du Vaudeville. Although the theater remained important, the vaudeville's arena expanded once the periodical *Dîners du vaudeville*—founded and animated by the same men responsible for the theater's success—became equally important to the embodiment and publicization of the vaudeville's new image.

[53] *Journal de Paris*, 3 ventôse an V.

[54] Note on théâtre du Vaudeville in *Décade philosophique*, 10 frimaire an VI; Deschamps, "La différence entre le drame et le vaudeville," *Dîners du vaudeville*, no. 2 (brumaire an V).

[55] Desfontaines, "La nécéssité d'un théâtre du Vaudeville," *Dîners du vaudeville*, no. 1 (vendémiaire an V).

[56] See, for example, "Ronde chantée la journée de l'ouverture du théâtre du Vaudeville," by Barré, Radet, and Desfontaines, *Dîners du vaudeville*, no. 38 (brumaire an IX).

[57] On the institutional continuities between Directory and Empire, see Lefebvre, *Napoleon*, vol. 1; Hunt, Lansky, and Hanson, "Failure of the Liberal Republic."

[58] Police to Grand Juge, 20 fructidor an XI and 11 vendémiaire an XII, AN, F[18] 39 nos. 107, 131; report on *spectacles* by Petit, 4 messidor an VIII, AN, F[7] 3688[20]; statement from minister of police published in *Journal des hommes libres*, 29 brumaire an VIII.

[59] On Desorgues see Michel Vovelle, *Théodore Desorgues, ou la désorganisation* (Paris, 1985). For other cases, see Ernest d'Hauterive, ed., *La police secrète du Premier Empire* (Paris, 1908), vol. 1, items 745, 750, 1022; vol. 2, items 144, 1458, 1480; vol. 3, items 601, 721.

[60] Brigitte Level, "Le Caveau moderne," *A travers deux siècles: Le Caveau, société bachique et chantante, 1726–1939* (Paris, 1988).

[61] Level, *A travers deux siècles*.

[62] Level, *A travers deux siècles*, pp. 183–97.

[63] On *goguettes* see Pierre Brochon, *Béranger et son temps* (Paris, 1979); Edgar Leon Newman, "Politics and Song in a Parisian Goguette: The Lice Chansonnière, 1830–1848," *Maryland Historian* 12, no. 1 (Spring 1981); Claude Duneton, "Histoire de la goguette," *La goguette et la gloire* (Paris, 1984).

[64] Brochon, *Béranger et son temps*, pp. 9–10.

[65] Thomas Bremer, "Le chansonnier comme franc-tireur: Charles Gilles et la chanson ouvrière politique pendant la deuxième moitié de la Monarchie de Juillet," in *La chanson française et son histoire*, ed. Dietmar Rieger (Tubingen, 1988), p. 173.

[66] Quoted by Bremer, "Chansonnier comme franc-tireur."

[67] See T. J. Clark, *The Painting of Modern Life: Paris in the Art of Manet and his Followers* (Princeton, 1984).

Conclusion

[1] For scholarship that treats revolutionary political culture, see the Introduction. For a useful overview of scholarship on Old Regime political culture see Roger Chartier, *The Cultural Origins of the French Revolution*, trans. Lydia G. Cochrane (Durham, N.C., 1991).

[2] Quoted in Brochon, *Béranger et son temps*.

[3] Michel Vovelle, "*La Marseillaise*: La guerre ou la paix," in *Les lieux de mémoire*, vol. 1, *La République*, ed. Pierre Nora (Paris, 1984).

Bibliography

ARCHIVAL SOURCES

ARCHIVES NATIONALES (AN)

Series F^7: Police Générale.
Series F^{1}7: Comité d'Instruction Publique.
Series H^2: Bureau de la Ville de Paris, carton 2103.
Series W: Juridictions Extraordinaires, Tribunal Revolutionnaire.
Series DXXXVIII: Comité d'Instruction Publique, cartons 2–5.
Series AF II: Comité de Salut Public, cartons 32, 67.
Series BB^{18}: Ministère de la Justice, Corréspondance générale de la Division criminelle, cartons 745, 764.
Series BB^3: Ministère de la Justice, Affaires criminelles, cartons 81^1, 222.
Series C: Assemblée Nationale, carton 168.
Series DI§2^1: Dons et hommages faits aux Assemblées.
Series F1^c III Seine 27: Esprit public et élections.

ARCHIVES DÉPARTMENTALES DE LA SEINE (AS)

Series VD*: cartons 2029, 2042, 2053, 2737, 2768, 2770, 3410, 3411, 5984.
Series D1U^1: carton 35.
Series DQ^{1}0: carton 7.

ARCHIVES DE LA PRÉFECTURE DE POLICE DE PARIS (APP)

Series Aa: Procès-verbaux de Police.

Bibliography

BIBLIOTHÈQUE DE L'ARSENAL (BA)

Manuscripts (BA MSS)

5134: Entrées et sorties de la Bastille.
7083: Nouvelles à la main, lettres de Paris [1777–79].
10,319; 10,628; 10,633; 10,734; 10,832; 11,117; 11,420; 11,428; 11,441; 11,448; 11,501; 11,741; 11,749: Archives de la Bastille.

Collection Rondel

Series Ro: manuscript nos. 13,962, 14,008, 14,026, 14,003, 14,020.
Series Rt: manuscript no. 5276.
Series Rf: manuscript no. 19,568.

BIBLIOTHÈQUE NATIONALE (BN)

Manuscrits fonds français (BN MSS ff)

6685–87: "Mes Loisirs" par le libraire S.-P. Hardy (1786–1789).
7005: Receuil de pièces historiques sur la Revolution, documents sur les théâtres (1790–1798).
7574: Cabinet du Président Durey de Meinières, receuil de pièces diverses, vers, noëls, chansons.
21741: L'Administration et la police de Paris: livres.
22070; 22087; 22092; 22093; 22116; 22136: Collection Anisson-Duperron sur la librairie et l'Imprimerie.
25570: Receuil de plusieurs pièces concernant le Regiment de la Calotte (1734).
13713: Journal des événements survenus à Paris, du 2 avril au 8 octobre 1789, par un clerc du procureur au Châtelet.
12755: Receuil de discours, vers, et chansons pour et contre la Révolution française.

Manuscrits nouvelles acquisitions françaises (BN MSS naf)

312: Receuil de lettres autographes et de documents historiques de l'époque révolutionnaire.
3040: Biographies théâtrales.
3043: Papiers concernant le théâtre de l'Opéra.
3055: Receuil de papiers relatif au théâtre du Vaudeville.
6620: Receuil de chansons, la plupart de la periode révolutionnaire.
9192–93: Papiers Ginguené, Mémoires et documents relatifs à l'instruction publique pendant la Révolution.

BIBLIOTHÈQUE DU SÉNAT/BIBLIOTHÈQUE DE LA CHAMBRE DES DÉPUTÉS

Manuscript, 1421.

Bibliography

BIBLIOTHÈQUE HISTORIQUE DE LA VILLE DE PARIS (BHVP)

Manuscripts, folios 773, 777.

BIBLIOTHÈQUE VICTOR COUSIN

Manuscripts, folios 117–18.

PRINCETON UNIVERSITY, FIRESTONE LIBRARY SPECIAL COLLECTIONS (PU)

(Ex) Dc141.C6 nos. 407(2)–548: French Revolutionary songs from the *Cornwall Burnham Rogers Collection of Song sheets and Pamphlets of the French Revolution.*

PRINTED PRIMARY SOURCES

Affiches de la Commune de Paris, 1793–94, reimpression edited by Albert Soboul. Paris: EDHIS, [n.d.]

Ah! ca ira. Chanson nouvelle sur la fête du 14 Juillet 1790. [Paris]: Simon & Jacob Sion, 1790.

Almanach des prisons, [by Coissin]. Paris: Michel, an III.

Almanach du Père Duchesne. Paris: Imprimerie de Tremblay, [1791].

Anthologie Française, ou chansons choisies, depuis le 13eme siècle jusqu'à présent. Attributed by Barbier to Monnet. N.p., 1765.

[Bachaumont]. *Mémoires secrètes pour servir à l'histoire de la République des Lettres en France depuis MDCCLXII jusqu'à nos jours.* London: John Adamson, 1777–1789.

Bagneris, Citoyenne. *La Citoyenne Bagneris à la Convention Nationale.* [Paris]: Imprimerie de la Feuille des Spectacles, an II.

———. *Couplets adressés à mon epoux pour le jour de sa fête.* [Paris]: Imprimerie de la Feuille des Spectacles, n.d.

Barbier, E. J. F. *Journal historique et anecdotique du Regne de Louis XV.* Paris: Jules Renouard et Cie., 1847.

Barré, Yves. *La Chaste Suzanne: pièce en deux acts melée de vaudevilles.* [Paris]: "se trouve au théâtre et chez Maret," 1793.

Barré, Yves, and François Pierre Auguste Léger. *L'heureuse décade, divertissement patriotique en un acte et en vaudevilles.* Paris: Libraire du théâtre du Vaudeville, an II.

Brossette, Claude. *Du Vaudeville. Discours prononcé à l'Académie de Lyon en 1729*, published with introduction and notes by Achille Kuhnholtz. Paris: Comptoir des Imprimeurs Unis, 1846.

Ça Ira. Dictom Populaire. Avec Accompagnement du Clavecin, par Mr. André de l'Academy Royale. [Paris]: Frère, n.d.

Cantique nouveau sur l'air du cantique de S. Roche. N.p., n.d.

Chansonnier de la Montagne, ou Recueil de Chansons, Vaudevilles, Pots-pourris, et Hymnes patriotiques par différens auteurs. Paris: Favre, an II.

Chansonnier patriote, ou Recueil de Chansons, Vaudevilles et Pots-pourris patriotiques par différens auteurs. Paris: Garnery, an I.

Chenier, Marie-Joseph. *De la liberté du théâtre en France*. N.p., 1789.

Citoyen en Bonne Humeur. Bouillon & Paris: Belin, 1789.

Condorcet, M.-J.-A.-N., "Fragments sur la liberté de la Presse" (1776), *Oeuvres*, vol. 11. Paris: Didot, 1847.

Confédération Nationale, du 14 Juillet 1790, ou description fidèle de tout ce qui a précédé, accompagné, et suivi cette auguste cérémonie, no. 2. Paris: Imprimerie de Simon et Jacob-Sion, 1790.

Convention Nationale, Comité du Salut Public. *Arrêtés du Comité du Salut Public, relatifs aux monuments publics, aux arts, et aux lettres*. Paris: an II.

Des Essarts. *Dictionnaire universel de police*. Paris: Moutard, 1785–1787.

Desfontaines de la Valée, Guillaume François Fouques Deshayes. *Les mille et un théâtres, opéra-comique en un acte et en vaudevilles*. Paris: Salle du théâtre du Vaudeville, 1792.

Détails de la fête nationale du 14 juillet, arrêtés par le Roi. [Paris]: Garnery, 1790.

Dictionnaire laconique, veridique et impartial, ou Etrennes au Demagogues sur la Révolution française. "A Patriopolis . . . l'an troisième de la prétendu liberté."

Dîners du Vaudeville. Paris: "Imprimeur des Dîners," an V–an VII, an IX.

Duvergier, J. B. *Collection complète des Lois, Décrets, Ordonnances, Règlemens et Avis de Conseil d'Etat*. Paris: Guyot & Scribe, 1825.

L'Elève d'Epicure, ou Choix des chansons de L. Philipon la Madeleine, de l'Académie de Lyon; précédé d'une notice sur Epicure et sur le Caveau; et suivi de quelques contes en vers. Paris: imprimerie Delamarre, [an IX?].

Encyclopédie, ou Dictionnaire Raisonné des Sciences, des Arts et des Metiers, par une Société de Gens de Lettres. Neufchatel: Samuel Fauche, 1765.

Etrennes au Beau Sexe, ou la Constitution Française mise en Chansons, suivie de Notes en vaudevilles constitutionnels. Paris: Imprimerie Royale, 1792.

Etrennes des Troubadours, chansonnier lyrique et anacréontique pour l'an VIII. Paris: Gaillot, an VIII.

Etrennes Dramatiques, à l'Usage de Ceux qui fréquentent les Spectacles, par un Amateur. Paris: Garnier, 1798.

La France Régénérée, et les traîtres punis. Paris: Imprimerie Valleyre, [1789].

Le Grand Oculiste du Champ de la Tuerie, cidevant de la Fédération, ou la Cataracte enlevée aux aveugles Parisiens. N.p., n.d.

Grétry, André Ernest Modest. *Richard, coeur de Lion*. Bruxelles: n.d.

Hardy, Siméon-Prosper. *Mes Loisirs. Journal d'Evénements tels qu'ils parviennent à ma connaissance*, vol. 1. Paris: Libraire Alphonse Picard et fils, 1912.

Haute Cour de Justice. *Copie de l'instruction personnelle au representant du peuple Drouet*. Paris: Imprimerie Nationale, an V.

——. *Copie des pièces saisie dans le local que Baboeuf occupoit lors de son arrestation*. Paris: Imprimerie Nationale, an V.

Instruction sur les mauvaises chansons et sur les saints cantiques. Paris: Benoit, 1779.

La Joie du peuple à la vue des préparatifs que l'on fait au Champ-de-Mars, par G——. N.p., n.d.

Ladré. *Ah! Com' Ça Va, les bons François trompés par les Noirs*. N.p., n.d..

LeBrun. *Odes Républicaines au peuple français*. Paris: Imprimerie Nationale de Lois, an III.

Leclerc, Jean-Baptiste. *De la poésie, considerée dans ses rapports avec l'éducation nationale.* Paris: Imprimerie Nationale, 1793.

——. *Essai sur la propagation de la musique en France, sa conservation, et ses rapports avec le gouvernement.* Paris: Imprimerie Nationale, an IV.

——. *Rapport fait par Leclerc (de Maine et Loire) sur l'établissement d'écoles spéciales de musique.* Paris: Imprimerie Nationale, an VII.

Léger, François Pierre Auguste. *L'Auteur d'un moment, comédie en un acte et en vaudevilles.* Paris: Salle du théâtre du Vaudeville, 1792.

Lois et Actes du Gouvernement. Paris: Imprimerie Royale, 1834–1835.

La Lyre d'Anacréon, choix de romances, vaudevilles, rondes de table, et Ariettes des pièces de Théâtre les plus nouvelles et les meilleures, avec figure et les airs notés [by Mercier de Compiègne]. Paris: Favre, an VII.

Manuel, Pierre. *La Police de Paris dévoilée.* Paris: Garnery, an II.

Marchant, Frédéric. *La Constitution en vaudevilles, suivis des droits de l'homme, et de la femme et de plusieurs autres vaudevilles constitutionnels.* Paris: Libraires Royalistes, 1792.

Melpomène et Thalie Vengées, ou Nouvelle Critique Impartial et Raisonnée, tant de differents théâtres de Paris, que des pièces qui y ont été représentées pendant le cours de l'année dernière. Paris: Marchand, an VII.

Mercier, Louis Sebastien. *Entretien du Jardin des Tuileries de Paris.* Paris: Buisson, 1788.

——. *Paris pendant la Révolution (1789–1798), ou le nouveau Paris.* Paris: n.p., 1862.

——. *Tableau de Paris,* nouvelle édition. Amsterdam: n.p., 1782.

Mercier (de Compiègne). *Concerts républicains, ou choix lyrique et sentimental.* Paris: Louis, an III.

Mervesin, Joseph. *Histoire de la poésie française.* Paris: Pierre Giffart, 1706.

Meyer, Frédéric Jean Laurent. *Fragments sur Paris.* Translated from the German by General Dumouriez. Hamburg: n.p., 1798.

Morgan, Lady. *La France.* Translated from the English by A. J. B. D. Paris and London: Truettel & Wurtz, 1817.

Nougaret. *Chansons de Guerre, pour les soldats français, au moment de combattre les ennemis de la République et de la Liberté; suivies des nouvelles Minerves.* Paris: Debray, an II.

Nouveau chansonnier patriote, ou Recueil de chansons, vaudevilles, et pots-pourris patriotiques, par différens auteurs. Lille and Paris: chez Deperne & chez Barba, an II.

Les Nouveaux Troubadours, recueil lyrique, no. 1. Paris: au Bureau, rue S. Thomas du Louvre, an V.

Organisation du Conservatoire de Musique. Paris: Imprimerie de la République, an V.

Organisation du Conservatoire de Musique. Paris: Imprimerie du Conservatoire de Musique, an VIII.

Peltier, J. *Dernier Tableau de Paris, ou Récit historique de la Révolution du 10 Août 1792.* London: chez l'auteur, 1794.

Person. *Chants Républicains, et Poésies Patriotiques.* Paris: chez Basset et chez Dufart, [an III].

Piis, Antoine. *Hymne à l'imprimerie.* N.p., n.d.

——. *Le mariage du vaudeville et de la morale.* Paris: Salle du théâtre du Vaudeville, an II.

Pitou, Louis-Ange. *Les déportés de fructidor,* annotated by Albert Savine. Paris: n.p., 1909.

——. *Le désespoir du peuple contre les agioteurs.* [Paris]: "se trouve rue Percée," n.d.

——. *La queue, la tête et le front de Robespierre, en vaudeville.* [Paris]: "se trouve rue Percée," n.d.

——. *Voyage à Cayenne.* Paris: n.p., 1807.

Prousinalle, M. de [Roussel]. *Histoire secrète du tribunal révolutionnaire.* Paris: Lerouge, 1815.

Pujoulx, J. B. *Paris à la fin du 18ème siècle.* Paris: Brigite Mathé, an IX (1801).

Radet, Jean-Baptiste, and Guillaume Desfontaines. *Couplets des citoyens Radet et Desfontaines, détenus à la maison d'arrêt de Laforce [sic], adressés au Conseil Général de Paris pour réclamer leur liberté.* N.p., n.d.

Receuil de chansons patriotiques, no. III. [Paris]: Simon & Jacob Sion, n.d.

Receuil de chansons, vaudevilles, et arriettes, qui ont été chantés avec succès sur les théâtres de Paris, depuis le commencement de la révolution jusqu'à présent, avec les air notés. Paris: Fr. Dufart, an IV (1796).

Receuil des couplets d'annonce chantés sur le théâtre du Vaudeville, depuis la première représentation d'Arlequin Afficheur jusqu'à ce jour, précédé d'une notice historique sur ce théâtre, par E. A. Dossion, secretaire. Paris: Capelle, an XI (1803).

Recueil d'hymnes patriotiques chantés aux séances du Conseil Général de la Commune, par les citoyens de la première requisition et de l'armée révolutionnaire. N.p., 1793.

Restif de la Bretonne, Nicolas. *Nuits de Paris, ou le Spectateur Nocturne.* London: n.p., 1788.

La Revue des théâtres, ou Suite de Melpomène et Thalie vengées, 3d year. Paris: Marchand, an VIII.

Rouget de Lisle, Joseph. *Hymne dithyrambique sur la conjuration de Robespierre et la Révolution du 9 thermidor.* [Paris]: Imbault, n.d.

Ruellan, Adrien-François. *Te Deum en Français, ou Hymne de réjouissance et d'actions de grâces à Dieu, pour toutes les fêtes et cérémonies publiques, patriotiques et décadaires de l'année, et un avis préliminaire.* Paris: Rochette, an III.

Savary des Bruslons, Jacques. *Dictionnaire universel de commerce.* Paris: Jacques Estienne, 1723.

Souvenirs du Baron Hüe, officier de la chambre du roi Louis XVI et du roi Louis XVIII (1787–1815), publiés par le Baron de Maricourt, son arrière-petit-fils. Paris: Calmann-Lévy, n.d.

Les Spectacles de Paris, et de toute la France, ou Calendrier historique et chronologique des théâtres. Paris: Duchesne, n.d.

Vues proposées dans l'Assemblée des Amis de la Constitution, séante aux Jacobins Sainte-Honoré, pour éclairer le peuple de la campagne, le 21 Septembre 1791. [Paris]: Imprimerie du Patriote François, n.d.

Bibliography

JOURNALS

Les Actes des Apôtres.

A Deux Liards, A Deux Liards, Mon Journal.

L'Ami des Lois, ou Memorial politique et littéraire, par Poultier et une Société de gens de lettres.

L'Ami du Roi, des Français, de l'ordre, et surtout de la vérité.

Annales patriotiques et littéraires de la France, par une société d'écrivains patriotes et dirigé par M. Mercier.

L'Anti-Royaliste, journal de la rue de Chartres.

Chronique de Paris.

La Clef du Cabinet des Souverains. Paris: Gratiot puis Panckouke.

Courrier de Paris, ou Chronique du Jour, par Imbert, Labatut, et de la Platrière.

Courrier de Versailles à Paris, de Antoine Joseph Gorsas. Known subsequently as: *Courrier de Paris dans les provinces; Courrier de Paris dans les 83 départements; Courrier des 83 départements; Courrier des départements.*

Courrier Républicain, par Poncelin.

Débats du procès instruit par la Haute Cour de Justice, contre Drouet, Baboeuf, et autres; recueillis par des sténographes. Paris: Imprimerie Nationale, an VI.

La Décade philosophique, litteraire, et politique, par une société de Gens de lettres, an VI & an VIII.

Le Disciple des Apôtres.

Les Evangalistes du jour. Paris: Garnery, "l'an premier de la Liberté."

Feuille du Salut Public, par une société de gens de lettres (par A. Rousselin).

Gazette de Paris, de Rozoi.

Gazette française, par Fievée et J.-Ch. Poncelin.

Les Grands Sabats, pour servir de suite aux Sabats Jacobites, [par F. Marchant].

Journal de Paris.

Journal des Halles, 1790.

Journal des hommes libres de tous les pays, ou le Républicain, rédigé par plusieurs écrivains patriotes. an V–an VIII.

Journal des Muses, par une Société de Gens de Lettres. Paris: Imprimerie de Didot, jeune, an V–an VII.

Journal des Rieurs, ou le Democrite français, par Martainville.

Journal des Spectacles, published by Boyer.

Journal du Palais-Royal.

Journal en vaudevilles.

La Légende d'orée, ou les Actes des martyrs.

Messager du Soir, ed. by Isidore Langlois & Lunier.

Le Rambler, ou le Rodeur.

Les Rapsodies du jour, par Villers.

Le Rédacteur, "par une société de gens de lettres." an V–an VII.

Le Républicain, ou Journal des hommes libres de tous les pays.

Le Républicain universel, later, *Républicain français.*

La Rocambole des journaux, "rédigée par dom Religius Anti-Jacobinus et compagnie."

Les Sabats jacobites, par F. Marchant.

Bibliography

PRINTED SECONDARY SOURCES

Albert, Maurice. *Les théâtres des boulevards (1789–1848)*. Paris: n.p., 1902.

Aulard, Alphonse. *Paris pendant la réaction thermidorienne et sous le Directoire*. Paris, 1898; New York: AMS Press, 1974.

——. "La presse officieuse sous la Terreur," and "L'art et la politique en l'an II," *Etudes et leçons sur la Révolution française*, 1st series. Paris: F. Alcan, 1905.

——. "La querelle de la *Marseillaise* and du *Réveil du peuple*," *Etudes et leçons sur la Révolution française*, 3d series. Paris: F. Alcan, 1902.

Baecque, Antoine, de. *La caricature révolutionnaire*. Paris: Presses du CNRS, 1988.

Baker, Keith Michael. *Inventing the French Revolution*. Cambridge: Cambridge University Press, 1990.

Barbier, Pierre, & France Vernillat. *Histoire de France par les chansons*. Paris: Gallimard, 1956–1957.

Barnes, Clifford. "Vocal Music at the Théâtres de la Foire." *Recherches sur la musique française classique*. 8 (1968): 141–60.

Bellanger, Claude. *Histoire générale de la press française*, vol. 1. Paris: Presses Universitaires de Françe, 1969.

Bergeron, Louis. *France under Napoleon*. Trans. R. R. Palmer. Princeton: Princeton University Press, 1981.

Bertaud, Jean-Paul. *Les Amis du Roi: Journaux et journalistes royalistes en France de 1789 à 1792*. Paris: Librairie Académie Perrin, 1984.

Bianchi, Serge. *La révolution culturelle de l'an II*. Paris: Aubin, 1982.

Bonnet, Jean-Claude, ed. *La carmagnole des muses*. Paris: A. Colin, 1988.

Bordier, Henri-Leonard. *Le chansonnier huguenot au 16e siècle*. Paris: n.p., 1870.

Bouloiseau, Marc. *La République jacobine*. Paris: Seuil, 1972.

——. "Robespierre vu par les journaux satiriques (1789–1791)." *Annales historiques de la Révolution française*, no. 152 (1958): 28–49.

Bourdieu, Pierre. *Distinction: A Social Critique of the Judgement of Taste*. Trans. Richard Nice. Cambridge: Harvard University Press, 1984.

Boyd, Malcolm, ed. *Music and the French Revolution*. Cambridge: Cambridge University Press, 1992.

Brécy, Robert. "La chanson révolutionnaire de 1789 à 1799," and "La chanson babouviste." *Annales historiques de la Révolution française* 53, no. 244 (1981) and 54, no. 249 (1982).

Cabanis, André. *La presse sous le Consulat et l'Empire (1799–1814)*. Paris: Soc. des Etudes Robespierristes, 1975.

Censer, Jack. *Prelude to Power: The Parisian Radical Press, 1789–1791*. Baltimore: Johns Hopkins University Press, 1976.

Charlton, David. *Grétry and the Growth of the Opéra-Comique*. Cambridge: Cambridge University Press, 1986.

Chartier, Roger. *The Cultural Origins of the French Revolution*. Trans. Lydia G. Cochrane. Durham, N.C.: Duke University Press, 1991.

——. "Culture as Appropriation: Popular Cultural Uses in Early Modern France." In *Understanding Popular Culture*, ed. Steven L. Kaplan. New York: Mouton, 1984.

——. "Intellectual History or Sociocultural History? The French Trajectories." In Dominick LaCapra and Steven Kaplan, eds., *Modern European Intellectual History: Reappraisals and New Perspectives.* Ithaca: Cornell University Press, 1982.

Cornette, Joel. *Un révolutionnaire ordinaire.* Seyssel: Champ Vallon, 1986.

Darnton, Robert. *The Great Cat Massacre.* New York: Basic Books, 1984.

——. *The Literary Underground of the Old Regime.* Cambridge: Harvard University Press, 1982.

David, Martine, and Anne-Marie Delrieu. *Aux sources des chansons populaires.* Paris: Belin, 1984.

Davis, Natalie Z. *Culture and Society in Early Modern France.* Stanford: Stanford University Press, 1965.

——. *Fiction in the Archives: Pardon Tales and Their Tellers in Sixteenth-Century France.* Stanford: Stanford University Press, 1987.

Desan, Suzanne. *Reclaiming the Sacred: Lay Religion and Popular Politics in Revolutionary France.* Ithaca: Cornell University Press, 1990.

Egret, Jean. *The French Pre-Revolution, 1787–1788.* Trans. Wesley D. Camp. Chicago: University of Chicago Press, 1977.

Engerand, Fernand. *Ange Pitou, agent royaliste et chanteur des rues (1767–1846).* Paris: E. Leroux, 1899.

Farge, Arlette. *Dire et mal-dire: L'opinion publique au XVIIIe siècle.* Paris: Seuil, 1992.

——. *Fragile Lives.* Trans. Carol Shelton. Cambridge: Harvard University Press, 1993.

——. *Vivre dans la rue à Paris au XVIIIe siècle.* Paris: Gallimard, 1979.

Farge, Arlette, & Jacques Revel. *The Vanishing Children of Paris.* Trans. Claudia Miéville. Cambridge: Harvard University Press, 1991.

Fiaux, Louis. *La Marseillaise: Son histoire dans l'histoire des français depuis 1792.* Paris: Fasquelle, 1918.

Fournier, Edouard. *Histoire du Pont Neuf.* Paris: Dentu, 1862.

French Caricature and the French Revolution. Catalogue for an exhibit at UCLA. Chicago: University of Chicago Press, 1988.

The French Revolution and the Creation of Modern Political Culture. volumes 1–2. Oxford: Pergamon Press, 1987–1989.

Furet, François. *Interpreting the French Revolution.* Trans. Elborg Forster. Cambridge: Cambridge University Press, 1981.

Furet, François, and Denis Richet. *La Révolution française.* Paris: Hachette, 1965.

Garrioch, David. *Neighborhood and Community in Paris, 1740–1790.* Cambridge: Cambridge University Press, 1986.

Gauthier, Marie-Véronique. *Chanson, sociabilité et grivoiserie au XIXe siècle.* Paris: Aubier, 1992.

Gendron, François. *La jeunesse dorée.* Québec: Presses Universitaires de Québec, 1979.

Godineau, Dominique. *Citoyennes tricoteuses: Les femmes du peuple à Paris pendant la Révolution française.* Paris: Alinea, 1988.

——. "Masculine and Feminine Political Practice during the French Revolution, 1793–year III." In *Women and Politics in the Age of the Democratic Revolution,* ed.

Bibliography

Harriet B. Applewhite and Darlene G. Levy. Ann Arbor: University of Michigan Press, 1990.

Gorceix, Septime. "Antoine-Joseph Gorsas, journaliste et conventionnel (1753–1793)." *L'Information historique* 15, no. 5 (1953): 179–83.

Grand-Mesnil, Marie-Noelle. *Mazarin, la Fronde, et la presse*. Paris: A. Colin, 1967.

Greenlaw, Ralph. "Pamphlet Literature in France during the Period of Aristocratic Revolt, 1787–1788." *Journal of Modern History* 29, no. 4 (1957).

Guillaume, Jacques. *Procès-verbaux du Comité d'Instruction Publique, Convention Nationale*. Paris: Imprimerie Nationale, 1891–1907.

Habermas, Jürgen. *The Structural Transformation of the Public Sphere*. Trans. Thomas Burger. Cambridge: MIT Press, 1989.

Hahn, Roger. *The Anatomy of a Scientific Institution*. Berkeley: University of California Press, 1971.

Hampson, Norman. *A Social History of the French Revolution*. London: Thames & Hudson, 1963.

Hardman, John, ed. *The French Revolution: The Fall of the Ancien Regime to the Thermidoran Reaction, 1785–1795*. New York: St. Martin's Press, 1982.

Hatin, Eugene. *Histoire politique et littéraire de la presse en France*. Paris: Poulet-Malassis, 1860.

Hauterive, Ernest d', ed. *La police secrète du Premier Empire*, bulletins quotidiens adressés par Fouché à l'Empereur. Paris: Libraire Academique Perrin, 1908.

Hesse, Carla. *Publishing and Cultural Politics in Revolutionary Paris, 1789–1810*. Berkeley: University of California Press, 1991.

Hesse, Carla, and Laura Mason. *Pamphlets, Songsheets, and Periodicals of the French Revolutionary Era*. Princeton and New York: Princeton University and Garland Press, 1989.

Hunt, Lynn. *Politics, Culture, and Class in the French Revolution*. Berkeley: University of California Press, 1984.

Hunt, Lynn, David Lansky, and Paul Hanson. "The Failure of the Liberal Republic in France, 1795–1799: The Road to Brumaire." *Journal of Modern History* 51, no. 4 (1984).

Hyslop, Beatrice. "The Theater during a Crisis: The Parisian Theater during the Reign of Terror." *Journal of Modern History* 17, no. 4 (1945).

Isherwood, Robert. *Farce and Fantasy: Popular Entertainment in Eighteenth-Century Paris*. New York: Oxford University Press, 1986.

———. "Popular Musical Entertainment." *International Review of the Aesthetics and Sociology of Music* 9, no. 2 (1978).

Jam, Jean-Louis. "Fonction des hymnes révolutionnaires." in *Les fêtes de la Révolution*, ed. Jean Ehrard and Paul Viallaneix. Paris: Société des Etudes Robespierristes, 1977.

Jouhaud, Christian. *Mazarinades: La Fronde des mots*. Paris: Aubier, Montaigne, 1985.

Julia, Dominique. *Les trois couleurs du tableau noir: La Révolution*. Paris: Belin, 1981.

Kennedy, Emmett. *A Cultural History of the French Revolution*. New Haven: Yale University Press, 1989.

Bibliography

Lefebvre, Georges. *The French Revolution.* Trans. Elizabeth Moss Evanson, J. H. Stewart, and J. Friguglietti. New York: Routledge, 1964.

——. *Napoleon*, vol. 1, *From 18 Brumaire to Tilsit.* Trans. Henry F. Stockhold. New York: Columbia University Press, 1969.

Leith, James. "Music as an Ideological Weapon during the French Revolution." *Canadian Historical Association Report,* (1966), pp. 126–39.

Level, Brigitte. *A travers deux siècles: Le Caveau, société bachique et chantante, 1726–1939.* Paris: Presses de l'Université de Paris–Sorbonne, 1988.

Lough, John. *Paris Theater Audiences in the Seventeenth and Eighteenth Centuries.* London: Oxford University Press, 1957.

Lyons, Martyn. *France under the Directory.* Cambridge: Cambridge University Press, 1975.

Mason, Laura. "*Ca ira* and the Birth of the Revolutionary Song." *History Workshop,* no. 28 (Fall, 1989).

——. "Mixing Media: Songs." In *Revolution in Print: The Press in France, 1775–1800,* ed. Robert Darnton and Daniel Roche. Berkeley: University of California Press, 1989.

Mazauric, Claude. *Babeuf et la conspiration pour l'égalité.* Paris: Editions Sociales, 1962.

Ménétra, Jacques-Louis. *Journal of My Life,* with an introduction and commentary by Daniel Roche. Trans. Arthur Goldhammer. New York: Columbia University Press, 1986.

Michaud, Joseph-Fr., and Louis Gabriel Michaud. *Biographie universelle,* new edition. Paris: Didot, 1843.

Monin, Hippolyte. *L'Etat de Paris en 1789.* Paris: D. Jouaust, 1889.

Mukerji, Chandra, and Michael Schudson. "Introduction: Rethinking Popular Culture." In *Rethinking Popular Culture: Contemporary Perspectives in Cultural Studies,* ed. Chandra Mukerji and Michael Schudson. Berkeley: University of California Press, 1991.

Murray, William J. *The Right-Wing Press in the French Revolution: 1789–1792.* Suffolk: Boydell, 1986.

Ong, Walter. *Orality and Literacy: The Technologizing of the Word.* London: Methuen, 1982.

Ozouf, Mona. *Festivals and the French Revolution.* Trans. Alan Sheridan. Cambridge: Harvard University Press, 1989.

Packer, Dorothy. "'La Calotte' and the eighteenth-century French Vaudeville." *Journal of American Musicological Society* 26 (1973).

Paulson, Ronald. *Representations of Revolution.* New Haven: Yale University Press, 1983.

Pierre, Constant. *B. Sarrette et les origines du Conservatoire National.* Paris: Delalain Frères, 1895.

——. *Les hymnes et chansons de la Révolution française.* Paris: Imprimerie Nationale, 1904.

——. *Le Magasin de musique à l'usage des fêtes nationales et du Conservatoire.* Paris: Fischbacher, 1895.

Raunié, Emile. *Chansonnier historique au 18ème siècle.* Paris: A. Quantin, 1879.

Bibliography

Revel, Jacques. "Forms of Expertise: Intellectuals and 'Popular' Culture in France (1650–1800)." In *Understanding Popular Culture*, ed. Steven Kaplan. New York: Mouton, 1984.

Roche, Daniel. *Le Peuple de Paris*. Paris: Aubier, Montaigne, 1981. Translated by Marie Evans under the title of *The People of Paris*. Berkeley: University of California Press, 1987.

Rogers, Cornwall B. *The Spirit of Revolution in 1789*. Princeton: Princeton University Press, 1949.

Root-Bernstein, Michèle. *Boulevard Theater and Revolution*. Ann Arbor: University of Michigan Press, 1984.

Rudé, George. *The Crowd in the French Revolution*. Oxford: Clarendon, 1959.

Sewell, William H., Jr. *A Rhetoric of Bourgeois Revolution: The Abbé Sièyes and "What Is the Third Estate?"* Durham, N.C.: Duke University Press, 1994.

——. *Work and Revolution in France: The Language of Labor from the Old Regime to 1848*. Cambridge: Cambridge University Press, 1980.

Slavin, Morris. *The Making of an Insurrection: Parisian Sections and the Gironde*. Cambridge: Harvard University Press, 1986.

Soboul, Albert. *The Sans-Culottes: The Popular Movement and Revolutionary Government, 1793–1794*. Trans. Remy Inglis Hall. Princeton: Princeton University Press, 1980.

Starobinski, Jean. *Jean-Jacques Rousseau: Transparency and Obstruction*. Trans. Arthur Goldhammer. Chicago: University of Chicago Press, 1988.

——. *1789: The Emblems of Reason*. Charlottesville: University Press of Virginia, 1982.

Sydenham, M. J. *The Girondins*. London: University of London, Athlone Press, 1961.

Tackett, Timothy. *Religion, Revolution, and Regional Culture in Eighteenth-Century France*. Princeton: Princeton University Press, 1986.

Tiersot, Julien. *Les fêtes et les chants de la Révolution française*. Paris: Hachette, 1908.

——. *Histoire de la chanson populaire française*. Paris: Plon, 1889.

——. *Rouget de Lisle: Son oeuvre, sa vie*. Paris: n.p., 1892.

Tønnesson, Kare. *La défaite des sans-culottes*. Oslo and Paris: Presses Universitaires d'Oslo, 1959.

Vaccaro, J.-M, ed. *La chanson à la Renaissance: Actes du 20ème colloque d'Etudes humanistes du Centre d'Etudes supérieurs de la Renaissance de l'Université de Tours*. Tours: Van de Velde, 1981.

Vovelle, Michel. *La chute de la monarchie, 1787–1792*. Paris: Seuil, 1972.

——. "La Marseillaise: La guerre ou la paix." In *Les lieux de mémoire*, vol. I, *La République*, general editor Pierre Nora. Paris: Gallimard, 1984.

——. *Théodore Desorgues, ou la désorganisation*. Paris: Seuil, 1986.

Walter, Gerard. *Babeuf et la Conjuration des Egaux*. Paris: Payot, 1937.

Weber, William. "Learned and General Musical Taste." *Past and Present*, no. 89 (1980).

Welschinger, Henri. *Le théâtre de la Révolution*. Geneva: Slatkine Reprints, 1968.

Woloch, Isser. *Jacobin Legacy: The Democratic Movement under the Directory*. Princeton: Princeton University Press, 1970.

Woronoff, Denis. *La République bourgeoise de thermidor à brumaire*. Paris: Seuil, 1972.

Index

Index

Index

Mercier, Louis-Sebastien: and language, 30–31; and political culture, 27–29, 50, 186–87

Messager du soir, 136, 153

Les Mille et un théâtres (Desfontaines), 74–75, 78–79, 203

Monarchy, celebration of, 26

Montagnards: encouragement of culture, 127; songs about, 112, 119, 134–35; and Thermidorian reaction, 132, 138, 139, 142, 151

National Assembly, 46, 49–50, 58, 62; celebration of, 36; and festival of Federation, 42–44

National Convention, 86–87, 104, 107; contributions of songs to, 90, 110–11; and *Marseillaise / Réveil du peuple* debate, 140–44, 146, 151; song policies, 102, 120–29, 161–64, 207, 211, 217–18; after Thermidor, 130, 132–33, 138–40, 147–48, 200. *See also* Dantonists; Jacobins; Montagnards; Robespierre, Maximilien

National Institute of Music: creation and responsibilities of, 102, 121–23, 159–60; and musical performances, 127, 141

Newspapers: changing publication rates of, 36, 62–63, 105, 114–15; and *Marseillaise / Réveil du peuple* debate, 136, 138, 146–47; opinions about songs, 35, 40–41, 57–60, 101–2, 113, 152–53, 201–3, 211, 215–17; and political culture, 39, 61–63, 72, 93–94, 183, 185, 213; royalist, 48–49, 53–54, 64–65, 79–80, 178; satiric, 67–70, 80–84, 89–90; and theatrical performances, 48, 51–52, 75, 77–79, 86. *See also* Representation; *individual journalists; individual newspapers*

Nouveautés. See Market

Nouveaux troubadours, 196–97

Observateur sans-culotte, 113

Old Regime: attitudes toward songs, 9–10, 20, 30–35, 41, 215; notions of honor, 27–29; political culture of, 5, 18–20, 24–25, 29, 36–37; political songs, 25–29; revolutionary references to, 39–41, 66, 85–86, 132–33, 194–96; song culture of, 15–18, 22–24. *See also* Censorship; Streetsingers

Opéra: impact of August revolution on, 105; under Old Regime, 23, 70, 162; revolutionary performances in, 72, 100

Opéra-comique, 24, 162

Oral culture: impact on song culture, 17–18, 22, 28, 122–23, 220; and political culture, 28–29, 53, 99, 220; and print culture, 2–3, 25–26, 44–45, 61–62, 64, 99, 223n4. *See also* Appropriation; Performance

O Richard, ô Mon Roi: appearance of, 46–48; and revolutionary politics, 51–52, 54–55, 57, 60, 215–216

Où peut-on être mieux qu'au sein de sa famille?, 37, 55–57

Ozouf, Mona, 5, 163, 209, 212

Paris Municipal Council: and sans-culottes, 107, 110; and song publication, 121, 160; and théâtre du Vaudeville, 86–87, 89

Paris Parlement, 29, 34, 36

Parody, 53, 197–98; and *Ça ira*, 48–49; and *La Marseillaise*, 82, 149–50. *See also* Satire

Pastoral songs, 197–98

Patriotism: marketing of, 115–19; official encouragement of, 123; among sans-culottes, 109–12, 125; and war, 93–94, 144, 189, 192–93. See also *La Marseillaise*

Pedagogy: and cultural elites, 201–2; official projects for, 122–24, 164–65; among sans-culottes, 115–17; and singing, 108, 128, 205–6, 211, 216, 219. *See also* Public instruction

Peltier, Jean-Gabriel, 65

Performance: flexibility of, 3, 18; indeterminacy of, 72, 112–13, 123–24, 181–83, 220; and *Marseillaise / Réveil du peuple* debate, 136–37, 153–54, 168–69; as political expression, 54–55, 98, 107–10, 128, 131, 166–67, 175–77, 211; and royalism, 148–51

Piis, Antoine: Old Regime career of, 24, 74; and théâtre du Vaudeville, 86, 89, 118

Pitou, Louis-Ange, 147, 179–83

Poetry: and hymns, 41, 120, 163; and songs, 194, 196

Poissardes. See Market women

Police: and *Marseillaise / Réveil du peuple* debate, 144, 146, 150–51; and political songs, 25–26, 28–29, 120; and public singing, 158–59, 166–68, 170–71, 190–92, 203–5, 207; and streetsingers, 21–23, 31, 169–70, 181–83, 189; and theaters, 168–69

Political activism: and *Ça ira*, 50, 52–54, 57, 59–60; criticism of, 126, 128–29, 211–12; decline of, 188–93, 206–7; and *La Marseillaise*, 98, 101; and popular tunes, 36–37; restriction of, 200–201; and *Réveil du peuple*, 136–37, 146, 154; and revolutionary singing, 39–40, 105–10, 158, 166–67, 176–77, 183, 216–19

Political culture: in contemporary scholarship, 5–8, 209–10, 222n13; growing conservatism of, 184–86, 206–8; heterogeneity of, 11, 102–3, 128–29, 131, 144–45, 151–54, 210–14; of the Republic, 101–2, 104–6, 132–33; revolutionizing of, 4, 36, 39–40, 54–55, 59–60

Index

Pont-neuf, 20, 73, 224n17
Pont Neuf, 15, 20, 23, 30, 162
Popular culture: definition of, 8–9, 31–33; and revolutionary change, 4–5, 9–12; songs as, 16–17, 19–20, 35–36, 58–60, 66–67, 69–70, 100–2, 108–9, 124–25, 158–59, 183, 208, 214–20. *See also* Aesthetics; *Ça ira*; *La Marseillaise*; Taste
Prairial insurrection, 139, 166, 168
Press. *See* Newspapers
Professionalization, of songwriting, 12, 157–65, 195–96, 218
Public instruction, 104, 120–24, 126–27, 158; changing objectives of, 158, 161, 163, 165–66, 201. *See also* Pedagogy

Radet, Jean-Baptiste, 74, 86–89
Rapsodies du jour, 178
Reformation, and songwriting, 18–19
Religious songs, 18–19
Révolutions de France et de Brabant, 63–64
Révolutions de Paris, 42–43, 63, 68, 69, 77–78, 93, 98
Representation: and the idea of popular culture, 9–10, 12, 16, 35–36, 215–18; of songs, 4, 30–33, 40–41, 57–60, 63–64, 102, 128, 185, 208, 210–11
Republicanism: attacks on, 137, 151–52, 182; and Babouvists, 174–76; under Directory, 184, 186, 193, 207; and *goguettes*, 205; heterogeneity of, 128–29, 209, 211, 214; and sans-culottes, 105–10, 216; and songbooks, 117, 127; in théâtre du Vaudeville, 89; during Thermidorian reaction, 138–39, 142–43, 151, 153. See also *La Marseillaise*
Réveil du peuple: appropriations of, 146–47; broadening popularity of, 138–39, 146–47; criticism of, 145–46; defenses of, 140–45; under Directory, 190; lyrics, 134–37; partisan popularity of, 137–38, 148; significance of, 129–31, 150–52; tune, 135. See also *La Marseillaise / Réveil du peuple* debate
Revolution of 10 August: commemoration of, 117, 129, 142, 151; consequences of, 80, 84, 100, 104
Richard the Lion-Hearted: performances of, 47–48, 51–52, 64
Rivarol, Antoine, 65
Robespierre, Maximilien, attacks on, 82, 132, 136, 138, 151, 231n23; and culture, 83–84, 93; as legislator, 124–25; popular discussion of, 113
Rocambole des journaux, 68, 79, 83
Rouget de Lisle, Claude-Joseph, 94, 96–97. See also *La Marseillaise*

Rousseau, Thomas: and *Les chants du patriotisme*, 115–17, 119; government subsidies to, 121–23, 216
Royalism: and *Ça ira*, 47–49, 53–54; under Directory, 168, 170, 181–83, 188; opposition to, 81, 97, 211; and *O Richard, ô Mon Roi*, 45–48, 51–52, 54–55; and satire, 65–69, 78, 80, 178; and song culture, 57–60, 211, 215–17; and theaters, 51–53, 169; during Thermidorian reaction, 131, 139, 147–48, 149–54, 173. *See also* Pitou, Louis-Ange; Satire; Théâtre du Vaudeville

Sans-culottes: attitudes toward songs, 112–13; culture of, 105–10, 211, 217–18; and National Convention, 120, 123–24, 125–28, 146, 200, 216; songs about, 111–12, 122; and Thermidorian reaction, 137, 144
Sarrette, Bernard, 121, 165
Satire: revolutionary criticism of, 11, 80, 83–84; and royalism, 62, 65, 67–70, 78, 89–90, 150, 152, 154, 158; and vaudevilles, 73, 75, 195, 203. See also *Les Actes des Apôtres*; *Courrier*; Théâtre du Vaudeville; *Dîners du vaudeville*; Vaudeville
Singing practices: breadth of, 2, 9, 16–17, 24–25; and revolutionary change, 12, 105, 186
Streetsingers: Old Regime, 15–17, 20–21, 23–24, 34–35; policing of, 22, 169–70, 181–83; revolutionary, 162–63, 167, 179, 225n29; status of, 22, 24, 31–32, 180–81, 189. *See also* Ladré; Pitou, Louis-Ange
Suleau, François, 65
Supreme Being, cult of, 111, 127

Taste, 195–96, 202, 218, 249n34
Te Deum: and *Ça ira*, 50; and festival of Federation, 41, 44; and *La Marseillaise*, 100
Terror: criticism of, 134–36, 138, 140, 142–46, 150–51, 190, 198–201, 218; dismantling of, 125, 129–30, 132–33; impact on culture, 104–6, 114–15, 124, 131. See also *Réveil du peuple*
Theaters: audiences, 48, 51–52, 64, 70–72, 78–79, 86–87, 146, 150–51; and commercialism, 61–62, 73, 79, 84; liberty of, 70, 72–73, 75; pedagogic value of, 41, 71, 78, 88–89; policing of, 148, 150–51, 157, 168–69; singing in, 52–53, 137, 141, 147–49; and staged songs, 24, 61–62, 100, 141, 147. *See also* Market; *O Richard, ô Mon Roi*; Vaudeville; *individual theaters*
Théâtre de la rue Feydeau, 100, 134, 149
Théâtre du Vaudeville: controversial plays of, 74–78, 85–87; and entertainment, 202–3; establishment of, 73–74; and market, 70,

Index

Théâtre du Vaudeville (*cont.*)
79, 84, 117–19; and *La Marseillaise*, 100,
149; and republicanism, 87–90

Thermidor: commemoration of, 141–42, 144,
146, 150–51, 186–87; significance of, 7–8,
129–32, 160, 211

Thermidorian reaction: broadening of, 138–
39, 180; emergence of, 129, 132–37; significance of, 130–31, 142–46, 151–54, 190,
199–200, 217–18. See also *Marseillaise /
Réveil du peuple* debate

Transparency, 68–69, 109, 111

Tuileries section, 84, 87, 118

Tunes: allusiveness of, 19, 37, 67, 73; as identification, 18, 180; and memorization, 2, 25;
popular, 2, 18, 23

Vaudeville: composition of, 73, 224n17; defined by Boileau, 24, 79; as entertainment,
197–98, 202–3, 250n52; republican definition of, 88–90; and satire, 75, 78; in theaters, 73–75, 84, 202. See also *Les Dîners du
vaudeville*; Théâtre du Vaudeville

Veillons au salut de l'Empire, 138, 141, 148,
175–76

Vendémiaire insurrection, 147–48, 166–67,
176, 181

Vive Henri IV, 37, 55–57

Vovelle, Michel, 97

War: criticism of, 41; enthusiasm for, 12,
93–94, 103, 192–93, 212, 219; impact on
culture, 55, 100–1, 104–5, 188; promotion
of, 58, 98–99, 109, 118; songs about,
67–68, 94–96, 109, 112, 122, 192–93,
198–99. See also Army; *La Marseillaise*; Patriotism

Women. See Market women